R.D. Chantrell (1793–1872)

and the architecture of a lost generation

Arch[t]

DESIGN FOR
A NEW CHURCH & PARSONAGE HOUSE AT
MIDDLETON, IN THE PARISH OF ROTHWELL, YORKSHIRE.

R.D. Chantrell (1793-1872)

and the architecture of a lost generation

Christopher Webster

Spire Books Ltd

PO Box 2336, Reading RG4 5WJ
www.spirebooks.com

Spire Books Ltd
PO Box 2336
Reading RG4 5WJ
www.spirebooks.com

CIP data:
A catalogue record for this book is available
from the British Library
ISBN 978-1-904965-22-0

This book has been published with grants from the Leeds Philosophical and Literary
Society and the Paul Mellon Centre for Studies in British Art

Designed and produced by John Elliott
Text set in Bembo

Frontispiece: Middleton, Leeds, St Mary's church and vicarage (R.D. Chantrell, 1845-9),
engraving from a drawing by Chantrell, probably produced to encourage fundraising,
c.1844. (*Lambeth Palace Library*).

Contents

For my mother, with whom, as a child in Morley,
I enjoyed my earliest experiences of Chantrell
buildings.

Acknowledgements

My involvement with Chantrell began in 1976 when Derek Linstrum suggested him to me for an MPhil at York. Following completion, and the adaptation of parts of it for a handful of publications, Chantrell was largely put to one side while I pursued other research interests. Coming back to him, his many remaining buildings and the documents he left in order to write this book has been a real pleasure, rather like renewing contact with a series of familiar friends.

Stimulating discussions with Professor Linstrum about Chantrell and his contemporaries continued long after the degree was awarded and I shall always be grateful to him for his wisdom and encouragement. Anyone who has worked on Leeds architects will join me in acknowledging his unparalleled knowledge and enthusiasm for the designers of his native city, as well as his generosity in sharing that knowledge. My acquaintance with Terry Friedman goes back even further and it is a pleasure to record here my gratitude to him for many hours of convivial conversation about Georgian architecture, as well as for helpful comments about my Chantrell text. I have always considered myself fortunate to have been contacted by Andries Van den Abeele in 1980. The unexpected arrival of a letter from him in connection with his own research on two of Chantrell's brothers in Bruges proved to be the beginning of a long friendship and several academic collaborations. Sections of this book dealing with Chantrell's family and with the Bruges Cathedral commission would have been much thinner without his kind assistance. My understanding of the complex and sometimes contradictory artistic world that Chantrell inhabited benefited much from the academic stimulus of my former colleagues Hilary Grainger, Mike Hope and Gillian Salway.

Colin Cunningham and Michael Port – as well as Terry Friedman – generously agreed to read sections of the book and I am indebted to them for many corrections and helpful comments, although any errors of fact or interpretation are entirely my own.

I have received valuable assistance from a number of organisations and individual archivists, and wish to record my thanks to: West Yorkshire Archives Service in Leeds and Wakefield, especially Stefanie Davidson and Vicky Grindrod; Geoffrey Foster and his staff at the Leeds Library; the Thoresby Society in Leeds and its former Librarian, Joan Newis; Sir John Soane's Museum, especially Susan Palmer and Stephen Astley; Lambeth Palace Library, especially Clare Brown.

I am grateful to the following for taking time to answer specific questions: Paul Barnwell, Elizabeth Bee, Oliver Bradbury, Gwen Brown, Tim Brittain-Catlin, Ann Clark, Trevor Cooper, Janet Douglas, Kevin Grady, David Hall, Rosemary Hill, Simon Lindley, Michael Meadowcroft, David Neave, Alexandra Wedgwood and Susan Wrathmell.

In the course of a project that has spanned so many years, a number of friends have assisted in various ways and it is with pleasure that I record my thanks to: Sarah Brown, Trevor Cooper, Susan Harrison, Trevor Harrison and Christine Taylor. I am especially grateful to Graham West who has, with unswerving generosity and kindness, assisted me out of numerous technical difficulties that I encountered in arranging the text and illustrations. I am indebted to Peter Hirschmann who has been a constant source of support and encouragement.

A number of people have kindly supplied photographs including: Albert Booth, Mike Collins, Isobel Combes (Diocese of Derby DAC), Roger Hatfield, Colin Hinson and Richard Tinker. Karen Haslam of Blacksheep Photography not only took photographs for me but also significantly enhanced images that I and others had taken. I am deeply grateful to her for her remarkable technical expertise as well as for her patience and good humour.

Finally, I would like to pay tribute to the team at Spire Books: Geoff Brandwood, John Elliott and Linda Hone. They have not only done an accomplished job in editing, correcting, designing and marketing this work, but are to be congratulated for a whole succession of valuable books on important but neglected architectural topics.

Christopher Webster
Barwick in Elmet, 2009.

Introduction

The period between Waterloo and the establishment of Ecclesiology, from 1815 to the mid-1840s, is the focus of this book. And it is a much neglected period of architectural history. It delivered a handful of well-known buildings – for instance, Brighton Pavilion, the National Gallery and much of Buckingham Palace – but produced neither the elegance and inventiveness of late eighteenth-century Classicism nor the vitality of the mid-nineteenth century Gothic Revival. More significantly, it continues to be widely seen, just as Pugin and the Ecclesiologists wanted it to be seen, as artistically moribund, devoid of any originality, riddled with unethical or corrupt practices, a period mired in the final death throes of a worn out Classical tradition, after which British architecture was saved from utter degradation only by the vigour of a newly found interest in the Middle Ages, and a new generation of Gothic exponents. In this context, perhaps the most engaging accounts are ones that stress either the stylistic variety and extravagance of late-Georgian country houses, or, more recently, ones that repeat the caricature of Pugin's *Contrasts* and the Cambridge Camden Society's numerous pamphlets. The twenty-first century is in danger of surrendering to a largely fictitious 'Puginisation' of the period which is not only grossly misleading, but seriously marginalises the many achievements of a whole generation of architects.

We already know much about the careers of John Soane, John Nash and Thomas Hope – as well as A.W.N. Pugin – whose interests have dominated our understanding of the age, but there are other stories to be told. Looked at from different perspectives – and perspectives that are no less valid – this is a period of real importance, and a re-evaluation of it is long overdue. It was at this time that architecture emerged as a recognisable profession, with the Institute of British Architects being founded in 1834; the availability of architectural services reached the provinces; there were considerable technological advances which certainly changed, even if they didn't quite revolutionise, architectural design and construction; there was a huge growth in the demand for buildings and, more importantly, in the demand for buildings designed by architects to satisfy an increasingly discerning clientele. There was, indeed, a shift away from Classical dominance towards a greater acceptance of Gothic, but not on the scale many recent writers have suggested, and, significantly, often the drive for Gothic came from outside the profession, especially for churches. All these issues are addressed in the first chapter, a substantial account which, in a number of ways, offers a revision of this remarkable period: it reveals the professional world that Chantrell would inhabit. And it provides the context for our examination of his dynamic career, as in all these issues Chantrell was not simply responding to external events, but was central to our conception of them. What better way to understand the period than by examining the life of one of the profession's workhorses? Indeed, Chantrell's career reveals much about the wider issues of architectural activity in this period, and in many ways, he is much more representative of the profession as a whole than is Soane, Nash, Hope or Pugin.

Robert Dennis Chantrell (1793-1872) enjoyed the finest architectural education available in Britain as a pupil of John Soane, then professor of architecture at the Royal Academy, and a committed Classicist. This is one of very few studies of a Soane protégé and one that examines architectural education in the period. While a student, Chantrell no doubt envisaged a career modelled on that of his teacher, designing Classical public buildings and country houses from a London office. The reality was to be very different. He chose instead to settle in Leeds, then a rapidly expanding industrial town that offered considerable opportunities to an ambitious and able young architect, and he was among the first of many of them to offer architectural services there. Certainly, there was employment to be had but, at the same time, he was having to establish the demand

London, University College (W. Wilkins, 1827-8). Dull or pedantic, perhaps, and bigger than most, but stylistically entirely typical of the huge number of competently designed Classical public buildings erected after Waterloo. (T.H. Shepherd and J. Elmes, *Metropolitan Improvements*, 1827, opp. p. 124).

for it where almost none had existed before. Consideration of Chantrell's career in fact illustrates all the issues that make this such a compelling period for study and it allows historians ample scope to scrutinise the changes taking place.

There are other reasons for examining Chantrell and his work. Most interestingly, he was not simply following the slow drift towards Gothic, but was actually helping to lead it. Although it was probably more to do with expediency than any deeply held affection for the style – at least initially – he nevertheless reinvented himself to become the region's principal Gothic exponent. Indeed, the bishop of Ripon was moved to pronounce him 'one of the first architects in all the north of England',[1] following many years of exemplary church work. This was no mean achievement. As we shall see in the next chapter, church work in the Gothic style could hardly have been undertaken in less auspicious circumstances: there were few helpful models for a building type that served a very different function from its medieval counterpart and there was little lead from the country's principal architects or the Commissioners of the 1818 Church Building Act who were paying most of the bills. Yet there was a clear demand for Gothic from the northern church-building committees and the worshippers they represented which prompted Chantrell and his colleagues to work heroically to satisfy their stylistic ambitions, supported by less than generous budgets. Chantrell was one of the few architects who could perform consistently well in these hostile circumstances. And it was not just in the design of new churches that he excelled – he became an expert at restoration jobs and an antiquary whose academic pronouncements were eagerly absorbed by amateur historians fascinated by the newly fashionable cult of the medieval. There was a moment, in the mid-1840s, when he might, without too much arrogance, have believed himself to be in the very highest echelons of the Gothic camp. The intellectual background in which the Gothic Revivalists between Nash and Pugin operated is another theme of the book and an aspect of this period that has hitherto been neglected.

Perhaps most crucially, this was a time of immense change in the practice of architecture. Whether they are examined on the level of stylistic developments, the growth of middle-class patronage, the emergence of new building types and constructional techniques, or the services architects offered to society, the thirty years after Waterloo laid the foundation for what we now think of as Victorian architectural practice. And it is a period ripe for revision. Chantrell's career is a microcosm of the events which lead to the invention of the modern architect; it is also a fascinating story.

1

Architecture in post-Waterloo England: a Time of Change

By the mid-1840s, the battle for Gothic to be taken seriously – and made virtually compulsory for Anglican ecclesiastical commissions – had been fought and won, although the Classical tradition remained a powerful force in British architectural thinking. So far as Chantrell was concerned, the production of Classical designs was by then but a distant memory. Despite his training with Soane that was overwhelmingly Classical in focus, and his early preference for the style, by 1840 he had unquestionably re-aligned himself with the Gothic camp. But in the 25 years after Waterloo, he and most other architects were much exercised by stylistic and other professional debates. Investigation of these is thus rewarding for historians, as well as being surprisingly neglected by them. This chapter seeks to establish the pre-1840 architectural climate, the one in which Chantrell would pass the formative part of his career. It was a period when so many aspects of British life were undergoing fundamental changes and these form a useful context for our examination of the architectural profession.

A question of style

More than half a century ago, Sir John Summerson concluded that the post-Waterloo period was 'the time for the general practitioner – and the general dealer in styles.'[1] A similar theme of stylistic diversity has underpinned subsequent books. 'In Regency architecture we find a variety ... which no other period can equal', David Watkin wrote in 1982.[2] John Morley's *Regency Style* of 1993[3] continues the interpretation, beginning the 'Exterior Architecture' section with the sub-heading: 'The Stylistic Quandary' and proceeding to rationalise the stylistic divisions with chapters headed 'Classical Styles', 'Gothic Styles' and 'Exotic Styles' (**1.1**). And Giles Worsley ends his *Classical Architecture in Britain: the Heroic Age* with the opinion that '[after 1815] no one style of architecture was dominant'.[4] There is much to commend these interpretations of the material.

1.1: London, the Egyptian Hall, Piccadilly (P.F. Robinson, 1812-13). A very rare example of the apparently widespread taste for the Exotic. (T.H. Shepherd and J. Elmes, *Metropoliotan Improvements*, 1827, opp. p. 157).   .

Perhaps the major compositional innovation of the period around 1800 was the picturesque, and if an architect sought to exploit its principles, almost *any* style was more compatible with its emphasis on asymmetry than Classicism. The ascendancy of the picturesque can be traced from James Wyatt's Lee Priory, Kent (*c.*1785-90), running through his Fonthill Abbey, Wiltshire (1796-1812), to be taken up by John Nash at Killymoon Castle, Ireland (*c.*1801-3), Cronkhill, Shropshire (1802), and Ravensworth Castle, Co. Durham (begun 1808). Indeed, no-one better personifies the 'stylistic diversity' interpretation of the age than Nash. Admittedly some of the astonishing variety that he demonstrated at the beginning of the century was subsequently curtailed, but around 1815 he could still be found moving through Gothic, Tudor, *cottages ornés*, Claudean Picturesque and a whole range of Classical idioms, as well as the Exotic at Brighton Pavilion. Comparing the latter to 'a grim monument to the Greek Revival' by Smirke of the same date, Watkin was moved to conclude they were so inconsistent that they 'can seem the products not merely of different ages, but of different cultures'.[5]

Unquestionably then, stylistic diversity is easily identified but a crucial question is this: are the designs of Wyatt, Nash and one or two others evidence of a fundamental shift in the mainstream of architectural thinking and a rejection of Classicism, or simply an interesting byway, telling us more about the artistic independence of a relatively small group of exceptionally wealthy patrons than they do about the demise of Classicism's long domination of British architecture? The iconic building of the age is surely Prince George's Pavilion – and with its Classical plan, Moorish domes and fantastic Chinese interiors, what could be more indicative of a cavalier attitude to stylistic propriety? – but to imply that it is somehow characteristic of the architecture and the architectural patronage of the age is grossly misleading. This chapter seeks to re-examine the apparent stylistic variety[6] of the quarter century after Waterloo and suggest that while the 'diversity' story is an exciting and often compelling one to tell, we should not be seduced by it to the extent that we overlook an alternative one: that Classicism maintained its dominance well into Victoria's reign,[7] and that the fledgling pre-1840 Gothic Revival came about largely despite the architectural profession rather than because of it.

The Classical tradition

Architectural education – such as it was – is a useful place to start. Here, undeniably, Classicism dominated and it did so in a number of ways. The tenure of Soane and Cockerell as professors of architecture at the Royal Academy covers the period from 1806 to 1859,[8] and it would be hard to find two more committed Classicists. Of course, only a fraction of practitioners benefited from actually hearing the lectures, but the professors gave a lead – albeit a sometimes reactionary one – which filtered down through the strata of the

1.2: Athens, the Theseion. (J. Stuart and N. Revett, *The Antiquities of Athens,* vol. 3, 1794, ch. 1, pl. 3).

profession *via* extensive coverage in late-Georgian periodicals. Not just in London in the early nineteenth century, but widely through Europe since the Renaissance, Classicism and academic dogma formed a convenient alliance in a way that none of the alternative styles could begin to match. Classicism was capable of being taught according to a set of rules, and the same rules could be applied to the assessment of the students, and exploited for the wider role of the critic. Those journals which regularly commented on British architectural matters in this period, for instance the *Edinburgh Review,* the *Westminster Review, Gentleman's Magazine* or the *Quarterly Review,* devoted much space to the issue of 'originality', a desirable quality situated at an imprecise point between the undesirable qualities of 'imitation' at one extreme and 'novelty' at the other.[9] Crucially, these debates were almost entirely developed in the context of Classicism. Perhaps this is not surprising; the principles of Classicism were readily capable of assimilation by the interested patron or layman. There was thus a hierarchy in which all levels, from the professor to the man in the street, could consider and evaluate a design according to a set of widely-agreed, objective criteria. It allowed patrons to talk intelligently to architects, building committee members to debate rationally and constructively with each other, and dinner party guests to demonstrate their artistic understanding to their fellows. Architecture that followed these principles could, in the hands of a genius be awesome; in the hands of the least able practitioner,[10] it might often be dull, but it could never be dire. When faced with the challenge of conceiving an impressive entrance front for a new mansion or market hall, grafting the portico from some Greek temple – conveniently illustrated in impeccable detail in Stuart and Revett's *Antiquities of Athens* (**1.2**) – onto an otherwise plain façade was straightforward; to adapt the west front of Lichfield Cathedral for the same purpose – despite equally precise illustrations in Britton's *Lichfield Cathedral* (**1.3**) – was almost impossible. Indeed, at a time when few buildings had more than three principal storeys, a style which relied for much of its effect on soaring height was unlikely to be the profession's preference. There were, then, a range of vested interests dependant on the survival of the Classical tradition and keen to marginalise stylistic alternatives which were seen as intuitive, arbitrary and lacking defined principles.

Perhaps the most reliable barometer of taste is the architectural book trade. At the level of volumes destined as much for the gentleman's library as for the professional office there is ample evidence that the concept of eighteenth-century connoisseurship, dominated by the Classical tradition, lingered well into the nineteenth century.[11] Here we could point to William Wilkins' *Antiquities of Magna Grecia* of 1807 and *The Civil Architecture of Vitruvius* of 1812-17; the final, belated, volume of Stuart and Revett's *The Antiquities of Athens* in 1816 and new editions of earlier volumes (first editions 1762 and 1794) in 1825-30; a new edition of Robert Wood's *Ruins of Palmyra* (first edition 1753) in 1829; and for modern Classical buildings, there was George Richardson's two-volume *New Vitruvius Britannicus,* the final editions of which appeared in 1808 and 1810, and which would still be seen as current after 1815, as well as new editions of Woolfe and

1.3: Lichfield Cathedral. (J. Britton, *The History and Antiquities … of Lichfield*, 1820, pl. 2).

Gandon's *Vitruvius Britannicus*, IV and V (first editions 1767 and 1771) in 1819. Other pioneering eighteenth-century works which reflected their authors' commitment to Classicism continued to be widely available in new, post-Waterloo editions: Robert and James Adam's *Works in Architecture* from the 1770s was completed only in 1822, and new editions of the earlier volumes appeared at the same time while William Chambers' *The Decorative Parts of Civil Architecture*, originally published in 1759, appeared in new editions in 1825, 1835 and 1862. Perhaps most important for our study were the books aimed firmly at the second tier of the architectural profession as well as at the more ambitious builder or carpenter. For this market the books are essentially practical, often encompassing aspects of geometry, mathematics and perspective, and the model designs they provide – whether for a mansion, a fireplace or an architrave – are overwhelmingly Classical ones, frequently including instructions for setting out the five orders. Here one could include William Pain's *The British Palladio* and *The Builder's Companion,* the final editions of which came out in 1804 and 1810 respectively. His *The Practical House Carpenter* with editions in 1815 and 1823, long after the author's death in *c*.1790, contained a series of adaptable designs. All were Classical including the single church.[12] In addition there was Andrew George Cook's hugely popular *The New Builder's Magazine* with editions of 1817, 1818, 1819, 1820, 1821 and 1823, itself largely a revision of John Carter's *The Builder's Magazine* of 1774-8. Finally there were the numerous block-busters from Peter Nicholson, all of which contain almost entirely Classical designs, although a small number of Gothic ones creep into post-*c*.1840 editions. These include: *An Architectural Dictionary* with editions from 1819 to the 1860s; *The New Practical Builder* which ran to eight editions from 1823; *The Builder and Workman's New Director,* of 1825 with numerous later editions. Only his *A Theoretical and Practical Treatise on the Five Orders of Architecture,* with four editions from 1834, includes some coverage of Gothic alongside the much greater number of Classical examples.

Cook and Nicholson will repay attention. Cook even contrives to define Gothic in Classical terms: 'That which deviates from the proportions, character etc of the antique … The abundance of little, whimsical, wild, and chimerical ornaments are the most normal characters. The profiles of these are generally very incorrect.'[13] Even more interesting for our enquiry is Cook's comment on contemporary architecture which accompanies 'his' design for a Gothic church, actually one of Carter's from the 1770s:

> The Gothic Architecture was for these few years past, fallen greatly under the censure of the immoderate admirers of Grecian Architecture, yet if we candidly consider, we shall find both styles have their separate beauties in use. The Grecian taste certainly best suits those public buildings such as palaces, courts of justice, exchanges, hospitals, music-rooms, banqueting-rooms, museums etc, but for religious structures Gothic, undoubtedly, might be preferred … This little digression [most of the book's plates are accompanied by no more than a brief, entirely factual description] is meant to take those partial impressions from the minds of the students which they may likely have imbibed, that Gothic Architecture is a depraved taste, and ought never, on any account, to be introduced, and to remind them and others that Gothic Architecture has been ages back the taste of England, and not entirely be led away by Grecian Architecture alone, because it is the invention of foreigners.[14]

On the one hand, Cook promotes and confirms Classicism's monopoly of secular projects, yet on the other gives a forceful endorsement of Gothic's value in ecclesiastical work, a theme to which we will return. Nevertheless, only seventeen of the book's 177 plates are other than Classical and of these, there is just one church (**1.4**), a 'Gothic Mansion' (actually a triangular castle of Carter's), a few garden buildings and some church furniture.

The 1823 edition of Nicholson's *The New Practical Builder* devotes 112 pages to an entirely standard rehearsal of the Classical orders; his account of 'Antient Architecture of Great Britain' is concluded in less than four, largely plagiarised from Chambers, Gwilt,

Plate CX.

1.4: 'The Plan and Elevation of a Design for a Church'. (A.G. Cook, *The New Builder's Magazine,* c.1820, pl. CX). This is the only design for a church among the 177 plates in this widely read pattern book. The plate, which bears John Carter's name, first appeared in 1770s. The plan is idiosyncratic by English standards and the six spaces at the sides of the nave suggest, somewhat incongruously, Italian Baroque inspiration.

Britton and Milner. He does, though, conclude that 'the antient architecture of our country [is] ... at the present period, in high estimation,'[15] although his chapter 'On the Beauty of Buildings' is implicitly Classical.[16] The book is concluded with 47 plates[17] of designs. The town houses, doorways and shop-fronts – even the two designs for churches (**1.5**) – are all Classical, but there are a handful of Gothic and Tudor villas.

An interesting book of architectural theory is John Billington's *The Architectural Director being an Approved Guide to Architects, Draughtsmen, Students, Amateurs and Builders* – with a sub-title of 'The Pocket Vignola' – of 1833.[18] Its 383 pages of letterpress provide a theoretical and historical account; anyone reading the 'history' section could be forgiven for concluding that medieval Gothic had never existed and the 55 plates are exclusively Classical. Gothic is acknowledged in a chapter entitled 'On True Taste in Architecture': 'An enthusiasm for what is termed Gothic architecture is extremely prevalent at the present day; and amongst those who praise [it] there are men of good understanding ... but whose judgement being perverted by a vitiated taste, confound themselves with a crowd of admirers possessing neither scientific principles not taste ... they are erecting monuments of ignorance [they produce] models proving that we have not ... thrown off the barbarism of our ancestors ... the only true architecture is that of the ancients.'[19] Pugin would face an uphill struggle in some quarters.

1.5: 'Principal Elevation of a Chapel'. (P. Nicholson, *The New Practical Builder, and Workman's Companion*, 1823, pl. XXIII). The plate reappeared in most of Nicholson's many books over the next twenty years.

1.6: London, the New Corn Exchange, Mark Lane (G. Smith, 1827-8). This is just one of many neat Classical buildings erected in London in the late-Georgian period. The façade reveals an imaginative use of the Greek repertoire which, according to Elmes, 'produced one of the most agreeable compositions in the city' and included the cornice 'crowned by a magnificent blocking course of extraordinary height and boldness'. (T.H. Shepherd and J. Elmes, *Metropolitan Improvements*, 1827, p. 146-7 and opp. p. 131).

For those outside the profession, James Elmes' *A General and Bibliographical Dictionary of the Fine Arts* of 1826 is similarly biased. 52 pages are devoted to the 'Architecture' entry in which the Middle Ages warrants just three-quarters of a page and where Gothic is discussed it is in terms of its opposition to Classical principles. Elmes' *Lectures on Architecture* of 1823 is also revealing. Predictably, the bulk of the eight lectures dwell on antiquity, even the 65 pages of Chapter 7 – 'On the Origins and History of Architecture; in Great Britain and Ireland' largely manage to circumvent the Middle Ages and instead concentrate on Roman remains. His brief conclusions about Gothic we will address later.

As late as 1839 it was deemed expedient to publish as a separate volume the *Treatise on Architecture and Building* taken from the recent *Encyclopaedia Britannica*. This was by William Hoskin FSA, and represents yet another rehearsal of the by then standard Classical bias. The 51-page 'History of Architecture' is comprehensive, even including a paragraph on Indian architecture and two on Jewish, but the three-and-a-half pages on Gothic is hardly a balanced coverage. And when it comes to the section on 'Elements of

Beauty in Architecture' the discussion is explicitly or implicitly in Classical terms apart from a single sentence on Gothic. One could cite many other examples but the point is surely made.

Finally we come to the question of what was actually being built, and the answer is that in the 25 years after Waterloo, those engaged in building – whether individuals or committees – were almost united in wanting a Classical structure, apart from church-builders to whom we will turn later. The exceptions to this rule are rare: once we move below the very top of the country house market where a few powerful individuals had the aesthetic confidence to chose an alternative – and the wealth to gamble on its critical success – the vast majority of suburban villas and town houses remained stubbornly Classical; a school might be Tudor, but for other public buildings, as Cook had proposed, there was rarely any stylistic debate for the subscribers.[20] The pages of Shepherd and Elmes' *Metropolitan Improvements* of 1827 reveal a London dominated by sophisticated Neo-Classical landmark buildings (**Intro.1, 1.6**),[21] just as Shepherd and Britton's *Modern Athens! … or Edinburgh in the Nineteenth Century* would do four years later for Scotland's capital. In the provinces, *Lancashire Illustrated,* also of 1831, showed the recent public buildings of Liverpool, Manchester and Salford had not deviated from

1.7: Manchester, the Royal Institution (C. Barry, 1824–35). This is a particularly majestic example of the provincial demand for Classicism at this time. The church on the extreme right is St Peter's – Classical again – by James Wyatt, 1788-94, with a tower added by F. Goodwin, 1824. (*Lancashire Illustrated*, 1831, opp. p 67).

the Classical tradition (**1.7**), and the outstanding example, Liverpool's St George's Hall, had yet to be started. From Dobson's Newcastle to Busby's Brighton, it would seem not unreasonable to conclude that the architectural leadership of the post-Waterloo period was in the hands of the Classicists serving a satisfied, if conservative, clientele.[22] And even Nash, that apparent luminary of architectural diversity, actually built far more in the Classical style than in any other.

The Gothic alternative

Despite all the foregoing evidence to support the Classical cause, interest in Gothic was both tenacious and increasing. Central to our enquiry is the nature of its support. Chris Brooks' masterly assessment of the Gothic Revival[23] reveals a remarkably diverse range of constituencies, each exploiting Gothic for its own ends; one can do no better than rehearse his findings. He starts with politicians as well as those engaged in political discourse, theories of government and models of social organization where, for disparate ends, 'the Gothic past [was] claimed by radicals [as well as] conservatives'.[24] In the late eighteenth century it was a useful ally of those seeking to promote the British virtue of trade and commerce, as well as for those wishing to assert their patriotism.[25] Simultaneously, those with literary interests as wide as Shakespeare and 'bardic' poetry felt an obvious leaning to Gothic.[26] By the early nineteenth century, it could be adopted to show anti-French Revolutionary sentiments; by those keen to regain a lost, more chivalrous, pre-industrial age, as well as those seeking to give an historical legitimacy to industrial change; by those with Romantic leanings in the arts; and by those who enjoyed dressing up to stage a tournament. It provided compelling entertainment at playhouses and dioramas, and was a natural confederate for the readers of Gothic novels and the army of Walter Scott's devotees.[27] It offered a focus of study for those denied a European Grand Tour and obliged to travel in Britain, as well as providing the perfect man-made landscape accessory for the traveller seeking picturesque scenery. Importantly, the medieval past was the academic foundation for British antiquarianism, the growing popularity of which can be attested by the numerous societies that it spawned and the shelves of books devoted to British antiquities that were published.[28] To quote Rosemary Hill, 'A new taste was coming over the public sensibility, a new feeling for history and a thirst for information about the past. The Middle Ages no longer seemed merely dark and primitive, they were picturesque and romantic.'[29] To take just one example that neatly draws together a number of strands, William Wordsworth's hugely popular *A Guide Through the District of the Lakes,* which ran to five editions between 1820 and 1835 is instructive. Exploration of the remote Lakes region could satisfy those with any or all of the following passions: poetry; the picturesque; landscape painting; the power of nature; and Romanticism in general. Wordsworth begins his *Guide* with a chapter entitled 'Directions and Information for the Tourist':

There are three approaches to the Lakes through Yorkshire; the least advisable is the great north road by Catterick … The traveller, however, taking this route, might [visit] Barnard Castle … The second road leads through more interesting country beginning at Ripon, from which place see Fountains Abbey [and] Jervaux Abbey … The third approach … is through Leeds [which allows exploration of] Kirkstall Abbey [and] Bolton Abbey.[30]

For Wordsworth and his readers, it was axiomatic that the post-Waterloo traveller seeking picturesque scenery in the Lake District would have a keen interest in antiquarian matters.

There was, then, a vast range of interest groups which shared a Gothic passion in the late-Georgian period but so far we have not encountered a single architect. Indeed, even when we examine the authorship of those mansions that were being built in the Gothic style, we discover that a significant minority, including several major examples, were, in fact, designed not by professional architects but by amateurs, Christopher Hussey going so far as to state, 'two or three convinced amateurs were the most authentic exponents of the [late Georgian] period's aspirations [for Gothic]'.[31] Certainly there were a significant number of non-Classical houses erected in the early nineteenth century, but if the many Tudor examples are excluded from the count, relatively few genuinely Gothic examples are left. Their builders' precise motives are unlikely ever to be known, but it might reasonably be argued that, in the majority of cases, it came down merely to fashion[32] – with all the superficiality the term implies – rather than any deeply held belief in the style's qualities.[33] Much has been made of the mercantile origin of large swathes of the period's aristocratic stock. Was not their fondness for the 'old English' style – which, anyway, was more usually Tudor rather than Gothic – simply another example of what J.M. Robinson noted as their 'smother[ing themselves] in neo-feudal trappings and Norman-sounding suffixes in order to sound more "blue blooded"'?[34] It all suggests a rather less high-minded interpretation of events than Brooks'. Furthermore, if one accepts that at this time the architectural 'profession' was more usually seen as trade, it is even less likely that its members could do more than follow the stylistic bidding of its paymasters.

On the other hand, there were architects among the antiquarian fraternity. One could point to John Carter, whom we have encountered already, and Thomas Rickman whose *An Attempt to Discriminate the Styles of English Architecture,* first published in 1817 with many later editions, was a seminal work (**1.8**). And there was L.N. Cottingham busy producing some exemplary cathedral restorations. But among the architects responsible for the period's most memorable Gothic work – for instance James Wyatt, John Nash or Jeffry Wyatville – 'there was no proper feeling of the true spirit of Gothic architecture,'[35] claimed a critic as early as 1838, and it is thus debatable whether Wyatt and his colleagues led the fashion or merely made professional capital from its popularity. Until the next phase of the Revival is entered in *c.*1840, and we encounter the magisterial figures of A.W.N. Pugin and the Camdenian protégés, it can reasonably be argued that the profession

1.8: Plate v of T. Rickman's *An Attempt to Discriminate the Styles of Architecture in England,* 1st ed., 1817.

generally displayed little real commitment to Gothic, even if most of its members were content to compete for a Gothic commission if one came their way. However, is this claim not contradicted by the vast amount of literature on medieval architecture which appeared in the late Georgian period led by the prolific publisher John Britton? Here it is important to ask a supplementary question: how much of it was aimed specifically at the profession? The answer is that Britton, ever the consummate entrepreneur, saw his fortunes resting primarily with antiquaries, those interested in topography and the amateur historian; architects were rarely his target market.

A theme Britton rehearses in various places is this:

> England contains many magnificent examples of [Gothic architecture] … one cannot refrain from wishing that Gothic structures *were more considered, were better understood* and *in higher estimation* than they hitherto have been. Would that our Dilettanti, instead of importing the gleanings of Greece; or our Antiquaries, instead of publishing loose, incoherent prints, encourage persons duly qualified to undertake *correct, elegant publications of our cathedrals,* and other buildings before they totally fall to ruin, it would … preserve a remembrance of an *extraordinary Style of Building.*[36]

Of course, Britton was anxious to promote his own publishing initiatives in the area of British antiquities and is hardly an objective commentator. Nevertheless, here, as with much else from his presses, his sights are on connoisseurs and antiquaries rather than the architectural profession. Britton's *Descriptive Account* of his works was published in 1849, after nearly half a century of enterprise and by which time he could, not unreasonably, have claimed a key role for himself in the, by then, successful Gothic Revival. However, even here he remains modest, preferring to take credit for having encouraged and served the growing topographical and antiquarian constituencies rather than the profession. His early series, *The Beauties of England and Wales* (10 volumes, 1801-14) 'was of topographical rather than architectural interest.'[37] His commitment to a lay readership is even more explicit in the 'Introduction' to the third volume of the *Architectural Antiquities of Great Britain,* 1812 (**1.9**): acknowledging that some subscribers had expected a 'History of Medieval Architecture', Britton claimed it had always been his intention merely to issue a 'miscellaneous collection of views'. While a 'chronological [survey] in geometrical elevation, section and plan … it is admitted would be most useful and interesting to the professional architect, and the scientific antiquary; but the artist, the amateur and the greater number of readers, require variety, picturesque effect and general views. The work is addressed to each of these classes [i.e., not architects or scientific antiquaries].'[38] However, even if the profession had not been Britton's principal market, his books nevertheless 'offered the architect and the scholar accurate details of medieval architecture to copy or to study.'[39] By the *Cathedral Antiquities* (14 volumes, 1814-35) Britton seems to have been aware that a new market was developing – the late-Georgian architect struggling to understand Gothic principles – one he was beginning to exploit. Thus in

1.9: Beverley, East Riding of Yorkshire, Beverley Minster, south transept. (J. Britton, *Architectural Antiquities of Great Britain*, vol. v, 1826). Although appearing to be a perspective drawing, the transept's façade is, in fact, a flat elevation and contained all the information needed for adaptation to contemporary usage.

the 'Introduction' to *Salisbury* – the first volume of the series – of 1814 he includes, 'in planning and executing the present work, the Author has sought to inform and gratify the architect and antiquary by geometrical elevations and details; and the connoisseur and artist, by such views of buildings as display its most interesting and characteristic features [i.e. perspective views, as well as those interested in] ancient sculpture'.[40] And ten years later, for the 'Introduction' to *Wells,* he was able to claim 'the architect [has] long known and appreciated [the] utility ... of the *plans, sections etc*' of the earlier volumes in the series.[41] For his joint publishing venture, *Specimens of Gothic Architecture,* (2 volumes, 1820-3) with text by E.J. Willson and plates by Augustus Pugin, the profession was clearly identified, the title page even including that the 'Specimens ... [were] calculated to exemplify ... the practical construction of this admired class of architecture'. The '100 engravings are entirely different in style and character from those of Mr Britton's contemporary publications, being exclusively geometrical elevations and sections with a scale to each subject,'[42] intending that they would 'undoubtedly prove the greatest use to architects'.[43] What is of seminal importance to our study is that, in the early 1820s, a seasoned publisher could anticipate a clear demand for a book, the preface of which, although short, offered assistance to the designer at the most basic level. It tentatively proclaimed principles of Gothic architecture analogous to those that had served the Classical architect so well and which, by this period, were so thoroughly established that they hardly needed rehearing. But the study of Gothic architecture was still in its infancy – 'most architects had no idea where to begin to study or analyse medieval buildings',[44] and Willson felt compelled to return to first principles, complaining,

> Whether a design is for a mansion, a cottage, or a church, does not appear to have entered into the calculations of many builders. They blunder on with some confused notions of pointed arches, slender columns, and embattled parapets; and at length produce a nondescript building ... [which] unfortunately excites prejudice against, and erroneous opinions of, a class of architecture, which is susceptible of great beauties and impressive combinations. It is to obviate a repetition of such blunders, and such follies, that the present Work is produced: and, at the same time that it furnishes genuine materials for the Architect to work from, it supplies the amateur with a criterion for reference, and to guide his judgement.[45]

Willson proceeds to more detailed 'Remarks on Gothic Architecture and on Modern Imitation', the latter essentially a survey of post-Reformation Gothic failures which concludes by pointing out that Greek and Gothic have their 'own proportions and characteristic features which cannot, without impropriety, be transferred to the other.' The designer must use 'the best models ... and must endeavour to *think* in the manner of the original inventors'. He will not be led 'to servile imitation [but will be] at liberty to build in the ancient styles.'[46] Clearly, both publisher and authors believed that remedial education was necessary and the book's huge success confirmed their prediction. But what it did not offer was clear guidance to the architect unsure of the best way to design a modern Gothic church as it is essentially a book of details; they are carefully chosen and accurately recorded, but it remained for an architect to devise for himself the best way to exploit these details in a modern design. The same was true of J.P. Neale's *Views of the most interesting Collegiate and Parochial Churches in Great Britain*, of 1824. As we shall see, this was no simple task.

It is, perhaps, surprising that the success of *Specimens,* and one or two other books from Britton, did not produce a flood of volumes from other publishers aimed specifically at architects to match those produced from the Classicists, discussed above – there were no Gothic equivalents of the primers from Cook and Nicholson. There was no review of recent Gothic work that could be seen as promoting good practice in the way the various editions of *Vitruvius Britannicus* had done for Classicism, and there appears to have been only one book devoted to the design of modern churches, W.F. Pocock's *Designs for Churches and Chapels of various styles and dimensions ... with estimates ... ,* of

1819 (**1.10**, **1.18**). Pocock had already published books of villa designs and household decoration, and appears to have had no experience of church design although he claimed 'the circumstances in which I have been placed for many years past, having led me to study Ecclesiastical Architecture, which is not quite in the general line of practice ... '[47] However, the production of the book would seem to be entirely opportunistic; there is no evidence that he had given much attention to church design and his understanding of Gothic was, even by the standards of 1819, lamentable.[48] It has already been noted that Nicholson's two examples of modern churches were Classical. Yes, there were numerous books on the theme of villa residences that included a variety of Gothic and Tudor models,[49] but all these books are stylistically neutral – their examples range across the stylistic alternatives – none could claim to offer a Gothic manifesto in the way that some post-1840 volumes did, for instance the Ecclesiological Society's *Instrumenta Ecclesiastica* of 1847, the Brandon brothers' *An Analysis of Gothic Architecture* of the same year or the anonymously authored *Churches and Chapels in the Norman and Gothic styles* of 1844. Do we conclude that this indicates there was no market for such a book around 1820 because architects did not have sufficient interest in the subject to make it a financial success, or that architects' understanding of modern Gothic had matured to the extent that such a book would have been superfluous? The latter seems unlikely.

The considerable number of publications on aspects of Gothic that appeared in the post-Waterloo period was primarily aimed at the antiquarian market where 'controversy ... raged over two principle points, one concerning the nomenclature of the style and

1.10: 'Elevation of a Church in the Gothic style'. (W.F. Pocock, *Designs for Churches and Chapels*, 1819, pl. xxiv). This was the period's only book devoted to the design of churches and chapels, and although Pocock thought the composition 'exhibits a bold tower', his understanding of Gothic was clearly limited.

the other the origin of the pointed arch',[50] neither of which was high on the agenda of most architects. Britton identified 66 pre-1822 texts which he analysed in *Architectural Antiquities*;[51] modern discussion of them – and some slightly later ones – can be found in Kruft,[52] Pevsner[53] and Watkin[54] and need not detain us here. Additionally, there were many volumes on specific cathedrals and churches. Where these books include a list of subscribers they are instructive. Members of the clergy, aristocracy and gentry, schoolmasters and members of antiquarian societies dominate; architects appear only rarely. Few lists are as long as the 535 recorded in Marmaduke Prickett's *An Historical and Architectural Description of the Priory Church of Bridlington* of 1831, but only one architect, Rickman, is included.

Central to the architects' problems with Gothic was the issue of identifiable principles. To a generation of architects which had mastered the skills of Classical design by first learning a set of axioms of composition and proportion,[55] it is not surprising that it believed that the route to success in Gothic lay in mastering *that* style's distinct principles. But first they had to be identified as 'unhappily no medieval Vitruvius had collected and transmitted them'.[56] As early as 1809 Thomas Kerrick had realised the problem: '[until] the principles and rules by which [medieval churches] were designed … are discovered, all our attempts to build in the Gothic Style must be unsuccessful';[57] 34 years later, the issue was no less pressing for J.M. Neale, one of the Cambridge Camden Society luminaries:

1.11: Carlisle, the Newsroom and Library (T. Rickman, 1830-1). This was a rare example of a post-Waterloo public building which used the Gothic style.

'That there is a proportion observed between every part of an ancient church is an unquestionable fact; we feel it to be so, though we cannot at present explain the rules, nor analyse its principles.'[58] Elmes, in his *Lectures on Architecture* which we encountered in the discussion on Classical authors, continues the theme: after praising the achievements of York, Westminster Abbey and St Albans he concludes: 'Gothic architecture disdains the trammels and the systems of the schools [i.e., of Classical rules]; nevertheless it has its own laws … although they have not yet been arranged into a grammatical form.'[59]

Two books, ostensibly concerned with Gothic principles should be noted here. There was John Kendall's *An Elucidation of the Principles of English Architecture Usually Denominated Gothic* of 1818 and Matthew Bloxam's *Principles of Gothic Architecture,* first edition 1829, with nine further editions over the next 30 years. Those seeking insight from Kendall are likely to have been disappointed; he at least attempts clarification, but only at the most basic level. After a rambling 'Elucidation' he offers, 'To the experienced architect the principles here laid down may be so obvious as to be deemed almost useless; the many heterogeneous attempts to erect buildings in the pointed manner prove, however, that they are not sufficiently attended to.'[60] Eventually, we reach the chapter on 'The Principles', but it offers little enlightenment. Four are enumerated: 'I. The pyramidal form … II Buttresses, or external support … III. The peculiar form of the arch, composed of segments of circles … IV. The clustered column … [for which] no rules regulated the proportions'.[61] At least he includes 23 plates, mainly of Exeter Cathedral where he was surveyor, which an architect might have found useful, but this was not a book destined to educate the profession in any meaningful way. Bloxam's book is rather more useful, but it was hardly a set of 'principles' in the sense that it had distilled a set of identifiable rules to guide the struggling designer. However, its many little illustrations do at least supply a corpus of useful details and it offers systems for setting out the curves of arches, yet it was as much a pocket book for the 'church spotter' as a manual to sit by the drawing board.

A fundamental failing in all the books on the subject of the 'principles' of Gothic architecture was their authors' inability to realise that only by entirely abandoning the ways in which the Classical language had been analysed and applied could an architect become truly proficient with Gothic. It was a lesson that would not begin to be appreciated until the mid-1840s. Post-Waterloo architects recognised the sublime effects of York or Salisbury and they can be forgiven for believing that the way to repeat the success of these works was by identifying the principles that guided their creators, as they could, for instance, with Rome's Colosseum. For a generation weaned on the Classical rules, a realisation that success with Gothic required intuition, imagination and an exploitation of, to quote Soane, 'what is absolutely arbitrary',[62] was surely challenging.[63] E.B. Lamb was moved to complain in 1835 'The study of ancient [Gothic] architecture is fraught with difficulties, one book is examined after another … but very few can give satisfactory information, fit for practical purposes.'[64] Some even doubted that there *were* any principles waiting to be discovered and, despite the sublime qualities of medieval

1.12: London, part of the east side of Regent's Street (J. Nash, *c*.1824). T. Davis, *The Architecture of John Nash*, 1960, p. 102, refers to it as 'a clumsy composition in the neo-Greek style …[a] grotesque composition …ugly vase-shaped columns' and it might well have been the sort of debased Classicism that the correspondent in the *Architectural Magazine* had in mind when he wrote' it is not the use but the *abuse* of Grecian forms of which I complain' (vol. 2, 1835, p. 339). (T.H. Shepherd and J. Elmes, *Metropolitan Improvements*, 1827, opp. p. 98).

cathedrals, if 'Gothic was based on "no true principles", [it] therefore had "no real hold on the enlightened intellect;" with moral, political and scientific progress its allure was destroyed.'[65] Not until almost the middle of the century was the issue being addressed with confidence.[66]

The Architectural Magazine

J.C. Loudon's *Architectural Magazine* ran for five years from 1834 to 1838. It was the first journal devoted to architectural matters and, while it was not exclusively aimed at the profession,[67] it provides a useful barometer of architects' interests. It arrived almost twenty years after Waterloo and might have provided the definitive documentation in our stylistic investigation, yet on many issues it was demonstrably neutral. Loudon had already established his catholic stylistic interests in earlier publications,[68] for instance his *Encyclopaedia of Cottage, Farm and Villa Architecture* of 1833, and that impartiality continued in the *Magazine*. However, for those seeking to identify the stylistic preferences in the 1830s, several conclusions can be reached. Firstly, the 'modern style' of the period was set firmly in the Classical tradition. The volumes contain numerous theoretical articles, for instance 'On Conveniency in Architecture',[69] 'On Taste in Architecture',[70] or 'On Effect in Architecture'.[71] Most contain few explicit references to style, yet there is an underlying assumption that what is being discussed is Classical examples. However, other articles cover a range of specific stylistic alternatives, as do the model designs of, for instance, villas or churches, and the books reviewed.

In trying to understand the underlying stylistic attitudes of Loudon, his contributors and his readership, one important conclusion is supportable: Classicism might be *the* style of the age, but that did not absolve it from criticism; far from it. Classicism had to endure its fair share of vitriol: from Soane and Wilkins, at the top of the profession, to the designers of modern shop fronts at the bottom, none was spared from the wrath of the critic. Typical in sentiment was this: 'it is not the *use* but the *abuse* of [Grecian forms] of which I complain'.[72] Central here were the conflicting ideals of 'imitation' and 'originality' – the 'purity' of Greek architecture seemed beyond question yet its application to contemporary building types was often deemed wanting (**1.12**). Indeed, Classicism had all the characteristics of a once proud style reduced to a feeble and debased dotage. Gothic likewise had detractors and admirers – and was mired by the 'imitation versus originality' debate just as much as Classicism – but, crucially, one senses it was a style in the ascendancy.

A few quotations will provide a flavour of the *Magazine's* attitudes: 'Gothic has too many details … no architecture is more disposed … to produce effect than Greek Doric';[73] modern Classical adaptation was often criticised yet there was praise for Wilkins' porticoes at the National Gallery and London University;[74] 'our ancient church architecture is again in the ascendancy, proudly triumphing over the various abominations of the dark ages … which commenced at the Dissolution';[75] 'Gothic was invented … for obtaining magnificence in places of worship and none other … it should properly be called 'the architecture of churches [and not used for secular work]';[76] 'The study of Gothic has inoculated the British architectural world with a mania for [Gothic] but little anticipated by its admirers of twenty years ago';[77] discussing the rebuilding of the Royal Exchange, the writer urged architects to 'eschew Gothic … and instead develop the early palatial style of modern Italy'.[78]

It would be going too far to suggest that the *Magazine* identified Gothic as the salvation of contemporary architecture's various shortcomings, yet it seemed to offer a welcome vibrancy in the face of Classicism's malaise, and one that helpfully reflected those qualities of 'Britishness' brought to the fore, in part, by the debates engendered by the Houses of Parliament competition to which we will turn presently.

Looked at from a different perspective, we might conclude issues of style were of only limited concern to the journal's professional readership: the quality and integrity of the design was more important than its stylistic cloak. Furthermore, a significant proportion of the *Magazine's* content is well removed from the stylistic arguments.[79] In these contexts the rival claims of Classical or Gothic must have seemed old-fashioned or irrelevant and, inevitably, a few voices asked why the age had not developed a style of its own. Perhaps the single most significant conclusion to be taken from the *Architectural Magazine* adds little to our stylistic investigation but suggests that the day was fast approaching when the real challenges for the profession would not be concerned with the use of past styles but with satisfying an increasingly educated and demanding public requiring ever greater levels of comfort, efficient planning and functional convenience, demands that could best be met by exploiting new materials and production processes, and best provided by a properly organised and regulated profession in which the public could enjoy confidence.[80] This was an age of change and the new age would be at least as concerned with a building's functional achievements as it would be with its stylistic niceties.

The Palace of Westminster competition, 1835

The old Palace of Westminster was destroyed by fire on the evening of 16 October 1834. Its passing was mourned by neither the legislators who had struggled with its ill-planned accommodation nor architectural commentators who despised its lack of magnificence or even coherence. But among antiquaries and the wider public, it had a historical resonance that was treasured. For the profession, the new Palace of Westminster would be the biggest and most prestigious architectural commission in British history, and it is not surprising that individual members sought to influence the conditions of the competition on terms that best suited themselves: naked self-interest was wrapped in all sorts of supposedly higher architectural ideals. The debates which surrounded the competition were perfectly timed to make a very useful case study for our investigation into the stylistic attitudes of the profession.

There had been calls for new Houses of Parliament in the eighteenth century and the prospect of a prestigious new building was, to quote Summerson, 'that project on which ... were focused the hopes of British architecture'.[81] A number of architects responded with essentially speculative schemes, for instance William Kent in the 1730s, Robert and James Adam in *c*.1762 and John Soane in the 1770s and later. All were Classical – Soane even referred to his as a 'Senate House' – and what subject could be more appropriate for a monumental, academic Classical essay? However, architects underestimated the power of historical precedent; Wyatt's alterations and additions for the House of Lords (from 1799) were appropriately Gothic, a style that acquired new national legitimacy[82] at the time of Britain's struggle with France, and Soane even had to demolish his partially completed Classical façade to the adjacent Court of King's Bench and replace it with a Gothic design following a vitriolic attack from a handful of M.P.s with strong stylistic preferences.[83] (**1.13**) Following the fire, the profession might have anticipated that it would not have an easy ride trying to please a group of opinionated patrons adept at getting its own way.[84]

Only a year before the fire, several architects were consulted about building a new House of Commons; their proposals were overwhelmingly Classical, and only a matter

1.13: London, the Palace of Westminster, the King's Entrance (J. Soane, 1822-4). Even a Classicist like Soane felt compelled to use Gothic for his new work at Westminster. (T.H. Shepherd and J. Elmes, *Metropolitan Improvements*, 1827, p. 146-7 and opp. p. 154).

of months after the fire, and before the details of the competition were announced, C.H. Tatham chose to exhibit his unsolicited proposal for rebuilding.[85] Predictably, it was Classical; indeed what architect of this period would have believed he could produce a better chance of securing the ultimate commission of a lifetime in any other style? Thus when the parliamentary Committee for Rebuilding[86] published its conditions in June 1835, especially that entries must be either Gothic or Elizabethan in style, they must have been greeted with a mixture of dismay and disbelief by a profession already dreaming of Greek and Roman extravaganzas; Gothic might be popular for churches and occasionally for villas, but 'no one had ever suggested that a large secular public building should be designed in that style'.[87] The official reason for the stylistic prescription was 'the peculiar charm of Gothic architecture in its associations; these are delightful because they are historical, patriotic, local and intimately blended with early reminiscences.'[88]

Arguments in favour of a Classical scheme appeared from outside the profession – several published 'Letters' from 'W.R. Hamilton Esq. to the Earl of Elgin' led the way – but initially the architects themselves were remarkably quiet. Charles Fowler was a rare exception: he complained that the stipulation of Gothic or Elizabethan was 'likely to preclude the best ideas … as it encourages architects to copy past examples rather than' seek originality.[89] An anonymous writer claimed 'It must be evident that, in the

Gothic style, the intended structure cannot aspire to more than third-rate character,'[90] while another did not object to Gothic but saw Elizabethan as 'mongrel buildings [and] among the blemishes rather than the beauties of art … Gothic … may be considered … as properly ecclesiastical or collegiate … but for a senate house, what are its recommendations?'[91] 'Mr Hakewill … an advocate of the Classic style … compare[d] Gothic to a weed and the Classical style to a flower' in expressing his preferences.[92] Benjamin Ferrey 'readily conceded that much dissatisfaction and regret [was] felt by the practitioners in Grecian and Roman architecture' although he was more sanguine about the stipulation.[93] Others objected to any proscription: 'For our part, we exceedingly regret that the Commission did not leave the choice of style to the competing architects'[94] and 'those who were invited to send in designs should not only have been left to choose the style of architecture, but also the site.'[95] But generally, the 97 architects who submitted designs were too busy, or too politically astute, to complain; once Barry was announced as victor, in Clark's wonderfully pithy words, 'ninety-six disillusioned architects were free to voice their dislike of Gothic.'[96] The *Architectural Magazine* summed up the situation: 'We certainly think a better design than any exhibited [in the public exhibition of entries] might be produced in the Italian manner … [One might assume this] exhibition will show the state of architectural talent in this country. This is by no means true, as the unfortunate restriction of the committee … restricted the style to Gothic or nondescript Elizabethan; it will only show the ingenuity with which architects have tortured the forms of the ecclesiastical architecture to the purposes of a senate house to be erected in the nineteenth century.'[97] In later editions, the journal noted: 'many of those [architects] that might have been expected [to submit designs] have decided to stand aloof; one reason might be that the style was restricted to Gothic or Elizabethan[98] … why not [allow] that style of architecture we behold at Greenwich [English Baroque] … we regard prescribing the style as Gothic as … altogether unworthy of the present age.'[99] Despite winning the third prize with an Elizabethan design, David Hamilton was moved to lament 'Gothic barbarism is again to be allowed to triumph over the masterpieces of Italy and Greece … Let it not be said that we run away from our own [Classical] principles when an opportunity is offered of placing before the eyes of Europe what we can effect … Gothic architecture having in truth, no strict rules of proportion, size, height, mouldings, decoration being all arbitrary, you will there indeed be safe from criticism.'[100] Even two years after Barry's victory, letters of complaint were still being written[101] and perhaps the debate would have continued further had Loudon not ceased publication of the *Magazine* in 1838. Few spoke in favour of the Gothic restriction. An article in 1835, probably by Loudon, was balanced in its judgements;[102] Benjamin Ferrey also produced some reasoned stylistic support for Gothic.[103] Only a paper by the young A.W.N. Pugin enthusiastically endorsed the committee's stylistic preferences.[104]

What conclusions should we draw from this episode in which professional attitudes to a range of issues were laid bare? One senses a Classical old guard which either shunned

1.14: Manchester, St Matthew, Camp Field (C. Barry, 1822-5). An expensive and impressive design – paid for entirely by the Church Building Commission – although one that could hardly be seen as having much archaeological fidelity. (*Lancashire Illustrated*, 1831, opp. p. 90).

the competition altogether, or grudgingly struggled to produce a passable non-Classical scheme. Only among a small section of younger architects does there appear to have been enthusiasm for Gothic. Central to the profession's problems was the question of precedent: there was nothing remotely close to a medieval parliament building capable of acting as a model. But this perceived problem reveals much about the profession's anxieties; it was not enough that ecclesiastical Gothic might be adapted, or – to paraphrase Soane – that individuals try to imagine what a medieval architect *would* have done if asked to design a parliament building. It seems the profession felt on safe grounds only if it could quote historical precedent for its design decisions and could point to respectable sources for mass, proportions and details. It appears that it was an age that was not simply in awe of the studiously studied Classical models to an extent that they now enjoyed an authority that seemed to limit adaptation, but that this misplaced deference to the past was perhaps even more stultifying for the Goths. It was the perfect illustration of the conflicting demands of 'imitation' and 'originality' to which we have referred above. A further revealing point is this: 'We would have preferred an Hellenistic style, or a variant such as ancient Roman; for the beauty of these styles is less subject to local and contemporary preferences than is the Gothic style. A public building intended to last for centuries, must not owe its beauty to a whim of fashion.'[105] Surely this is the crux of the issue: Classicism, it seems, represented a series of timeless values; Gothic was deemed to be but a transitory fad.

On a wider level, we might seek to consider the rebuilding in the context of professional practice. Coincidently, the Westminster fire and formation of the Institute of British Architects were virtually concurrent.[106] But what does this commission reveal about the state and status of the profession? That parliament chose to manage the competition itself, refused to include professional assessors and even failed to consult the profession about the most efficacious means of obtaining its new home would seem to suggest the profession was by no means held in high regard.

Did the committee reach the right stylistic decision? By 1850, long before the building was completed, its style 'had ceased to please refined taste [and] the New Palace was condemned as a stylistic travesty, and a grossly expensive one at that'.[107] However, the parliamentary supervision of the projects and the project management of the huge undertaking came to be seen as exemplary. And despite the unashamed historicism of its style, in terms of its use of new materials and construction techniques, and in its provision of services such as heating and ventilation, it was ground-breaking. Whatever mid-century critics might have felt about Barry's particular brand of Perpendicular, few by then would have dreamed of questioning the Gothic prescription. Perhaps better than any other building project, it showed the real power of popular sentiment for the medieval past and all the political, religious and historical associations it encompassed.[108] It was surely this rather than any lead from the architectural profession that eventually terminated Classicism's long dominance of British architecture.

The design of churches

A survey of the churches of the post-Waterloo period might reasonably lead to the conclusion that, despite the Classical preferences clearly displayed by architects in other building types, the profession at least concluded that Gothic was the better style for ecclesiastical commissions. A.G. Cook, whom we have already encountered, had come to this conclusion as early as 1820 and it seems a fair summary of the built evidence: 'The Grecian taste certainly best suits those public buildings such as palaces, courts of justice, exchanges, hospitals, music-rooms, banqueting-rooms, museums etc, but for religious structures Gothic, undoubtedly, might be preferred ... [He proceeds to compare St Paul's with Westminster Abbey] We may very easily and seriously tell which has the greater effect on the mind ... which conveys the more devout ideas, which fills the senses with the greater attention to the heaven above us ... [and] on life to come ... Therefore condemn not Gothic entirely, but as occasion serves, and subject requires, give preference to it.'[109] Yet even for church work, a closer examination of the profession's stylistic attitudes suggest that it was far from being united behind Cook's philosophy. So from where did the enthusiasm for Gothic churches proceed? First, we need to consider the church building context.

The majority of new churches in this period were the products of the 1818 Church Building Act,[110] (**1.14**) and those that were financed by other means were much influenced by its lead. At this point we should examine the stylistic pronouncements of the Commission that administered the Act. The administrators of the previous two post-Reformation church building initiatives – that which followed the Fire of London and the so-called Queen Anne churches – consciously chose to build in the most fashionable architectural style of the day, Baroque.[111] However, the Commissioners for the 1818 Act seem to have been more concerned with practical matters like durability and, in the words of the Act's much-quoted Section 62, 'providing proper accommodation for the greatest number at the least expense'.[112] But to dismiss entirely the Commissioners' architectural ambitions in this way is misleading; elsewhere they required 'that the character be preserved, both externally and internally, of an ecclesiastical edifice for divine worship according to the rites of the United Church of England and Ireland'.[113] And more explicitly, one of the leading Commissioners, Archdeacon Wollaston, sent a long letter to George Jenner, the Commission's secretary, in August 1819. He was unhappy with some of the early designs 'We get most crude devices: tasteless and unauthorised exterior; ill-arranged interior ... anxious as I am that the work be done economically ... at the same time [it should be done] handsomely because we are supporting the National Religion'.[114] But while the Commission might have been determined to have dignified buildings, it appears to have been ambivalent about the style that would best satisfy this ambition, as Wollaston continued: 'Of an exterior ... we may have either a Greek dress ... or a Gothic dress, and we may adopt the one or the other.'[115] The three Crown Architects, Nash, Smirke and Soane, who were asked to submit specimen schemes, provided between them many alternatives in a range of Classical and Gothic idioms. Smirke's were predictably in a severe Greek style, but even Soane was coaxed to invent a Gothic design as well as a Norman one. Nash's ten proposals were certainly varied, or, according to Summerson, 'the impression they give is that everybody in the office was allowed to have a go'.[116] We can, then, reasonably conclude that the Commission had no intention of setting a stylistic lead and that its ambivalence was both reflected and confirmed by its professional advisors, the Crown Architects.[117] Thus the stylistic debates were delegated to the local committees that were required to promote the design of its choice;[118] the approval of the Board, after consulting its Building Committee and the Crown Architects, was almost entirely dependant on issues such as size, cost and durability, and was rarely influenced by the design's style.

Although often dismissed as 'cheap', the Commissioners' churches were, in fact, substantial building projects, especially the first wave in the 1820s; for many recipient communities, the new church would be by far the most expensive building ever to appear in the area. The Commission's initiatives were also a major boost to the architectural profession; literally dozens of relatively high-budget projects were available for the ambitious architect to pursue. At a time when building activity was still recovering from the long and debilitating war with France, the Commission's largesse represented valuable stimulation and it is unlikely that many architects would have willingly passed by such opportunities for the sake of personal stylistic ideals. If a local committee wanted a certain style, there would, surely, be no shortage of architects willing to oblige. Chantrell himself usefully illuminates the point. Writing to Soane in January 1821, seeking guidance in the creation of a church design in a convincing Gothic dress, he included, 'I should wish to present a Grecian or Roman design, but the objections to them, made by the Local Committee, would be so strong that I fear my labour would be entirely lost, still I must say that I consider the present a firm opportunity for restoring the best examples of Greece and Rome.' Earlier in the letter he wrote, 'I expect to be strongly opposed by some persons in this and the neighbouring towns who have submitted to the county mania for plain Gothic works.'[119] 25 years later, an article he published in *The Builder* included the statement, 'though generally well grounded in Greek and Roman architecture [the architects of the Gothic churches of the 1820s] found themselves called upon to construct works utterly at variance with Greek and Roman principles; and having no time to study or collect data were required at once to compose works in the unfamiliar style.'[120] It will be rewarding to enquire further into the attitudes of local committees, presumably reflecting parochial preferences, in an attempt to test Chantrell's statements.

George Steuart's St Chad, Shrewsbury (1790-2), and S.P. Cockerell's St Mary, Banbury (1790-7), are the well-rehearsed examples of late-eighteenth century churches. And they are both Classical. Indeed, Terry Friedman's extensive research reveals that of the eighteenth century's total of 520 new or entirely rebuilt churches, 451 – or 86% –

were Classical.[121] Nevertheless, there is evidence of changing attitudes before the end of the century,[122] and by the early years of the next one, Classicism had lost its clear dominance of church building. Associative values were increasingly prized and Gothic's popular image as the style of traditional worship acquired a new significance. For a social stratum rather lower than that which employed Steuart and Cockerell, arguably it was a significance that had never entirely disappeared; and for the educated middle classes, Gothic also chimed perfectly with the growing popularity of British antiquarianism as a respectable pastime. For all, war-induced patriotism provided Gothic with a new resonance. These associative values were increasingly alluded to in publications aimed at the general reader. Although not the first, Carter's account of being moved by Gothic's 'pale religious light'[123] and 'nothing can be more in character and better adapted to a place of worship, than that awful style of building [called Gothic] … Grecian and Roman architecture should be confined to mansions and other structures of ease and pleasure',[124] helped establish attitudes. In 1806 Loudon claimed the 'general effect of a [Gothic] cathedral … far surpasses that of any Grecian building in producing that exhilarating sublimity which is so analogous to the purpose for which they are erected. This may be felt when comparing the effect of Westminster Abbey, or York Cathedral, with St Paul's.'[125] Britton's publications tended to be more objective, but included references to Gothic's capacity to 'command awful veneration'.[126] And in 1824, J.P. Neale noted 'the interior of [St Mary's Abbey, Shrewsbury] has still much of that solemn dignity which inevitably fills the mind with religious awe to the excitement of which, ancient Cathedrals and Monastic Churches, contribute in a degree so far beyond all other ecclesiastical structures, that the art of man has ever yet produced.'[127] The link between spiritual experience and Gothic architecture was a compelling one, or as the Revd G.A. Poole explained it twenty years later, 'Greek art is beautiful, Gothic art is sublime'.[128] Thus we can identify as examples of this popular taste the four new churches in the parish of Simonburn, Northumberland, of 1815-17, simple but unmistakeably Gothic. Coming to the debate from a different angle was the Revd Hammond Roberson of Liversedge, West Yorkshire, who from 1812 onwards, sought to promote not just Gothic tokenism, but medieval arrangements that would allow compliance with Prayer Book rubrics, and was highly influential. Even an architect of Soane's status was not immune from this popular sentiment. As well as supplying specimen designs, Soane also secured three jobs from the Commissioners; one of them, Holy Trinity, St Marylebone, London (1826-7), seems to have been a particularly frustrating project for the architect. The Vestry – in effect the local committee – wanted Gothic and was belligerent. After submitting several alternative Classical models, none of which, for various reasons, was greeted enthusiastically, Soane was obliged to compose a Gothic scheme in an attempt to placate his clients. This was only abandoned in favour of one of the previously rejected Classical designs on the basis of its claimed excessive cost.[129] Another major architect whose Classical ambitions were thwarted by his patron was C.R. Cockerell. His design for a new church in Birdsall, East Riding, for Lord

1.15: London, St Mary's Chapel, Somers Town (W. Inwood and H.W. Inwood, 1824-7). It is a particularly grim example of Commissioners' Gothic and the one singled out by A.W.N. Pugin for ridicule in *Contrasts*. (T.H. Shepherd and J. Elmes, *Metropolitan Improvements*, 1827, opp. p. 163).

Middleton 'with a tetra-style Ionic portico' of 1822 was rejected in favour of a Gothic composition by John Oates of Halifax,[130] a competent but unremarkable designer.

Elsewhere, we can point to a succession of architects who would normally be considered skilled Classicists but who produced some decidedly mediocre Gothic churches and we might reasonably enquire why this was. The ecclesiastical commissions of Lewis Vulliamy, Francis Bedford and William Henry Inwood will repay investigation in this respect. All had undertaken travel in Italy, Greece or Asia Minor, Vulliamy and Bedford were trained in the offices of Classicists, and Bedford and Inwood authored important books of Classical archaeology. Their major secular works are all Classical. Inwood, working with his father, designed arguably the best Classical church of the period – St Pancras (1819-22) – and several other good ones; he also designed one of the least convincing of the Gothic examples, St Mary, Somers Town, London (1822-4) (**1.15**), a church pilloried by Pugin, the *Gentleman's Magazine*, Clarke and Summerson, the latter referring to it as, 'one of the most pitiful bungles in the way of Gothic revivalism ever perpetrated.'[131] Elsewhere he showed no sympathy with the style. Bedford designed nine churches including 'four … scholarly Greek Revival [ones] with effectively-designed steeples';[132] some of his Gothic designs are quite without redeeming features, for instance St George, Newcastle-under-Lyme (1827-8). Only Vulliamy used Gothic extensively in his church work. While he could, on occasions, produce a good Gothic design, he also produced some dull ones. A similar pattern can be seen in the provinces. The Leeds-based architect John Clark, who came from Edinburgh, subsequently enjoyed considerable success exploiting the Classical idioms he learned in Scotland for a range of Yorkshire public and private commissions. Yet when he came to design his sole new church, he made a rare, and hardly convincing, Gothic foray. The case of John Dobson of Newcastle is also revealing. He is best remembered for his elegant Classical buildings in the city's centre, but his extensive country house work demonstrates an early use of Tudor as well as more predictable Greek motifs. For his few churches, the style was pedestrian Gothic – Summerson judging that, for ecclesiastical architecture, he displayed 'no aptitude whatever' – and for his major one, St Thomas, Newcastle, he seems to have produced both Classical and Gothic alternatives with the committee choosing the latter.[133] In all these cases – and many others that could be quoted – it seems not unreasonable to conclude that the architects were responding, reluctantly, to what Chantrell identified as the lay 'mania for Gothic'. Local committees were, indeed, in a powerful position to dictate matters of style.

On the other hand, we can point to architects for whom the Gothic preferences of the local committees seem merely to have confirmed an existing interest in the style and a belief in its suitability for churches, although the list is not a long one. Thomas Rickman and Thomas Taylor come to mind. Rickman was self-taught and produced a number of compelling Gothic designs before 1818, sometimes working in conjunction with the wealthy ironmaster, John Cragg. Subsequently, he produced many more churches, including some that rank among the best of the period, especially when he was working for a wealthy private patron, although he was adept at producing Classical designs too. Taylor began his career with a competent Classical design for the new Court House in Leeds, but went on to design a succession of good Gothic churches, beginning with the much admired Christ Church, Liversedge (1812-16), for the Revd Roberson. Although several of them were hardly archaeologically accurate, they nevertheless revealed Taylor's commitment to the style for ecclesiastical commissions.

It was not just the associational value of Gothic that endeared it to local committees and thwarted the profession's Classical ambitions; cost was also a factor in Gothic's favour. Port suggests the Commission's insistence on traditional materials might have contributed to the decreasing popularity of Classicism: a Classical church required a portico, and one carved in stone would inevitably be expensive. A Classical church also required a tower to distinguish it from a non-conformist meeting houses, whereas a Gothic design might need only a small bell-cote to denote its function if funds were tight.[134] Taylor believed

Gothic windows were cheaper than Classical ones and produced detailed costings to prove the point,[135] although initially Chantrell believed that 'the buttresses, pinnacles, indented parapets and other appendages will cause the expense of Gothic to exceed considerably that of Grecian or Roman.'[136]

A further reason for thinking that the profession was by no means united behind Gothic church building initiatives is that, aside from those with Classical inclinations, a range of alternative ideas were put forward. These included calls: to develop the Anglo-Norman Style;[137] to design circular churches with concentric rings of seats focused on a central pulpit, 'it is quite inappropriate to design modern protestant churches on the model of a Roman Catholic Cathedral';[138] to exploit Lombard-Romanesque for cheap churches;[139] to go back to Wren's city churches for inspiration, '[they] are almost the perfection of Protestant church building'.[140] A few years later, other works looked to 'natural geometry' as a means of going 'beyond' the present pointed system of architecture,[141] and to the exploitation of iron as the ideal material for all building types instead of masonry.[142]

What conclusions can we reach about the choice of style for church-building in the pre-1840 period? A fondness for Classicism lingered in London and occasionally elsewhere through the 1820s, although generally, the preference was for Gothic. The driving force for it seems to have come from outside the profession; the associative value

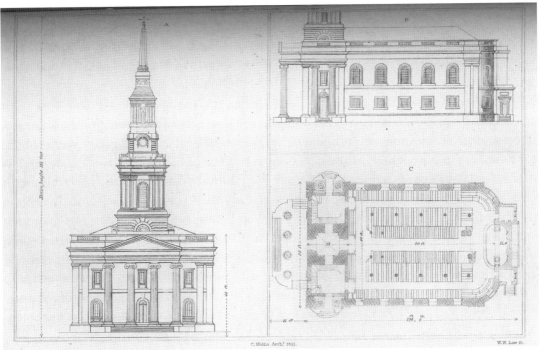

1.16: London, All Saints, Poplar (C. Hollis, 1821-3). The design was typical in both its plan and west elevation of many Classical churches of the period. (A. Pugin and J. Britton, *Illustrations of the Public Buildings of London*, vol. 1, 1825, opp. p. 176)..

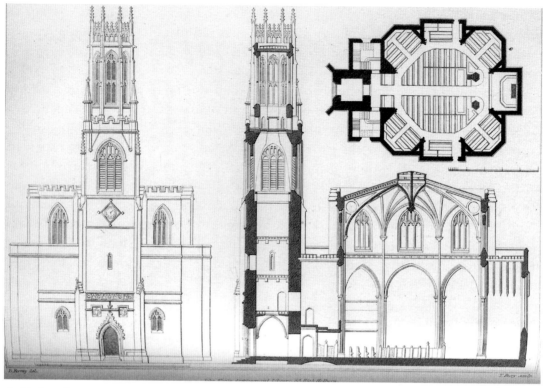

1.17: London, St Dunstan's-in-the-West, Fleet Street (J. Shaw, 1831-3). Although the tower has a convincingly medieval lantern, the novel plan would have rendered the church as of little use to those architects seeking an adaptable model of modern Gothic. (A. Pugin and J. Britton, *Illustrations of the Public Buildings of London*, 2nd ed., 1838, opp. p. 187).

of Gothic in this period was a central concern of those privately funding or contributing to projects, those administering them at a local level, as well as for ordinary worshippers.

There was at least general agreement about the floor plans of new churches, regardless of their style. Wren had claimed his St James, Piccadilly (1676-84) was the ideal Protestant church, 'beautiful and convenient, and as such, the cheapest I could invent'.[143] It was the model for James Gibbs' St Martin-in-the-Fields in London (1722-6), an arrangement that was much copied during the eighteenth century, and Soane's starting point when asked by the Commissioners to recommend a plan.[144] This arrangement – a rectangular body with a shallow 'chancel' and vestries at either side forming the (liturgical) east end, and a tower flanked by stairs to the galleries at the other (**1.16**) – became almost ubiquitous, but not before a variety of alternatives were considered. The Crown Architects' specimen designs included an imaginative set of plans – for instance, cruciform and octagonal – but it seems cost quickly ruled them out.[145] Interestingly, the first volume of Augustus Pugin and John Britton's *Illustrations of the Public Buildings of London*, the one that contained the capital's churches, first appeared in 1825. Among its plans are several interesting

1.18: 'Design for a Church in the Gothic Style'. (W.F. Pocock, *Designs for Churches and Chapels*, 1819, pl. xxix). This is another of Pocock's idiosyncratically decorated Gothic designs.

alternatives to the Wren/Gibbs rectangle: the domed St Stephen's, Walbrook, by Wren, and the circular St Peter-le-Poor, by Jesse Gibson; the 1838 edition included the octagonal St Dunstan's –in-the-West, by John Shaw of 1831-3 (**1.17**). None of them seem to have diverted architects from the Wren and Gibbs models that the book also illustrated. This was the Commissioners' favoured arrangement, although it seems not to have been made explicit; how it could best be presented in a Gothic dress was left to individual architects to resolve. Some, like Inwood and Bedford, failed miserably; others, for instance Rickman, produced some exceptional work. Between these extremes, practitioners like Francis Goodwin and Chantrell worked hard to overcome the difficulties presented by the unfamiliar style coupled with far from generous budgets and they should be commended for their efforts. Their task was compounded by a lack of suitable models in published form; there were almost no useful publications of post-Reformation Gothic designs; as we have seen already, A.G. Cook's *New Builder's Magazine* of 1820 included only a single church and that was a 1770s design of Carter's with unorthodox transepts and somewhat at variance with the preferred early-nineteenth-century model; the two examples of churches in the other widely read manual, Nicholson's *New Practical Builder* of 1823, were Classical. Those in W.F. Pocock's *Designs for Churches and Chapels*, of 1819[146] – apparently the only book of the immediately post-1818 period devoted to this building type – were pedestrian and the Gothic ones inept (**1.10**, **1.18**); it is not surprising the 1835 edition was savaged in the *British Critic*.[147] Pugin and Britton's *Illustrations* was a sound survey of London churches and, as if to confirm the profession's preferences, the majority of the examples were Classical. There was, in short, nothing that provided real assistance to the struggling middle-order Gothic practitioner.[148] The Crown Architects offered few adaptable models, and the other leading architects of the day were conspicuous by their absence from the church-building arena. Furthermore, of the architects of this period generally deemed to be proficient at Gothic work, L.N. Cottingham had almost no engagement with new churches and preferred to concentrate his undisputed skills in restorations;[149] Anthony Salvin, despite Jill Allibone's claims for his 'pioneering' Gothic work,[150] and exceptional understanding of the style, produced little ecclesiastical work before the 1830s; George Webster of Kendal,[151] another pioneer, was busy with domestic work and his churches are unremarkable.

Any attempt at an objective assessment of these Gothic churches still has to overcome the Ecclesiologists' bigoted and comprehensive dismissal of them which lingers on in folk-lore, if not in academic circles, even into the twenty-first century.[152] The Ecclesiologists needed their condemnation to be convincing in order to promote their own architectural agenda, and they did a very thorough job on both counts.[153] However, at the time of their construction, the churches of the 1820s and 1830s were generally well received and widely admired, the chairman of the subscribers at Bordesley, Birmingham, being moved to write to the Commissioners that 'the solidity of the monument [Goodwin] had raised will mark for many centuries the good taste of the present age'.[154] Some were very fine and the few that escaped the unsympathetic hands of ecclesiological modernizers are often stately and impressive.

Architecture: a profession or a trade?

The status and remunerated activity of those claiming the title 'architect' is another central theme in the study of this period. It is an issue that has already been touched on and it will appear again in Chapter 3. On the one hand, Soane had established the architect's professional responsibility in the oft-quoted passage from his *Plans, Sections and Elevations of Buildings* of 1788,[155] and Soane was fond of the term 'professors' to imply the exalted intellectual status of architects. However, half a century later it was still possible for Pugin's caricature of architectural practise in *Contrasts* to have a resonance. The first plate was 'dedicated … to the trade' and in it the author pillories such issues as architectural education and expertise, the absence of any stylistic integrity and the popularity of cheap modern materials as economical alternatives to traditional ones. Perhaps more damning for the profession – since the caricature was rehearsed before a much wider audience – was the inclusion of Seth Pecksniff as one of the principal characters in Dickens' *Martin Chuzzlewit* of 1844. Here the 'architect' is a man who 'had never designed or built anything' and whose income was derived from the collection of rents and 'the reception of pupils' whose families or guardians paid not inconsequential premiums in expectation of an education that failed to materialise. When his pupil Chuzzlewit wins a competition to build a new grammar school, Pecksniff claims the design as his own.[156]

The foundation of the Institute of British Architects in 1834 was a milestone and, to some extent, sought to define the practice of architecture in the mind of the public at a time when professional bodies already existed for surveyors and engineers. On the one hand, the establishment of the IBA can be interpreted as representing architecture's coming of age, 'as an expression of growing professional confidence and increased maturity.'[157] On the other hand, it can be seen as 'an expression of insecurity',[158] the need to 'raise the public perception of the profession',[159] and protect it from builders, rent-collectors, surveyors and engineers, all of whom cast a covetous eye over the architects' territory. To some extent, the upper end of the profession was insulated from this threat and was able to continue reasonably genteel practice in the eighteenth-century manner well into Victoria's reign. However, for those lower down the scale, the issue was more pressing. Especially in the provinces where, traditionally, the majority of buildings were designed by the builder who erected them, what was perceived as the 'extra' expense of the architect was likely to be seen as an extravagance. And settling that issue only led to the next: was architecture an essentially intellectual pursuit, or a species of the building trades?

Arguably, the patronage of the Church Building Commission was crucial in establishing the architect's importance and his responsibilities. Its work reached almost every medium-sized town in the country and it demanded standards of professional competence on which it was uncompromising. It was at least as concerned with matters of construction, budgeting and management as it was with composition. It was meticulous about communication, the approval of drawings and the fees paid to architects. Significantly, it promoted standards that few of the builder/architects or surveyor/architects could achieve which further helped separate architects from builders and define their respective roles. The Commissioners' belief that the employment of a competent architect was the best means of securing a well-designed, durable structure at a fair price – as Soane had argued – was widely followed. It was a model ideally suited to the committee patronage which defines much of the huge post-Waterloo building scene throughout England. For the committee assembled to erect a mechanics' institute, a corn exchange, a school or a market – even down to the erection of a modest house for a schoolmaster – the rule was unambiguous: whenever public money was being spent on building, it was essential for all concerned that an architect be employed to control the finances and manage the tradesmen. However, progress in defining the architect's responsibilities was far from straightforward: where was the line to be drawn? Should an architect be employed to cure a smoking chimney or clear rats from the drains? Where he designed a new market hall to replace an old one, should he be expected to value the materials from the demolished building and arrange their auction? Should he advise on the sums to be paid by tenants in his recently completed row of shops, arrange advertisements for lessees and subsequently collect the rents? There was still much work to be done in defining the architect's special calling.

The 1840s

In 1840, Chantrell's career still had a decade to run, but this is a convenient point at which to close the discussion of the professional and stylistic debates. By then he was a very well-established church architect, the completion of his Leeds Parish Church and Bruges Cathedral jobs would soon further enhance his status, and he was widely seen as something of an expert in medieval archaeology. Apart from a handful of Tudor-style schools, he had nailed his colours firmly to the Gothic mast – at least in public – and there was no profound stylistic debate to engage him.

In the wider context of English architecture this is also a sensible place to draw this chapter to a close. The path of the country's architecture in the 1840s would be very different from that of the 1820s and 1830s, and with a largely new set of leading characters. By the end of 1840 Hope, Nash, Soane, Wilkins and Wyatville were all dead. Only Smirke of the leading early-nineteenth-century figures lived on, but designed little after 1838 and retired in 1845. Importantly, historians now have at their disposal an excellent, if short, recent account of the 1840s.[160] From the very beginning of that decade a shift in architectural direction is discernable. Alongside the easily identified demands that stylistic change was urgently needed are more obscure, but no less real, indications that calls for change had already attained critical mass – a future Gothic supremacy was beginning to be discussed as something inevitable.[161]

One of the points that seems to emerge in the quarter century after Waterloo is that while there wre certainly differences of opinion on a range of architectural matters, there was no discernable avant-garde. The Classicists might be dismissed as reactionary, but even among the Goths and the other stylistic camps, there was little discernable passion for their cause. Those favouring Greek or Gothic did so using very much the same language and reasoning as their stylistic opponents, and for those who remained outside the conflict, many of the best architects could work with equal ease in any of the stylistic alternatives. Conversely, the confluence of the writings of A. W.N. Pugin, the theological radicalism of the Oxford Movement and the liturgical and architectural innovations of the Cambridge Camden Society gave a new energy to architectural thinking after 1840, 'not so much because the Gothic was yet the dominant style … nor because Gothic buildings were always the best … but because the Goths and their admirers were young, vocal and closely engaged with the issues of the day'.[162]

2

Childhood, Architectural Education and the Beginning of a Career

The Chantrell family

The little we know about earlier generations of the Chantrell family suggests lower middle-class status. However, it is with Chantrell's father that the family's fortunes take a distinct move up the social scale; like many at this time, he identified, and was able to exploit, opportunities presented by the processes of industrialisation and the infrastructure necessary to support them.

Chantrell's great-grandfather, Thomas, died in Salisbury and his great-grandmother Mary (née Speakman) died in London.[1] Their son Robert [I] (1734-1811) was born in Oxford. He was a grocer and his wife, Dinah (née Messman) (1735-1807), was born in London.[2] They had three children: Thomas (1762-1830),[3] Robert [II] (1765-1840)[4] and Mary (1777-1847).[5] The birthplace of Thomas and Mary is not known, but Robert [II] was born in London[6] and perhaps the family lived there. He married Mary Ann (née Dennis) (1776-1829), who was born in Newington[7] and perhaps it was through her that that they came to settle in the area and acquire the property in Crown Row,[8] Walworth, then in the parish of Newington.

Robert [II] and Mary went on to produce seven children; the records of their places of birth present valuable evidence of the remarkable travels of the family as Robert sought to develop his mercantile activities. Their first child, Robert Dennis – the subject of this book – was born in Newington in January 1793[9] but by 1794 they were living in Ostende when Mary Ann was born.[10] Probably as a result of the beginning of the war with France, they were back in Newington when George was born on 12 August 1795.[11] They do not appear in the Newington rate book at this date,[12] but in 1797 and '98 Robert was paying rates on the tenth property in Crown Row.[13] He appears in a 1799 directory as living in East Street, Walworth where, interestingly, his profession is listed as 'private',[14] although he does not appear in the rate book as living anywhere in the parish in that year.[15] In fact the family had moved to Hanover, then a British

2.1: Bruges, a picturesque view of one of the canals with the tower of the Cloth Hall in the background.

possession, and were living in Ritzbuttel in August 1799 when Louise was born[16] and they were in Cuxhaven, on the North Sea coast of Germany, in 1801 for the birth of William.[17] In 1803, Hanover was occupied by the French army and no doubt for this reason, the Chantrells were back in Ostende for the birth of Suzanna later that year.[18] Finally, in 1805, they undertook the short journey to Bruges (**2.1**) where their last child, Emily Sophie, was born on 3 November.[19] Despite the on-going war with France, life in Bruges must have been both congenial as well as advantageous for Robert's business; they spent the rest of their lives there and invited various members of Robert's extended family to join them (**2.2**). Robert Dennis was the only one of them to leave the city to

2.2: Bruges, Cemetery, the Chantrell burial plot showing the memorial to Chantrell's mother and other members of his close family.

return to their roots in England. However, the property in Crown Row was not given up as we shall see later; perhaps it continued in Chantrell ownership as both an investment and as a useful residence for not infrequent trips back to London.

Robert was one of a number of entrepreneurs from across the Channel who chose to make Bruges their home and commercial base – forming a thriving English enclave[20] and, apparently, conducting their lives almost entirely in the English language – since it offered considerable advantages for those with the foresight to exploit its opportunities. He appears in the Bruges directories listed, usually as 'commissionaire' or occasionally 'proprietaire'; he is known to have had extensive interests in the shipping, forwarding, importing and exporting of goods.[21] The entrepreneurial flair demonstrated by Robert was developed further by his second and third sons, George and William. George married into what was, in effect, the Belgian aristocracy and both brothers had extensive connections with politicians, leading lawyers and high-ranking civil servants which they exploited to further their enterprises. These advantages, coupled with their own business flair, enabled them to be highly successful in ventures as diverse as the manufacture of armaments and the commercial cultivation of orchids. Between these extremes were included ship-owning, sugar production, railway construction and public works.[22]

Bruges at the opening of the nineteenth century was, and remains, a highly picturesque city, full of historic buildings from all periods (**2.3**). Half a century later Chantrell was to write enthusiastically about the tall, 'picturesque gables ornamented with arches and tracery … On entering the ancient town … we are reminded of the olden times by its gates which are closed at 9.00 every night … the fortifications have long been dismantled, but the broad moat still surrounds the town's ramparts'.[23] It must have made an impact on Robert Dennis arriving as a 12-year-old and perhaps it was here that he began his interest in the built environment. And we know he grew up surrounded also by his father's art collection; in *c.*1800 Robert had begun to collect pictures,[24] and his son no doubt acquired something of the father's enthusiasm for the visual arts. Robert also dealt in art; despite the French blockade, he was one of a number of successful dealers buying works of art cheaply on the war-torn continent and exporting them to England. Some of the best pieces he kept for himself and the Bruges directories note he possessed a '*cabinet de peintures*'; for a public exhibition in 1837 he lent seven works and he was also a benefactor of the Academy of Painting and Architecture in Bruges. On his death, his collection was auctioned in 174 lots.[25] Such was the interest that the sale was preceded by a two-day public exhibition in the *Grande Salle* of the Town Hall.[26]

We know little of Chantrell's time in Bruges, although he later referred to 'a small church appropriated to the use of the English Protestants … in the Rue d'Ostende' where, presumably, the family worshipped. He believed it to be one of the 'few fine

2.3: Bruges, the Town Hall. Nineteenth-century engraving. (*Andries Van den Abeele*).

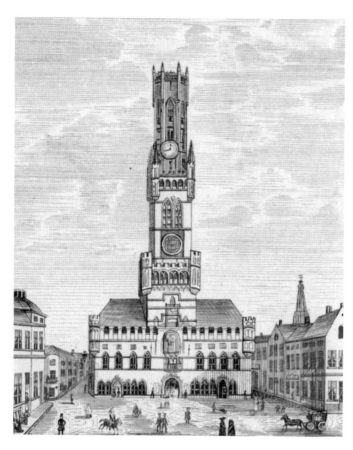

2.4: Bruges, the Cloth Hall on the Grand Place. Nineteenth-century engraving. (*Andries Van den Abeele*).

specimens of [the] Italian style of Church façade'[27] to be found in the city, but this assessment might have been informed by later study. Most interestingly, in one of several later accounts of buildings in West Flanders he referred to the tower of the cloth hall (**2.4**) 'when, after the Peace of Amiens, I was with my father, a *'detenu'* and in 1805 when preparations were being made for an [invasion of] England, I have seen with a telescope an English blockading squadron from this belfry.'[28]

In 1807, when Chantrell was 14, he was articled to John Soane and thus began his formal involvement with architecture. This meant leaving behind the warmth and security of family life, but as compensation, he was about to enjoy the best architectural education available anywhere in Britain. His father had chosen wisely.

This account of the Chantrell family now moves on to 1841. It has long seemed likely that Chantrell's arrival in Leeds was guided by something other than good fortune and perhaps a link to the town is beginning to emerge. A family member in Leeds sending news of the town's prosperity and growth, and one capable of offering introductions to potential patronage would be a plausible explanation for the young man's decision to move to the town. Certainly, no Chantrells were recorded in Leeds before our architect so any family link must have come *via* the female line.[29] At the 1841 census, three of Chantrell's children – twenty-five year old John Boham, twenty-four year old Elizabeth

Caroline and twenty-two year old Mary Louisa – were living not in their parent's house, but at Green Gates Farm near Bramhope, about eight miles north of Leeds.[30] It was the home of John Barstow (d. 1850), listed as a 'farmer', and his family. Three years later, J.B. Chantrell married one of Barstow's daughters, Mary Ann. In 1841 she would have been only 17 and it seems highly unlikely that the three Chantrells were at the house on the strength of the engagement; indeed had such an arrangement existed then, it would have been a good reason for JBC *not* to have been living there. Kinship is surely a much more plausible explanation for the Chantrells' presence, with the engagement occurring later.

Was Barstow sufficiently prominent to be in a position to promote Chantrell's career around 1819? Probably not; he is not recorded on any of the major building committees of the period or, indeed, in any other influential role. However, John Barstow's father, William, is described as being from 'Middleton [between Wakefield and Huddersfield] and afterwards of Halifax'[31] which might help to explain Chantrell's stay in Halifax prior to his arrival in Leeds. In the absence of more specific information, perhaps correspondence from the Barstows detailing the remarkable changes that were taking place in the West Yorkshire industrial centres, coupled with the offer of familial support, was sufficient to lure Chantrell to what Bigland, writing in 1812, described as 'one of the greatest manufacturing districts in England, or even the world.'[32]

An architectural education

Quite what lead the family to consider an architectural career for the eldest son is not recorded. We might speculate that the young Chantrell spent his leisure time sketching the old buildings of Bruges and showed aptitude for it, or it might have been concluded by his father – a successful entrepreneur with a real interest in the visual arts – that architecture could usefully combine the worlds of business, construction and art. And what made Robert think of Soane as a teacher for his son? Here we may have a less speculative answer: it seems likely that Soane was one of Robert's clients for works of art prior to 1807. Certainly such a relationship existed in 1820[33] and probably started much earlier. Since we know that many of Chantrell's fellow pupils were the sons of Soane's friends or business acquaintances, such an explanation seems plausible.[34] Whatever the reason, the choice of Soane as teacher was a most fortunate one for the young Chantrell. Soane usually had no more than four or five pupils at any one time and these young men enjoyed what was, without doubt, the most thorough education available in England at this time. The advantages were several. As a practitioner, Soane was at the very top of the profession with a string of prestigious commissions for public buildings and private mansions. Secondly, Soane cared passionately about style and had developed his own unique contribution to the Classical tradition. While it is true that James Wyatt might have challenged for Soane's professional crown, it is now undisputed that the latter had a depth of scholarship, subtlety and originality that put his work on a plane quite beyond Wyatt's facile style-mongering. Thirdly, Soane was appointed

Professor of Architecture at the Royal Academy – a post he was to hold for thirty years – in the year before Chantrell's arrival. This was certainly a prestigious appointment but more importantly, it was while Chantrell was in his office that Soane was undertaking the research for his annual lecture course, producing the lecture diagrams – some of which Chantrell drew – and, it seems safe to conclude, perfecting the nuances of his syllabus on his own pupils prior to the lectures in the Academy. Fourthly, Soane cared passionately about the need for professional standards in the practice of architecture at a time when such high-mindedness seemed either unnecessary or positively inhibiting to the majority of 'architects' for whom designing buildings was only one of a number of business activities.[35] But Soane's vision of the profession proved to be the way forward and Chantrell was later to benefit from the standards and principles which Soane had instilled in him. Finally, there were the unquantifiable educational advantages to be gained simply from being at 13 Lincoln's Inn Fields – Soane's remarkable London home and office (**2.5**). The extensive museum, the library and the drawings collection, plus the constant opportunities to engage in discussions with others committed to architecture, must have been significant factors in the pupils' development.[36] Watkin notes an 1812 publication which refers to the house as 'an academy for the study of *architecture* upon principles at once *scientific* and *philosophical*' and himself suggests Soane conceived it as 'a setting in which students could learn about architecture through casts, models, books, and drawings [In this way] the building became a three-dimensional version of the [Royal Academy] lectures.'[37]

Chantrell's indentures were signed on 14 January 1807, shortly after his fourteenth birthday.[38] The document states the apprenticeship is to last for seven years – to 14 January 1814 – and that Soane will provide his pupil with 'board, lodgings[39] and wearing apparel'. In exchange Robert Chantrell is to pay Soane 100 guineas.[40] Fourteen was not an untypical age to arrive,[41] although the fee was lower than most fathers paid.[42] What is striking is that the indenture was usually signed after the pupil entered the office 'as there was usually a probationary period of some weeks or longer';[43] Chantrell did not enter 13 Lincoln's Inn Fields until 15 June 1807, five months after the indenture was signed.

In the early nineteenth century, there was no requirement for an architect to have specific skills or qualifications, and many set themselves up in practice with none at all. However, for those seeking an education prior to entering the 'profession', this was almost always gained in the office of an established architect, either as a pupil, an assistant or a clerk.[44] The quality of the education obtained in this way varied considerably and the system of pupilage in particular was readily open to abuse. At its worst the pupil was not only exploited as unpaid labour, but the principal could actually derive a substantial income by simultaneously taking several of them without any precise obligations in return. George Wightwick, destined to be Soane's last pupil, recorded his earlier 'training' with the surveyor-architect Edward Lapidge between 1818 and 1823. 'No instruction … was ever given … I expected to find a tutor, I found only an employer … I

2.5: 'The Dome' of 13 Lincoln's Inn Fields, Soane's house. The watercolour, by Soane's assistant George Bailey, reveals something of the atmosphere of Soane's remarkable home and office where Chantrell passed his student days. (*Sir John Soane's Museum*).

2.6: 'Detail of the Tuscan order of Vitruvius', one of Chantrell's early student drawings. Soane's Day Books reveal that the first few months of each pupil's education were spent in copying drawings of the Classical orders. (*Sir John Soane's Museum*).

found in short I had paid my premium for the opportunity of self-instruction ... for the advantage of serving my master and picking up such information as might lie in my way.'[45] On the other hand, some architects took seriously their responsibilities to their pupils and a combination of office experience, site visits and some instruction of the principles of design and construction produced a steady stream of satisfactory architects. However, the education offered by Soane was in a league of its own.

The period of Chantrell's pupilage saw Soane engaged on most of the buildings which are now seen as his major artistic achievements: Chelsea Hospital (1809-17); the Picture Gallery and Mausoleum at Dulwich (1811-14); 13 Lincoln's Inn Fields (1812-13); and the Bank of England (the commission ran throughout the 1807-14 period). Chantrell could not have chosen a more auspicious time to be in Soane's office, but the education which *his* pupils received went well beyond menial tasks to assist their master with his projects. Indeed relatively little time was spent on Soane's buildings; the majority of their time was occupied on a syllabus of theoretical study devised by the master in the belief that architecture was essentially an intellectual activity. Soane was meticulous in recording and storing the minutiae of daily office activity and as a result, we have unparalleled information about education as a Soane pupil, including the day books in which are recorded the daily activities of everyone in the office.

Soane cared passionately about architecture and demanded commitment from his pupils. The opening section of his first RA lecture includes the warning 'from earliest youth not a moment must be lost by him who desires to become a great architect,'[46] and it might be concluded that this pronouncement guided office practice; the indentures record office hours as 7.00 am to 7.00 pm in the summer and 8.00 am to 8.00 pm in the winter. However, the day books note that most pupils arrived between 9.00 and 9.30 am throughout the year. Much of the time was spent drawing, specifically in copying prints and drawings of: Classical orders and ornaments (**2.6**) – e.g. 21 August 1808 'Copying the Composite Order'; ancient Classical buildings – e.g. 29 October 1811 'About the Ruins of Paestum'; Italian, French and English Renaissance architecture – e.g. 24 August 1811 'Section of a Church from Palladio'. Time was spent on drawing Soane's own current projects, although it seems clear that this was for the benefit of the pupil rather than the master, e.g. 13 May 1812 'About Dulwich Mausoleum'. In addition to large-scale office copies of project drawings, Soane also kept a series of books of more manageable, small-scale drawings – somewhat bigger than A3 in 21st century terms – of his designs, especially plans, elevations and sections of them. His pupils spent many hours in 'copying a drawing of [a specific building] for The Book', although in reality, there were numerous books. As Chantrell's time in the office coincided with the beginning of Soane's professorship at the RA, he and his handful of colleagues spent much time in the preparation of the remarkable large-scale lecture illustrations.[47] In addition, time was spent on preparing accounts. This was something on which staff worked spasmodically and often all together, presumably at various stages of individual contracts; the accounts for 'The Bank' [of England] consumed huge amounts of time. Interestingly, what the students did *not* do was produce designs of their own. It seems almost unbelievable that Soane would not have considered the ability to create original compositions as a key skill for his young charges, yet there is no mention of such exercises in the day books. A possible answer is that this sort of task was set as homework. Nevertheless, nowhere in the day books has Chantrell written anything like: 'tutorial with Mr Soane to consider my recent design for a Royal Palace'. In this context, it is instructive that Chantrell's RA exhibits in 1812 and 1813 were submitted from his home address, not Soane's office.[48]

Soane kept much of the work produced by his pupils. Only occasionally is it signed, although often drawings are dated and by cross-checking with the day books it is sometimes possible to identify the work of individual pupils. Those that can be attributed to Chantrell reveal competent artistic ability. Perhaps in an attempt to perfect these abilities, Soane had Chantrell spend almost the whole of his last year out of the office producing drawings of London buildings (**2.7**).

An analysis of the day book entries reveals a course of study that was undeniably conservative; chronologically it ran from the Greeks and Romans, through Palladio, Vignola then to the English architects Jones, Wren, Burlington, Kent and Chambers. And there, somewhat surprisingly, it concluded. There is no mention of the leaders of

2.7: 'The east side of Fitzroy Square, London', watercolour by Chantrell, 1813. This large-scale drawing was produced as one of the many diagrams that Soane used to illustrate his Royal Academy lectures. (*Sir John Soane's Museum*)..

European Neo-Classicism, no mention of the early-nineteenth-century *avant garde,* no mention, even, of Soane's own mentors such as Dance or Holland, or of the theorists Blondel or Laugier whom we know he admired. One week in 'drawing urns from Piranesi' – by then the book was half a century old – seems to have been the extent of Chantrell's exposure to progressive ideas.

Some time – although relatively little – was devoted to a number of practical skills that students would need once in independent practice. Accounts, which involved examining bills of quantity, calculating costs and checking these against tradesmen's or suppliers' invoices have already been mentioned. Occasionally, two or three pupils would go out to measure a specific building or site and produce plans;[49] Bolton claimed that 'pupils … visited works in hand, in pairs, and had to take sketches … they must in this way have acquired excellent ideas of the construction actually in execution',[50] and Richardson adds 'This practice seems to have been unique to the Soane office and formed an essential part of the training.'[51] We know that Chantrell, George Underwood and Thomas Lee went out to draw Chelsea Hospital in 1810, and that Chantrell and Underwood subsequently were at the New Bank Building in the City for the same purpose.[52] Chantrell spent several days at Dulwich in the summer of 1812 (**2.8, 2.9**) and on 17 July 1813 he was sent to take 'a plan, elevation and section of Dr Bell's House, Westminster'.[53]

What the pupils did not do was *assist* Soane with his current projects; that was the role of the office assistants and draughtsmen. Arguably, this was another aspect of Soane's high-mindedness; having received fees to educate his pupils, perhaps the prospect of using them as unpaid labour was abhorrent, despite the undoubted benefits the pupils would have received in so doing.[54] Alternatively, perhaps he found their 'help' more trouble than it was worth. Whatever the answer, apprenticeship was essentially a theoretical course of study. Yet despite the fact that the day books record almost hour-by-hour how Chantrell was occupied for six and a half years, it gives little insight into the philosophical framework that underpinned pupilage. This is where our considerable knowledge about Soane's activities as Professor of Architecture at the Royal Academy is invaluable. While there is no suggestion that Soane saw the RA syllabus and that followed by his own pupils as interchangeable, nevertheless, there was much overlap, and the texts of the lectures[55] – and the voluminous notes produced by the professor in their preparation[56] – usefully amplify Soane's syllabus as recorded in the often bald details of the day books.[57] Yet with all this material to guide us in seeking to establish Soane's philosophy, clarity remains elusive; the contradictions are as prevalent as the certainties. At the heart of our dilemma – and, indeed, probably Soane's too – was the issue of originality.

Everything that is known about Soane suggests he wanted passionately to promote a great school of English Classicism and correct the many failings and lost opportunities in contemporary London monumental architecture in order to make the city a worthy rival of Paris or ancient Rome. And surely his students – both at the RA and at 13 Lincoln's Inn Fields – must have longed for guidance through a series of universally valid

2.8: 'View of the Mausoleum and part of the Picture Gallery of Dulwich College', watercolour by Chantrell, 19 June 1812. Pupils spent a small amount of their time visiting Soane's projects as a means of gaining an understanding construction methods. (*Sir John Soane's Museum*).

principles that would assist them to respond to Soane's call. They listened in vain. Soane, it seems, lacked the dogmatism, or perhaps the confidence, to codify his philosophy in a set of basic rules of composition. We may, of course, commend his modesty; perhaps he believed laying down a set of rules would be seen as arrogant and certainly the concept of self-discovery was a central part of Soane's interest in the Enlightenment, yet we may conclude he erred too far in the other direction.

A superficial reading of the day books and lecture texts suggests almost an obsession with copying the great works of the past. Surely these exemplars must constitute a set of rules? However, this is to misread Soane's rationale. The study of the past was only the starting point for architectural composition, not an end in itself. 'By referring to first principles, the uncertainties of genius will be fixed, and the artist enabled to feel the beauty and appreciate the value of ancient works, and thereby seize the spirit that directed the minds of those who produced them.'[58] And knowledge of the great works of the past, no matter how extensive, was of little use without 'judgement'. At the heart of Soane's rationale was his identification with 'Enlightenment thinkers who believed that problems could be solved by a return to origins, and that truth could be attained through reason'.[59] Soane pointed out that even in the best products of antiquity, students would find no consistent use of detail or proportion 'but let not the young artist be dismayed with these difficulties; rather let him consider them as a means of calling forth all the energies of his mind, the power of his thought, and the exercise of his judgement.'[60] In lecture 11 he points out 'Imitation of masters is not required in Architects … It may make [them] humble mannerists, but this method of study will never make a great artist.'[61]

What, it seems, above all else Soane wanted to impart to his students was the ability to tread their own path through the labyrinth of Classical theory. '[You must be] intimately acquainted with not only what the ancients *have* done, but endeavour to learn what they *would* have done. We shall thereby become artists not mere copyists.'[62] Soane's claim that 'Art cannot go beyond the Corinthian order'[63] was not so much a prescription for the order's universal use as a clear statement that the basic ingredients of architecture already existed. What his students needed to find was their own recipe to exploit the ingredients. Was this sufficiently helpful for the students? Perhaps not, but then Soane was clear about the importance of intellectual skills for a successful architect and perhaps he felt that if the weaker students could survive only by 'spoon feeding' they should be abandoned to failure.

As Watkin points out, Soane struggled endlessly with the lectures' contents, constantly reading new books, re-reading old ones and amending his texts. If the result was often ambiguous or worse, perhaps some of the confusion resulted from Soane's own inability to identify his audience and its needs. The lectures often have a grandeur of ideas and language best suited to the great continental works of architectural theory that Soane admired so much; perhaps his texts would have been more appropriate had they been published as a contribution to the French Enlightenment than as lectures for an audience of adolescent youths of limited architectural experience or wider intellectual enquiry. In the context of our interest in Chantrell and his fellow students, we might reasonably question the extent to which Soane was equipping them with the skills they needed for late-Georgian practice.

This is an issue that will repay attention for not only might we legitimately feel instruction in the Classical tradition failed to capitalise fully on Soane's undoubted architectural skill, his extensive reading and his endless reconsideration of the syllabus, but we might also question his ability to anticipate the stylistic trends that would inform his students' careers. So far as Classicism was concerned, Soane's philosophy was, for the early nineteenth century, hopelessly old-fashioned. He was not so much equipping his students with a distillation of current cutting-edge thinking as summing up the situation as it existed half a century earlier. Had the lectures been delivered in (say) 1760 they might have offered a lead to the first generation of Neo-Classicists; by 1810 much of their content was obsolete.[64] Soane's reference to himself as coming from 'the Old Classical School'[65] is indeed instructive. Soane's pronouncements on what would become some of the central stylistic developments after Waterloo were equally unhelpful to his students. Here we must address his comments about the Gothic and Tudor Revivals and the picturesque in general.

For Soane, Gothic was a style essentially to be side-stepped. He surely saw it as an inconvenient interregnum between Rome and the Renaissance. There is no explicit record that Chantrell spent even a single day on medieval architecture.[66] The RA lectures

2.9: 'The west façade of Dulwich College', watercolour by Chantrell, 12 September 1812. (*Sir John Soane's Museum*).

follow a similar pattern. Students were urged to look at Gothic only 'for its effect in mass and detail' rather than 'for its taste'[67] and unsurprisingly, Soane avoided any attempt to codify its compositional principles; the following passage well illustrates the style's shortcomings for Soane: 'the comparative beauty of this mode [early Gothic] was soon lost in the subsequent works by a lightness of construction bordering on temerity, and in a blaze of ornaments crowded together, the details of which, resting on what is absolutely arbitrary, occasioned all the irregular whimsicality of form and capricious disposition so prevalent in the decorations of some of our great Gothic buildings.'[68] Put simply, a style that relied on 'temerity' or 'whimsicality', and on judgements that were 'arbitrary' rather than principled had no place in the study of great architecture. And yet he could not avoid grudging praise of Gothic's structural sophistication, its capacity to produce sublime effects in the viewer,[69] its 'pleasing gloom' and 'a boldness and lightness unknown … in any great works of antiquity'. Nevertheless, he concludes it has little relevance for current architecture – 'it is little calculated for the common habits of life'[70] – and that '[Gothic] must be considered by all inferior to the Grecian.'[71] Privately, Soane was more strident, almost paranoid, in his condemnation of modern Gothic; perhaps he recognised, no doubt reluctantly, the danger which it posed to his cherished Classical prospectus. 'The Gothic mania like the French Revolution carries all before it. It draws everything into its vantage in a mighty torrent/river that has burst its bounds … It destroys/pulls down and sweeps away every principle of ancient architecture and every idea of correct taste.' This was in one of his unused lecture drafts. Later, in 1822, he recorded in one of his many personal memoranda, 'In England we are covering the earth with Gothic churches, Gothic houses, Gothic castles which are in fact anything but Gothic unless Gothic and barbarism mean the same. [He notes that, in contrast, on the continent, Gothic is nowhere to be seen.] The most indolent and ignorant see beauties in this style of building which any with [a] Classical mind view with pity and contempt.'[72] In the light of Chantrell's subsequent career, it would be fascinating to know if Soane ever shared such extreme views with his pupils.

Soane's assessment of the Tudor style was no more balanced:

> [In the reign of Queen Elizabeth we find] the most extraordinary absurdities … Indeed so completely was the veil of ignorance and the clouds of darkness spread over the land that this licentious, whimsical and capricious mode continued unrestrained by scientific law and unfettered by reason until … Inigo Jones … restored … reason and philosophy … [and] correct taste.[73]

Finally, we must examine Soane's pronouncements about the picturesque. It seems there was much about the movement that interested him, yet he struggled to reconcile its asymmetry, its reliance on intuition, its stylistic superficiality and its opposition to Classical principles with his own frequently rehearsed preferences. 'An edifice, to be beautiful must be perfect in its symmetry and uniformity',[74] and '[there is] one other method now much in use although fatal to composition, I mean that of placing the offices at one side of the mansion … it is but a paltry makeshift and one seldom resorted to by any great artist'.[75] These two extracts make quite clear his conclusions about a movement that was already well established as a compositional philosophy by the time he was delivering his lectures.

There was a further aspect of professional training that should be addressed: the practicalities of construction and materials. Here we find Soane's lectures offering much sound advice and the theme usefully takes us to the next phase of Chantrell's life. While Soane clearly struggled to compose a coherent narrative from the extensive and often complex corpus of Neo-Classical theory, when he turned his attention to building construction he was demonstrably on more comfortable ground. For instance, lecture 12 contains much sound advice about the formation of chimney flues and ways to avoid dry rot.[76] He began the lecture by urging his audience to recognise the importance of a 'thorough knowledge of Construction and of the Nature and Quantity of [building materials] … Nothing is so well calculated to insure the Architect's success in life, as without knowledge, which can only be obtained by great experience and attentive observation, formed on real practice, all other attainment will be of little avail.'[77] Clearly, what Soane is struggling to say, but conscious of his own exalted status, as well as that of the Academy and his audience, is 'spend some time on a building site'. Soane was, himself, the son of a bricklayer, and Thomas Taylor (of Leeds) and Charles Barry were just two of many early-nineteenth-century architects to have spent time working for builders.

The final component of Soane's model of architectural education was foreign travel: having completed pupilage and read the great works of theory 'the student has then only to complete his studies by visiting foreign countries.'[78]

Soane's concept of a well-rounded architectural education thus had four components: articled pupilage; an acquaintance with the standard works of architectural theory; experience on a building site; foreign travel. When Chantrell's articles expired on 14 January 1814 he could reasonably feel he had satisfied the first two criteria, but what of the other two? His last day at Lincoln's Inn Field was 31 January; he had just celebrated his twenty-first birthday and a new phase of his life was about to begin. No doubt he left with mixed feelings. There must have been something comfortably familiar in the routine in the office and there was probably much illicit tom-foolery among the young men there; several of Soane's pupils later recorded fond memories of their master and of their time with him. And when, in 1836, Chantrell sought to become a member of the recently formed Institute of British Architects, it was to those with whom he had shared his student days that he turned for nomination.[79] But to return to 1814, foreign travel might have seemed the optimum activity after leaving Soane and such a plan would be followed by his former colleague George Basevi when his articles ended in 1816. However, two years earlier, the war with France rendered most of Europe closed to Englishmen. Anyway, Chantrell had other plans for life after Soane: marriage. On 12 February 1814

2.10: A miniature portrait by an unknown artist showing Chantrell at about the time he left Soane's office. The painting remains in a private collection in Bruges. (*Andries Van den Abeele*).

he married Elizabeth Caroline Boham at St Mary Magdalene, Bermondsey.[80] The couple went to live in the Chantrell property at 6 Crown Row, Walworth. Since all of Chantrell's immediate family was still in Bruges and much of his extended family had chosen to move there, we might have expected him to have joined them after pupilage but that was not to be. And what of Chantrell's post-Soane professional ambitions? From knowing how he spent almost every day of the previous six-and-a-half years, the story suddenly becomes much less clear. It is known he was in Halifax in 1818, but there is a four-year gap where the few facts must be linked by a degree of speculation.

Certainly he set himself up as an architect, although the details are sparse (**2.10**). He appears in Underhill's *Triennial Directory of London, Westminster and Southwark … for the years 1817, 1818 and 1819,* published, probably, in 1817. This was the principal directory covering the Walworth area and Chantrell is listed under 'Architects' as well as 'Nobility and Gentry'. Both entries give his address as 6 Crown Row, Walworth. His attempts to establish a practice probably started earlier but the previous edition of Underhill's *Directory,* in 1814, would have involved the collection of data in 1813, just before he left Soane. In the Royal Academy's Summer Exhibition of 1814 he showed a 'view of a design for a series of dwelling houses intended to form one side of a square',[81] no doubt hoping that it would attract the attention of potential patrons. In February 1815 his first child was born and in the register of births[82] the father is listed as 'architect', and later that year it is likely he submitted a design for the competition for the new London Institution building.[83]

Whether Chantrell secured any architectural commissions at this time is questionable, but it is certain he could hardly have chosen a less auspicious time to launch his career. The war with France had almost halted building in London,[84] and there were already a number of distinguished architects who could find little or no employment in this period.[85] And since Chantrell's 'office' was in a village on the outskirts of London, his opportunities of employment were further limited.[86] It is not inconceivable that he had an allowance from his father and actually led a rather *dilettante* existence, essentially 'playing' at architecture but achieving little professionally. However, there is one tantalising piece of evidence that points in a different direction. When Chantrell's second son was baptised in March 1816, the father is described as 'surveyor'[87] unlike the entry for the first son's baptism where he appears as 'architect'. Now it is true that, to a considerable extent – and certainly in the mind of the layman – these two labels were interchangeable, but it is inconceivable that anyone brought up with Soane's robust attitude to professional standards would have been indifferent to the distinctions of skill and status the terms

2.11: Halifax, West Yorkshire, the medieval parish church. The lithograph, by Nathaniel Whittock, *c*.1837, shows the building with the tower pinnacles that Chantrell restored. (*Leeds University Library, Special Collections*).

implied; perhaps Chantrell really *was* working for a surveyor. This would be a perfectly reasonable conclusion and both Soane and Chantrell would have seen such career development as beneficial and positive: it was the ideal way for Chantrell to supplement his essentially theoretical training with the practical knowledge we know Soane saw as an invaluable foundation for a successful architectural career.

The birth certificate thus places Chantrell in Newington in March 1816 and he is listed there in the local directory published in 1817, but perhaps compiled in late 1816. At some point he left London and by 1818 appears in Halifax (**2.11**). When he arrived there and, perhaps more perplexingly, why he should even know of the place let alone seek employment there, is a complete mystery. But in Halifax he undoubtedly was: much later in his career he wrote a letter to *The Builder* which included 'In the year 1818 [I restored] the parapet and pinnacles of the parish church in Halifax';[88] correspondence from Chantrell in early 1819 concerning the Leeds Public Baths competition gives his address as 'Blackwell, Halifax';[89] and perhaps most interestingly, in 1821 a letter from Chantrell to Soane included 'My success in [securing the Baths commission has] lead to my removal from Halifax where, since I had the pleasure of waiting upon you, I have resided as assistant to an architect, whose principles and ideas differed so widely from mine that I found I could never expect to reap any benefit from the connection ... '[90] And who was this architect whom Chantrell was assisting? There were only two architects practising in Halifax at this time, William Bradley and John Oates. An examination of the Halifax parish church accounts reveals that it was Bradley to whom payments were made in 1818 for work on the tower and they make no mention of Oates.[91] By way of confirmation, the diary of Ann Lister of Shibdon Hall, near Halifax, records that Bradley was 'not a man to be depended on – very idle – never right in his estimates – not fit to be an architect.'[92] Yet despite Bradley's dubious professional integrity, it is unlikely Chantrell's time with him was wasted. Chantrell emerges early in 1819 to begin independent practise in Leeds as a fully rounded young architect; the transition from the genteel, academic world of Soane's office to the cut and thrust of the Yorkshire building site, which Chantrell seems to have accomplished with relative ease, probably owed a good deal to what he learnt in Halifax.

3

Post-Waterloo Leeds

If Chantrell was destined not to be a successful London architect, he could hardly have chosen a better provincial location than Leeds as a base from which to establish his practice, nor a better time to do it. In 1820, the town could reasonably claim to be one of the most industrially advanced towns anywhere in the world and would soon have the fifth largest population in the country. It was already thriving and it was about to get much bigger and much wealthier. Inevitably, that meant more building and more opportunities for an ambitious architect.

But it wasn't just the town that was developing. In the 35 years after Waterloo, the architectural profession too was undergoing profound change and it was in centres like Leeds that the new caste of architect was being formed. Of course, after 1850 architects can still be identified working as they had done before 1815 – building large country houses, churches or hospitals from a London office – but after Waterloo architects became more involved with new building types, such as banks, markets, schools and villas for the middle classes; with new building materials and processes; and with working outside London. Increasingly, they were employed to erect buildings that, earlier, would have been designed by the builder responsible for their construction. Central to their new-found demand was the ability to satisfy rapidly changing and increasingly sophisticated stylistic nuances. But perhaps more important was the growing belief that the architect's supervisory role was the best way to police the worst excesses of the building trades and achieve a sound, well-constructed building; an extra 5% for the architect's services was widely deemed to be money well spent, even by blunt Yorkshire merchants.[1] Thus in the provinces, an architect in *c.*1800 was a rare animal, but by 1850 every medium-sized town had one or two and a big one might have twenty or thirty. Despite Chantrell's entirely traditional and, in some respects, very conservative programme of education, he belonged to a generation of architects who went out into territory hitherto essentially closed to the profession to develop aspects of practice largely ignored by Soane. For those brave enough to exploit the new possibilities, the reward was a comfortable and sometimes prestigious practice (**3.1**).

3.1: Leeds, view looking up Park Row, *c.*1840. At the extreme right is John Clark's Yorkshire District Bank, 1836, the principal subject of the lithograph being Clark's Commercial Buildings of 1826-9. The pedimented building that can be seen in the middle distance is Thomas Taylor's Court House of 1811-13 and further up Park Row, also on its left-hand side, is Chantrell's Philosophical Hall. The only building not to reflect the town's fondness for Classicism is John Child's St Anne's R.C. church at the top of the street. (*A Stranger's Guide to Leeds,* 1844, frontispiece).

Leeds' importance throughout the period under discussion derived from its pre-eminent position in the West Riding woollen industry,[2] 'the principal seat of woollen manufacture in England' began the account of the town in the 1822 directory. The production of cloth in Leeds was not inconsiderable – following sluggish investment in new mills and machinery during the French wars, there was a huge growth in the 1820s which saw production triple in the decade – but more important was the town's role as the principal location in the finishing and marketing of cloth produced elsewhere in the West Riding, for instance Halifax or Bradford. Leeds benefited from local coal supplies for its steam engines, and by being well served with transport links to other parts of the country, and to seaports for world-wide exports. Industrial production brought engineers and founders, and as the marketing centre for the industry, Leeds attracted a full range of allied trades and professions including finance and banking (**3.2**), insurance, warehousing, legal services, commission agency, transport etc. All these activities needed offices, factories or workshops, the expanding population needed housing and when not at work, it needed shops and markets for consumer goods, and buildings to satisfy leisure and cultural pursuits.

The building boom

Chantrell kept an office in Leeds for 32 years, closing it in 1851. In the 30 years covered by the censuses of 1821 to 1851 the population rose from 83,943 to 172,270[3] and the housing stock from 11,191 to 21,215.[4] More importantly for the employment of architects was the increase in public buildings and those for worship, usually enumerated on the town's maps. Netlam and Francis Giles' plan of 1815 lists 48 of them, Charles Fowler counted 54 in his map of 1821, and in his revised editions of 1826, 1831 and 1844, the numbers were 82, 140 and 205 respectively.[5] We can conclude, therefore, that during Chantrell's stay in Leeds, somewhere between 150 and 200 new public

3.2: Leeds, Yorkshire District Bank (John Clark, 1836). From a photograph of *c*.1870.

3.3: Leeds, Leeds Library, Commercial Street (Thomas Johnson, 1807-8). From an engraving based on a drawing by the Leeds architect Thomas Taylor.

or religious buildings were constructed. Fowler actually sub-divided his list into four categories: churches; chapels; charitable buildings, law, commercial; other buildings. We can reasonably conclude that several of the law or commercial buildings could well have been modest conversions of late-eighteenth-century houses in the town's west end rather than entirely new buildings, although the group certainly did include some new structures. Nevertheless within these bald statistics is included clear evidence of the demand for the services of architects, and the extent to which it was increasing. All the new churches, chapels, schools, markets, and the bigger banks and institutions were the work of an architect.[6]

The increase in the number of religious and public buildings can also be enumerated from the pages of the local newspapers, especially the *Leeds Intelligencer* which seems to have taken a special interest in building activities, usually linking them to the concept of civic improvement and Leeds chauvinism. An 'invitation to tender' aimed at the building trades, might appear two or three times per year in the early 1820s, by the mid-1830s this rose to five or six and by the 1840s there were dozens. Further evidence appears in the notices of newly completed buildings; in the six years 1834-9, for example, the paper made reference to at least 45 new religious or public buildings – including 17 Nonconformist chapels – erected in the town, most overseen by an architect.[7]

In the eighteenth century, the various cloth halls were by far the most ambitious additions to Leeds building stock. However, while they continued in use through Chantrell's stay, their importance in the marketing process declined and no new ones were added. And important buildings for leisure – the Leeds Library (**3.3**), the Music Hall, the theatre and the Assembly Rooms – already existed when Chantrell arrived, although he was to make modest alterations to the first two. The town also possessed a fine hospital. After Waterloo, the main additions to the Leeds townscape were buildings for retail and commerce: the South Market (1823-5), the Central Market (1824-7), the Commercial Buildings (1825-9), the Corn Exchange (1826-8) and a small number of impressive banks. Alongside these came Chantrell's Public Baths (1819-20) and Philosophical and Literary Society Hall (1819-22). Later the town acquired some very substantial new or extended schools.

Then there were houses. Leeds had developed a substantial middle-class enclave of elegant terraced houses in the west of the town as the Park Estate was developed from *c.*1779. For perhaps two generations, the area supplied most of the housing needs of the town's more genteel residents, but as early as *c.*1800 we can identify a new trend: the suburban villa in the northern 'outer townships' of Woodhouse, Headingley or Potternewton. The motivation was two-fold: the national rise in the popularity of the villa was underscored, in the case of Leeds, by the increasing air pollution on the western side of the town caused by a number of very substantial, recently erected nearby mills.

3.4: Leeds, St Paul, Park Square (probably by Thomas Johnson, 1791-3). This elegant design reflected the still dominant taste for Classical churches at the end of the eighteenth century. (T.D. Whitaker, *Loidis and Elmete*, 1816, opp. p. 69).

However, squares and terraces did not altogether lose their appeal, they just moved further away from nuisances. As late as 1840 architects were still producing such schemes, although rarely were they completed on anything like the scale and extent that their developers first hoped.[8]

The stylistic and suburban model of villa dwelling was established in Leeds by two exceptionally wealthy citizens: John Gott, a mill-owner, and John Blayds, a banker. Gott's villa is at Armley, a mile-and-a-half west of the town centre, Blayds' is at Oulton, about four miles south of the town. Both lay in extensive gardens laid out in the first decade of the nineteenth century by Humphrey Repton and both houses were Classical, designed by Robert Smirke and built in the second decade. In terms of scale and the eminence of the designers, it was a pattern few could afford to emulate, but together they established the fashionable model which others eagerly sought to follow, albeit on a more modest scale. The result was dozens of neat Classical villas, each in a garden of an acre or two, and dotted all around the northern suburbs, usually between one to three miles from the town. A few are to be found south of the river too. All were built in the first half of the nineteenth century and all would have been architect-designed. Sadly, only a handful have documentary links to a specific architect, but we can surmise their erection was a significant source of employment for the profession in Leeds.[9]

The development of the architectural profession in Leeds

To cater for the town's increasing needs, the profession expanded,[10] a growth recorded conveniently in the town's directories. There are no architects in the 1798 edition, one in 1800, four in 1814, five in 1822, six in 1830, eight in 1834, ten in 1837, eleven in 1843, thirteen in 1847 and nineteen in 1851 when Chantrell's office closed. Interesting as the statistics are, they nevertheless reveal little of the many subtleties which together constitute practice in this period. What we are seeing in Leeds was a microcosm of a national pattern of provincial practice in this half-century during which the title 'architect' initially implied no specific training, set of competencies or service to the public, but which evolved to a situation in the middle of the century where it suggested a professional expertise broadly as we understand it today. Chantrell was to be in the vanguard of this change.

The situation is nicely revealed by an examination of the five men listed in the 1822 directory. Two of them, Taylor (**3.5**) and Chantrell, can be categorized as the higher end of the group: both were London-trained, no doubt coming to Leeds having identified its potential, both specialised in the design and superintending of building projects and neither mixed architecture with related activities to any notable extent. Taylor conveniently announced his arrival in Leeds; had Chantrell done the same, his puff would, no doubt, have followed the same pattern:

[Thomas Taylor's] DESIGNS having been approved for the NEW COURT HOUSE … with his other Engagements in the County will render him stationary

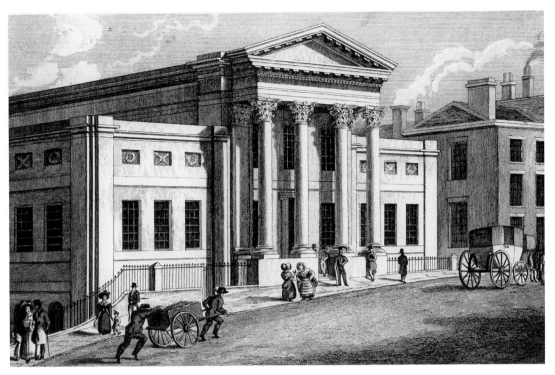

3.5: Leeds, Court House (Thomas Taylor, 1811-13).

in Leeds, where he will be happy to receive the Commands of those who might have Occasion for his Professional Services, in which he flatters himself enabled to give Satisfaction, as during a Period of Eight Years Practice under Mr James Wyatt, the present Surveyor-General, he was in the Habit of making Plans, Elevations and Sections ... and from Five Years Practice under Mr Andrews, builder of eminence in London ... he is enabled to calculate Estimates upon an unerring Principle, and further trusts from having made careful studies of all the superior French Buildings, he is enabled to arrange Architectural Decoration in a superior Style; Specimens of which may be seen in several distinguished Mansions in this Neighbourhood.[11]

The other three men listed as 'Architect' in the directory were rather different. Benjamin Jackson is recorded as the designer of a small number of modest buildings, but appeared more often in the newspapers or other documentation offering existing houses and commercial buildings for rent, selling building land, acting as a building surveyor or producing road widening schemes. Joseph Cusworth had been a pupil of Taylor's, but his design work was confined almost entirely to the most modest of alterations, spending most of his time as a building surveyor. Of Henry Chambers, despite twelve years in the Leeds directories in the 'Architects' section, not a thing is known other than he was a Commissioner for the Leeds Water Works in 1818. What Jackson, Cusworth and Chambers demonstrate is firstly anyone could call himself an architect in the hope of securing employment and secondly, the style 'architect' could encompass a wide and imprecise range of services. Other Leeds 'architects' of this period acted as rent collectors, sellers of building materials as well as suppliers of building services. But of all the occupations this wide range of activities subsumed, 'architect' was the one that implied the highest social standing and the one that offered the greatest – if unlikely – opportunity for fame and wealth. This concept of self-aggrandisement is neatly illustrated by another Leeds character, William Lawrance. He designed and built several substantial, neat but unremarkable terraced houses in Park Square in the 1790s, describing himself as 'carpenter, joiner and architect' on the leases.[12] He appears at this time in the directories as a 'joiner and cabinet maker', but in the editions of 1809, '14 and '16 he has re-branded himself as 'architect'; his elevation was announced in the *Leeds Mercury* of 17 January 1807 when he informed 'his numerous Friends that he has declined the Business of Joiner and Carpenter ... [and] begs Permission to offer his Service to the Public as an ARCHITECT, SURVEYOR and VALUER OF BUILDINGS, and to inform them, that he intends carrying out the Business of RAFF-MERCHANT[13] on his premises in Simpson's Fold, and shall be happy to receive a Share of their commands.'

There is useful evidence to flesh out the often blurred line between the role of the

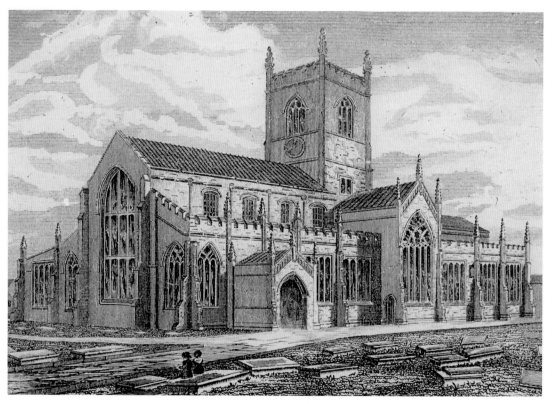

3.6: Leeds Parish Church, the building shown here was demolished in 1838 to be replaced by Chantrell's new church. (R.W. Moore, *Leeds Parish Church and its Ancient Cross*, 1877, opp. p. 2).

architect as we understand it today and those lower down the scale who aspired to the profession. For instance, we can see a perceived differentiation between those buildings that needed the services of an architect and those that did not in terms of their stylistic pretension. When, in 1801, William Lindley, the eminent Doncaster architect was asked to prepare plans for the new market place and shambles in Rotherham, he declined on the grounds that in his opinion the buildings were 'intended to be so plain and simple in construction' that the assistance of a professional architect was unnecessary.[14] Not surprisingly, the standards – in terms of style, project management or durability – of the builder/architects were often questionable. The new parish church at Keighley, erected in 1805, was within a generation condemned: ' ... ugly ... like a meeting house ... dilapidated ... the work of a common builder ... '[15] And in 1826 Chantrell was called in by the chapelwardens in Hunslet, Leeds, to 'extricate them from their difficulties and manage the accounts'[16] three years into a project to enlarge the chapel started by the estate agent/surveyor/architect Benjamin Jackson whom we have just encountered; in the following year, the ICBS requested Chantrell to inspect the parish church at Glossop, Derbyshire, the nave and chancel of which had recently been rebuilt 'most injudiciously and in very bad taste'[17] by the Sheffield surveyor/architect Edward Drury.

This pattern of men moving into the ranks of the architects from the building trades or of combining limited design work with loosely allied businesses continued throughout the first half of the century and – although more rarely – beyond, but it became increasingly unusual as the practice of architecture came to be seen by the public as a more clearly defined activity, a situation assisted by the formation of the Institute of British Architects in 1834. Nevertheless, as late as 1846, the young Robert Kerr in his *Newleafe Discourses* still felt compelled to call for an 'improved division of labour ... whereby the real Architect might be relieved from the inspection of sewers and cesspools and wells, and the shoring up of old houses, and the rating of dilapidations, and the ventilation of foul cellars and the fitting up of stables, and the curing of smoky chimneys, and the exclusion of rats, and all such like 'Architecture' ... '[18] Certainly there is an element of sarcasm in Kerr's narrative, but there was also much truth. Back in Leeds, the arrival of John Clark from Edinburgh in the late 1820s and, later, the emergence of a number of home-grown firms like Perkin and Backhouse, who were competent and prolific designers, further strengthened the ranks of the 'professional' architects like Taylor and Chantrell by demonstrating a level of sophisticated design awareness and professional service that the local builder/architects or surveyor/architects could not match. Ultimately, it led to a near permanent gulf between the various activities with the architects – based very much on the Soane/Chantrell model – emerging with the ultimate status and income.

In the second half of the eighteenth century, long before Leeds could boast any architects, the profession had been established in York, the county town, 24 miles away, as a rare provincial provider of such services. There, a small number of practitioners, lead

3.7: Leeds Parish Church, interior of the old church. The watercolour by Joseph or John Rhodes is taken from the west end of the nave looking east. The organ and east gallery effectively cut the nave off from the chancel, although the altar and bare chancel can just be seen in the distance in the centre of the image. (*Leeds City Libraries*).

by John Carr, enjoyed successful careers, largely engaged in the building and extending of country houses and other estate structures, including churches, for the aristocracy and gentry of northern England. In these commissions they were working for the 'landed interest' not industrial wealth, and the distinction was keenly observed. A brief diversion to consider aspects of the York-based profession will repay examination in the context of the pioneering developments in Leeds.

Given the profession's early base in York one might have imagined it looking acquisitively at building development in Leeds and other West Riding woollen towns. However, this was rarely the case. True, York's Watson and Pritchett secured some 'town' commissions, but for the most part, York architects seem consciously to have shunned industrial patrons. The division was symptomatic of a more general rift, neatly summed up by a writer in 1837: 'Though Leeds was formerly connected with some of the principal families of the West Riding, some of whom made it their place of residence, others sustaining offices in its Corporation and others interested themselves in the transactions of its affairs, it has long been totally abandoned by the aristocracy. Three distinguished noble families reside within a few miles of it [at Harewood, Temple Newsam and Methley] but are seldom seen in its streets; the independence of manufacturing wealth being inconsistent with both the pride and dignity of rank.'[19] Perhaps the York architects feared working in Leeds might compromise their rural bread and butter; whatever the reason, they largely gave Leeds a wide berth.[20] The same pattern existed in reverse: almost never did a Leeds architect receive the patronage of the landed gentry. Its highest social strata looked to London: Bretton Hall (15 miles south of Leeds) was extended by Jeffry Wyatt in *c.*1815; Methley Hall (8 miles south-east of Leeds) was substantially remodelled by Anthony Salvin in 1830-6; Decimus Burton enlarged Grimston Park (14 miles north-east of Leeds) in 1840; and for the modernisation of Harewood House (8 miles north of Leeds) Charles Barry was employed. The next social division looked to York architects including Peter Atkinson (*c.*1776-1843), his sons John (1807-74) and William (1811-86), or Charles Watson (*c.*1770-1836) whom we have already encountered. That country house work – the staple ingredient of so many provincial as well as London practices– was implicitly denied to the Leeds architects, further underlines the extent to which the town's architects were toiling to establish markets for their services where they had not hitherto existed.

In considering Chantrell's career, it is almost inevitable that we focus on his buildings. However, we should not overlook the fact that, seen in a different context, he occupies an important position as a leading member of a generation who forged a new chapter of architectural provision in the major industrial towns by defining the architect's identity, creating a clear demand for his services where little had been recognised earlier, and by setting new standards of professionalism in their delivery.

4

Chantrell in Leeds

We shall never know if Chantrell's arrival in Leeds was but the latest step on a carefully choreographed career plan or just one of life's accidents, but, like so much of his existence so far, it seems another example of the young man's good fortune. It appears that there were relatives in the town and perhaps they provided both information about its opportunities and promises of employment.[1]

Establishing a practice

Chantrell's residence in Leeds and the opening of his office in Saddle Yard, Briggate, can be dated precisely to 15 March 1819,[2] and from hereon the story of his life can be chronicled with much greater precision. By which of his Christian names do the many documents that are available for the study of this part of his career refer to him?

4.1: Leeds, Public Baths (R.D. Chantrell, 1819-21). The crude engraving, taken from the bath's shareholders' handbook for 1837-8, is the only known illustration of the building.

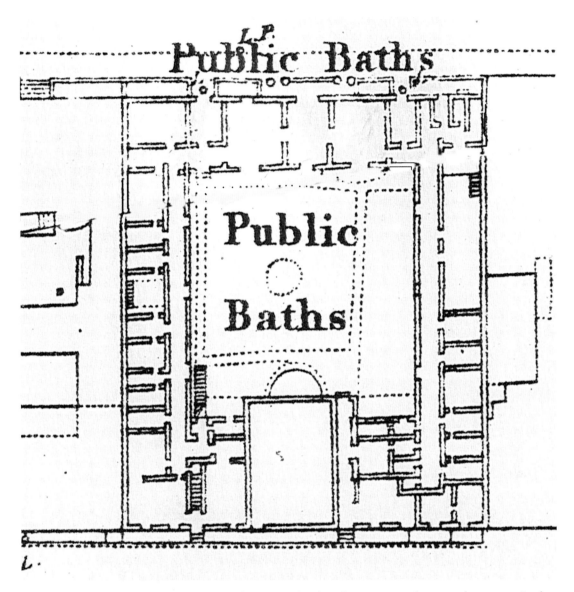

4.2: Leeds, Public Baths (R.D. Chantrell, 1819-21). The plan suggests the complex comprised a series of relatively small rooms arranged around a central courtyard. The plan is taken from the O.S. map of 1850.

Interestingly, rarely is there anything but 'Mr Chantrell'; only the signatures on letters and drawings – 'R. Dennis Chantrell' – reveal that it was by his mother's maiden name that he chose to be identified.

The Leeds woollen industry was slowly, but very definitely, picking up after the uncertainties of the wars with France and the next 25 years were to produce unparalleled prosperity; a prosperity that would be marked, in part, by new buildings to improve and ornament the town. Chantrell was just 26 but despite his youth and inexperience, it would not be unreasonable to claim that he made something of a triumphal entry: he had just secured the Public Baths commission (**4.1, 4.2**) – despite submissions from a number of distinguished architects from around the country[3] – and had already entered the competition for the Philosophical and Literary Society's new hall (**4.3, 4.4**), a keenly sought job for which he would be announced the victor in just two months time.[4] He had thus secured the first two commissions for new public buildings in the town since Thomas Taylor was appointed to build the new court house back in 1811.

An examination of Chantrell's addresses reveals that the decision to move to Leeds pre-dates his winning of the baths[5] competition and must have been made in the belief that the town offered both opportunities and limited competition. Chantrell would have known of Taylor – the only other metropolitan-trained professional architect – and must have concluded there would be enough work to keep both of them busy;[6] Taylor, no doubt, viewed Chantrell's arrival rather less sanguinely.

That the merchants of Leeds would trust their hard-earned subscriptions in the hands of an unknown 26-year-old seems remarkable, but perhaps this is simply an indication of the pace of change that was bringing prosperity to Leeds and the already established belief that innovative thinking – whether for mechanical processes, marketing or transport –

4.3: Leeds, Philosophical and Literary Society Hall (R.D. Chantrell, 1819-21). Pen and wash drawing by W.R. Robinson. (*Thoresby Society, Leeds*).

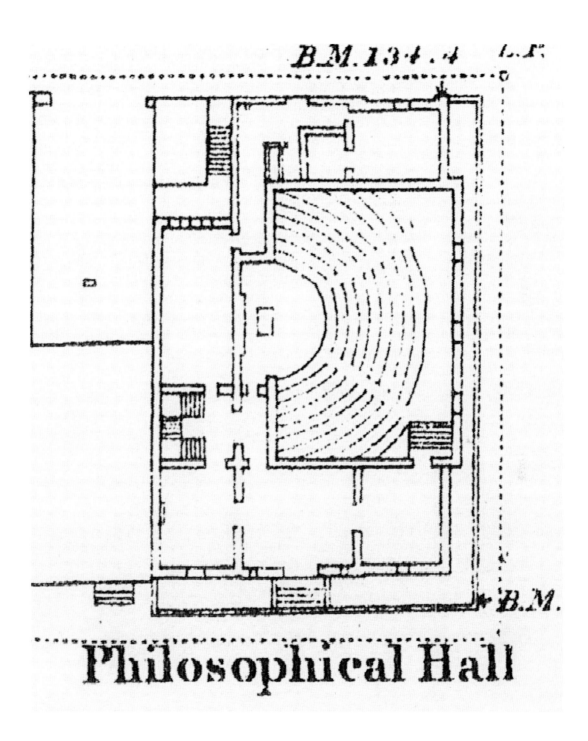

4.4: Leeds, Philosophical and Literary Society Hall (R.D. Chantrell, 1819-21). The plan is taken from the O.S. map of 1850.

should not be dismissed lightly, no matter how youthful the innovator. Interestingly, of the great figures then driving Leeds' industrial pre-eminence, Benjamin Gott (1762-1840) and John Marshall (1765-1845) – the two most significant mill-owners and entrepreneurs of this period – and the engineer Matthew Murray (1765-1826) had all reached prominence in their respective businesses by their mid-twenties. Or perhaps Chantrell's overnight success suggests he already had the support of an influential patron, perhaps in some way connected to the Tory *Leeds Intelligencer,* a theme to which we will return.

Over the next two years, work progressed on these two commissions and we can imagine Chantrell making the short round trip from his office to the two building sites on an almost daily basis with rolls of drawings tucked under his arm. It wasn't London, but he would have felt a sense of satisfaction that he was 'someone' in a town that was not only important, but appeared to offer almost limitless opportunities in the post-Waterloo boom. On a more prosaic level, he was acquainting himself with Leeds' building practices as well as the builders – many of whom he would use regularly over the coming years – and it also enabled him to meet members of the two building committees who would call to discuss changes and monitor progress, many of whom were to become loyal patrons of Chantrell in private and public works over the next 25 years.

The baths, situated in Wellington Street, near the present City Square, consisted of 'two separate and complete suites of apartments … for ladies and gentlemen'.[7] It was

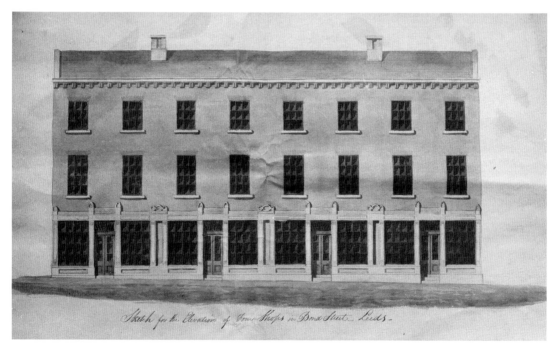

4.5: Leeds, unexecuted design for four shops for William Hey, intended to be built in Bond Street, now Commercial Street (R.D. Chantrell, 1820). (*WYASL*).

4.6: Leeds, alternative unexecuted design for four shops for William Hey (R.D. Chantrell, 1820). (*WYASL*).

described as 'a highly elegant and classical, though diminutive building … The entrance is marked by two couples of Ionic columns supporting an entablature, and a rich chiselled panel, where, among the foliage is seen the esculapian serpent; at the end of the building are coupled pilasters.'[8] The only record of the building, demolished in the nineteenth century, is a crude engraving on the front of the *Baths Company Handbook, c.*1838. It suggests the composition was a scaled-down version of the east end of Soane's Lothbury façade of the Bank of England of 1795.

The Philosophical Hall was in nearby Park Row and like the baths was part of the most fashionable area of the town, the west end. The hall was a rare Leeds loss to German bombing, although it had been extended and significantly altered in 1861-2. It contained a lecture room in the form of an amphitheatre, library, laboratory, and galleries for the display of items of natural history. In plan, the building was rectangular and its two principal façades were adjacent to each other, facing Park Row and Bond Street. It was of two storeys, the lower one rusticated and the upper adorned with Doric pilasters. Descriptions of the hall in the nineteenth century usually included the word 'handsome', whereas the same publication would use 'elegant' for the baths. The distinction was a nice one; the home of a society established to promote culture in its broadest sense would not have been seen as the appropriate recipient of the more fashionable motifs used to give the baths a veneer of stylishness.

The *Leeds Intelligencer* of 10 June 1820 announced proudly that His Majesty's Commissioners had agreed to fund three new churches in Leeds and there was the expectation of others for the neighbouring towns. Taylor must have viewed the news contentedly for he would have felt confident of securing some of the commissions; whether Chantrell too was exercised by the statement – prophetic as it was for his fledgling career – is less certain. He was still busy with the baths – not finished until August 1821[9] – and the Philosophical Hall – opened in April 1821.[10]

These two commissions did much to help Chantrell establish himself. The buildings were used by the principal inhabitants of the town and so far as contemporary newspaper articles and guide books were concerned, both buildings were viewed as real assets to Leeds and credits to their architect. Chantrell was involved in a relatively minor dispute with the Philosophical Hall's carpenter, Michael Webster, that later cast a shadow over Chantrell's career – discussed below – but the useful connections he made with the subscribers more than outweighed this difficulty, at least for the time being. The patronage of William Hey and Benjamin Gott usefully illustrate the point. Hey was a subscriber to the baths and a council member of the Phil. and Lit. In 1820 he commissioned Chantrell to design a block of four shops for him in Bond Street[11] and might well have employed him for the two houses he erected in Albion Place a few years later.[12] The shops (**4.5, 4.6**) were of three storeys, the upper two being quite plain, but on the ground floor, the shop doors and large windows displayed a profusion of fashionable Grecian motifs. Much of it was derived from the ornament of Soane's bank's Tivoli Corner, but applied without restraint and – as was often the case with shop fronts at this time – any desire for archaeological propriety.[13] Gott was a member of the Baths Building Committee and he was not only on the Phil. and Lit's Council but also laid the building's foundation stone. Between 1823 and 1847 Chantrell enjoyed a succession of commissions from him for work in Armley and Leeds.[14] The relationship between the two went beyond that of architect and building committee member and as early as 1820, they were on sufficiently good terms for Gott to introduce Chantrell to Sir James Graham of Headingley; soon after, Chantrell designed a small chapel for Graham's estate,[15] although it seems not to have been built.

1821 was a significant year. The opening of the baths and Philosophical Hall generated much interest, there were some useful, if modest, secular commissions and, most momentously for the rest of his career, there was a major Gothic church and a small addition to another one. The secular jobs involved alterations to the Leeds Library (**Cat. 16**) and the town's music hall. The fees were small but again Chantrell was working on buildings used by that sector of the town's population he was keen to court. In addition, he was invited by the Harrogate Baths Charity to produce a design for a suite of baths for the use of the poor. The project was supported by the earl of Harewood who chaired the charity, and although it failed to raise sufficient funds to complete the project, Chantrell benefited from yet more useful connections and publicity. It is likely that his first executed Gothic design was the new 'belfry' at Bramley (**4.7**, **4.8**), a tiny but architecturally interesting turret capable of holding perhaps just one bell. It was an irregular octagon in plan with openings on the four long sides, crowned by a modest spire.[16] His commission can have been only a few pounds but, like William Hey and Benjamin Gott, the chapelwardens at Bramley joined the list of Chantrell's satisfied clients and, over the next twelve years, repeatedly returned to him for designs for extending the chapel, building wholly new ones and erecting a new vicarage. But the real landmark of the year was securing his first new church, Christ Church, Meadow Lane, Leeds, one of the three new churches financed largely by the Church Building Commission, a big, commanding edifice with a suitably generous budget.

In between the announcement that Leeds was to have three new churches – in June 1820[17] – and confirmation of the architects chosen – in May 1821 – Chantrell must have regretted the partiality of his stylistic training. Although he believed the work of the Commissioners to be 'a firm opportunity for restoring the best examples of Greece and Rome', he was sufficiently pragmatic to appreciate the prevailing mood in Yorkshire that had 'submitted to the county mania for plain Gothic works … I should wish to present a [Classical] design, but the objections to them by local committees are so strong that I fear my labours would be entirely lost'.[18] Many years later, he claimed it was the clergy who, 'where they had sufficient influence, induced Local Committees to adopt [Gothic] for their new churches.'[19] And Thomas Taylor had already established a fashion for modern Gothic through a series of highly regarded pre-Commissioners' era churches.

Never one to let a lucrative commission slip through his fingers, Chantrell made a two-pronged effort to enlist Soane's support and attempted to redress the limitations in his training. In anticipation that Leeds would receive funding, Chantrell's father wrote to Soane on 16 May 1820 stating that his son had requested Soane to 'get your friends to exert their interest with the Commissioners in [his] behalf'.[20] Subsequently, on 6 January 1821, while Chantrell was agonizing over his submission mindful of the impending 1 March deadline, he also wrote to Soane,

> I take the liberty of applying to you for advice … On the economical style recommended by the clergy, and as I am informed, approved by the Commissioners, I conceive it will be impossible to obtain the pleasing effect of our cathedrals, or such parish churches as those of Bristol, Manchester, Hull etc with an area sufficient to contain 1,200 and a preparation for galleries to contain eight hundred in addition, unless the plan be made a great length in proportion to the breadth, which I should consider injurous to the sound at the west end, and also to the external effect; the productions of Mr Taylor in this district have given great satisfaction to the Archbishop of York and other exalted ecclesiastics, and his later design for Pudsey Church is, I am told a more extended model of those executed and as you of course have inspected it, you will be enabled to judge whether my task is well or ill informed by my differing in opinion with his admirers … [21]

4.7: Bramley, Leeds, Bramley Chapel, nineteenth-century watercolour of the east end, remodelled 1731-2. The top of Chantrell's spire on the south transept can be seen in the top centre. (*Thoresby Society, Leeds*).

It would be interesting to know if Chantrell had made research visits to the churches at 'Bristol, Manchester, Hull etc' or whether he knew them simply through engravings. Closer to home, he could have studied the large parish church at Wakefield and he already knew Halifax's. The extensive monastic remains at Kirkstall, on the fringes of Leeds, and Fountains, some twenty miles away might have supplied useful details as he attempted to become proficient in Gothic. He was probably an eager purchaser of

4.8: Bramley, Leeds, Bramley Chapel, unexecuted design for east and north extensions (R.D. Chantrell, 1822). (*Lambeth Palace Library*).

Auguste Pugin's 1821 offering *Specimens of Gothic Architecture* – arguably the first book aimed at the architectural profession as a reliable primer – but in January, publication was still several months away.[22]

Thus early in 1821, we find Chantrell clearly lacking any sense of conviction as he contemplated his drawing board and earnestly seeking Soane's advice. He had yet to build anything in the Gothic style and his first efforts to be constructed – the Bramley 'belfry' of 1821 and a proposed addition to Armley Chapel in 1822 – were anything but sophisticated and, anyway, still in the future. From this unpromising scenario apparently emerged his remarkably elegant design for the Meadow Lane church. The story is told in Chapter 7. It was the beginning of Chantrell's career as a church architect and Gothic expert, and a much-admired building.

Chantrell was certainly imaginative and diligent when it came to self-publicity. From the early 1820s he accepted commissions in which his artistic, as opposed to architectural, skills could be displayed. On a number of occasions, he produced perspective views of the locality intended for sale as engraved prints (**4.9**), as Taylor had been doing for some time, or to illustrate corners of maps and plans produced by the Leeds surveyor, Charles Fowler.[23] In September 1822 he exhibited at the Yorkshire Horticultural Society 'a design and elevation for a residence, and plan of four acres of garden and pleasure grounds' which was 'much admired'.[24] To put in context the ingenuity of Chantrell's self-promotion, although the activities of the YHS were noted in the newspaper, there was no other notice of the display of architect's drawings at its meetings. Finally, the Northern Society for the Encouragement of the Arts was revived in 1822 after a lapse of eleven years.[25] The venue for its exhibition was the Leeds Music Hall's Picture Gallery, a room transformed the previous year when Chantrell added top lighting. Alongside Anthony Salvin, Thomas Taylor and others, he exhibited 'several clever architectural designs and views'[26] in the architecture section.[27] Subsequently he exhibited with the Society in

4.9: Leeds, the junction of Park Row and Infirmary Street, engraving, based on a mid-1820s drawing by Chantrell. (*Author's collection*).

1823, 1825 and 1830, all the occasions on which modern architectural drawings were accepted for display. However, the most valuable and consistent publicity came via the pages of the *Leeds Intelligencer*. Quite why this should have been the case is not clear. Certainly the paper was keen to publicise new or proposed buildings in that they were a tangible manifestation of the town's increasing status and prosperity, but often they were mentioned without qualitative comment or the name of the architect. Conversely, almost all of Chantrell's designs were noted – often at the planning, foundation stone laying as well as completion stages – and were usually accompanied by enthusiastic approval. In the 1840s, as Chantrell's churches increasingly came to be seen as buildings of national importance, the paper carried lengthy accounts almost certainly written by Chantrell himself, although his authorship was not acknowledged. Some examples will usefully illustrate the point. On 20 October 1838 the paper reported the erection of the new organ screen at St Mark's, Woodhouse, Leeds – a minor commission by most standards – adding 'the honour of the design belongs to Mr Chantrell'. Two weeks later it announced the opening of St George's, Leeds, the first new church in the town for a decade, a landmark in that it was the first to be financed by private subscription and it was a substantial structure on a prominent site in the town's fashionable west end. The consecration was reported in detail but there was no mention of the church's architect, John Clark, who by this time had achieved some prominence in the town, an issue that will be discussed later. The school which Chantrell built in Meadow Lane (1841-2) was a modest structure erected to the meanest of budgets and was thus of the most limited architectural pretension. However, as it 'approached completion' the paper predicted it would be a 'spacious and elegant structure',[28] and its opening was greeted with a degree of rhapsody barely surpassed for the opening of Brodrick's magnificent Town Hall sixteen years later.[29] Then there was the paper's lengthy defence of Chantrell's position concerning disagreements over the Philosophical Hall and the Central Market *à propos* the Commercial Buildings competition in 1825 which we will reach shortly. It seems that Chantrell diligently kept the editor informed of his projects and the editor dutifully reported them, usually in the most laudatory terms. Quite why this was so is not clear, but the consistency of the support was invaluable.

After only a few years in Leeds, Chantrell could survey his short stay in the town with considerable satisfaction and his rising fortunes were reflected in his address. In late 1820 or early 1821 he left his first office in the Saddle Yard – not the most salubrious part of town – for an office and residence in Bank Street, and in November 1821 he 'informed his friends and the public that he was removed from his house and office in Bank Street to Park Row, near the Philosophical Hall. NB his house and office in Bank Street to let'.[30] Park Row was not quite the best address in town, but it was in the best area and suitably close to his most important building for the latter to have been a useful advertisement of his talent. The family remained there[31] until July 1833. The Chantrells arrived at Park Row with five young children and another on the way. A further two were to join them during their stay there. All eight children survived well into adulthood and seem to have enjoyed comfortable middle-class existences; two of them we will encounter later in connection with their father's profession.

1823 was to bring further successes. The year started auspiciously with the foundation stone-laying ceremonies for Chantrell's new churches at Meadow Lane and Taylor's at Quarry Hill. It was a joint event, the cause of much rejoicing, and an impressive procession of 'the mayor, corporation, clergy of the parish, churchwardens, subscribers [for providing the sites], freemasons … [was] formed at the Courthouse and proceed[ed] from thence to the Parish Church and after attending divine service'[32] proceeded to the sites of the two churches. A special place of honour was allotted to 'the architects, carrying their plans, and the plates.'[33] For the next three years, until the consecration, periodic accounts of progress, always positive, appeared in the *Intelligencer*. But the major event of 1823 for Chantrell was his securing the job of building the South Market in Leeds (**7.1-4**), a striking design and a huge budget, £23,000 – twice that of Christ Church and almost four times that of the Philosophical Hall – with a correspondingly large commission for the architect. The market was part of the rapid expansion of retailing facilities in Leeds in the mid-1820s and architecturally, was the most exciting. The finished building consisted of a cross for the sale of butter, eggs and poultry, 23 butchers' shops and stalls, 16 shops for miscellaneous purposes, 88 stalls, 9 slaughterhouses, and 18 dwelling houses on the upper floors of the shops. The most compelling part of the scheme was the striking circular 'cross' at its centre in the form of a Neo-classical temple.

During 1823 and 1824, the Leeds newspapers reflected the general sense of optimism – sometimes bordering on euphoria – resulting from the prosperity of the era and the physical changes taking place in the town. Occasionally it was nothing more than the suggestion for a beneficial project, but more usually it was a report of something tangible happening: 'scarcely a week elapses that we have not had the pleasure to announce some project for improving and adorning the town',[34] the *Intelligencer* waxed at the end of 1824, and Chantrell, still carrying all before him, must have entertained hopes that some of these 'projects' would require his services. Another tantalising report appeared in the *Intelligencer* six months earlier concerning the strike in the local building trades. Chantrell took the side of the employers, perhaps predictably, and was quoted as having said 'There are five gentlemen who were on the point of commencing building but who had instructed him to say that they would not proceed until the workmen had consented to work at the present prices.'[35] While we have information about the architects responsible for the major public and religious buildings erected at Leeds at this time, little is known of the more minor projects and even quite major private ones. The two quotations above give some idea of the extent of building activity at this time, but at the same time remind us that for the majority of schemes, especially private business or residential ones, rarely have details of the architects involved survived. A rare exception came in 1825: Chantrell advertised for 'Joiners and carpenters … for a large dwelling house about one

4.10: Armley, Leeds, Armley Chapel, proposed extension (R.D. Chantrell, 1825). (*WYASL*).

mile from Leeds … cottages will be provided on the spot for such workmen as may require them at the customary rent.'[36] The wording suggests this was all so commonplace, yet it was not a typical request, indeed it was more-or-less unique in the Leeds papers and appeared probably because the tradesmen engaged for the project had suddenly withdrawn and replacements were needed urgently. Just how many other 'large dwelling houses' Chantrell designed we will never know but it is likely these projects formed an important sector of his output.

On-going work at Meadow Lane church and the completion of the South Market must have occupied much of 1824 and both projects received helpful coverage in the *Intelligencer*. Not untypical was: 'With the South Market and the attraction caused by the highly enriched Gothic church at Meadow Lane, both executed from the designs and under the direction of Mr Chantrell, this end of town will be much enlivened.'[37] These comments are all the more interesting in the context of the other two Commissioners' churches – at Quarry Hill and Woodhouse – then in the course of erection; beyond accounts of the foundation stone-laying ceremonies and consecrations, there were no progress reports nor mentions of their respective architects. But Chantrell's apparently faultless debut on the Leeds stage could not last for ever and so it was that in this year his reputation took a knock, although not before almost winning another major commission, one that would have been the biggest of his career: the Central Market. A new covered market had first been proposed in 1822 but it was not until April 1824 that plans for what became known as the Central Market were requested. The budget was a massive £30,000[38] and apparently Chantrell won the competition. So far he had secured all four of the big public building jobs since his arrival in the town as well as a substantial church. Perhaps it was too good to last. So far as the Central Market was concerned, although his scheme was chosen, he was not formally appointed because he 'would not furnish working drawings … that injurious delay was the result and that the Committee were compelled to apply to another quarter: to which it is replied, that he [Chantrell] in the outset had furnished all the Drawings, Plans, Estimates, etc. customary in such cases – that he only waited till he should be actually appointed the Architect, to furnish the Working Drawings – That the latter would have been very expensive, and that in no instance are they supplied before the Architect is chosen.'[39] On the face of it, this sounds more like a minor misunderstanding that was easily rectifiable; that it was not resolved to everyone's satisfaction suggests more fundamental differences and entrenchment on one or perhaps both sides. Subsequently, Francis Goodwin was appointed and the foundation stone of his building was laid on 26 November 1824.[40]

The fall-out over the Central Market, galling as the loss of such a big job must have been to Chantrell, was essentially a private spat. However, matters erupted onto the public stage the following year in connection with the Commercial Buildings competition. The project, the grandest of all the public buildings connected with marketing and commerce in Leeds,[41] was first proposed in 1824 and early in 1825, six architects – Chantrell and Taylor from Leeds, plus Charles Barry, Francis Goodwin, Anthony Salvin and John Clark – were invited to enter a closed competition. Once the entries were submitted, the committee deliberated for seven weeks during which the newspapers provided an eager public with accounts of the assessors' discussions and details of the various designs. Such was the public interest in the competition that the *Intelligencer* carried very lengthy accounts of each entry, enumerating merits and defects: 'none of [the designs] is free from objections or undeserving of praise'.[42] Of Chantrell's design it reported, 'Our chief objection is that too florid an order of Architecture has been adopted and the ornaments are too numerous. In internal arrangements, the position of the Coffee-Room relatively to the News Room, appears to us a striking defect. At the same time, the general merits of the design are so great that we only regret our inability to do justice to them at present.'[43] The *Mercury*, in a much less detailed evaluation of the entries, went so far as to say his design was 'enthusiastically received by many of the shareholders.'[44] The reason why the *Intelligencer* was unable to say more of Chantrell's design was that the article was largely taken up with a robust defence of the wider issues of his professional position, another striking example of the paper's outspoken defence of him.

> The remaining design is Mr Chantrell's; but before we attempt to specify its defects or merits, we shall presume to advert to some rumours recently circulating respecting Mr Chantrell himself, which, unless disposed of would render all remarks upon his

production a mockery. We come then broadly and directly to the point. It is stated, that some prejudice prevails against this gentleman for his professional conduct relative to the Philosophical Hall and the Central Market, and that in consequence, if his Designs and Plans, etc. for the Commercial Buildings, were unexceptionable, they would still be rejected by the Subscribers at large, as well as the Committee. Now if this be fact, may we not ask, without pretending to be Mr Chantrell's advocates, whether it would not have been fairer towards him and the Subscribers not to have invited him to send in a Design at all in the present case? Why solicit him to become a competitor for a prize, if, whatever his deserts, he is foredoomed never to obtain it? No gentleman surely could wish to make a scape-goat or a stalking-horse of one member of a profession for another or for others – and particularly at the expense of the Subscribers generally: for though disapproved of, Mr Chantrell's Design, like the rest of the unfortunate ones, must be paid for. We confess indeed that these reflections created at first a sort of conviction in our minds, that the report in question had no substantial foundation, and to satisfy ourselves, and be just to our readers, we enquired further into the matter. We have thus found that two distinct charges, enveloped in the usual atmosphere of general inculpation, are preferred against Mr Chantrell, and these charges, with Mr Chantrell's answers to them, are as follows. The first charge respects the Philosophical Hall, and assumes a double shape – namely that the expenditure much exceeded the estimate, and that owing to the Architect's negligence, the Joiner employed in one part of the building American Pine, instead of Memel timber. The answer to the former is, that the Committee for erecting the Hall, made great alterations in the Design, after it was, with its accompanying estimate approved of – and secondly, that in the progress of the work, they interfered without previously conferring with the Architect, and introduced further alterations to a considerable extent, by which the aggregate cost was swelled to a larger amount than originally set down. On the subject of the timber employed … Mr Chantrell alleges, and the allegation is admitted on the other side, that he was the first to detect the American Pine, and that after three months contest, he succeeded in having it taken out of the building and Memel timber substituted. The other charge is that Mr Chantrell would not furnish working drawings for the Central Market [this section of the article has been quoted above]. We think then, if nothing be extenuated or suppressed in the foregoing statement, that the prejudice towards Mr Chantrell is unfounded and unjust, and that any attempt to exclude him from a fair chance of the Commercial Buildings, on such grounds, ought to be resisted. Having said so much, however, upon the preceding and in our opinion the material points as regarding this gentleman, our criticism of his Design … must be extremely brief … [45]

This supportive article was timed so that undecided shareholders might rally behind Chantrell's submission, but in the end it did little good and Clark was announced victor a week later.[46] (**3.1**) He was from Edinburgh, although he seems to have built almost nothing in the city, despite the massive amount of construction in progress there. And interestingly, he was the only one of the six entrants who had no apparent link to Leeds

4.11: Leeds, Christ Church, Meadow Lane (R.D. Chantrell, 1821–6). (*English Heritage/NMR*).

either from entering earlier competitions in the north of England or displaying drawings with the Northern Society. Quite how he came to the notice of the shareholders for their closed competition remains a mystery.

The national boom of the first half of the 1820s, of which Leeds had been an obvious beneficiary and which had provided the confidence for so much building in the town, finally broke towards the end of 1825. The reports of expansion, proposed 'improvements' and chauvinistic accounts of newly opened facilities found so often through 1823 and 1824 evaporated, replaced in late 1825 and through 1826 by accounts of bankruptcy. And it produced a double blow: not only were potential shareholders or philanthropists now unwilling to part with their money for building projects, but much that had already been collected for intended schemes was lost as the banking houses suffered financial ruin. So far as Leeds was concerned, 1825 was a watershed: the Commercial Buildings was the last major public building before the slump and not until the 1830s did a degree of prosperity and confidence return to the town. For Chantrell too, 1825 was a watershed; never again did he erect a major Classical public building although his career in Leeds still had more than twenty years to run. And when prosperity returned, his dominant professional position was challenged by John Clark who by this time had left Edinburgh and settled in Leeds.[47]

Public pronouncements from concerned, disappointed or grievously wronged unsuccessful entrants in nineteenth-century architectural competitions are legion; it was a system ripe for abuse by those involved as organisers, assessors and entrants. If Chantrell was aggrieved that those who had initially given him such unswerving support seemed now to have turned against him, he was by no means alone in feeling that this system of patronage was rotten. One of the last projects in Leeds to escape the recession was the new Corn Exchange, a relatively modest structure with a budget of £12,500, the competition for which occurred in 1825 and generated a short, but very significant letter to the *Intelligencer* from Thomas Taylor. In answer to rumours in some of the local papers that he had been an unsuccessful entrant for the job, he stated he had been 'unjustly represented' and that his many appointments on 'government churches prevented [him] making plans on speculation.'[48] We do not know whether Chantrell was similarly uninterested in this competition – eventually won by the almost unknown Samuel Chapman of Harrogate[49] – but Taylor's aloofness might well have struck a chord with Chantrell. Of even more significance was Taylor's premature death – he was only in his late forties and at the height of his career – announced just a few months later.[50] This is a convenient point at which to review Chantrell's situation.

In a number of ways, there are parallels in the careers of Chantrell and Taylor: both were the product of the offices of leading London architects, and neither had obvious Leeds connections, but settled in the town on the strength of winning a competition for a major public building, having identified huge potential in the West Riding for further employment. However, there was a fundamental difference: while Chantrell sought

4.12: Lockwood, Huddersfield, Emmanuel (R.D. Chantrell, 1826–30).

commissions where he could exploit his Classical training and stylistic preferences, Taylor had enjoyed a very successful career designing Gothic churches, a practice unique in northern England. In the relatively small circle of Leeds' professional class, it seems unlikely that Chantrell and Taylor's paths didn't cross from time to time. As newcomers to the town they probably felt an instant bond and as their careers were following different directions, they could meet largely without professional rivalry. Did Chantrell identify the rather more congenial working arrangements enjoyed by Taylor, free from the partiality, vagaries and inconsistencies of lay committees? The Commissioners' and their surveyor were rigorous in their standards, but they were consistent – once a design was approved, changes were rare – and most beneficially, they did not require architects to expend their energy on competitions. Furthermore, while budgets were extremely tight, once agreed they were not susceptible to variation and thus financial disputes were rare.

A stylistic reorientation

And so we return to March 1826: Taylor had just died and had several churches either about to be started or in the course of erection,[51] thus there were certainly jobs to be taken over if not quite a practice to be inherited. His Majesty's Commissioners had announced an additional grant of half a million pounds for church building and had

4.13: Netherthong, near Huddersfield, All Saints (R.D. Chantrell, 1826-30). The church is broadly similar to that at Lockwood although there are many differences, particularly in the arrangement of the staircases at either side of each church's main entrance. (*Leeds University Library, Special Collections*).

identified many West Riding towns and villages in need of more church room; Chantrell's Meadow Lane church (**4.11**) had recently been consecrated with much pomp and he enjoyed the public assessment that it was the best of the three Commissioners' churches in the town and was a great credit to his professional skill; finally, he must have despaired at the prospects for public building in the town – as we have seen, investment was almost non-existent and anyway he must have felt deeply hurt at the way he had been both abandoned and slandered by some of the leading townsmen who had initially welcomed him so warmly. What is clear is that Taylor's demise could hardly have come at a more auspicious time for Chantrell.

Seven years in Leeds and three impressive public building had undoubtedly established Chantrell's reputation in the town, but his achievements in the field of ecclesiastical Gothic were not inconsequential. Aside from Meadow Lane, he had built the new bellcote at Bramley Chapel and, significantly, had advised on the design and cost of a substantial addition as well as a wholly new church, he had made an addition to Armley Chapel and designed various other extensions there, he had designed a small chapel for Sir James Graham and had proposed additions to Rawdon Chapel. It was a not unimpressive list for an architect who, only five years earlier, had written to Soane desperate for guidance.

4.14: New Mills, Derbyshire, St George (R.D. Chantrell, 1827–31). (*Isobel Combes, courtesy of Derby DAC*).

Maybe he had discovered that Gothic was not such a strange beast after all. Whether he envisaged that courting further ecclesiastical commissions would be just a temporary diversion until the economy recovered and secular work reappeared or whether he recognised that the time had come for a fundamental shift in career focus takes us back to speculation. Nevertheless, we can identify early signs that Chantrell's interest in Gothic went beyond expediency. By the end of 1827[52] he was deemed to be sufficiently expert in medieval architecture to be quoted by the local antiquary Norrisson Scatcherd in his *A Dissertation on Ancient Bridge Chapels* of 1828: 'Since writing this treatise, I have seen Mr Chantrell, the Architect, who allows me to say, he coincides in my opinion, and thinks the Chapel [on Wakefield bridge] was built about 1340'.[53]

Taylor's obituary noted he had 'made drawings for, and been appointed architect for the new churches at Manchester, Ripon and Almondbury.'[54] Manchester was reassigned, at Ripon his design was executed by Lees Hammerton[55] but, it seems, Almondbury was not so wedded to Taylor's submission. The CBC meeting of 26 September 1826 was read a letter from the vicar of Almondbury stating that 'Mr Chantrell will soon furnish you plans of Lockwood and Netherthong.'[56] (**4.12**, **4.13**) These were approved on 11

November, but not sanctioned by the CBC's Building Committee until 5 May 1827. Apparently a crowd of 10,000 witnessed the foundation stone layings in 1828 and at their consecrations in 1830 there were also extensive celebrations; Lockwood was described as 'exceedingly handsome … from the designs of our gifted townsman, Mr Chantrell … in the old gothic style of the 14th century.' But it wasn't just the parishioners of Almondbury who were impressed: the Commissioners in London were demonstrably satisfied with Chantrell's performance. In May 1827 they had 'requested [him] to go to Glossop [in Derbyshire] to view the site [of the intended new church at New Mills] and prepare new designs.' This is significant as more usually the Commissioners waited for a parish to appoint an architect.[57] Clearly there had been problems with the parish's choice and in a relatively remote area, alternative expertise must have been limited. Thus the Commissioners turned to the reliable Chantrell. The result was St George, New Mills, opened in 1831 (**4.14**, **4.15**, **7.14**, **8.2**, **Cat. 29**). Similarly in 1827, when the Vicar of Dean in Lancashire wrote to the Commissioners asking if it could supply a design for the proposed new church at Horwich in his parish, it requested its surveyor, J.H. Good, to 'examine the drawings in his office to ascertain whether there be any

4.15: New Mills, Derbyshire, St George (R.D. Chantrell, 1827–31). The photograph shows the interior before the reordering of 1898.

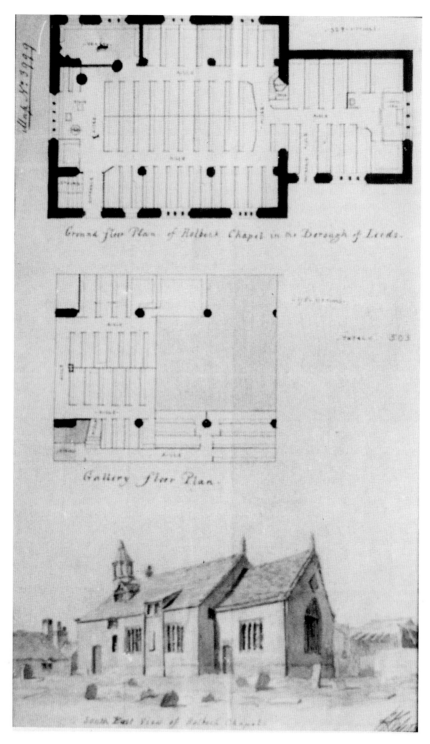

4.16: Holbeck, Leeds, old chapel. The drawing, by Chantrell, accompanied the application to the CBC.

design by Mr Chantrell applicable for the new church [at Horwich].' Although he found there was nothing of the size required and the job ultimately went Francis Bedford, clearly Chantrell was the Board's first choice. And a similar situation occurred at Hyde, Cheshire, probably in 1828, when the Commissioners 'ordered' him to look at the site and prepare designs, although again he was not appointed. However, at this time he was successful in securing the commissions to build new churches at Holbeck (**4.16, 4.17**) and Kirkstall (**4.18, 4.19**) in Leeds and at nearby Morley (**7.10–13**). All three churches were constructed in the late 1820s and early 1830s. These three, with New Mills, shared a broadly similar basic design using the Early English style and having an impressive spire.

The six new churches built at this time for the CBC – the four above plus Lockwood and Netherthong – not only kept Chantrell busy in the six years immediately after the shift in his practice's focus, but they lead to further ecclesiastical work. For instance, almost certainly on his first visit to Glossop to discuss New Mills, he was asked to report on the state of the parish church, recently the subject of an extensive rebuilding programme by the Sheffield surveyor/architect Edward Drury (**4.20**). Chantrell found his work to be 'injudicious and in very bad taste' and was immediately engaged to rebuild

4.17: Holbeck, Leeds, St Matthew (R. D. Chantrell, 1827–32). The watercolour, by W. R. Robinson, shows the tower without the spire which Chantrell intended. The spire that eventually completed the composition is by W. Hill, added in 1860. The school, to the right of the church, was also by Chantrell, 1839–40. (*Leeds Library and Information Services*).

4.18: Kirkstall, Leeds, St Stephen (R.D. Chantrell, 1827-29). Watercolour, by W.R. Robinson. (*Leeds Library and Information Services*).

the nave and rectify Drury's blunders, a project completed in 1832. Also related to these two Glossop jobs was an invitation to produce a scheme for repewing Bakewell church in *c*.1830. And from the two new churches in the parish of Almondbury – Lockwood and Netherthong – came the commission for repewing and repairing the parish church there in 1829. In the same year he was consulted about a new church at Lothersdale, near Skipton. The project came to naught, but interesting work would follow in this area geographically new to him. And in Leeds, the late 1820s saw him engaged on alterations at his own Christ Church, Meadow Lane, as well as to the churches at Woodhouse and Hunslet.

This period certainly saw him busy, but budgets were tighter than in the earlier 1820s. Meadow Lane's £10,555 – from the Commissioners' 'First Grant' – must have seemed

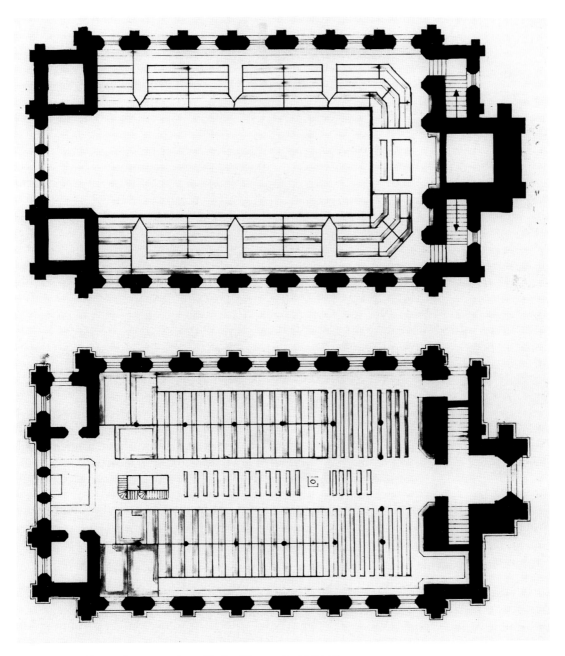

4.19: Kirkstall, Leeds, St Stephen (R.D. Chantrell, 1827-9).

luxurious compared to the less than £4,000 for each of the six late-1820s churches financed from the Commissioners' 'Second Grant'. And as he contemplated his fee of £13 9s. 5d. for the new west gallery at St Mark, Woodhouse, he must have reflected nostalgically on the more than £1,000 that the South Market had brought him only a few years earlier. Yet worse was to come. By about 1830, the funds of the Commissioners

Parish Church Glossop in Derbyshire
South Elevation shewing the proposed alteration of the Windows and door

4.20: Glossop, Derbyshire, All Saints. The tower and chancel were medieval, but Chantrell rebuilt the nave, 1827-32, as shown in this 1827 drawing of his. (*Lambeth Palace Library*).

were largely exhausted; they continued their work for a further 25 years, but their grants were significantly reduced and they required a much higher proportion of a project's cost to be born by the parish. From the ICBS – never a rich organisation in the context of the demands made of it – a grant of usually no more than £250, and often £50 or less, could rarely be more than a useful addition to an otherwise healthy subscription list. Private munificence would be the way forward, but the era of generous benefaction as a fashionable pastime was still some way off. For the 1830s, pragmatic – as opposed to elegant – additions and alterations were the only viable means of tackling the desperate shortage of church room in the rapidly expanding industrial towns. Fees were modest but at least it was a type of project with which Chantrell had had ample experience and at which he could excel. In this category should be placed repewing and proposed – but unexecuted – additions to St Oswald, Guiseley (1830-3) (**4.21, 4.22, 8.3**), the reconstruction of a usable space in the ruined nave of All Saints, Pontefract (1831-2) (**Cat. 30-2**), the addition of a new 'transept' and repewing at Bramley Chapel (1833) (**4.23, Cat. 5**) and a substantial alteration and addition to Armley Chapel (1833-4)

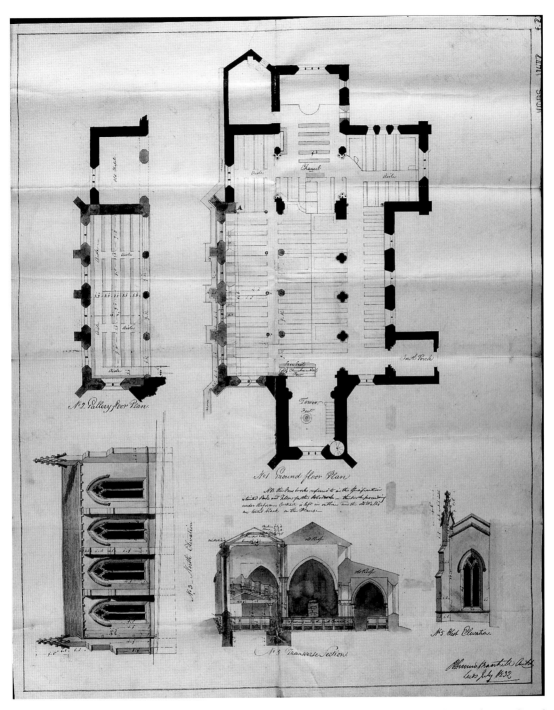

4.21: Guiseley, West Yorkshire, St Oswald. This drawing of 1832, by Chantrell, shows the medieval church before work commenced. (*Lambeth Palace Library*).

4.22: Guiseley, West Yorkshire, St Oswald, Chantrell's largely unexecuted proposals of 1832 for rebuilding the north aisle and re-seating the church. *(Lambeth Palace Library)*.

(**4.24-26, Cat. 1, Cat. 2**). At the last of these, Chantrell managed to add nearly 400 extra seats, at a cost of £1,030, to bring the total for this small chapel to 963. It was a remarkable feat, but entirely typical of the ingenuity being shown in the face of demands for more accommodation. Even lower down the list of prestigious appointments was the repair of the storm-damaged tower at St Stephen, Kirkstall (1833), and the eradication of dry rot at St Paul, Birkenshaw (1835). Not until the middle years of the decade did any commissions for new churches present themselves. Christ Church, Skipton (1835-9), St Michael, Headingley, Leeds (1836-8), and Christ Church, Lothersdale, near Skipton (1837-8), were the results. Funds remained limited: Lothersdale's budget, a staggeringly low £650, included a modest tower and provided 400 seats (**Cat. 25**, **Cat. 26**); Headingley cost only £2,500 for 600 seats and much of the old fabric had to be used to contain expenditure (**4.27**). In looking collectively at his church work of the period prior to the commencement of Leeds Parish Church in 1837, a commission that was to reinvigorate and transform his career, we can conclude it was all competent – remarkably so when the budgets are considered – and some of it was both elegant and convincingly antiquarian, for instance the new north aisle which he proposed for the neglected medieval church at Guiseley (Compare **4.22** and **8.3**). The interior of Pontefract presents a *tour de force* of Decorated vaulting, even if it is of only wood and plaster (**Cat. 30-2**). But the most remarkable of the mid-1830s churches is at Skipton: it is a church which looks forward

4.23: Bramley, Leeds, Bramley Chapel, view from the south-west. The chapel was built in the seventeenth century and had a school attached to it occupying the two western bays. Chantrell built the south transept – the right-hand part of the illustration – in 1833, re-using the bell-turret he had designed in 1821 but with a new, much taller spire.

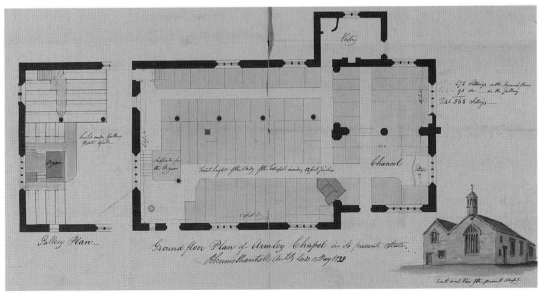

4.24: Armley, Leeds, Armley Chapel. Chantrell's 1833 drawing showing the chapel before his enlargement. (*Lambeth Palace Library*).

4.25: Armley, Leeds, Armley Chapel. Chantrell's proposals included rebuilding the south and west walls, building the small tower, substantially widening the north aisle and building a much bigger gallery. (*Lambeth Palace Library*).

to many of the architectural and liturgical innovations of the next decade (**4.28–31**). The driving force behind the project was Christopher Sidgwick, a member of a wealthy local family who held strongly to High Church principles and who would become a churchwarden of the completed building. He was not only instrumental in raising money for the project and then having some involvement in its management, but it would seem he was also involved in its planning: 'the interior arrangements were made under the direction of Christopher Sidgwick whose object it has been to make it precisely conformable to what was designed by the Reformers of the Church of England and make it easy for the officiating minister to observe the Rubrics to the strictness of the letter.'[58] It would be helpful if we knew more about this man whose written account of the Skipton church predicted so much of the language and attitude of the Ecclesiologists, but seems not to have belonged to any of the key national organisations. Certainly he was friendly with the Revd Hammond Roberson, who, as early as 1811 was stressing 'not only the Doctrines, but the sacraments and other Rites and Ceremonies of the Established religion',[59] and seems to have taken something of a lead in High churchmanship in the West Riding. Both Sidgwick and Roberson later appear to have been associated with the Revd Dr Walter Farquhar Hook, the new vicar of Leeds, appointed in 1837. Although

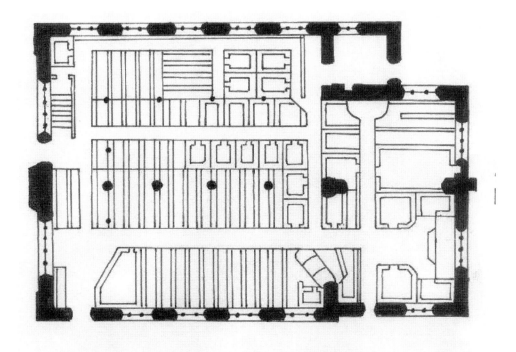

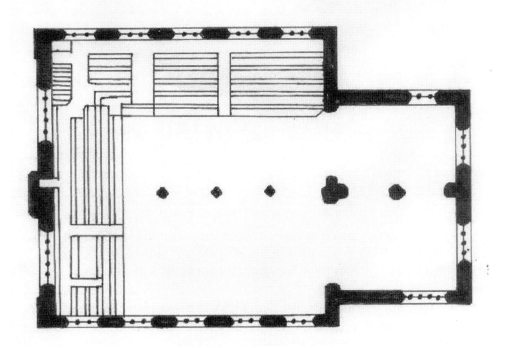

4.26: Armley, Leeds, Armley Chapel. A redrawn version of Chantrell's 1833 plans to show the new accommodation. (*Mike Collins*).

4.27: Headingley, Leeds, St Michael (R.D. Chantrell, 1836-8). The rebuilding of an earlier church used the existing nave foundations but added two transepts to increase accommodation. Mid-nineteenth-century photograph. (*Author's collection*).

there remains much to be uncovered about this group, it seems clear that Chantrell was well positioned to provide architectural flesh for their ritualistic bones.

The rebuilding of Leeds Parish Church (1837-41), the most important of all his projects and a commission that transformed his status, presides over his practice like a Colossus (**4.32, 7.15-17, Cat. 17-21**). Effectively, it divides his career into two parts and before we address it, it would be helpful to examine Chantrell's secular work of the 1830-7 period.

Despite the ecclesiastical successes of the late-1820s and the professional reorientation that followed, Chantrell was not entirely absent from the town's secular projects in the 1830s once the economy recovered from the mid-1820s depression. However, his status in the town was significantly marginalised. This might well have been a continuation of the prejudice that we encountered over the Commercial Buildings competition, but was certainly not helped by the decision of the competition's victor, John Clark, to settle in Leeds. Clark was quickly established as the most successful architect in the town[60] and, through the 1830s, carried all before him as Chantrell had done in his first six years

4.28: Skipton, North Yorkshire, Christ Church (R.D. Chantrell, 1835-9). (*Roger Hatfield*).

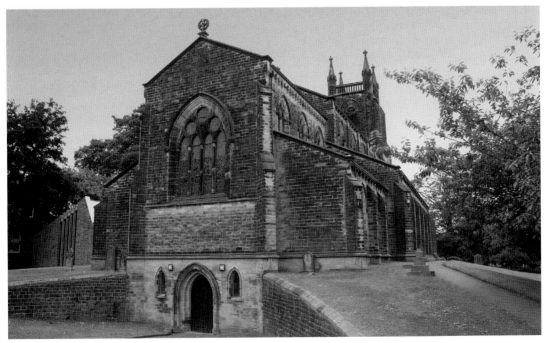

4.29: Skipton, North Yorkshire, Christ Church (R.D. Chantrell, 1835-9). The scheme included a crypt for fee-generating interments. (*Roger Hatfield*).

4.30: Skipton, North Yorkshire, Christ Church (R.D. Chantrell, 1835-9). (*Roger Hatfield*).

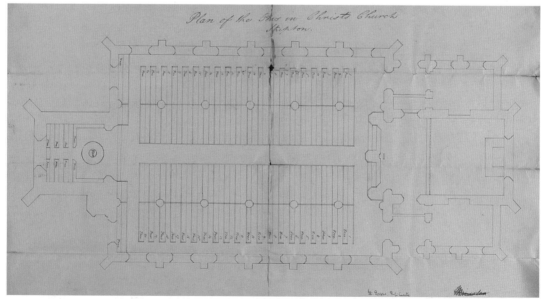

4.31: Skipton, North Yorkshire, Christ Church (R.D. Chantrell, 1835-9). Plan, perhaps by Christopher Sidgwick, one of the churchwardens and the driving force behind the project. (*Lambeth Palace Library*).

4.32: Leeds Parish Church (R.D. Chantrell, 1837-41). Lithograph by Richardson and Hawkins of 1841 apparently recording the arrival of those attending the re-dedication. (*Author's collection*).

there. In the decade Clark designed a number of important public buildings in and around Leeds, as well as several very substantial suburban mansions. He was adept at the Classical vocabulary he had acquired in Edinburgh and these triumphs must have served to confirm Chantrell's felicitous Gothic diversion. There is, though, another important dimension to the issue of the architectural crown in relation to Clark and Chantrell: Clark was very much the local architect; Chantrell now operated on a regional platform. That is not to say that Clark obtained no work outside the town, but he was busy mainly supplying Leeds with the full range of public and private buildings that a prosperous and expanding town required. Conversely, Chantrell – as the region's most accomplished church architect – was working over a much bigger area. And in an age when the architect's status lacked a precise definition or social position, Clark might just about be dismissed as a general dealer in architectural services, albeit, a very successful one. In choosing to specialise in churches, Chantrell had undoubtedly picked the higher end of practice: his patronage from the clergy could hardly have been more prestigious, and via Gothic's associations with antiquarianism and scholarship, he had successfully positioned himself well beyond those aspects of architectural practice that continued to bring it into disrepute.

4.33: Leeds, Court House (Thomas Taylor, 1811-13, wings altered by R.D. Chantrell, 1834). Taylor's building is illustrated in 3.4. (*Leeds Library and Information Services*).

The secular work that reached Chantrell in this period was minor: internal alterations to the Leeds Library in 1828 and 1835, additions to the wings of Taylor's Court House, first proposed by Chantrell in 1827, but not carried out until 1834 (**4.33**). Of the bigger projects in Leeds in the 1830s, Chantrell entered the General Cemetery competition in 1833; it was won by Clark, and Chantrell was not even short-listed. He didn't bother to enter the workhouse competition in 1835, again won by Clark;[61] whether his were among the 'nearly 50 plans submitted for the Corn Exchange'[62] in 1836 is not known. Given Clark's ability to handle the Classical vocabulary, it might have been predicted that Chantrell would stand little chance of success for the cemetery job, despite having produced a design which 'suggested such arrangements as were usual in the days of the Romans',[63] but it must have been truly galling to have been beaten into second place in the competition for the new Gothic church at Mount Pleasant, Leeds. This church, dedicated to St George, and situated in the fashionable north-eastern fringe of the town, was an early example of a new church built by private subscription; it was a commendable initiative, but it was, predictably, open to the partiality of all 'shareholder' projects of the period when it came to choosing an architect. Most depressing of all for Chantrell was the mediocrity of Clark's winning submission: far from being a worthy victor, it was actually a distinctly indifferent pastiche of several Chantrell designs from the late 1820s with an ineptly decorated spire. Also in 1836, Clark was appointed to rebuild the tower of Leeds' seventeenth-century Gothic St John's, a job that might have seemed logically destined for Chantrell. Only once were the tables turned. In 1830, and despite going to the trouble of submitting three alternative designs, Clark failed to secure the relatively modest job of building the new tower of Hunslet chapel. Chantrell's preferred design is not without interest. The existing chapel, a plain Georgian design of little architectural merit, and for which almost any style of tower might have been deemed appropriate, was significantly enlivened by Chantrell's Soanian composition, the most overt of his few architectural tributes to his former master (**4.34, Cat. 12**).

Central to the practice of an architect like Soane's were country house commissions and Chantrell might reasonably have expected such work to come his way, although there is little evidence it did. True, documentation of private commissions survives rarely, especially outside the muniments rooms of the great estates, and there are plenty of medium-sized West Yorkshire suburban villas that might be by Chantrell, but only two domestic commissions in the 1820s and 1830s have been positively identified and only

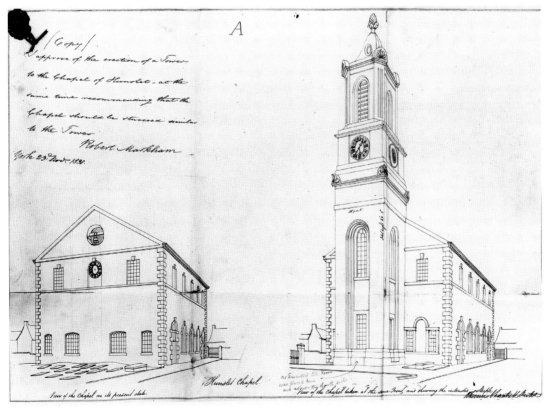

4.34: Hunslet, Leeds, Hunslet Chapel. Chantrell's 1830 drawing shows the 1744 building 'at present' on the left, and with his proposed tower on the right. This was the most Soanian of all Chantrell's compositions. (*WYASL*).

4.35: Armitage Bridge, near Huddersfield, Armitage Bridge House (R.D. Chantrell, 1828). North front.

one was for a new house. This was Armitage Bridge House at Armitage Bridge, near Huddersfield, for the mill-owner John Brooke (**4.35–36**). There Chantrell designed an unremarkable Classical five-bay, two-storey villa. The outside is plain but the interior contained two fine 'star-fish' ceilings[64] modelled on Soane's own breakfast room at 12, Lincoln's Inn Fields which Chantrell would have known well. The stable block too was replete with Soanian motifs. The house was completed in 1828 and must have resulted from Chantrell's appointment to build the nearby Lockwood church. Chantrell went on to complete several other commissions for the clearly well-satisfied client. The other country house commission was Rudding Park near Harrogate where Chantrell was employed (probably) from the late-1820s to the mid-1830s (**4.37–38**). This is a medium-sized country house rather than a villa, described in 1818 as a 'spacious modern mansion recently erected', attributed to the Wyatts or their circle. Although it might not have been entirely completed at this date, it was certainly sufficiently finished to be inhabited. In 1824 it was bought by Sir Joseph Radcliffe and subsequently he employed Chantrell, among other things, to eradicate an outbreak of dry rot. We know he was there in 1834 but not when he started or finished. An undated abstract of the tradesmen's bills, which is not complete, shows expenditure in this one phase alone of over £11,000. Since a mansion of this size could have been built from scratch for around £20,000, Chantrell's job must have involved much more than simply taking out decayed timbers and making good. The account includes £2,500 for masonry. Since the entire mason's bill for Chantrell's bigger churches would be around £2,000,[65] it seems likely that he made substantial additions to Rudding, including, perhaps, the stable block which displays certain Soanian characteristics.

The 1830-7 period was indeed something of a low point in Chantrell's career, but the contacts that came via his church appointments often brought with them commissions for small but nevertheless significant related buildings such as parsonage houses and church schools. They are testament to the satisfaction he had given in earlier commissions for the same clients. In this category can be placed the parsonage for Kirkstall church (1834-5), and the schools attached to the churches at Quarry Hill, Leeds (1829), St Peter's, Morley (c.1832), and that at Armitage Bridge, near Huddersfield (c.1835). Additionally, he designed a school and set of almshouses at Armley, Leeds (1832). All are nominally Gothic and economically detailed using a pared down, if sometimes incongruous, Early English vocabulary and simple lancet windows.

In 1833 the Chantrells, now with eight children, moved from Park Row to Oatlands, a house just beyond the northern boundary of the built up part of the town, although his office remained in Park Row for a further ten years.[66] Oatlands had a large garden and must therefore have been much more suitable for the children than their former town house, but in other respects it was a curious choice for a style-conscious architect. Photographs of the now-demolished building suggest it was a rather rambling farmhouse, perhaps of eighteenth-century origin, and totally without architectural pretension (**4.39**).

4.36: Armitage Bridge, near Huddersfield, Armitage Bridge House (R.D. Chantrell, 1828). South front.

4.37: Rudding Park, near Harrogate, North Yorkshire. Although the house was begun in 1807, perhaps by one of the Wyatts or their circle, Chantrell undertook significant work there in the late 1820s and early 1830s.

There is no evidence that its owner made any alterations or additions to it. Despite the less glamorous nature of much of the early-1830s employment, Chantrell remained very busy and thus financially secure, yet the new house was hardly a fashionable villa; perhaps it suggests that life there was relaxed, informal and family orientated. We might picture him sitting in his new study with its books and architectural fragments arranged on the model of Soane's remarkable house, vaguely aware of the noise of his children in distant rooms as he read in his *Intelligencer* of the early events of what would become the Oxford Movement, or a year later, of the terrible fire that had engulfed the Palace of Westminster. Both events would have a profound affect on his career, although it is unlikely that he had any inkling of their significance for the reception of Gothic as he read these accounts. The controversial choice of 'Gothic or Elizabethan' as the stylistic stipulation for Westminster – the country's most important secular building project – had no immediate impact on Leeds' fondness for Classicism. It would be another quarter-century before Gothic was selected as the style for the new infirmary and Beckett's Bank in Park Row, and by then, Chantrell was long gone.

Chantrell was forty in 1832 and, as well as making valuable contributions to the Leeds skyline, he was also becoming more conspicuous in the town's affairs as one might have predicted for an established member of the professions. His eldest two boys had been enrolled at the Grammar School in 1829[67] and their father had joined the Leeds

Library by 1827.[68] He had joined the Philosophical and Literary Society soon after its formation and although his membership had lapsed in the late 1820s[69] following his disputed fee, he rejoined in 1839.[70] The *Intelligencer* of 20 January 1831 carried a letter to the editor from Chantrell following the 'late fire in Commercial Street' in which great damage was caused. He made several sensible suggestions, principally that a series of taps should be installed beneath the town's pavements so that fire-fighters would have easy access to a water supply. Later that year, the Leeds Gas Light Company appealed against the rates levied on it by the overseers. Subsequently a group of architects, land surveyors and solicitors were asked to value the property; the architectural contingent comprised Chantrell and Lees Hammerton.[71] On one level it was a mundane activity but it was precisely the sort of parochial dispute that was given extensive coverage in the *Intelligencer*. In January 1835, Chantrell was elected one of nineteen Commissioners for the recently passed Leeds Improvement Act.[72] He chaired the meeting of 5 March,[73] but did not seek re-election for the following year.[74] In 1837 he became a freemason, joining the Lodge of Unanimity in Wakefield[75] before transferring the following year to the Lodge of Fidelity in Leeds.[76] Also in that year the *Intelligencer* trumpeted the proposed formation of the Leeds Zoological and Botanical Gardens[77] and quickly noted that Chantrell was both a shareholder and a member of the provisional committee of management;[78] subsequently he was elected to its Council.[79]

In July 1836, Chantrell was elected as a fellow of the recently established Institute

4.38: Rudding Park, near Harrogate, North Yorkshire, stable block. This building, much more Soanian than the mansion, might well have been part of Chantrell's commission.

4.39: Leeds, Oatlands. This was Chantrell's home for the latter half of his stay in Leeds, although there is no indication the architect made any significant changes to this (probably) eighteenth-century building. (*Leeds Library and Information Services*).

of British Architects,[80] the first Leeds practitioner to be designated in this way. He was clearly honoured by his elevation and the following year presented the Institute with a copy of Palladio's *Il Quattro Libri delle Architectura*, the French translation published in 1726.[81] At a time when anyone could style himself 'architect' regardless of training or talent, belonging to this professional organisation represented an important statement of Chantrell's conception of architectural practice, and his own role within it. Later in 1837, he gave a lecture to the Institute on 'Methods of Quarrying Stone at Springfield Quarry near Leeds'.[82] It was hardly profound scholarship but its delivery in London suggests he already had his sights set on a role within the national architectural scene.[83]

The summer of 1837 was enlivened by a short trip to the continent, probably to Bruges,[84] but the key event of the year so far as Chantrell's career was concerned was the arrival of the newly-appointed vicar of Leeds, Dr Hook. He was inducted to the living on 15 April and within two weeks had announced ambitious plans for the church. He was a man of vision and energy, 'the greatest parish priest of the nineteenth century'[85] and one who believed the spiritual renewal of his new parish was inseparable from the physical renewal of its principal church – 'a dirty, ugly hole of a church'[86] he called it – 'I see a handsome church is a kind of standing sermon'[87] was typical of his energising calls.

The rebuilding of Leeds Parish Church, antiquarian fame and local celebrity

The restoration of Leeds Parish Church – initially a relatively modest proposal to increase accommodation but which culminated in a near complete rebuilding – lasted four years. It was a project which, quite simply, transformed Chantrell's career; to describe the latter as moribund in 1837 would be unfair although it had certainly lost the edge of the previous decade, yet even before the Parish Church was completed, signs of Chantrell's enhanced status are easily detected.[88] The importance of the project cannot be overestimated, and not just for its architect's reputation: it was the biggest new church in England since Wren's St Paul's, a building predicted by the higher end of the Anglican fraternity to be a beacon for the long-awaited drive to reclaim the industrial towns from the grip of Nonconformity, and a physical manifestation of the theological revisions of the Oxford Movement.[89] For Chantrell too it was a seminal event. Throughout its construction, the *Intelligencer* provided regular eulogies and even before completion we can note more prestigious commissions coming Chantrell's way. However, it was following the rededication in 1841 that he acquired his real celebrity status, an event attended by the archbishop of York, three diocesan bishops and 300 clergy. And it received coverage in the national press: Chantrell was indeed famous. But in seeking to place the building in the context of his career, it would be a mistake to see this as some sort of fortunate break, rather we should interpret it as the culmination of two decades of often prosaic church work; what had formerly been mundane and unremarkable, the regrettably mean budgets which compelled alteration rather than new construction at (say) Glossop or Bramley, was now, on the heroic scale of Leeds Parish Church, simply sublime. It was as if his Gothic apprenticeship was finally completed and if there was any good fortune to be identified it was the rededication's concurrency with the national shift in architectural taste: Classicism was giving way to the popular and widespread interest in Gothic.

Back in 1837, the initial repewing proposal was accompanied by a £2,000-2,500 price tag; it was precisely the sort of economical job at which Chantrell was adept and for which Clark might have been aloof (**4.32, 7.15-17, Cat. 17-21**). The 1841 bill amounted to just less than £30,000, of which Chantrell received a handsome £1,570. A tantalising question is this: had a total rebuilding on this scale been envisaged in 1837, might the rebuilding committee have given serious consideration to Clark's candidacy?

It was while Chantrell was in the middle of this project that he would have heard news from his family of the fire in Bruges Cathedral where, on 19 July 1839, the roof and part of the tower were destroyed. Among those invited to tender for the repairs was Chantrell's younger brother William, a prominent Bruges businessman and entrepreneur. Soon the brothers were collaborating, Robert Dennis offering the architectural expertise and William the organisational. They secured the commission and with remarkably speed and efficiency, the roof was completed within a year, much to the delight of the citizens. Reconstruction of the upper section of the tower followed in 1843-6 and Chantrell proposed a wholly new west façade for the aisles and nave, although it was not executed (**4.40-2, Cat. 7**). He now had an international reputation and was, almost certainly, the first English architect ever to work on a continental cathedral.

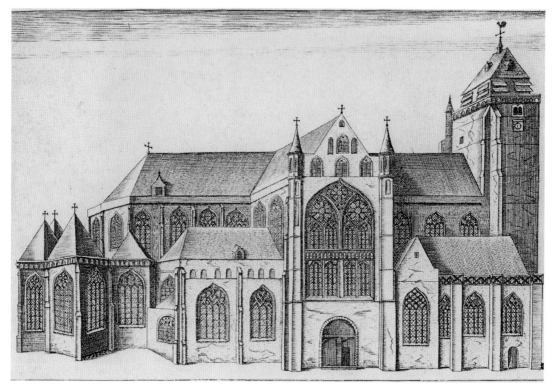

4.40: Bruges, Belgium, St Saviour's Cathedral. This engraving of 1641 shows the tower as it was before the fire of July 1839.

Chantrell emerged not just as the famous architect of the churches in Leeds and Bruges – accounts of the latter, predictably, appearing in the pages of the *Intelligencer* – and as a celebrated townsman in Leeds, but as an expert on all things medieval. He gave lectures, wrote learned papers, lent historic objects to public exhibitions, and was consulted extensively when the restoration of other medieval structures was envisaged. He had reinvented himself. No longer merely an architect, albeit now an exceptionally successful one, he was an antiquarian too,[90] replete with the resonance of gentlemanly scholarship and connoisseurship the term implies.

After the publicly aired fallout surrounding the Central Market and Commercial Buildings projects, discussed above, the rebuilding of the parish church seems to have brought Chantrell back into the exclusive fold of the Leeds oligarchy. In 1838 he gratuitously offered to design a temporary pavilion for the Leeds Tradesmen's Conservative Association's third annual dinner (**4.43**). Having been defeated in 1835 in the first municipal elections following the Municipal Corporations Reform Act, the Conservatives were intent on reasserting their importance and the 1838 dinner was to be a conspicuous symbol of the party's drive for power. The Tory *Intelligencer* was euphoric and could scarcely contain its enthusiasm for the event and especially the

4.41: Bruges, Belgium, St Saviour's Cathedral. Chantrell's drawing of 1840 showing his proposed termination to the tower. (*State Archives, Bruges*).

4.42: Bruges, Belgium, St Saviour's Cathedral. Chantrell's substantial termination to the tower of 1843-6 was further extended in 1866-72 by the present flèche.

4.43: Leeds, temporary pavilion for the Leeds Tradesmen's Conservative Association. (R.D. Chantrell, 1838). (*Leeds Library and Information Services*).

4.44: Farnley Tyas, West Yorkshire, St Lucius. (R.D. Chantrell, 1838–40). (*Albert Booth*).

4.45: Farnley Tyas, West Yorkshire, St Lucius. (R.D. Chantrell, 1838–40). (*Albert Booth*).

'palatial' – if temporary – surroundings in which it was to take place. It was indeed a useful means for Chantrell to ingratiate himself with this influential group. And in the following year, the rift with the Philosophical and Literary Society appears to have been healed as Chantrell delivered a lecture entitled 'An Historical Account of the late Parish Church in Leeds with some Observations relating to ancient fragments discovered during the removal of various parts of the building'.[91] This, coupled with the offer of his services without charge to remodel the Society's museum in 1839 must have been accepted by the Society as suitable penance on Chantrell's part and later that year he was re-elected to membership. In subsequent years he delivered lectures on 'Italian Architecture',[92] on 'Gothic Architecture'[93] and in 1843, on the 'Geometric Principles of Gothic Architecture',[94] a subject to which we will return in a later chapter. His public profile was further enhanced by his membership of the committee for the Leeds Public Exhibition in 1839 and his loan of various items – historic artefacts, architectural models

4.46: Honley, West Yorkshire, St Mary. (R.D. Chantrell, 1840-44).

and drawings, ancient coins etc. He lent further items to the Bradford Exhibition in 1840 and to a second exhibition in Leeds in 1843.

In 1840, Chantrell's father died. He was certainly both a prominent and a wealthy citizen of Bruges and must have left a substantial estate. Chantrell's mother had died eleven years earlier and although several of his siblings survived, as the eldest son, his inheritance was likely to have been considerable. This, plus the increase in professional fees in the c.1840 period might have led to his being more selective in the jobs he undertook, although the evidence would suggest otherwise. In 1839-40 he was eradicating dry rot at St John, Dewsbury Moor, he designed a new schoolroom for Ermysted's Grammar School, Skipton, in 1840 (6.3), for a fee unlikely to have exceeded

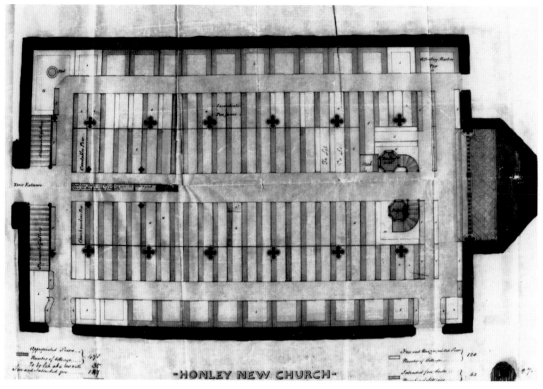

4.47: Honley, West Yorkshire, St Mary (R.D. Chantrell, 1840-44). (*WYASL*).

£10, and in 1842-4 he found time to re-roof the church at Golcar, West Riding, a repair that had defeated several architects following initial construction only thirteen years earlier. In 1840 alone, he was involved in at least twenty different projects. But it was the design of new churches that dominated the rest of his period in Leeds. After securing the Leeds Parish Church job he was appointed to build new churches – all in Yorkshire – at Farnley Tyas, near Huddersfield (1838-40) (**4.44-45**), Pool, near Otley, (1838-40) (**Cat. 33, Cat. 44**), Batley Carr (1839-41) (**Cat. 3, Cat. 4**), Cowling, near Skipton (1839-45) (**Cat. 8**), Honley, near Huddersfield (1840-43) (**4.46-48**), Shadwell, near Leeds (1840-2) (**4.49, Cat. 35**), Leven, East Riding (1840-5) (**Cat. 22-23**). There were repairs or alterations to the churches at Chapel Allerton, near Leeds (1839-40), Cleckheaton, West Yorkshire (1839-40), Earlsheaton, Dewsbury (1840), Holy Trinity, Leeds (1840-1), Heckmondwyke (1840) and Frodingham, Lincolnshire (1840-2). The new churches displayed the full stylistic range: Norman, Early English, Decorated and Perpendicular. To complete his stylistic virtuosity were a number of Tudor schools (**4.50**) and houses, and most remarkable of all, the Baroque tower of Holy Trinity (**4.51-52**). This last was modest in cost but visually elegant and enduringly popular as an addition to the Leeds skyline. The church, built in 1722-7, in a style perhaps best described as

4.48: Honley, West Yorkshire, St Mary (R.D. Chantrell, 1840-44). (*Albert Booth*).

4.49: Shadwell, Leeds, St Paul (R.D. Chantrell, 1839-42).

provincial Gibbsian, initially had an elegant tower and subsequently acquired a wooden spire. The spire was destroyed in a storm and replaced by Chantrell's delicate three-stage stone 'spire', a confection of various compositions published by Gibbs.[95] At a time when Baroque was probably at its least fashionable, it was a brave and remarkably successful solution; clearly Chantrell had lost none of his Classical panache. The spire had not the least function beyond the aesthetic and it is surely a testament to the influence Chantrell now wielded that he succeeded in prosecuting the scheme.

It seems Chantrell, like Soane, was intent on passing his practice to the next generation and at least two of his sons, John Boham (1815-99), his second son, and Henry William (1826-77), his fourth son, were educated in their father's office.[96] Subsequently, in 1842, John entered partnership with Thomas Shaw, Chantrell's former clerk of works at Leeds Parish Church, as Chantrell and Shaw.[97] This seems not to have been a happy relationship and after the dissolution of the arrangement in 1845, father and son worked together under the style 'Chantrell and Son'. Perhaps John was ill-suited to the calling and seems to have done little alone. Given the number of Chantrell's engagements and modest wealth, one might have anticipated he would use his son, with or without Shaw, as a convenient vehicle for less interesting jobs, but this seems not to have been the case. He did at least allow them to take credit for some projects but an examination of the documents show the father still firmly at the helm.[98] Henry acted as clerk of works at Honley and Denholme Gate, but, as was the case with John, seems to have lacked commitment and thus, like Soane's, Chantrell's architectural ambitions for his sons came to nought.

A project from this period with an importance beyond its size or budget was the restoration of the remarkable Norman church at Adel, near Leeds. Chantrell rebuilt the west gable and bellcote in 1838-9 and re-roofed the chancel in 1843 (**7.18-20**). The significance of the project was archaeological rather than architectural: by the early 1840s there was popular interest in ancient survivals such as this and Chantrell emerged as the local specialist. His paper 'Observations on the Ancient Roof of the Church of Adel …' was published by the Yorkshire Architectural Society (probably) in 1845 and reprinted in the *Institute of British Architects Papers* in 1847.

There is evidence that Chantrell's antiquarian interests stretched beyond his own restoration projects. In 1842, reflecting the growing interest in 'ecclesiastical architecture, antiquities, and design, [and] the restoration of mutilated remains',[99] it was proposed to form what soon became the Yorkshire Architectural Society.[100] Hook chaired the first preliminary meeting of nine interested men, eight of whom were clergy. Chantrell might

4.50: Hunslet, Leeds, National School (R.D. Chantrell, *c.*1840-3). The illustration shows a tile decorated with a transfer print taken from a drawing by Chantrell. (*Thoresby Society, Leeds*).

4.51: Leeds, Holy Trinity (William Etty, 1723-7; wooden spire added subsequently). The early nineteenth-century engraving shows the tower before the 1839 hurricane.

4.52: Leeds, Holy Trinity. Chantrell added the top three stages to the tower to replace the damaged spire in 1839–40.

4.53: Rise, East Riding of Yorkshire, All Saints (R.D. Chantrell, 1844-6).

have been the one layman, but certainly he was an early member of Society – becoming a life member for the sum of £5 – and the following year was part of a sub-committee formed to steer the Society's first project: the restoration, by Scott and Moffatt, of the Chantry Chapel, Wakefield.[101] Also in 1843, he joined the Cambridge Camden Society – later the Ecclesiological Society – the most strident of the national groups aiming to push Anglicanism in a higher, more ritualistic direction and seeking to revive church arrangements necessary for the correct enactment of the prayer book rubrics. There is no evidence that Chantrell held any particular opinions about churchmanship, but explicit alignment with the views of those seeking 'correct' new churches and church restorations was on the verge of becoming, as Chantrell must have predicted, a most useful means of securing commissions. This is not to suggest that his membership was entirely opportunistic, although at a time when the most appropriate form of church design was a matter of contention, Chantrell could not reasonably sit on the fence. His church work thus far – especially Skipton, Leeds Parish Church and Adel – had placed him perfectly to anticipate the Ecclesiological revolution and now he had found the perfect vehicle to legitimise his design decisions. Sadly, the Ecclesiologists were not

4.54: Rise, East Riding of Yorkshire, All Saints (R.D. Chantrell, 1844-6).

quite so enthusiastic about their new recruit and often reviewed his churches with little enthusiasm, but he remained a member until at least 1856.[102]

An important adjunct to his work as antiquarian and architect was his research on 'The Geometric System applied by the Mediaeval Architects to the Proportions of Ecclesiastical Structures', the 'discovery' of which occurred in 1842. Its first public airing seems to have been a lecture for the Leeds Phil. and Lit. in 1843,[103] repeated, perhaps with modifications, for the Institute of British Architects in 1847[104] and publication in *The Builder*[105] the same year. While the validity of the theory – discussed in Chapter 7 – might be questionable, it seems to have enabled Chantrell to produce a set of fine church designs in his final years in Leeds: Rise, East Riding (1844-6) (**4.53-54**), Middleton, near Leeds, (1845-6) (**7.22-25**), King Cross, Halifax (1844-7) (**4.55-56**), Armitage Bridge, near Huddersfield (1844-8) (**5.1-4**), St Philip, Leeds (1845-7) (**4.57-58**) and others. Finally there was the substantial new parish church in Keighley (**7.26-29**), an attractive finale to his Yorkshire career. Several projects remained unfinished on his departure and

4.55: Halifax, St Paul, King Cross (R.D. Chantrell, 1844-7).

4.56: Halifax, St Paul, King Cross. The illustration shows Chantrell's drawing for his proposed decoration of the east wall, 1847. It specifies vivid blues, greens and reds on a cream background and texts from Exodus with 'all the letters capitals and coloured red'. (*WYASW*).

4.57: Leeds, St Philip (R.D. Chantrell, 1845-7). From a mid-nineteenth-century lithograph by Pulleyn and Hunt of Leeds.

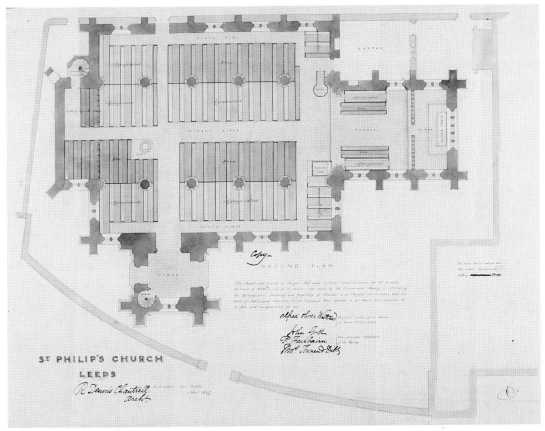

4.58: Leeds, St Philip (R.D. Chantrell, 1845-7). (*Lambeth Palace Library*).

he seems to have managed them by post and occasional visits from London. Chantrell and Son retained an office in Leeds until 1851, although essentially no new projects appear to have been started.

It was at the beginning of 1847 that he announced his removal to London,[106] although he had been spending increasing amounts of time away from the town since the mid-1840s and, it seems, playing a decreasing role in its affairs as London beckoned. We have already noted several of his publications and he had joined the Archaeological Institute of Great Britain and Ireland at some point between its foundation in 1844 and 1846 when he was a member of the Architecture Committee.[107] At the Institute's annual meeting at York that year he read a paper 'Observations on an Ancient Pillar found in taking down the old Parish Church of Leeds'.[108] In moving to London he was, it would seem, seeking to position himself to exploit his archaeological and architectural expertise on a national stage.

ROBERT DENNIS CHANTRELL, F.SA., F.R.IBA.

Architect of Leeds Parish Church, 1841.

4.59: Anon, a drawing of Chantrell, presumably made during his last years in Leeds. Although he is listed as 'FSA' it seems likely the writer confused this with Chantrell's membership of the Archaeological Institute of Great Britain and Ireland. (*Thoresby Society, Leeds*).

5

Chantrell in London

At the beginning of 1847 Chantrell announced his move from Leeds to London[1] and thereafter, he appears to have had little to do with the town beyond the completion of projects started before his departure. A combination of inheritance and professional success had made him sufficiently wealthy not to engage in paid employment and it would be easy to associate transfer to London as retirement; certainly, there is no evidence to suggest the move south was an attempt to secure metropolitan commissions. He had just celebrated his 54th birthday and was at the height of his professional success; if he tired of the rigours of practice, he was unlikely to have welcomed idleness.[2] A career reorientation seems a much more likely motivation for a move to London. But first, we need to try to disentangle the timing of the move.

January 1847 might well have marked Chantrell's departure from Oatlands, his Leeds home, but we know he had at least two addresses in London before 1847[3] and is recorded as spending time there through the early 1840s.[4] The *Intelligencer* announcement gave his 'new' address as 21 Lincoln's Inn Fields, but he had occupied the property in 1845, and perhaps earlier. This, and his giving up his Leeds office in 1843 – professional communications came to Oatlands thereafter – all suggest the move south was a gradual one rather than a sudden break. From 1847 until he left London for the south coast (probably) in 1862, he occupied a series of houses and evidence from a variety of sources is not consistent. His precise address is fairly unimportant in the context of this study, except for one respect: the location of his office and thus the extent of professional activity. *Kelly's London Post Office Directories* list him as 'architect' at 21 Lincoln's Inn Fields in 1848-50. No other address is given at this time suggesting this was his home too. However, the editions of 1850, 1851 and 1852 continue to list him as an architect in Lincoln's Inn Fields, but also include him in the 'Court Division' at 4, St Mary's Road, Canonbury, suggesting the office was sufficiently important to justify its own address. From 1853, he does not appear in the architects list but continues in the Court Division

5.1: Armitage Bridge, near Huddersfield, St Paul (R.D. Chantrell, 1844-8). The church was badly damaged by a fire in the 1980s and the design was modified in the rebuilding. Watercolour by H. Allen. (*Leeds University Library, Special Collections*).

in Canonbury, moving from 4 to 31 St Mary's Road from the 1856 edition. The 1861 and 1862 editions list him at 7 Park Place, Camberwell Green.[5]

Professional activities

Of more interest is the scope of his professional activities. This can, for convenience, be divided into a number of facets. Firstly, there were the unfinished Yorkshire projects. Of his seven new churches of the mid-1840s, Armitage Bridge (**5.1-4**), Halifax, Keighley and Leeds (St Philip), remained incomplete by the time of Chantrell's departure from Leeds; indeed Keighley was not consecrated until August 1848. Also, there were the parsonages at Armitage Bridge and Middleton (**Cat. 28**) which had lagged behind their churches awaiting further funds. In addition there were two small new projects which, although they were the result of earlier commissions, can best be dealt with here. These were the rebuilt bell-cote at Netherthong (1847) following storm damage (**5.5**), and a new chancel for Emmanuel church, Lockwood, Huddersfield (1848-9) – a remarkably early example of the initiatives to 'Camdenise' Commissioners' churches (**5.6**). The two jobs were small; if Chantrell was seeking to relinquish practice in Yorkshire why did he accept them? The likely explanation is that he did them as a favour for his long-time patron, John Brooke, effectively the 'squire' of this part of the Almondbury parish.

Chantrell and Son kept an office in Leeds until around 1850,[6] although little in the way of correspondence, and certainly no drawings, seem to have emerged from it. Tenders for Middleton's vicarage were to be sent to Chantrell and Son's Leeds office,[7] but this was a rare instance. Important documents passed through Chantrell in London and there is scant evidence of contact between father and son.[8] A much more significant source of local assistance seems to have come from John Wade, Chantrell's trusted clerk of works over many years, who seems to have superintended most of the unfinished projects.[9]

Secondly, there was his academic research. That there is no evidence that he sought metropolitan commissions underlines the fact that his move south must have been for other reasons. The answer is surely that he sought to establish himself as an antiquary, one with expert knowledge of ancient rather than modern church building. His experience was now exceptional and London would suit this academic objective much better than Leeds. To some extent it was an audacious plan, yet one not entirely doomed. In the mid-

5.2: Armitage Bridge, near Huddersfield, St Paul (R.D. Chantrell, 1844–8). The painted decoration seen at the top of the photograph, might be original as Chantrell specified similar embellishments at Halifax at this time. Early twentieth-century photograph. (*WYASW*).

5.3: Armitage Bridge, near Huddersfield, St Paul (R.D. Chantrell, 1844–8). Early twentieth-century photograph. (*WYASW*).

1840s, he possessed a rare blend of architectural and archaeological experience where churches were concerned. It was a level of expertise few could match and for a short time, following the deaths of Rickman in 1841 and Cottingham in 1847, but before the new generation of ecclesiological protégés had made its mark, his achievements were almost unparalleled. To underpin this ambitious plan, Chantrell's address in Lincoln's Inn Fields, just a few doors from Soane's former home and office, was surely no accident. By then it was the Soane Museum, curated by George Bailey, Chantrell's contemporary as a Soane pupil. No doubt Chantrell called regularly and enjoyed its unique ambiance. In moving to the square, might Chantrell have hoped to become the doyen of Gothic scholarship in the way that Soane had championed Classicism? The contents of Chantrell's will certainly suggests he had a not inconsiderable collection of drawings, fragments and artefacts.[10] We need to consider his credentials.

Towards the end of the previous chapter we noted some of his lectures and publications. By the early years of Victoria's reign the history and buildings of the Middle Ages was no longer the preserve of an educated elite, but had moved into the realm of the popular imagination, a development perhaps personified by the cult following for Scott's Waverley novels. On a more specialised level, the 1840s saw the introduction of numerous societies intent on stimulating the new-found interest in Gothic remains – the diocesan architectural societies – and there was a range of journals to disseminate discoveries and interpretations. Chantrell was ideally placed to capitalise on the new pastime. He had been a big fish in the Leeds pond, but London offered the real prizes. His

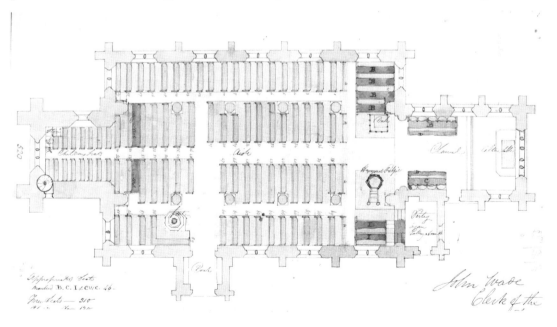

5.4: Armitage Bridge, near Huddersfield, St Paul (R.D. Chantrell, 1844-8). This plan was drawn by John Wade, Chantrell's much-employed clerk of works. (*Lambeth Palace Library*).

5.5: Netherthong, near Huddersfield, All Saints. This (probably) 1847 drawing by Chantrell shows his proposed rebuilding of the bellcote following a storm. The rest of the church is his work of 1826–30, shown in 4.13. (*WYASW*).

'Observations on the Ancient Roof … of Adel' was published by the recently founded Yorkshire Architectural Society in 1845; most conveniently, he was able to deliver it as a lecture to the Institute of British Architects in January 1847, within days of leaving Leeds. It was reprinted in the *Institute of British Architects' Transactions* later that year. The latter was both more widely read and more prestigious, and was the perfect *entrée* to his new life in London. Another piece of earlier scholarship was resurrected for the London audience: in 1843 he had given a lecture to the Leeds Phil. and Lit. 'On the Geometric Principles of Gothic Architecture', probably the piece of his research that would have been most highly regarded at the time, although largely dismissed today.[11] This was revised for a lecture to the much more critical audience of the Institute of British Architects on 17 June 1847, this time titled 'On the Geometric System Applied by Medieval Architects to the Proportions of Medieval Structures'.[12] Shortly afterwards it was published in *The Builder*.[13] Subsequently, extensive discussion of it was included in editions of Joseph Gwilt's *Encyclopaedia of Architecture* appearing through the second half of the century. In May 1847 he had been elected an ordinary member of the IBA's Council[14] and also in that year, the *Gentleman's Magazine* reported Willement's new

5.6: Lockwood, Huddersfield, Emmanuel. Chantrell replaced his earlier chancel of 1826–30 with this more 'correct' one in 1848–9..

stained glass windows presented to Leeds Parish Church by Thomas Blayds, including some positive discussion of the church itself.[15] And Chantrell's paper on the Leeds Parish Church cross, first heard at the Leeds Phil. and Lit. in 1839[16] and delivered to the Archaeological Institute's conference in York in 1846, mentioned in the previous chapter, was published in the conference *Proceedings* which eventually appeared in 1848 (**5.7**). It was also given as a lecture to the IBA[17] and subsequently published in the Institute's *Transactions*.[18] His arrival in London was thus accompanied by a not inconsiderable splash in its pond. However, this level of exposure to the new audience was not maintained[19] and *The Ecclesiologist* published several reviews of his recently completed churches which, if less damning than those of Blore's work, were hardly enthusiastic.[20]

The Incorporated Church Building Society's Committee of Architects

There was one important outcome of the early years in London that allowed Chantrell to exercise his experience and move in exalted circles: his work with the ICBS. Chantrell had had more than 25 years experience of the ICBS as a designer of new or altered churches that were the recipients of its grants; now he was to move to the other side of the funding process. Throughout that quarter-century, all matters of architectural supervision were handled by the ICBS Examining Architect, J.H. Good, another of Soane's former pupils. However, at its meeting of 21 February 1848, the Society's Committee agreed that 'Mr Good's Reports are very unsatisfactory as he only reports on the construction of the buildings' and it resolved 'to institute a system where architects can be sent to inspect works and the costs … be charged to the applicants.'[21] Perhaps this was a manifestation of the Camdenian-inspired revolution; the ICBS had, in the past, been interested only in increasing church accommodation and durability, never in 'correct' arrangements or archaeological preservation. However, fashions were changing. Consequently, a Committee of Architects was promptly established and its first meeting was held on 2 March 1848. Present were Raphael Brandon, R.C. Carpenter, J. Clark, Benjamin Ferrey, J.H. Hakewill, J.P. Harrison, Anthony Salvin and T.H. Wyatt. These eight, with the absent G.G. Scott, were to be divided into three groups of three, each meeting in rotation three times per year to inspect plans submitted. In addition to attending meetings, each architect had a geographical area of the country and was to be responsible for inspecting 'buildings in progress' in that area.[22] After a year, an amendment was carried by which a further three architects were to be added so as 'to make a more complete arrangement for dividing up England and Wales' and the new personnel were to provide a fourth member of each group. The recruits were Ewan Christian, David Brandon and Chantrell. Chantrell was allotted the diocese of York,[23] although he seems to have acquired Ripon too. He now belonged to the ultimate group of church architects and had thus achieved what he probably craved for a long time: recognition of his achievements. He was no longer a provincial practitioner, with all the disparagement that the term implied, but a London heavyweight.

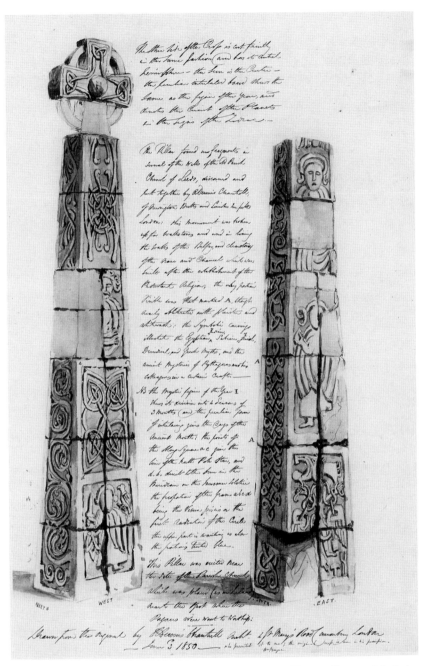

5.7: Leeds Parish Church, the ancient stone cross. Chantrell assembled the cross from fragments found built into the tower of the old parish church when it was being demolished. He claimed the stones as a legitimate part of his contract and took them to London when he left Leeds. They returned to the parish church following his death. Chantrell exploited his discovery in a number of lectures and articles. This sheet of drawings and text is dated 1850. (*Leeds Library and Information Services*).

Fangfoss Church Yorkshire
before its restoration 1849-50

5.8: Fangfoss, East Riding of Yorkshire, St Martin. This watercolour by Chantrell, made in *c*.1849, shows the old church which he replaced. This, and the matching watercolour of the proposed new church (5.9), suggest a leisurely preliminary visit to the village, perhaps staying for several days with the vicar. (*Lambeth Palace Library*).

Membership involved attendance at the committee's AGM and the three relevant sub-committee meetings. Additionally, there were numerous special meetings. Minutes rarely recorded individual contributions, but they note much concern about the need for care with restorations. Some projects generated extensive correspondence between the committee and the architect of the new church with members of the committee occasionally demanding revisions, such as thicker walls or more sturdy buttresses, and alternative construction details, set out in sketches within letters. Chantrell was a diligent attendee. Members also travelled to inspect projects, both during construction and on completion. Chantrell made many journeys north, no doubt exploiting the rapidly expanding rail network.[24] However, not all ICBS-financed projects appear to have received a site visit and it is difficult to understand how his choice was made beyond it being no more than an arbitrary sample. Some inspections were more predictable: in Sheffield, a half-completed tower had collapsed and in Whitby, the church had remained in an incomplete state for several years through lack of funds. Others might be explained by the archaeological interest of the church, although he omitted many important restorations. And perhaps some were chosen so he could visit old friends.

From the beginning, the Committee agreed that 'architects will supply plans for churches abroad but decline to do so for England so as not to out-do fellow professionals. However, they will gladly give free advice for restorations and erections etc.'[25] Concurrent with his membership of the committee were three interesting restorations within his diocese in the East and North Ridings – at Barmby on the Moor, Fangfoss and Malton – whether they resulted from some initial 'free advice' or whether the rule was relaxed is not clear.[26] What is undisputed is that the jobs were stimulating and, in the case of the first two, the cause of a new or enhanced friendship with the Revd Robert Taylor who, as vicar of Barmby, had responsibility for both churches.

St Martin, Fangfoss, was the first commission and historically, the most important (**5.8-10**). In his 1848 report Chantrell notes 'Fangfoss is perhaps one of the most interesting buildings to the antiquary that can be found in this county and it has so much beautiful carved material in a perfect state that I shall be glad to undertake its restoration. Fangfoss has once been a gem of Norman architecture.'[27] Taylor recorded his observations; presumably he accompanied Chantrell at the examination. '[He] discovered a vesica piscis (a fish's bladder) which he states is an ancient symbol of Christianity. We also found the master mason's private mark … Chantrell, in his rapture, declared these

5.9: Fangfoss, East Riding of Yorkshire, St Martin (R.D. Chantrell, c.1849-50). (*Lambeth Palace Library*).

5.10: Fangfoss, East Riding of Yorkshire, St Martin (R.D. Chantrell, c.1849-50).

last to be of great value.'[28] Detailed watercolour perspectives of the old and proposed churches survive. It was unusual for Chantrell to produce this type of illustration and they are, perhaps, indicative of an unusually lengthy and relaxed visit to inspect the site. The outcome was an attractive rebuild in the Norman style consisting of nave, chancel and pyramid-topped bellcote. The consecration in August 1850 prompted a lengthy account of the new church and its history in the *Yorkshire Gazette*, much of it written by Chantrell. Importantly, it was reprinted in the *Architect and Builders' Gazette* to reach a national audience.

While work at Fangfoss was in progress, Taylor asked Chantrell to inspect Barmby church. Both projects were recipients of ICBS grants which might account for Chantrell's involvement, or perhaps Taylor and Chantrell already knew each other. Certainly they were good friends subsequently.[29] At Barmby, Chantrell surveyed the dilapidated 'late second pointed … 14th century' church and rebuilt the nave and chancel in 1850-2 (**5.11, 5.12**).

Perhaps the most interesting aspect of these two commissions was not so much the buildings that were produced as the glimpse of relationship between architect and 'patron' that resulted. Most significantly, it reveals Chantrell the antiquary exercising his expertise and operating as the academic equal of Taylor, a graduate. While Barmby was in progress, Chantrell wrote to Taylor. It is the only personal letter known to have survived from the architect.

> I had the opportunity of becoming well acquainted with the delightful family of the Rev. Mr Duntze of Weaverthorpe [about 15 miles north-east of Barmby], as getting my feet wet and a severe cold I was obliged to call in medical attention and had I been with you or at home I could not have received greater attention. Mrs Duntze is a perfect lady yet thoroughly domesticated: the daughters – 1st Augusta, 2nd Mary, 3rd Jeaney, 4th Isabel, 5th Georgina, most agreeable young women and two younger girls will doubtless be like their sisters: the son who is at school – of course – I did not see. The weather was very bad – cold and snow daily. I went to Luttons to see the church (about 2 miles further from Sledmere) and we had a thunderstorm – two of the young ladies accompanied me, Augusta and Jeaney, and every evening I assisted them by sketching the antiquities of Weaverthorpe, Butterwick, Luttons and Helperthorpe churches, besides making them a set of pencil drawings illustrative of the changes in architecture from the Saxon period to the time of Elizabeth. Mr Duntze, unfortunately, had an attack of gout which deprived me of his society. I think Mrs Taylor and you will be delighted with the whole family … [30]

Here we see Chantrell meeting clerical families, presumably valued for his knowledge, and sometimes staying with them in connection with his projects, very much as an eighteenth-century architect would have done while supervising country house building. Finally we see Chantrell at the archetypal antiquary, out sketching local monuments for his own pleasure. Indicative of changing fashions, we note that his architectural syllabus for the Misses Duntze deemed the Classical orders irrelevant. Also reflecting mid-century taste, the letter includes Chantrell's enthusiasm for the Great Exhibition: 'I had intended to be here [in London] for the opening of the Exhibition … I have been there frequently and have not yet seen half … I hope both you and Mrs Taylor will come to see it … we will be glad to quarter you here … ' He was especially admiring of the Indian products but regrettably for our study, makes no comment about the building itself.

So far as ICBS inspections were concerned, it is clear Chantrell carried out at least a dozen in the mid-1850s. The dates of his visits suggest either that he made numerous short visits north or, more likely, spent several weeks over them and combined them with visiting his friends and family. Some details of his visit to Yorkshire in the summer of 1855 are recorded in two letters he wrote to the ICBS secretary. The second, of 14 August, was written from the Gargrave residence of Alfred Hopps, the husband of Chantrell's eldest daughter, Elizabeth Caroline. While there he had visited the relatively nearby churches Eastwood, near Keighley, and Skipton, and the next day was heading to the south of the county – presumably staying elsewhere – to visit projects in Sheffield and Brampton

5.11: Barmby on the Moor, East Riding of Yorkshire, St Catherine (tower medieval; nave and chancel, R.D. Chantrell, 1850–2).

Bierlow. By the end of that week he intended to be in Barmby Moor to stay with the Revd Taylor and his family; presumably he remained there several weeks as he inspected work at Spofforth church, near Harrogate, on 8 September. He was back in Yorkshire in November for more visits. The 14 August letter is helpfully informative about travel arrangements; he justified an unwillingness to revisit churches he had recently seen as

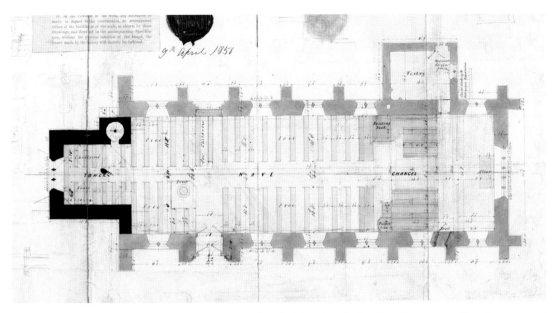

9th April 1850

5.12: Barmby on the Moor, East Riding of Yorkshire, St Catherine (tower medieval; nave and chancel, R.D. Chantrell, 1850-2). (*Lambeth Palace Library*)..

'travelling on country roads is difficult and expensive'. He proceeds to mention others he proposes to inspect: 'Whitby is the most remote but is on a direct line of Railway and therefore readily accessible. Withernwick [in the East Riding] will take about 20 miles of carriage from the Bridlington railway and as it is in the hands of Mr Healey [Chantrell's former pupil] there will be no doubt that the report will be favourable … I find my visits to some places will be deferred as some of my friends are away on the (?)moors; but Barmby will be my (?)Central Station for the East [should you wish to contact me].'

After rebuilding Barmby church he seems to have undertaken no further design work until 1858 when he reconstructed the chancel of the largely Norman St Michael at Malton. The principle source is Whellan's *History* published just a year after the work which refers to 'Mr Chantrell the architect of the Incorporated Society'[31] and might explain his presence there, although no grant application was submitted and personal recommendation of the nearby East Riding clergy – Malton is just beyond the boundary of the North Riding – seems the more likely explanation.

Chantrell's final project was the rebuilding of the nave and chancel of St Michael, Peasenhall, Suffolk, 1860-1 (**5.13**). The project was paid for by John Brooke of nearby Sibton Park. This was the same John Brooke for whom Chantrell had build Armitage Bridge House near Huddersfield 32 years earlier and whose family and business had given him much employment throughout his career. It was fitting that his last commission should have come from a family who had been so loyal to him and, surely, admired his personal and professional skills. The finished church incorporated knapped flint walls, the

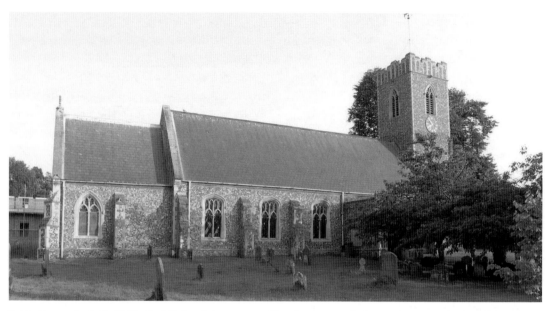

5.13: Peasenhall, Suffolk, St Michael (tower medieval; nave and chancel, R.D. Chantrell, 1860-1).

local tradition, but a novelty for Chantrell. His swan-song was reported in *The Builder*.[32]

Coincidentally, the very same page of *The Builder* reported that Leeds Parish Church had 'been renovated'. The twentieth anniversary of the re-opening must have seemed an appropriate opportunity for re-freshening the interior and while work comprised mainly cleaning, painting, gilding and improving ventilation, three new windows were added to the upper parts of the transepts to improve the light levels and 'the capitals have been re-carved, and the foliage deepened'. Stained glass replaced clear in several windows. Stone effigies of the four evangelists, carved by Dennis Lee and Welsh, were introduced at either side of the east window and the whole was superintended by Messrs Dobson and Chorley of Leeds.[33] While all this was, no doubt, a cause of celebration in Leeds, Chantrell was far from happy and the edition of two months later carried his response under the heading 'Interference With Architects' Works'. Clearly he had made an inspection visit before putting pen to paper. The first article had not mentioned Chantrell as the church's original architect, and was written using language that implied the recent work represented a series of improvements; Chantrell was at pains to point out, not unreasonably, that there is much more he would have done had funds been available then: 'the clerestory windows would have had pointed arches and [there would have been] an open roof of oak enriched with tracery, and coloured ... ' and added that in 1840 stone statues and large amounts of coloured glass were simply unacceptable to many worshippers. Finally, he claimed it was a professional discourtesy not to have been consulted.[34] A week later, E.M. Barry responded to claim a rather distant connection with the design of one of the new windows and added a suitable deferential apology.[35] This Chantrell accepted but repeated his attack on 'some architect of Leeds who is evidently no archaeologist' and concluded with a grumble about churchwardens.[36] His overall theme that, after twenty years, an architect should be able to revisit his works with a sense of pride would be hard to dispute.

What was, probably, the final development in Chantrell's long career came with his membership of the Pugin Memorial Committee. It was a body established 'to do honour to the memory of the late Augustus Welby Pugin, for his services in the promotion of true principles of Medieval Architecture' and raise a capital sum so that the interest it produced could fund a travelling scholarship, administered by the RIBA.[37] Chantrell was one of 96 on the committee; the appointment was, probably, little more than a reward for his 5 guineas contribution – most of those contributing £5/0/0 or more seem to have been invited – and the committee was divided roughly in half between the 'Working Committee' and the others. Chantrell was in the latter group. Nevertheless, his name appeared publicly with the great and the good of the profession. The committee was chaired by Beresford-Hope; Barry, Bloxham, the Brandons, Christian, Hardwick, Nesfield, Pearson, Scott, Teulon, White and M.D. Wyatt were there too. Had Chantrell joined simply to see his name in print alongside the profession's leaders, or had he really come to admire the man who, more than anyone else, had put an end to Soane's dream of a great and evolving British Classical tradition?

Meanwhile, his work for the ICBS continued, but not for much longer. Probably in late 1862, Chantrell moved to Eastbourne and this, coupled with the infirmities of entering his eighth decade, made attendance at the committee's meetings more difficult, although for the previous thirteen years, he had been one of the most diligent of its members. For the 1863 annual meeting and dinner, he sent the following letter of apology from Meads House, Eastbourne:

> My dear Clarke [the committee's secretary],
> I fear I shall not be able to devour rissoles and whitebait in [?some sauce] this year, should my leg[38] permit me to render myself at 7 Whitehall [the ICBS office] on 3 June but my [?]quota is at your service when we meet. I have located myself in this place, but 2 hours brings me to town yet as medics tell me I must avoid night air, I shall have to return at 4.00 pm and just as I land at home have to regret that I am 65 miles away from you. I return the ticket [for dinner] but hope I may live to meet you another year.
>
> I am, dear Sir, your faithful,
> R Dennis Chantrell.[39]

It was unfortunate that he missed the meeting as, in his absence, it resolved:

> members who from ill health or leaving practice in London regularly miss meetings be removed from the General Committee and become Honorary Members in which capacity they may still attend meetings and comment on the business …

The Committee resolved that as R.D. Chantrell is now in Eastbourne it would be better if he resigned as one of the London Committee of Architects and became an Honorary Member, but quite exceptionally, he can still keep his surveyorship of the Ripon Diocese if he wishes.

The following day, Clarke – clearly an accomplished diplomat – wrote to inform him:

> My dear Chantrell,
> We missed your familiar face at our little gathering yesterday at the Trafalgar – we hoped we might have seen you at the meeting first …
> We had an important meeting and among other matters initiated a new order of Honorary Members to be formed out of our own body. This has been done to meet the difficulty now beginning to arise of members of the London Committee living away in the country and who are unable regularly to attend the monthly meetings in Whitehall … Salvin has resigned in consequence of his being about to live in the country and we have elected him an Honorary Member.
>
> All our Committee desire as a mark of respect and regard to offer the same privileges to yourself and to relieve you of the necessity of travelling so far when inconvenient. We shall be glad to hear if this is agreeable …

Chantrell replied on 9 September:

> My dear Clarke,
> I am about to leave this place but have not yet met with a house to suit me therefore I do not wish to confine myself to London though I did mention last year that I was the short distance that would have permitted me when in health to attend the sub-committee regularly as I always have done – I beg therefore to resign that post and leave it with the General Committee to arrange as they may think proper – I can only express my regret at leaving my colleagues and shall be glad to hear that they attend more regularly than latterly – where ever I locate I hope often to be in London and shall look in at 7, Whitehall and be ready to assist as a customary amusement for the 'far niente' never will agree with me.[40]

He had attended his last meeting on 8 July 1863. The annual meeting in June 1864 confirmed Street as Salvin's replacement, and offered Chantrell's position to Butterfield although the latter declined and eventually J. Piers St Aubyn took the vacancy. There must have been a re-distribution of dioceses as Clarke appears to have inherited site visits for York.

The Committee's minutes record Chantrell as one of the most regular attendees and it seems he was packed off at the first sign of more frequent absence. On the other hand, ill health and distance were likely to present obstacles and perhaps it is unreasonable to suggest he was side-lined to honorary status prematurely; certainly, the correspondence is warm and cordial. Nevertheless, it is not difficult to imagine that, to the young Turks of the 1840s Gothic Revival like the Brandons and Christian, Chantrell – almost certainly the oldest member of the committee – and the slightly younger Salvin would have seemed reactionary in their attitudes. That Butterfield and Street were proposed as their replacements shows both the prestige of the committee and the generational gap represented by the two ousted members.

This would seem to represent the end of Chantrell's involvement with the profession, although he continued his membership of the RIBA until 1868. Nevertheless, the final decade of his life was not without incident. His wife, Elizabeth Caroline, died on 9 February 1863 at Seacombe, Cheshire,[41] perhaps while on a visit to one or other of her children, several of whom seem to have settled in the Wallasey/Liverpool area. However, a quiet life as a widower on the south coast was not to be; this final phase of his life suggests intrigue. We need to go back to the census of 1861. Kelly's *Directory* shows him at 7 Park Place, Camberwell Green in its 1861 and 1862 editions. The census reveals our architect as head of the household there, as we would expect, but no Mrs Chantrell. There might be some perfectly innocent explanation, for instance that she was away visiting family. Much more interestingly is that, along with the two young servants was one Mary E. Dear,[42] described as a 28-year-old unmarried painter, a visitor in the house. Five years later, she would be the second Mrs Chantrell, despite a forty-year age gap. They married at St Pancras old church on 2 December 1867, coincidentally, the place where Soane was buried thirty years earlier. How they met we shall probably never know, but the subject of her last RA exhibit, in 1859, is recorded as 'R Dennis Chantrell, Esq. FRIBA'; what better way for the two of them to become acquainted than via several intimate sittings for the portrait, although the painting could just as credibly represent the product of an established relationship as its beginning.

By 1864, Chantrell had moved from Eastbourne to Rottingdean, Sussex, probably to one or both of the properties mentioned in his will drawn up in 1868, 'Ivy Cottage and Rose Cottage … now occupied by me'.[43] More contentiously, the will, drawn up soon after the marriage, leaves all of his estate to his 'dear wife'. If she had pre-deceased him and there were any surviving children, the property would go to Charles Lamb 'of Brighton' or his wife, to be put in trust for 'Robert Dennis Chantrell's children born by the said wife who attain the age of 21.' No mention of the eight surviving children by his first wife. Clearly there had been a rift with them and the reason is not hard to detect. If Chantrell had, as the 1861 census hints, been engaged in a long-term adulterous affair with a woman not only younger than all his children, but only nine years older than his first grandchild, accusations of foolishness on their father's part and something rather more sinister as a motive for his bride would be easy to imagine. And just four years later, when Chantrell died, there was skulduggery over the assets in the estate. Initially it was valued at 'under £300'[44] but this was challenged by Chantrell's eldest son, Robert Dennis junior, and on 27 May 1874 'Administration of the effects of [Chantrell] was granted to [his son], probate granted in January 1872 being revoked. On 27 February 1874 in the case of Chantrell verses Chantrell and Lamb, judgement revoked the probate of the *altered will* [my italics] of the said deceased … '[45] In December 1880, the initial valuation of 'under £300' was raised to £12,000,[46] although it does not state how this was to be divided between the heirs.

Whatever motives she had for courting Chantrell, it would be pleasing to think that she made the final years of our old architect happy ones. They had a daughter, Marian Felicia Denise, baptised in Lewes, Sussex, early in 1869,[47] and perhaps the three of them had an enjoyable, if short, time together, in their pretty cottage not far from the sea. The only one of the 'antiquities' mentioned in Chantrell's will that we can identify is the ancient stone cross from Leeds Parish Church which he took with him when he left the town; no doubt it made an attractive feature in his cottage's garden[48] where he spent his last summer in 1871, perhaps maintaining an interest in his former profession via the pages of *The Builder* and reflecting on the huge changes in architectural design his career had witnessed. He died on 4 January 1872, just before his 79th birthday, at the Queen's Hotel, Norwood, Surrey.[49]

6

Chantrell's Office and Professional Practice

Chantrell's career spans a period of seminal importance in the development of the fledgling architectural profession and, as has been mentioned earlier, he was something of a pioneer in seeking to supply architectural services of the highest professional standards in the provinces. At a time when almost nothing has been published about the working practices of this sector of the profession, what follows, despite the mundane nature of many of its components, is not without interest. It is also a useful vehicle for material concerning the division of authorship in the 1840s between Chantrell, his son John and John's short-lived partnership with Thomas Shaw.

Notions of professionalism

Chantrell conveniently recorded his understanding of the architect's duties in a letter in 1851 to Charles Winn of Nostell Priory, almost certainly in answer to a request for advice following a dispute with some other architect Winn had employed:

> On receiving an order an architect has to make his design for approval by his employer, both for cost and for accommodation; on approval of the design, the working drawings and specifications become the next step towards the [?] advancement of the work. If an order is given for the work to cost £700 and I design one to cost £1,500 I have no right to charge for the design … For a building of £680 [presumably a figure supplied by Winn] I would say Design (of which you should have a copy of plans and elevations), drawings and specifications already to let the works, and inspecting (a [illegible word]) 5% on the amount of the tradesmen's bills being all of new materials.
>
> For time expended in making out amounts, travelling to inspect and expenses paid, according to the distance, say 5 journeys and 2 for first inspection of ground (site) and setting out the works; and lastly on charges for copies of them [presumably he means the working drawings and specifications], which might be done in a week by a clerk (or in most cases by a pupil) £2/2/0.

Many clerks may be obtained who can make very good copies of drawings at 20/- to 25/- per week leaving on the 42/- a profit.

I should consider myself in this case well paid with 10% and should conceive that I had no right to make my bill exceed that amount.[1]

There are just two statements which reveal something of Chantrell's concept of professional standards: in 1838, following delays in securing the ICBS's approval for his Holmbridge church design, the vicar suggested that Chantrell simply execute an earlier design by Henry Ward which already had approval. Chantrell declined, 'you … proposed to me that I execute another person's design which was quite unprofessional'.[2] And in 1841, following a request to him to tender for building work at Frodsham church, he wrote, 'as it is not professional, I should not contract for the execution of the work'.[3] All this suggests his model of professional practice was very much on the principles Soane would have instilled in him.[4] Apart from a couple of instances when Chantrell acted as an estate agent,[5] he seems scrupulously to have avoided any activities such as building or dealing in materials which the more high-minded architects of the period saw as sullying the profession's status. In June 1836 Chantrell joined the Institute of British Architects as a fellow. His four proposers were George Bailey, Edward Foxall, J.H. Good and Henry Hakewill. Bailey and Foxall were fellow pupils of Soane. Good, too, had been a pupil but much earlier although Chantrell knew him from his positions with the CBC and ICBS. The link to Hakewill is less obvious. Chantrell was the first Leeds architect to join the Institute,[6] and, indeed, was one of its earliest provincial members. Subscribing to the Institute's ethical standards is unlikely to have involved any compromises for him. Later, his widely publicised activities as a scholar and antiquary, and his membership of the Cambridge Camden Society and Archaeological Institute must have further enhanced his status among the Leeds professional classes.

Chantrell's first office in Leeds was in the Saddle Yard, where he set up his drawing board on arrival from Halifax in March 1819; in May that year, masons intending to submit tenders for the Philosophical Hall could view the drawings at 'Mr Chantrell's Office, The Saddle Yard, Briggate'.[7] The Saddle Yard was on the east side of Briggate, just below the present Queen's Court.[8] He was at Bank Street[9] by January 1821,[10] but the precise date of the move is not known. He did not remain there long and, on 26 November that year, the *Intelligencer*, 'inform[ed] his friends and the public he was removing from his house and office in Bank Street to Park Row, near the Philosophical Society Hall. NB, his house and office in Bank Street to let.' This would seem to have been 1 Park Row,[11] but by 1830 his office was listed as '11 and 12, Bensons Buildings, 2 Park Row'.[12] The numbering of properties at this time was not consistent, but even so it seems likely the office relocated. He remained there until the end of 1842[13] and for the rest of his time in Leeds − 1843-6 − he worked from Oatlands, his house.

Office staff

What office staff was there? Those who assisted Chantrell in his endeavours can be divided into pupils, office clerks and clerks of works. Of the pupils, the first one appears to have been Thomas Healey (1809-62). Healey came from Flockton, between Wakefield and Huddersfield. In 1829 he moved to Worcester and must, therefore, have been with Chantrell through the mid-1820s.[14] He returned to Yorkshire in 1847 to join James Mallinson in Bradford. They enjoyed a successful partnership in which, according to Healey's son, the latter was responsible for all the ecclesiastical work. Although this is not the place to examine Healey's career, he seems to have been adept at the Gothic style and Chantrell recorded several complimentary remarks about his former pupil's work.[15] Healey seems to have devoted much of his time in Worcester to drawing medieval buildings and probably perfected his skills there. However, and very interestingly, there also exist Gothic drawings from his time with Chantrell suggesting the latter saw it as an essential part of his pupil's education. And Healey might well have accompanied his master as the latter went out, in the early/mid 1820s, to visit notable Yorkshire examples seeking to make up for the deficiencies in his own training.

Ten years later, R. W. Moore was his pupil as were two of Chantrell's children, John Boham (1815-99), the second son, and Henry William (1826-77), the fourth son. In 1843, Moore, 'the late pupil of Mr Chantrell',[16] commenced practice on his own account and, at the same time, took over his master's former office in Benson's Buildings. He tells us he worked 'as pupil of the architect with whom I was during the whole time of pulling down the old [Leeds Parish Church] and [the] erection of the present edifice, and having had my fair share of making the working drawings and superintending the execution thereof'.[17] Given that pupilage normally lasted six or seven years, he would have entered the office in 1836 or 1837. Moore also gives us valuable information about Chantrell's sons: 'Henry William Chantrell … was brought up an architect, and … was in his father's office along with myself and his brother John during the whole period of pulling down the old [Leeds Parish Church] and … rebuilding the present edifice, and by and among whom most of the working drawings were made, and the execution of its several parts superintended.'[18] This seems unlikely; Moore, writing forty years after the event probably confused the two sons. Henry would only have been fifteen when the church reopened whereas John would have been ten years older. Moore also gives a vignette of pupilage: he recounts Chantrell's lecture to the Leeds Philosophical and Literary Society in 1839 on the old church and the ancient fragments discovered in its demolition, when 'I had the honour of assisting him therein by standing by his side, rod in hand, and pointing out the several parts of his drawings or diagrams as he described them.'[19] These diagrams were presumably produced especially to illustrate the talk and Soane's RA lectures come to mind. Moore produced little in independent practise, Henry was employed as clerk of works at Honley and Denholme Gate, but achieved nothing on his own account. John we will rejoin shortly.

6.1: Almondbury, West Yorkshire, All Hallows. Unsigned watercolour of *c.*1840. (*University of Leeds, Special Collections*).

What paid assistance was there in the office? The first character to whom we can put a name is J.P. Percy. He described himself as 'for some years assistant to Mr Chantrell', when he announced the establishment of his own practice as 'architect and civil engineer' in 1827.[20] Percy's contribution is interesting. We know he was clerk of works at Christ Church, Leeds, from 1823-6, but he also copied out the specifications in the tender documents before building work commenced implying he was in the office too. Given the short distance from Chantrell's office and the site of the new church, Percy might well have spent time assisting his master on other projects, but the title clerk of works usually implied someone who worked exclusively – or at least primarily – on the building site supervising and resolving day-to-day constructional issues, rather than a member of the office staff. However, perhaps we need to take a rather wider definition of the designation, and information about Chantrell's other clerks suggests a rather close relationship.

Almost every project beyond the minor ones would have enjoyed the service of a clerk of works; in most cases, their identity is unknown, but records of the Church Commissioners and ICBS are more enlightening. These tell us that Chantrell developed a pattern of using a small number of, presumably, trusted clerks to supervise several concurrent projects in a manageable geographical area and thus they can, legitimately, be seen as much valued assistants rather than as a man hired for the duration of a contract like the plumber or joiner. William Jordan was clerk of works for the new churches at Holbeck, Kirkstall and Morley, built more or less simultaneously in the 1828-32 period, and to broadly similar designs. In these circumstances, it is likely that many minor design decisions were delegated to him. Jordan was paid £224 compared with Chantrell's £167 for Holbeck; if we assume his fee at the other two churches was similar, we can understand why not all clerks followed Percy's career plan. Even more interesting is John Wade. He was clerk of works for the two similar and nearby churches at Lockwood and Netherthong – in the parish of Almondbury, near Huddersfield – erected in 1828-30, and was responsible for producing the pew rent plans for Lockwod in 1830.[21] Almost as soon as they were completed, he was dispatched to Glossop to act as clerk of works for the rebuilding of the parish church there. Of all Chantrell's major projects, Glossop was the furthest from Leeds and thus the one where he was most in need of a sound deputy. More revealing are two small, semi-independent jobs undertaken by Wade. The first was at the medieval parish church in Almondbury, in 1829 (**6.1**). Re-pewing of the ground and gallery floors was carried out, and the ICBS's completion certificate was signed by Wade; the two drawings which accompanied the certificate were signed 'John Wade, Clerk of Works, acting for Mr Chantrell, Architect' (**6.2**) and Chantrell seems to have

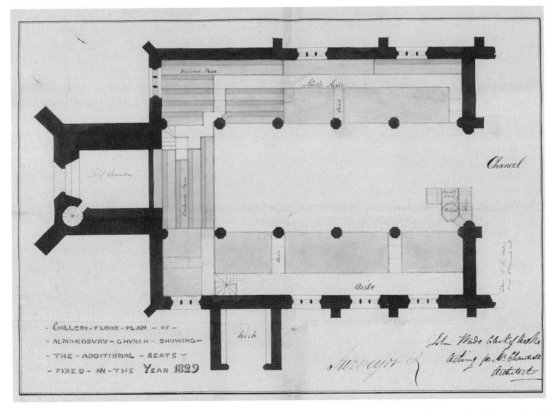

6.2: Almondbury, West Yorkshire, All Hallows. This plan was drawn by John Wade, the project's clerk of works. (*Lambeth Palace Library*).

6.3: Skipton, North Yorkshire, Ermysted's Grammar School, new schoolroom (R.D. Chantrell, 1839-41). Chantrell's building is on the right-hand side of the illustration. Almost certainly Chantrell sent Thomas Shaw, his clerk of works at Leeds Parish Church, to liaise with the school's trustees for this small commission in a distant location. *(Susan Wrathmell)*.

had no hand in their production.[22] The second was at Bakewell, Derbyshire, even further south than Glossop, where, in about 1830, Chantrell was invited to offer suggestions for repairing and increasing the accommodation in the parish church after Francis Goodwin's 1824 scheme was deemed too extravagant. Wade was dispatched to produce measured drawings and suggestions. The drawing subsequently presented to the vestry was made by Wade, but the proposed placing of the new pews was added by Chantrell who also made most of the annotations and at the bottom signed the drawing: 'John Wade, Clerk of Works acting for Robert Dennis Chantrell, Architect'.[23] Their relationship was a long one: in 1845-6 Wade was clerk of works at Lund, East Riding, he was at St Paul's Halifax, sharing the job with H.W. Chantrell in late 1844-7, and he was clerk for the building of Armitage Bridge church – for which he was paid a staggering £410 – and produced and signed the seating plan for the ICBS, although Chantrell signed it too, adding 'examined 13 July 1849'.[24] In 1848-9 he was back at Lockwood for the new chancel where he is recorded as having been paid '5% for superintending', an unusually large proportion of the total; presumably having produced the design, Chantrell did not make a journey from London to oversee this small project. The workmen's bills are annotated, 'the above is a correct account examined by Mr R.D. Chantrell, arch., London [signed] J. Wade, Clerk of Works. However, all payments for extra work were first approved by the addition of Chantrell's signature.[25] Was Wade employed continuously on other projects between Glossop and Lund?

Thomas Shaw was the clerk of works throughout the Leeds Parish Church reconstruction and subsequently in partnership with J.B. Chantrell. While still engaged at the parish church, Chantrell made use of him elsewhere: he was almost certainly the 'Mr Shaw' who attended meetings of the Ermysted's Grammar School's Trustees during discussions about Chantrell's new schoolroom in 1839 and '40, (**6.3**) and he signed contracts with tradesmen for the new parsonage at Dewsbury Moor in 1840 (**Cat. 9**). Could he have been the same 'Thomas Shaw' who was paid 1/- per week for 33 weeks unspecified work at Honley church in 1843?[26]

Of interest is Chantrell's detailed bill for the unexecuted Holmbridge church project, quoted below. It includes 'Clerk's time making out copies'; he doesn't refer to an 'assistant' or 'draughtsman'. Thus, it seems, Chantrell used the term 'clerk' to encompass both those who worked in the office – as indeed did many other architects at this time – and on site. Can we reasonably conclude he had a policy of employing men who spent some time in the office then, as circumstances demanded, were sent out, perhaps for several months, to supervise construction, or was there a clear distinction between '[office] clerks' and 'clerks of works'? If it was the latter, then we know little about the office staff, but what we know of office procedures would suggest the office was small, probably with only one 'assistant' at a time. Chantrell seems initially to have written all his own letters and reports, although from the late 1830s other hands can be detected.[27] The only name to emerge is that of S.J.W. Gawthorp who neatly wrote out the specifications for the new tower at Hunslet in 1830 and at the bottom added 'Per Procn. [per procurationem = through the agency of] R. Dennis Chantrell, Architect'. A clerk like Gawthorp would have been kept busy producing the numerous copies of specifications for tender documents and drawings where multiple quantities were needed.[28] Of the better quality, i.e. semi-presentational, drawings that have survived from before the very busy period after the commencement of the Leeds Parish Church project in 1837, all appear to be in Chantrell's hand.[29] However, more mundane ones are not. The CBC archive retains the plans used for the calculation of pew rents – essentially seating plans with the minimum of architectural information. Although Chantrell signed them, the rest of the writing, including the details of the value of each individual pew, is by someone else.[30]

The contribution of John Chantrell and the partnership of Chantrell and Shaw

Early in 1840 John, the elder of the two sons being groomed for the profession, was

6.4: Denholme Gate, West Yorkshire, St Paul (R.D. Chantrell, 1843-6). The watercolour, dated 1846, is by J.B. Chantrell, Chantrell's second son and sometime partner. (*University of Leeds, Special Collections*).

6.5: Denholme Gate, West Yorkshire, St Paul (R.D. Chantrell, 1843-6). The interior from a mid-twentieth-century photograph.

taken into partnership by his father and in some, but not all, references to the practice, the style Chantrell and Son was used. The 1842 directory – probably compiled in 1841 – notes 'Chantrell and Son' at 11 Benson's Buildings. Perhaps the arrangement was not a congenial one for either party; certainly it was short-lived, which leads us conveniently to Thomas Shaw who, as we have seen, had been the clerk of works throughout the parish church job. Perhaps Shaw was especially talented and identified by Chantrell as capable of better things;[31] perhaps he and J.B. Chantrell formed a strong bond as colleagues on the project. More likely, Chantrell senior identified in him the perfect practical skills to make up for any deficiencies in John's expertise. And thus, I would conclude, with much encouragement from Chantrell senior, the partnership of Chantrell and Shaw, architects, was launched in 1842 as a means of establishing an architectural career for John. Chantrell, it seems, assured their success by the promise of jobs – or at least the less rewarding aspects of jobs – he was happy to pass to them. The next issue, therefore, is to gain some understanding of the division of authorship in the projects from here onwards.

The first public notice of the new practice comes in a request for tenders for 'A house at Headingley'.[32] A month later, they sought tenders for '2 houses in Woodhouse Lane [Leeds]'[33] and two months after that for 'a Church of England School at Dewsbury'.[34] It was very many years since Chantrell had sought tenders for such minor projects; had the partnership succeeded in securing a 'new' area of work? Possibly, but a more plausible explanation is that Chantrell had *always* undertaken such jobs, but had not bothered to go through the time-consuming and laborious process of seeking tenders and had gone directly to his favoured tradesmen. In these three examples, probably the motivation was not primarily to obtain competitive prices, but to publicise the new practice. Who produced the designs? Of the bigger Chantrell schemes of the next few years, several of them appeared publicly at some point in the project's lifespan as Chantrell and Shaw jobs, for instance, St Paul, Denholme Gate (1843) (**6.4, 6.5**), All Saints, Rise (1844) (**4.53, 4.54**), St Paul, Halifax (1844) (**4.55, 4.56**) and St Andrew, Keighley (1845) (**7.26-29**). However, in all four of these, and most of the others, Chantrell subsequently – and convincingly – claims them as his own, almost as though he had treated the partnership simply as his assistants rather than as an autonomous practice. For instance, in discussing his Geometrical Principles he wrote, 'I have now some new churches in progress on this principle ... at Halifax ... Keighley',[35] and elsewhere he stated, 'upon this system ... I have ... erected the churches at ... Rise ... Halifax ... '.[36] More revealing is a letter he sent to the ICBS in 1847, 'I beg to return the Plan and papers for Denholme Gate Church for which I made the design ... for Messrs Chantrell and Shaw of Leeds ... ' and in 1845 he wrote to the ICBS, 'In consequence of several alterations made by Shaw and his setting all plans and specifications at nought, my son John has separated from him and I am examining all their works (as many as those which I entrusted to them) and rectifying the blunders committed by Shaw; I find the drawings given by Shaw to the contractors for ... Halifax ... to be at variance with my original designs ... '[37]

It might be imagined that in the period of the partnership, 1842-5, Chantrell would at least allow his son and Shaw full control of minor and unrewarding jobs, but even this seems not to have been the case. We can understand that he would take an academic interest in the part Norman church at East Ardsley where he was asked for a report, yet even the troublesome leaking roof at St John the Evangelist, Golcar (1842-4) and proposals for re-seating Hunslet chapel (1843-4) were jobs that remained very much under his personal control.[38] One is left to conclude that Chantrell junior and Shaw produced little on their own account, although Chantrell senior's letter to the ICBC – quoted above – suggests there were at least *some* of their projects that he had not 'entrusted to them'. Perhaps the Dewsbury National School (**6.6**) was one. Its distinctly Gothic character is at variance with Chantrell's Tudor schools of the period.

Although Chantrell was at pains to blame the duo's failure on 'Shaw's blunders', on the dissolution of the partnership in 1845 he immediately joined Jeremiah Dobson[39] and the two enjoyed some success in the region. Meanwhile, Chantrell and John re-formed their partnership reviving the style 'Chantrell and Son' with an office at 19 Park Row.[40]

6.6: Dewsbury, West Yorkshire, National School. The school, built in 1842-3, could be by either R.D. Chantrell or Chantrell and Shaw.

They maintained an office there until *c*.1850. Interestingly, John appears on his own in the 'Architects' section of the 1853 directory, although there is no evidence of any commissions at this time. The extent of John's known independent work is the school at Denholme Gate of 1846.[41]

The projects of Chantrell and Son, despite the departure of Chantrell to London only months after the formation of the new partnership, seem to have been entirely dependant on the father, essentially the finishing off of projects already started. Most significantly, the only two new jobs of the late 1840s had a clear connection to earlier commissions – Lockwood's new chancel and repairs to Netherthong's bellcote. Both were handled by 'Mr Chantrell of London', not Chantrell and Son in Leeds. Communication between London and Yorkshire does not seem to have presented insurmountable problems, although one might imagine Chantrell's absence would have been an ideal opportunity for John to have been given more autonomy. Probably Chantrell was no more willing to relinquish control – or perhaps had no more confidence in doing so – than he had been with Chantrell and Shaw, and the relationship with his son seems to have been uneasy. There is a letter in the ICBS archives concerning Denholme Gate church where the absence of any warmth between father and son is sadly palpable.[42]

Once in London, Chantrell seems to have worked from his various homes: 21 Lincoln's Inn Fields (mid-1840s-52), Canonbury (1850-9), Camberwell (1861-2).[43] However, *Kelly's Directories* for 1850, 1851 and 1852 show him as an architect at Lincoln's Inn Fields and under 'Court Division' at Canonbury, suggesting a separate office. There is no record of Chantrell's involvement in professional matters after his retirement from the ICBS Committee of Architects in 1863 by which time he was living in Eastbourne.

Related to the employment of office staff is the question of whether Chantrell employed a specialist perspective artist for his presentation drawings as Soane had done, as Dobson in Newcastle did at this time,[44] and many of the London architects did too. Unlike Dobson, whose practice was based on country houses and public buildings, there was little need for Chantrell to produce elaborate perspective drawings when courting ecclesiastical commissions. However, accounts of various public exhibitions in Leeds record perspectives of Chantrell's buildings,[45] now lost, that might well have been substantial virtuoso displays produced by a 'ghost'. However, the few perspectives that have survived – the Leeds Philosophical Hall and the South Market, for instance – would seem to be from Chantrell's hand. Indeed, we know that, occasionally, he produced perspective drawings of buildings he hadn't designed in order to, for instance, illustrate a town map or for commercial reproduction, suggesting such assistance would have been unnecessary.

Chantrell's fee structure

How much did Chantrell charge for his services? His fee structure, so far as we can deduce, was usually around 5% of the contracts for large jobs and an hourly or daily rate for small ones, 2 guineas per day in 1838, and rather less earlier in his career. There are just three itemised bills that are known: those for the west gallery of St Mark, Leeds (1832-3);[46] the unexecuted design for Holmbridge church (1837-8);[47] (**6.7, 6.8**) and for re-roofing St John, Golcar (1842-4).[48] They contain much tedious detail, but nevertheless give an insight into Chantrell's working methods.

Leeds, St Mark

1832	Dec. 3:	for attendance respecting the erection of a gallery;
	6:	for attendance to measure w. end of church;
	17:	plans for preparation of sketches;

19:	rough design for gallery;
20 & 23:	finished preliminary design and estimate; £2/9/0
1833 Jan. 4 to 8:	a set of working drawings comprising a plan, section and elevation and details with full specification of the several works, and writing notes to the several workmen informing them. Drawing a complete set of copies for them; £5/0/0
Jan. 19 - 24:	attendance to inspect works. Drawing several details at large; £3/10/0
July 31:	Altering vestry door heads; drawings for workmen and making out amount of all works; £1/4/6
	Set of drawings and scale of pew rents for Commissioners; £1/1/0

Total £13/9/5

Holmebridge, St David

1837	March 25:	For the design of a church to hold 500 on the ground floor, according to instructions given;
	April 2:	A fair copy of the plan;
	April 10:	Making drawings and calculating sittings;
	May 1:	Copies of plans on Ground and Gallery floors with sections, and calculating sittings;
	May 2:	Making estimates of the cost of the building;
	May 3-6:	Clerk's time making out copies;
	May 9-19:	Making working drawings and details for the Incorporated Society;
	May 31:	Completion of drawings;
	June 6-13:	Specifications and copies thereof;
	July 17:	Attendance at Incorporated Society in London respecting the drawings;
	Aug. 8:	Attending Incorporated Society in London when returning from the Continent;
	Dec. 4:	At Armitage Bridge taking instructions of new [word unclear] – alterations to suit the Society;
	Dec. 6:	Made out another plan and copy;
1838	Jan. 8:	Made plan of ground floor, description and alterations;
	Jan. 9:	Another plan, altering sittings, placing free seats in the middle aisle, and copy.

6.7: Holmbridge, West Yorkshire, St David (R.D. Chantrell, 1837–8), unexecuted. The drawings of the west end offered two alternatives: a tower without spire or, illustrated here, the tower with the spire drawing overlaid. The latter was estimated at an extra £150. (*WYASW*).

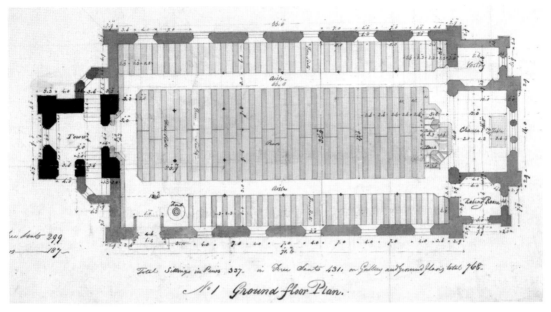

6.8: Holmbridge, West Yorkshire, St David (R.D. Chantrell, 1837-8), unexecuted. (*WYASW*).

The total time spent was 22 days. He charged 2 guineas per day and thus the bill amounted to £45/2/0. The account reveals some idea of the time involved in a single commission, and one that never progressed beyond conception.

Golcar, St John

> 1842-4
> Surveying church, making drawings and report: £5/0/0
> Making drawings and specifications and superintending the work: £12/0/0
> Travelling expenses, 9 journey: £8/0/0
> Clerk of Works, 3 weeks plus expenses: £6/12/0
> Total £31/12/0

Communications

Finally, there are questions surrounding communications: how did Chantrell manage projects over a relatively large geographical area? Central here is the issue of how often he inspected a substantial project? The only document to itemise visits relates to Armitage Bridge church, a project that spanned the years 1843-8, the last two of which he was in London. Here he seems to have made 24 journeys between 1 February 1845 and the consecration in May 1848 which produces an average of a visit every seven weeks. Even when he was living in London, he still visited every three months. Nevertheless, much could go wrong in seven weeks, a point which underscores the importance of having a reliable clerk of works. The Holmbridge proposal, as we have seen, appears not to have included a single trip to inspect the site yet the re-roofing of nearby Golcar church involved nine visits.[49] Elsewhere, Chantrell was always present to write a report on a dilapidated building and there is evidence that he was usually present for the consecrations of his churches, even travelling from London for that at Halifax in 1847. And in his London years, we know he made visits back to Yorkshire to inspect progress at, for instance, Barmby Moor[50] and Fangfoss.[51] Beyond personal visits, the postal and carrier services provided a reliable, if slow, service for delivering drawings or answering queries. The period's directories provide ample evidence of the extent of the service offered by a host of companies giving (usually) daily departures from Leeds to all parts of the country. The carrier service to London, for instance, took about four days. There are numerous references to drawings being sent in this way and later, by the new railway network.[52] In some cases, the client travelled to Leeds; perhaps it was a quicker and more efficient way of securing urgently needed information for a grant application or drawings to progress construction. The building accounts for Honley church include the following:

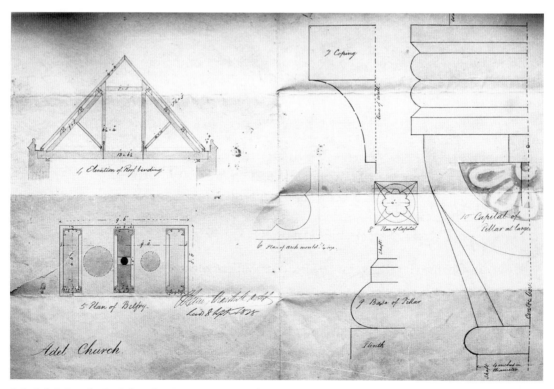

6.9: Adel, Leeds, St John the Baptist. One of Chantrell's working drawings, dated 1838, for the new bellcote for this Norman church. (*WYASL*).

6.10: Leeds Parish Church (R.D. Chantrell, 1837-41). One of Chantrell's working drawings showing the interior looking east. (*Lambeth Palace Library*)..

1841	Sept 10	Expenses to Leeds to see Mr Chantrell	3/-
	Sept 17	Paid carriage for plan	1/-
	Oct. 23	J. Stocks expenses to Leeds to see Mr Chantrell	10/-
	Oct. 27	Plans from Leeds by coach	1/-
	Nov. 14	Plan from Mr Chantrell for Incorporated Society	1/-
	Dec. 11	Postage for plans to Incorporated Society	1/6

How did Chantrell travel to his inspections? Little information about this has survived. He may have kept his own coach and coachman, but perhaps he simply hired them when needed. Later in his career he certainly exploited the expanding railway network wherever possible and for the Frodingham (Scunthorpe) project, he records that he took the train to Hull and the steam packet across the Humber.[53]

Chantrell made several references to his visits to London during his Leeds years to call at the ICBS or CBC offices to discuss current projects, although it is not clear that his presence there was primarily for business as on at least some occasions he was travelling through London going to or returning from the continent,[54] probably Bruges.

An interesting question is how well did Chantrell's office function? In the 28 years of his Leeds career, at least 140 commissions are documented and it is likely there were many more minor ones. Of the known ones, 37 can be considered major building projects, each of which, like Armitage Bridge church – discussed above – could have required 24 site visits and perhaps 100 days of work in the office.[55] The more minor commissions might involve an average of ten days of work. All this suggests a hectic schedule. How efficiently did Chantrell's system of communication between the office and the many building sites function? On the whole, it seems to have worked well although, especially in the very busy last ten years in Leeds, Chantrell must have needed real personal stamina, supplemented by a combination of a very well-managed office and a team of reliable clerks of works. An inspection visit to (say) Halifax or Armitage Bridge (15 and 20 miles from Leeds respectively) must have taken up most of a working day. For the church in Rise, Chantrell stayed for several days.[56] Inevitably, there were grumbles from employers that delays were caused by drawings that had not arrived on time – although in some cases this was demonstrably an excuse from a disorganised vicar – but in only two cases – at Frodingham in the early 1840s and Armitage Bridge in the late 1840s were there serious problems (for both these commissions see the Catalogue entries).

Chantrell's status in Leeds

Despite the controversy that surrounded the Leeds Central Market project (discussed in Chapter 4), Chantrell's Leeds career seems to have passed without the sorts of disputes and skulduggery that besmirched the careers of many of his contemporaries.[57] On the other hand, there are several references in Chapter 4 to the fact that Chantrell's early position as the town's principal architect was overtaken by the arrival of John Clark after the latter had won the 1826 competition for the new Commercial Buildings. Certainly there were a handful of instances in the 1830s of Chantrell and Clark competing for the same commission, and usually Clark was the victor. However, the situation will repay closer attention. What seems to have happened is that, yes, Clark carried off several prizes, but he might still just about be classed as 'trade', to use Pugin's derogatory term. Chantrell operated on a rather different plane. His move towards specialising in ecclesiastical work seems to have brought him considerable respect, a situation reflected in the *Intelligencer's* coverage of his projects. Clark's major buildings received favourable, if limited, notice, but Clark the man remained very much in the shadows, little better known than the masons and joiners he supervised. Perhaps it was simply that Chantrell was more adept at self promotion, but a close examination of the newspaper suggests Chantrell's church work and ecclesiastical patronage brought him celebrity and status altogether higher than Clark's. For the final ten years in Leeds – from the start of the Leeds Parish Church rebuilding – Chantrell's position in the town must have been exceptional among the architectural fraternity. Crucially, he had moved from being merely an architect, albeit an accomplished one, to become an antiquary as well, with all the trappings of gentlemanly scholarship the term implied. At a time when the architect's status still occupied a rather imprecise position between a trade and a respected profession, Chantrell's place in Leeds society was assured. His antiquarian lectures and publications, his willingness to offer views on all manner of antiquarian issues, his membership of prestigious organisations like the Yorkshire Architectural Association, Cambridge Camden Society, Archaeological Institute and RIBA, underlined his academic credentials. This, plus his personal friendship with the most dynamic clergy of the diocese for whom he had supplied designs to meet their progressive liturgical aspirations, gave him an exceptional status, not just 'one of the first architects in all the north of England', to quote the bishop of Ripon,[58] but a man whose endeavours fully justified the *Intelligencer's* epithet 'our gifted townsman'.

7

Chantrell the Architect

In this chapter, seven significant Chantrell buildings have been selected for examination as a means of identifying his interests, philosophy, development as a designer and his achievements. When seen in the context of the issues identified in chapter 1, these projects help establish Chantrell's place in the wider story of post-Waterloo architectural developments.

The South Market, Leeds, 1823-4

In the decade which followed Chantrell's pupilage with Soane, he must have anticipated a career in which he would be the author of a succession of Classical designs. This is what his training had prepared him for, and his few recorded thoughts on architectural style make his preferences clear.[1] Yet the South Market commission, secured only four years into his Leeds career, was his last new Classical public building.[2] It was also one of the biggest budgets he would ever be given.[3]

His first two public buildings – the Public Baths (1819-21) and Philosophical and Literary Society Hall (1819-21), both in Leeds – were competent, but unremarkable essays, essentially typical of their date and function. But the South Market was on an altogether higher plane (**7.1-3**). This ground-breaking scheme, as much a piece of town planning as of architecture, was a composition of exceptional quality and originality.

A public meeting in June 1823 resolved to proceed with the project and announced a competition as a means of securing a design.[4] The only other known entry was from Charles Fowler[5] who was awarded second premium and, remarkably, his plan survives.[6] A comparison between the Chantrell and Fowler proposals for this irregular site is instructive; whereas Fowler sought to mould the plot into a rectangle by 'losing' some of the east and west edges, Chantrell exploits it and, by an imaginatively placed circular centre, successfully resolves the awkward site. The design consisted of eighteen three-storey shops with living space above, facing outwards to Meadow Lane and Hunslet Lane, 9 slaughter houses, 118 stalls in roofed enclosures,[7] and at its centre, the remarkable cross.

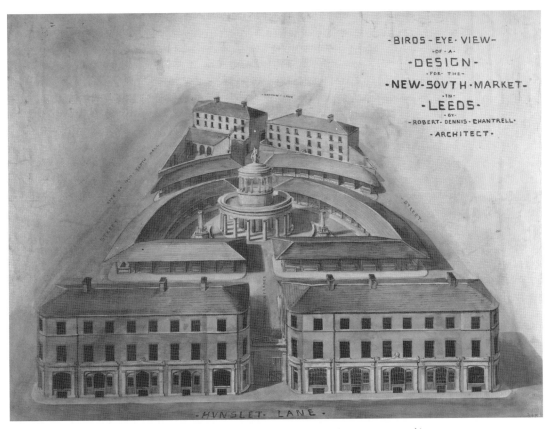

7.1: Leeds, South Market (R.D. Chantrell, 1823-4). (*Thoresby Society, Leeds*).

The completed cross – shown in a Chantrell drawing dated 30 July 1823 – consisted of two concentric rings each of twelve Doric columns, the centre ring supporting an upper floor with twelve attached columns crowned by a hemispherical dome surmounted by a tall statue – in essence, 'a circular temple'.[8] Within this cupola was a committee room. The flat roof covering the area enclosed by the concentric rings of columns was actually a reservoir which held water for the two fountains and 'to water the streets and causeways during the dry summer months',[9] the water being pumped there from a nearby well via an engine in the dome. But even more remarkable was a design for the cross – recorded only in a photograph of a drawing dated '1823', but, one assumes, an initial scheme, subsequently abandoned – which is one of Chantrell's most dramatic compositions for any project. It consisted of two concentric rings of sixteen stout, baseless Doric columns; the centre was either open or, perhaps, glazed.

On one level, the inspiration for this part of the design might well have been the central feature of the extensive Fish Market in Bruges, built in 1821, although the Belgian example is rectangular. No doubt Chantrell identified it as a modern design with a similar function, seen on one of his visits there. Another possible inspiration – and a rather more intriguing one – is Stonehenge.[10] Stonehenge was a structure that fascinated Soane[11] and

183

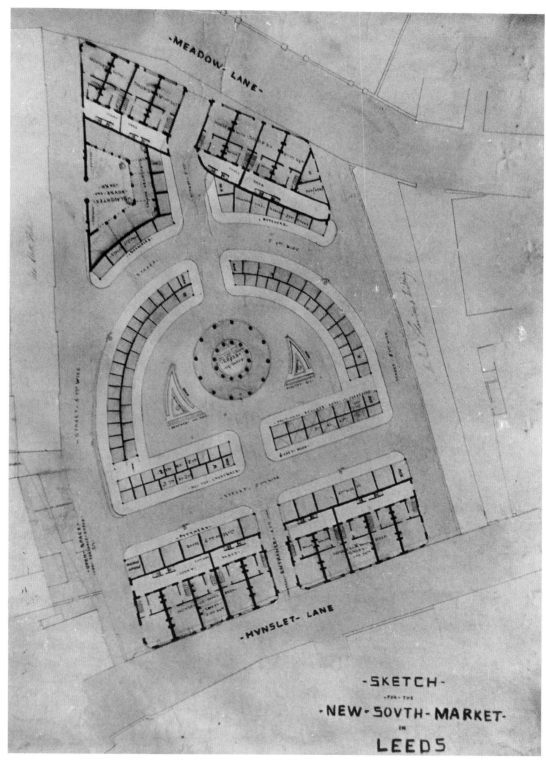

7.2: Leeds, South Market (R.D. Chantrell, 1823–4). (*Thoresby Society, Leeds*).

7.3: Leeds, South Market (R.D. Chantrell, 1823-4). This design, now known only from this illustration, was probably a preliminary scheme, later modified to that shown in 7.1. (*Leeds City Libraries*).

it is likely that his interest in it was conveyed to Chantrell during the latter's pupilage.

In 1823 there were few precedents for this sort of building. The older tradition of a market that comprised a permanent, but relatively small structure at its centre – usually referred to as the '[market] cross' – surrounded by temporary stalls erected and dismantled on market days, was still widely followed. The market hall as a large building containing all the traders under one roof was only just beginning to appear.[12] Chantrell's scheme is something of a hybrid.

The perimeter shops looked outwards and would have been open for business every day. These were dignified but orthodox, not unlike a row of four shops Chantrell had designed for William Hey, intended for Bond Street in Leeds, in 1820, and which could be found in most medium-sized towns of the period. The stalls, too, were unremarkable. But what lifts the project to a level of importance is the complexity of the overall arrangement in both a functional and aesthetic context. Much of its success rests on Chantrell's decision to dispense with any attempt at a rectilinear plan and exploit curved forms for the awkward site. This allows an efficient use of the available space by accommodating units of varying sizes. It also enabled a substantial slaughterhouse

7.4: Bruges, Belgium, the Fish Market (architect unknown, 1821). This building has a square central section surrounding an open centre. Chantrell had, no doubt, seen it on one of his many trips to the city and used it as a useful starting point for his Leeds design, 7.3.

to be slotted into the top left corner with an outward-facing entrance that was both discrete and discreet. The east-west axis focuses dramatically on the cross, a compelling composition made all the more impressive by the modest structures that surrounded it.

That Chantrell was capable of such an achievement, and so early in his career, suggests that, had he had the opportunities to secure further Classical commissions on this scale, a series of outstanding buildings might have been the result.

Christ Church, Meadow Lane, Leeds, 1821-6

This was Chantrell's first new church, the beginning of what would be an exceptionally successful career as an ecclesiastical architect, and as an expert in English buildings of the Middle Ages (**4.11, 7.5-9**). It might also have been his first Gothic essay, although we shall never know if the finished building was the design of 1821 that secured the commission, or a revised design that could have been several years later; the foundation stone was not laid until January 1823 and even after then, there was still time for many aspects of the design to be modified. The date is of significance for our study. It is known that Chantrell produced a drawing for an eastern addition, including a tower, for the chapel at nearby Bramley in August 1822 (**4.8**), and this provides a useful context in which to set the Christ Church project.

The Bramley design was composed with a very limited budget in mind, and is not without charm, but its almost naïve quality does not fit comfortably alongside – possibly, even later than – Christ Church. Furthermore, we have evidence that Chantrell was struggling in his attempt to produce a convincing Gothic design at this time; realising that the Church Building Commission's initiatives were likely to offer employment opportunities in Yorkshire, he wrote to Soane in January 1821 seeking advice:

> On the economical scale recommended by the clergy … and approved by the Commissioners, I conceive it will be impossible to obtain the pleasing effect of our cathedrals or such parish churches as those of Bristol, Manchester, Hull etc with an area sufficient to contain a congregation of twelve hundred … unless the plan be made of great length … I have learned that buildings however decorated, if without just proportion of the masses must offend the eye … yet even with good proportions this Gothic architecture requires many decorations to characterise it … I should wish to present a Grecian or Roman design, but the objections to them made by the Local Committee would be so strong that I fear my labour would be entirely lost … [13]

The foregoing confession of Chantrell's ignorance seems an unlikely context for the production of the Christ Church composition, an assured and accomplished design of real quality. How did he reach enlightenment so quickly? It is possible that Chantrell found himself in a situation where he could borrow from the work of another architect who had already overcome the obstacles that Gothic compositions presented? With this in mind, we must consider all three of the Commissioners' projects intended for Leeds in the early 1820s. Initially the three architects selected for them were Charles Busby (**7.7**), Edward Gyfford and Chantrell. However, Busby and Gyfford were later replaced by Taylor and Atkinson & Sharp respectively.[14] Busby had spent some time in 1820 and 1821 working in the office of Francis Goodwin, the most successful architect of the day at securing projects funded by the Commissioners. Indeed, so adept at this was he that the Commissioners were concerned that he would be unable adequately to supervise all his schemes, and resolved that no architect could work on more than six churches at any one time. Not wishing to see lucrative commissions slip from his grasp, Goodwin induced others, including his own clerks, to submit his designs as their own and if successful, the fee would be divided between the two of them. There is good reason for thinking that Busby's Leeds design was actually one of Goodwin's[15] and Busby later claimed that when he attended the Leeds committee he was 'astonished to find someone else with three sets of Goodwin plans'.[16] Busby was angry that, having secured the approval of the Leeds committee, his proposed iron roof construction here, and for a church in Oldham, were rejected by Nash and Smirke, and he also appears to have fallen out with Goodwin, probably over money. The outcome was that Busby sent several letters to the Commissioners and then printed his version of events in a pamphlet which

7.5: Leeds, Christ Church, Meadow Lane (R.D. Chantrell, 1821-6). The otherwise accurate mid-nineteenth-century watercolour shows the nave with only five bays whereas in reality it had seven. (*Leeds University Library, Specials Collections*).

he circulated. We are thus provided with a valuable insight into the devious workings of some prominent church architects, as well as illustrations of the two Busby/Goodwin rejects from Oldham and Leeds. How does Chantrell fit into this unsavoury business? It seems unlikely that Chantrell was one of Goodwin's collaborators,[17] but what is more likely is that the Leeds Committee was impressed by the Busby/Goodwin submission – which, let us not forget, they were forbidden to pursue by the Crown Architects only because of its roof construction – and quietly suggested that Chantrell might care to modify his original design to incorporate some aspects of it in his own scheme. Such a course would certainly account for the similarity between Chantrell's Meadow Lane church and the rejected Busby/Goodwin designs for Leeds and Oldham, as well as explaining the disparity between Chantrell's Bramley and Meadow Lane designs. Alternatively, and showing Chantrell in a more favourable light, perhaps Soane's answer

7.6: Leeds, Christ Church, Meadow Lane (R.D. Chantrell, 1821-6).

OLDHAM.

LEEDS.

70 Feet Front.

70 Feet Front.

C. A. Busby, delt.

C. A. Busby, delt.

7.7: 'Designs for churches in Oldham and Leeds' (C.A. Busby, *c*.1821). Busby, infuriated that he lost these two commissions because of perceived weakness in their novel roof construction, fought to be reinstated and published a pamphlet to set out his case. The illustrations – valuable records of his designs, very much in the manner of Francis Goodwin for whom he had worked – formed part of that paper.

to Chantrell's January 1821 letter, quoted above, was 'I suggest you go and look at some of the churches designed by Mr Goodwin which are much admired'.[18]

How much of the design is truly Chantrell's? We will never know but perhaps the crucial point is that by the time of its completion, he could emerge as an architect exceptionally well acquainted with the unfamiliar demands of Gothic church design, and then proceed to produce a succession of churches that were both undoubtedly his own designs, and very successful ones at that.

The plan of Christ Church is largely orthodox: a big rectangular body, a majestic west tower with gallery stairs at each side, and a shallow chancel. It was an arrangement he would rehearse many times over the next twenty years. The only slightly unusual feature is the low vestry placed directly below the east window – a feature to be found in several Goodwin designs – and the five-sided stair compartments that produce an interesting space around the font at the west end. Although the church was spanned by a single roof, both externally and internally the impression is given of a distinct nave and aisles; internally they were divided by the slender columns that supported both the galleries and the roof, made largely of cast iron. Almost certainly they would have been like those Chantrell designed for Lockwood a few years later: simple metal tubes – rather like very substantial drain pipes – to which were bolted strips of moulded wood so that, once painted, the composite component resembled a delicately carved stone column.[19] Also of interest internally is the treatment of the ceilings. Those over the aisles appear to have been flat, supported by low Tudor arches enlivened with geometrical tracery. On the nave side of the arcade, the shallow arches are enriched by ogee crowns surmounted with bold finials. Whether we should conclude the ceiling was a series of imaginative innovations or regrettable solecisms remains to be answered, but the effect was certainly stately.

Externally, the north, south and east sides are competent, but unremarkable, essentially Decorated details with the proportions of Perpendicular. The real triumph is the west front, the 'show' elevation. And it is here that the Busby/Goodwin influence is most obvious, indeed, Christ Church appears to be an amalgamation of Busby's published Leeds and Oldham designs. Having said that, most of the details of Christ Church's west elevation can be traced to readily available printed sources: Michael Port has identified the 'frieze patterned with quatrefoils in diamonds and with small triangular pediments over the main door, and the openwork battlemented parapets' as coming from King's College Chapel, Cambridge, illustrated in Britton's *Architectural Antiquities of Great Britain,*[20] and one can add that the ogee-crowned belfry opening and panelled tower walls could have come from Britton's *York Cathedral,* 1818, while the big, richly crocketed pinnacles, the battlements, window tracery and door hoods can be found in the plates of the first edition (1817) of Rickman's *Attempt.*

Of the first three Commissioners' churches in Leeds, Christ Church seems always to have been judged the best: 'the first in architectural beauty' claimed the town's 1835 guide book.[21] Even in the national context, it may reasonably be seen as one of the best of the Gothic examples from the early 1820s. Overall, it displayed a remarkable richness of effect, achieved by the selection of basic shapes of, for instance, tower, roof-line, buttresses and openings – the proportions of which could surely have been adapted from the more general principles acquired while with Soane – but these are expertly enhanced by the elaborate decoration applied to them, carefully selected from a range of extant medieval examples and printed sources. Chantrell had learnt how to apply decoration to mass; it was a skill that would serve him well in the future.

St Peter, Morley, 1828–30

The pair of churches that followed Christ Church were the ones at Lockwood and Netherthong. Their west ends used the much exploited St George's Chapel, Windsor[22]

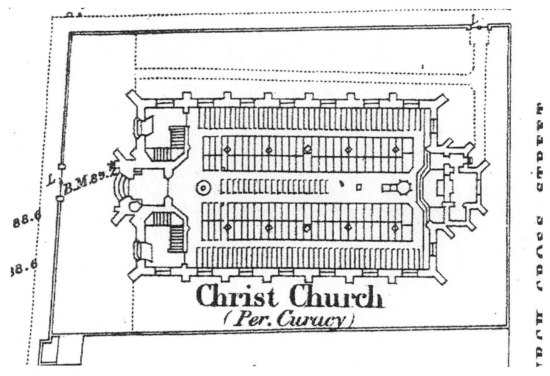

7.8: Leeds, Christ Church, Meadow Lane (R.D. Chantrell, 1821–6). The plan is taken from the 1850 O.S. map of Leeds

arrangement of a pair of octagonal towers[23] at either side of the nave's gable. But while the Windsor model is Perpendicular, Chantrell's adaptations of it used Decorated window tracery. Clearly he was not taking archaeological fidelity too seriously. However, for his next group of four churches, he kept scrupulously to Early English precedent.

The four churches are at Holbeck, Kirkstall, Morley (**7.10-13**) and New Mills. They were constructed more or less simultaneously, have similar budgets and offer almost exactly the same accommodation. If ever there was an opportunity to repeat a single design, this was surely it, yet all the four differ very significantly in their details. It was as if, having discovered the vast range of possible sources, Chantrell was overwhelmed with options and was anxious to accommodate all his findings in one design or another.

These four churches were products of the Commissioners' second grant era when budgets were significantly tighter than just a few years earlier and a number of architects had realised that Early English was the most economical of the three Gothic alternatives; discussing the Holbeck design, he wrote to the Commissioners, 'I have adhered to the style of the early part of the reign of Henry III which is the most economical that can be adopted and it possesses a degree of elegant simplicity rarely found in decorative examples of the 14th century as far as respects the contour.'[24] Further evidence of his new-found archaeological interests comes in other correspondence with the Commissioners at this time: 'I hope this style, which is a collection from some specimens of the 13th century will meet with [the Board's] approbation',[25] he wrote concerning New Mills, and of his rejected scheme for Hyde, Cheshire, he said, 'I have in progress a design in the Early English style (Henry III) partly on a model as far as respects the west front of Ripon Minster and the east part a composition from buildings of the same date which abound in this county.'[26] The Hyde design involved twin western towers – like Ripon – and although Chantrell pointed out that they would be no more expensive than a single, taller one, this might well explain why it was rejected in favour of Thomas and Walter Atkinson's more conventional scheme.

Chantrell was working on the Morley design shortly after Hyde and seems to have adapted the Ripon details here, too (**7.11**). In Morley's west front, the central doorway with a gabled hood over the arch, containing a trefoil set in a circle, and with the top of the gable just protruding above the sill of the window above, could all have been taken from Ripon. Furthermore, the two stages of triple-arches motifs with only the centre ones being open can be seen in Ripon's towers, and the non-diminishing, straight-sided tower buttresses, with a vertical bowtell moulding on each of the corners, also derive from Ripon.[27] However Ripon's towers do not have spires and sources for Morley's – and the other three in the group – are less obvious. Broach spires, like these, are not to be found in West Yorkshire, but Chantrell might have drawn inspiration from St Mary, Stamford, Lincolnshire, conveniently illustrated by Britton.[28] Alternatively, and perhaps

7.9: Leeds, Christ Church, Meadow Lane (R.D. Chantrell, 1821-6). The treatment of the ceilings is particularly interesting. (*English Heritage/NMR*).

7.10: Morley, near Leeds, St Peter (R.D. Chantrell, 1828–30).

more persuasively, he might have modelled Morley's spire on the medieval one at Glossop in Derbyshire (**4.20**), a church he was restoring as he was making the Morley drawings. The east end was another of the 'composition[s] from buildings of the same period [as Ripon] which abound in this county.'[29] He might well have been thinking of the north transept of Rievaulx, or the east end of Whitby Abbey. However, at Morley Chantrell continued the sill of the east window to form the hood-mould of the lower vestry windows, and specifies the chancel roof to be precisely parallel with that of the nave, contrivances which surely betray a Classical up-bringing that was difficult to abandon entirely (**7.14**).

7.11: Ripon Cathedral, west front. (J.R. Walbran, *A Guide to Ripon, Harrogate* ... , 1856, frontispiece).

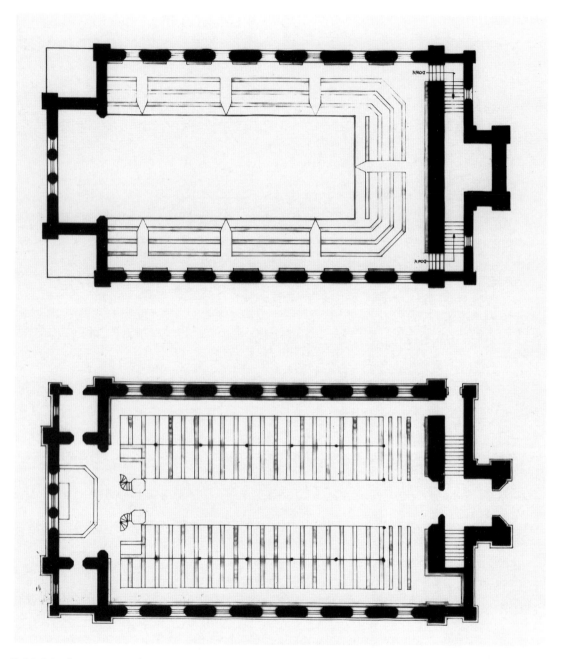

7.12: Morley, near Leeds, St Peter (R.D. Chantrell, 1828-30).

The first parliamentary grant had produced some expensive and impressive Gothic designs, but most of them remained unmistakeably of their time. Morley, for all its lack of pretension, ought to be seen as a remarkably early attempt to produce a serious essay using a consistent medieval vocabulary, based on diligent historical research. Importantly,

7.13: Morley, near Leeds, St Peter (R.D. Chantrell, 1828-30).

Chantrell now understood the significance of adopting a range of details from a single historical era – as defined by Rickman – rather than the essentially random selection that had characterised many of the 'first grant' churches of only a few years earlier. Interestingly, he is also aware of the importance of using local precedents. The single, relatively low-pitched roof unmistakably denotes a Commissioners' church, but overall it is a dignified composition. At just less than £3.00 per sitting, it was also one of the cheapest. Morley acquired a new chancel and lost its side galleries in 1885, seriously compromising Chantrell's composition. New Mills, the only one of the four churches largely unaltered, remains an impressive interior.

Leeds Parish Church, 1837-41

The history of this project and a detailed description of it can be found in the Catalogue; discussion here considers the reception of Chantrell's most important commission and

7.14: New Mills, Derbyshire, St George (R.D. Chantrell, 1827-31). Of the four Chantrell churches of the late 1820s, New Mills is the only one not to have had its chancel rebuilt. Although Morley's east end differed in its details, the photograph gives a good indication of the design of that church.

a church of national importance. On a local level, the project revitalised Chantrell's career; it was hardly flagging, but it had decidedly diminished since the arrival in the town of John Clark, the winner of the Commercial Buildings competition in 1826. The new church was the focus of tremendous Leeds chauvinism, and it, together with the newly-appointed vicar, W.F. Hook, was the centre of the revival of Anglicanism in the town. Leeds was justly proud of its own generosity in financing this huge project and it took pleasure in its magnificent new church – as a symbol of the town's piety, as an ornament and as a visible mark of improvement (**4.32, 7.15-17, 8.4, Cat. 18-21**). Chantrell basked in the general euphoria, and neither Hook nor the *Intelligencer* failed to include mention of his remarkable skill, ingenuity and taste alongside accounts of the project and the celebrations of its consecration. Its wider importance was acknowledged by the *Church Intelligencer* at the consecration: 'We trust we shall have no more churches built in the bald and beggarly style of dissenting meeting-houses, unworthy of God and discreditable to those who build them, but in the manner of the magnificent church at Leeds which stands as a noble monument to the taste, the sterling Christianity, and old-fashioned piety and spirit of Churchmanship of the town.'[30] The Revd G.A. Poole,[31] a prolific author of books and articles on church architecture, an advocate of Tractarian arrangements, and a commentator whose opinions should be considered seriously also published immediately after the consecration:

> The completion of the Parish Church of Leeds – the stately and appropriate beauty of this noble pile – and the deeply religious and ecclesiastical tone which pervaded the ceremony of its consecration, may ... be mentioned without apology, as having more than local interest, and promising no limited or transient effects on the ecclesiastical architecture of this kingdom.[32]

Later in the book, Poole noted 'the encouraging signs of a few beautiful and appropriate edifices, yet wearing the freshness of youth ... gives ... hope'. Singled out as examples were Newman's chapel at Littlemore, Rickman's Hampton Lucy and Oulton, but 'noblest among the noble [is] the Parish Church of Leeds.'[33]

The project heralded the beginning of the busiest part of Chantrell's career, but what of its longer-term significance? Initially, there was huge interest. The combination of the dynamic vicar and the magnificent new church was anticipated to be a vibrant model for the new, confident, Oxford-inspired brand of urban Anglicanism in the quest to reassert a sense of spirituality and halt the march of non-conformity. Its reopening was

7.15: Leeds Parish Church (R.D. Chantrell, 1837-41). The lithograph, probably from *c.*1841, seriously distorts the proportions, especially of the pinnacles. 7.16 is a more accurate record.

7.16: Leeds Parish Church (R.D. Chantrell, 1837–41).

greeted enthusiastically by clergy and laity alike. Chantrell must have anticipated that his building, the biggest new church since St Paul's Cathedral, and among the most expensive too, with its advanced chancel arrangement of choir and altar, would spawn countless imitations to enhance his fame. Sadly, Poole's euphoria was misplaced; the project had been overtaken by external events. In 1839, halfway through construction, the Cambridge Camden Society had been formed. Initially, its radical opinions about the design of churches and the form of services that should take place within them could be dismissed as the misplaced energy of the young. However, by the time of Leeds Parish Church's rededication, only two years later, the Society could boast the support of the primates of England and Ireland as well as twelve other bishops.[34] Had Leeds Parish Church been rebuilt just five years later, it would surely have been a very different building; as it was, attitudes to worship had changed so rapidly that it was old fashioned almost before its paint had dried. The galleries, the absence of a conventional chancel and chancel arch, the extensive use of 'unreal' materials, for instance cast-iron pew ends and *papier maché* gallery fronts, the curious arrangement of the ceilings – largely almost flat, but with a Decorated vault of wood and plaster over the crossing, and a fan fault over the altar – were all solecisms in the eyes of *The Ecclesiologist*. By 1847 it could be dismissed: '[it] can now only be studied as an historical monument. It had certainly been important as the first great instance … of the Catholic feeling of a church … and yet [it had] not been able to compass those points of church arrangement which are the result of study and patient research … [It is] not a Protestant preaching hall; nor … a church as we should like to build'.[35]

It has changed little since its opening. Today it is, perhaps, better than any other in the country, the church which conveys the liturgical dilemma of the Church of England at the very beginning of Victoria's reign; both literally and conceptually, the central space is a crossroads. The nave retains all the ingredients of a preaching box: every space downstairs crowded with pews and galleries above on three sides, all focused on the massive pulpit. However, the east end, with its prominent choir stalls and vast, open spaces both outside and inside the altar rails, anticipates much that we now associate with mid-Victorian ritualism.

Externally, the church has great dignity. It is dominated by the handsome tower which, most unusually, rises from the middle of the north front and leads to the north transept. The entrance, under the tower, is a space of almost Fonthillian proportions.

7.17: Leeds Parish Church (R.D. Chantrell, 1837–41). Lithograph, *c*.1841, by Shaw and Groom.

7.18: Adel, Leeds, St John the Baptist. Watercolour, by J. Rhodes, showing the church before the old bellcote on the west gable collapsed. (*Leeds Library and Information Services*).

7.19: Adel, Leeds, St John the Baptist. Unsigned watercolour, *c*.1840, showing Chantrell's bellcote of 1838-9, and the old chancel roof which he replaced in 1843. (*Leeds University Library, Special Collections*).

Although the church is now just outside the city centre, its slight isolation has spared it from the intrusion of Leeds' more recent developments. Diocesan reorganisations of the nineteenth century by-passed Leeds and thus Chantrell's great work was denied cathedral status. It remains as a parish church, but one of exceptional size and splendour, a church like no other in the country.

St John the Baptist, Adel, near Leeds, 1838 and 1843

The little Norman church at Adel was acknowledged locally as a building of special historical value. The *Leeds Guide* of 1803 pointed out that 'The Church is evidently of great antiquity',[36] but the noted Leeds historian T.D. Whitaker gave it more serious attention. His *Loidis and Elmete* of 1816 afforded the building three large plates and a lengthy description that included, 'here is undoubtedly one of the most entire and beautiful specimens of ancient architecture now remaining in the kingdom, but whether Saxon or Norman, remains to be determined.'[37] In 1842, between Chantrell's two commissions, it was chosen by the Revd Poole, whom we encountered above, for the opening instalment of his *Churches of Yorkshire,* a survey of the county's medieval churches, initially published in parts. Poole identified Adel as 'one of the most ancient structures in the county.'[38]

The work undertaken by Chantrell was modest in extent and cost, but coming at

7.20: Adel, Leeds, St John the Baptist.

the birth of the huge expansion of popular interest in this sort of ancient structure, and the emergence of the diocesan architectural societies in the early and mid-1840s, it underlines his pioneering commitment to this sort of work (**7.18-20**). It both led to other similar projects over the next decade and, perhaps more importantly, it helped to establish Chantrell's credentials as an antiquarian architect. In the years which followed the restoration, the church was the subject of several academic papers by Chantrell and others, and its importance was confirmed by G.E. Street accepting the commission of a more thorough restoration in 1878, with Norman Shaw having being consulted just a few years earlier.

Like so many ancient churches, it had been the subject of various insensitive alterations: new, lower pitched roofs appeared in 1686 and a west gallery was added early in the eighteenth century. Perhaps around the same time, a 'large rude wooden belfry like a farm pigeon house' – to quote Chantrell[39] – had been added which 'fell through decay in 1838, and a vestry meeting … [of] 1 September 1838 … resolved that the plans presented by Mr Chantrell … placing a double-niched bellcote to the crown of the west gable, should be adopted.'[40] Rather inelegantly, but no doubt for economy, the new section of roof was designed to merge into the existing shallow pitch. However, when work began, 'it was found that the groiling between the wall faces had been reduced to powder … [and] it was necessary to take [the gable] down to the square of the roof to enable it to bear the additional weight which had been proposed for it.'[41]

Probably in late 1842 or early 1843, 'the rector determined to raise the roof of the chancel to its former pitch.' Establishing the form of the original roof was problematic as there was no example that could be referred to with authority. 'In this state of the case, Mr Chantrell … had presented an elaborate design [showing] a treatment which he thought would best harmonize with the style of the building.' On one of his preliminary visits, Chantrell, accompanied by the rector's two clergyman sons, both of whom went on to prominent membership of the YAS, 'determined to examine the existing roof … [which] had been lowered and new fir trusses inserted.' This examination revealed to Chantrell fragments of a much older roof structure, largely decayed or dismantled but not removed in the later re-roofing. 'As soon as we reached daylight', Chantrell was able to 'sketch the form of the truss'. He concluded the roof had been an open one and designed a new one on this model, 'with partly new oak [but also] using the old materials as far as practicable'.[42] At the same time the 'two large incongruous windows, which had been substituted for the small original Norman ones' were returned to their original size using some old matching stone from the rector's out-building.[43]

A number of conclusions can be drawn from Chantrell's work at Adel, remembering that these two projects come either before or at the inception of the Cambridge Camden Society in 1839. Writing about the projects in 1847 Chantrell stated, 'it is indispensable that architects should not only keep pace with the clerical members of the local Architectural Societies, but be foremost in all antiquarian researches',[44] an early

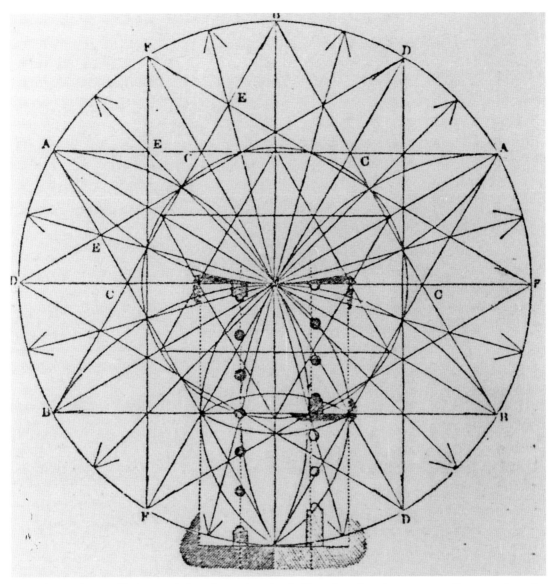

7.21: 'Mr Chantrell's System' showing what he believed to be the system of proportions by which all major medieval churches and cathedrals had been planned. (J. Gwilt, *Encyclopaedia of Architecture*, 1867, p. 973).

expression of interest in the subject from an established architect. Chantrell's desire to use as much old stone and wood as possible was also in advance of most restorers at this time as was his ability to compose 'missing' features; bellcotes were almost unknown in the Norman period, yet Chantrell successfully produced a design by adapting an Early English form to accommodate the Norman details. Thus the *Intelligencer* could report, almost certainly quoting Chantrell, that 'Adel Church … [has] just been improved by the erection of a turret at the west end of the church, exactly corresponding with the

7.22: Middleton, Leeds, St Mary (R.D. Chantrell, 1845-6). The watercolour, by J.B. Chantrell, shows the completed church. A comparison with the Frontispiece, which shows an earlier version of the design, reveals that the nave clerestory was omitted, but the attractive arcading under the west window was added. (*Leeds University Library, Special Collections*).

ancient style of architecture.'[45] Chantrell was able to gain much academic capital from the project: his paper 'Observations on the Ancient Roof of Adel Church' was printed in the *YAS Papers* (probably) in 1845,[46] it was read to the Institute of British Architects in January 1847[47] – coinciding with his arrival in the capital – and was included in the IBA's *Papers* for that year. His researches at Adel also appear in his work on medieval proportions; the dimensions of the church helped confirm the discovery of his system which is discussed below. An illustration of Adel's plan was included in the chapter on 'Medieval Proportions' in Joseph Gwilt's magisterial *Encyclopaedia of Architecture* which enjoyed great popularity in the mid- and late-century.[48]

St Mary, Middleton, Leeds, 1845 (or perhaps earlier)–1846

This was one of Chantrell's last new churches and an example of the group produced following his much-publicised identification of 'geometric principles' in 1842.[49] This was a remarkable, although now dismissed and largely overlooked phase of the rediscovery of medieval Gothic; while it enjoyed currency, Chantrell was one of its luminaries (**7.21**).

In the search to rediscover what were believed to be the 'lost' principles of Gothic, there was, in the first half of the nineteenth century, much interest in the idea that the leading medieval masons had developed a system of proportions which they applied to

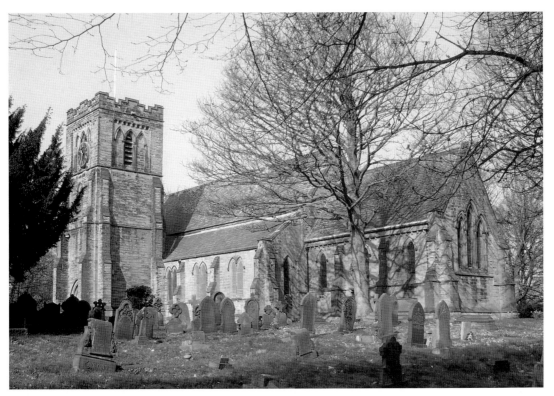

7.23: Middleton, Leeds, St Mary (R.D. Chantrell, 1845-6). The spire was removed due to mining subsidence in 1939 when the present parapet was added.

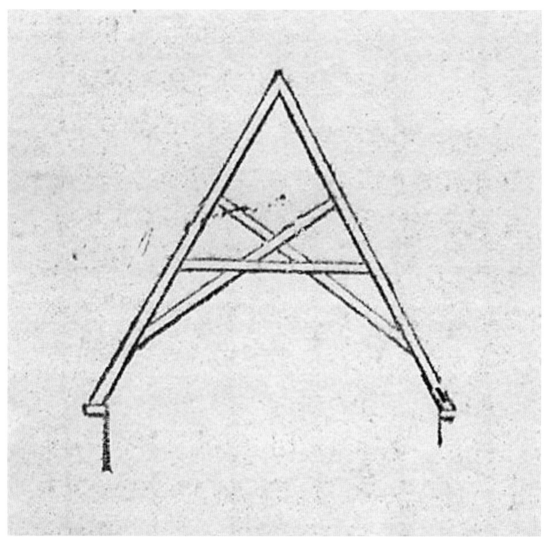

7.24: A diagram showing one of Chantrell's 'open' roof trusses. Having seen examples in several medieval buildings, Chantrell became an advocate for their use in modern churches. This one was specified for Rise church; a broadly similar design was used at Middleton. (*Civil Engineer and Architect's Journal*, April 1846, p. 100).

every part of the design for a cathedral or major church; this, of course, chimed perfectly with those schooled in the Classical tradition. It was, apparently, a system passed in secret from one mason to another, or kept within particular lodges,[50] and with the coming of the Renaissance, it ceased to be practised and as it had never been recorded, was forgotten. But while the principles might have been lost, the buildings which were based on them survived in large numbers and it is hardly surprising that some scholars sought to rediscover the system by carefully measuring its products. Chantrell was a key member of a small, but influential group that included Thomas Kerrick, R.W. Billings and C.R. Cockerell.[51] Shared by the different theoretical models proposed by individual members of this group was a shape known as the *vesica piscis,* or 'fish bladder'.[52] By sub-dividing a circle following a set of rules of almost labyrinthine complexity,[53] a series of points are established which provided a system of proportions and, at the same time, formed the positions of key parts of a plan – outer walls, inner arcades, etc – and can also be applied to elevations or openings. Such a system is hinted at in masonic ritual and Chantrell's induction into the craft in 1837 might have been a catalyst.

The ubiquitous adherence to such a system by an army of masons spread through Europe in the Middle Ages now seems implausible, and more recent scholars[54] are unconvinced.[55] However, whatever the theory's shortcomings, it seems to have given Chantrell a renewed confidence and the post-1842 churches form both a coherent and accomplished group. Those of the previous decade seem, in comparison, a disparate set. The 'discovery' also brought him national prestige as a theorist and antiquary. He gave a paper to the Leeds Philosophical and Literary Society in April 1843 'On the Geometric Principles of Gothic Architecture'. More significantly, he revised it as 'On the Geometric System applied by the Medieval Architects to the Proportions of Ecclesiastical Structures', delivered to the IBA in June 1847 and subsequently had it published in *The Builder*. That

7.25: Middleton, Leeds, St Mary (R.D. Chantrell, 1845-6). (*Blacksheep Photography*).

article included 'Upon this system, with great advantage and satisfaction, I have had erected the churches of Leven and Rise ... Middleton near Leeds, King Cross in Halifax; and those at ... Armitage Bridge ... and St Philip's in Leeds.'[56]

Middleton will repay further attention (**7.22-25**). It is instructive to compare it to Morley, discussed above, which shares many of the same basic elements, yet is unquestionably the less sophisticated design. However, in seeking to explain Middleton's 'success', we need to ask whether Chantrell's system alone provides the answer, or whether it benefits from the general development of ecclesiastical architecture after *c.*1840. Specifically, can we explain the greater visual interest in the Middleton design in terms of the new liturgical practices which demanded that architects experimented with more authentically pre-Reformation plans, rather than as a result of its 'correct' proportions alone?

Perhaps in the spirit of his medieval predecessors, at no point does Chantrell reveal in precisely *what* ways the proportions of Middleton − or any of the other churches in this group − benefit from the system. He does not, for instance, tell us that the length and breadth of the nave have a particular mathematical relationship, or that this is repeated, on a smaller scale, in the east window. However, Middleton certainly *appears* assured, it captures the spirit of Gothic convincingly, but is it mathematical certainty or intuition that directed its success? Let us return to the comparison with Morley. Both are Early English, they share broadly similar lancet windows and the towers and spires differ only in minor details. Yet for an 1840s critic, the 'improvement' at Middleton would have been beyond dispute. He might have pointed to the steeper pitch of Middleton's roofs, the explicit division of the components of the plan which provide more visual interest than Morley's block-like body, he might have identified the picturesque quality of Middleton's imaginatively placed tower, doubling as the south porch. On the inside, the prominent nave arcade and clear division between nave and chancel give a sense of intimacy, drama and spirituality absent in Morley's somewhat ponderous nave. The long chancel, and the altar raised on steps chimed perfectly with the new, more Tractarian worship. And the church contains a good open timber roof, a roof type that Chantrell was much taken with in the 1840s, regularly mentioned in his accounts of his churches, and in this respect, was well ahead of the Brandon brothers whose pioneering book on the subject did not appear until 1849.[57] St Mary's has some attractive details too, like the blind arcading under the west window, and the coupling of the diminutive lancet windows. But how much of this is concerned with a new understanding of proportion and how much can it be interpreted as the culmination of two decades of acquaintance with Gothic, both via his own work and that of his contemporaries? Whatever the answer, the church is undeniably attractive as well as providing a lead in the Tractarian revolution. Its asymmetrically placed tower was a model much copied in West Yorkshire in the middle of the century, for instance in several of the churches of Mallinson and Healey of Bradford.

St Andrew, Keighley, 1845-9

Keighley parish church (**7.26-29**) is included here both because it is a fine building, and also because an account of the project helps to explain the special skills which Chantrell possessed for this sort of rebuilding scheme, skills which differentiated him from many of his fellow architects at this time. And the account – which can only be fully narrated with sections of arguably tedious detail – also gives a flavour of the relationship between architect and patron. It was, surely, a story widely repeated throughout the country at this time.

The building history is unusually complicated. A faculty to rebuild the old church, adding galleries, was granted in 1805.[58] The tower, which was 'very ancient',[59] was to be retained. The finished church 'looked like a meeting house' which had been designed by 'a common builder'.[60] In the late 1830s it was decided to replace this in order to increase accommodation, but also because the roof was insecure.[61] The Bradford architect Walker Rawsthorne (d. 1867) was appointed and on 22 April 1839 an application was submitted to the ICBS. Rawsthorne estimated work would take only three months, although the vicar felt two years was a more reasonable estimate. In May 1839 the ICBS agreed a grant of £400 and the following month its surveyor, J.H. Good, approved the design although he felt the purlins and rafters were too far apart. Rawsthorne must have amended his designs and on 27 July 1839, Good pronounced them satisfactory. The faculty was

7.26: Keighley, West Yorkshire, St Andrew (R.D. Chantrell, 1845-9). (*Leeds University Library, Special Collections*).

7.27: Keighley, West Yorkshire, St Andrew (R.D. Chantrell, 1845-9).

granted in January 1841 for which Rawsthorne's plans are dated 12 December 1840.[62] They reveal an old-fashioned design: the inelegant elevations emphasise the two-storey nature of the interior, there are huge transepts and a shallow chancel. Interestingly, the proposed re-fenestration of the tower was not dissimilar to Chantrell's Christ Church, Leeds, of twenty years earlier (see above). The roof must have been modified yet again as Good was objecting to the 'new flatter roof' in his report of 15 January 1841. Then on 1 March 1841 the vicar wrote to the ICBS to say the whole scheme had been postponed since the parish could not manage without a place of worship while their church was being rebuilt. It was now proposed to build a small chapel in another part of the parish; when finished it could be used temporarily as the parish church while the old one was being rebuilt. This chapel – subsequently St John the Evangelist, Ingrow – was also designed by Rawsthorne.[63]

Nothing more seems to have happened on the parish church project until the *Leeds Intelligencer* announced on 11 January 1845 that 'Messrs Chantrell and Shaw [in reality R.D. Chantrell, see Chapter 6] have received instructions to prepare plans etc for the rebuilding of Keighley Parish Church'. Almost certainly the following month 'a meeting of the subscribers was held when the amended plans of Mr Chantrell were exhibited and agreed to, by which 600 additional sittings will be obtained without extending the structure beyond the old foundations except at the east end where the chancel is to be built. Part of the tower, which is very ancient and in a good state of preservation is to be retained.'[64] On 5 March 1845, the vicar informed the ICBS of developments: 'Mr Chantrell is busily engaged in preparing plans ... [which] will add 715 extra seats. This will cost £3,000 using the old tower, foundations and materials. Rawsthorn's plan would have produced 430 extra seats. His estimate was £2,700 but the work was let for £3,500. Rawsthorn would not even reply to our request for a cheaper scheme ... ' The vicar wrote again also on 5 March 1845 asking if the £400 grant was still available adding 'The Bishop has, I believe, made you acquainted with the circumstances which compelled us to employ a new architect – the justly celebrated Mr Chantrell.' Good approved Chantrell's designs on 12 May 1845 and on 13 June the ICBS issued a receipt for six drawings for this project. At about the same time the faculty was applied for with two drawings signed 'Chantrell and Son, June 1845' explaining the project involved: 'the removal of the nave and choir, or as much of the said parts as may be necessary and ... rebuilding on the site of the present church ... a new church and chancel ... 141 feet long and 62 feet wide'. The *Intelligencer* of 28 February 1846 carried an account of the foundation stone laying of four days earlier. The article includes the story of the abandoned Rawsthorne scheme. In December 1847 it was announced that 'the beautiful building is now fast approaching completion',[65] although the newspaper of 29 July 1848 still described it as 'nearly complete' adding 'the church is a fine specimen of Perpendicular Gothic of the 15th century, the whole being carried out with the greatest accuracy and will long remain a striking proof of the great fame of this celebrated architect ...' the church was consecrated on 11 August 1848, an event recorded in the *Intelligencer* eight days later accompanied by: 'taken as a whole there are few erections of the present day more

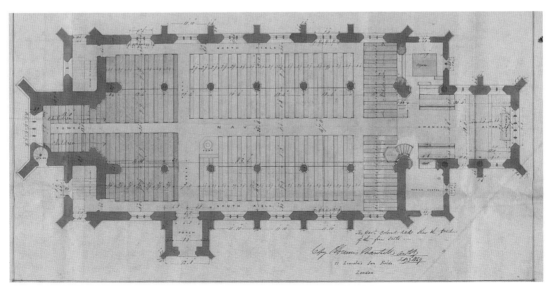

7.28: Keighley, West Yorkshire, St Andrew (R.D. Chantrell, 1845-9). (*Lambeth Palace Library*).

7.29: Keighley, West Yorkshire, St Andrew (R.D. Chantrell, 1845-9). (*Roger Hatfield*)..

creditable to the mind that designed it, although as students of church architecture there are a few details of which we cannot but regret the adoption [principally the placing of the choir stalls which, it argued, made the chancel too crowded] … it will accommodate 1,400 people and the cost of the rebuilding was £7,000 …' The certificate of completion is dated 3 February 1849 and was signed by Chantrell from his office in Lincoln's Inn Fields. Predictably, *The Ecclesiologist* was not impressed. Nevertheless, the review was unusually long and while the underlying theme is critical, much of the description is written without judgement.[66]

The finished church is Perpendicular with a largely rebuilt tower, nave with aisles, clerestory, galleries on three sides, and a long chancel with Camdenian arrangements. It was one of the projects that Chantrell conceived using his 'geometric principles' and it is one of his most successful late designs. From the exterior, it is a remarkably convincing example of a medieval town church.

What conclusions should we reach about Chantrell's contribution to the broader picture of the Gothic Revival? It is this: probably no other single career better reveals the evolution of church design in the period between the establishment of the 1818 Church Building Commission and the middle of the century. His early churches were indisputably inferior to Rickman's, but Rickman died in 1841 and thus achieved a dignified departure before the advent of ecclesiology. Goodwin, too, designed some fine compositions in the 'first grant' era when budgets were relatively generous, but struggled to adapt to the stringencies of the later 1820s; his St Mary, Bilston, Staffordshire, and St John the Evangelist, Derby, are neither impressive nor scholarly. Scott probably produced better churches than Chantrell in the 1840s, but entering practice in 1835 had missed employment from the Commissioners. The careers of Barry and Dobson share Chantrell's time-frame, but for both, church work was only an adjunct to their extensive secular projects. Cottingham could demonstrate greater expertise with large-scale restorations, but undertook few new churches. Chantrell stands almost alone as an ecclesiastical architect whose career spans the entirety of this seminal period in the evolution of church design. Arguably no other single career better reveals the sometimes subtle gradations ranging through the Commissioners' first grant, their second grant, the more humble 1830s projects that were the result of hard-fought for subscriptions, the early years of ecclesiology, and finally the liturgical and stylistic revolution of the mid-century. Towering over all of this is Leeds Parish Church, nationally, the greatest new church of its day.

8

Conclusion

Despite the religious divide, in one important way Pugin and the Ecclesiologists were united: both were remarkably adept at discrediting the generation of architects that came before them. The marginalisation of their predecessors was an essential part of the drive to see established their own highly subjective agendas. So effective were they in this respect that their own prejudices outlived them and became accepted as truisms. Now, more than a century and a half later, it is still difficult for historians to probe beyond the narrative they invented about late-Georgian architecture and worship. That 'the Victorian caricature of the Georgian Church of England as a lax and corpulent institution, consisting only of toadying place-hunters and squires rattling fire irons to stop over-long sermons lives on even today'[1] is a mark of the Ecclesiologists' dogmatism and bigotry. On every front, the reputation of Chantrell's generation suffered: its Classicism was dismissed as debased and not fit for a Christian country, its sterling attempts to come to terms with Gothic were pilloried as inept and incorrect, as uninspiring as the services they apparently contained; their attempts to establish architecture as an honourable profession were marginalized on the basis of the sack's few bad apples and instead labelled corrupt or self-seeking; and the late-Georgian diligence to find new materials and production processes that reflected the age's technological advances were dismissed and its inventions condemned as 'unreal'.

Any attempt to look objectively at the achievements of Chantrell's generation must reach beyond this received wisdom. And aside from this prejudice, the physical developments demanded by an expanding population have not been kind to most late-Georgian architects: the spread of towns and cities often left their churches without congregations, and the demand for bigger, more complex public buildings in the Victorian era swept away much that had been created by Chantrell's generation. Of the churches that survive, most suffered insensitive, Ecclesiologically-inspired changes, sufficiently drastic to destroy their intrinsic quality without entirely satisfying the new sensibilities. Often, the buildings – both secular and religious – live on only in old photographs or books, yet even a cursory look at a publication like *Illustrations of the Public Buildings of London*[2] or *Metropolitan Improvements*,[3] from the 1820s and 1830s reveals a succession of stunning now-demolished buildings, including several remarkable – mainly Classical – churches.

There were, undoubtedly, some dreary, cheap Gothic churches too (**8.1**) and the period contained its share of incompetent, lazy, and corrupt practitioners – Pecksniff must have been a readily identifiable character for Dickens' readers – yet are we in danger of missing much that should be celebrated?

What conclusions should we take away from a study of Chantrell's career? Firstly, the Classical tradition remained the dominant stylistic force nationally, at least until the mid-1840s. His few designs in this style show he could exploit its principles with fluency, and his South Market is an extraordinarily accomplished design. The success of John Clark – perhaps even more successful, although arguably less inventive, in the Classical tradition – shows the town's fondness for this style for public buildings; had Chantrell chosen not to devote his career to church work, there is every reason to believe he would have gone on to produce some exceptional Classical essays. Given Classicism's popularity in Yorkshire, how do we locate Chantrell's prolific work as a Gothicist? The answer is that well before Pugin and the Ecclesiologists, Gothic was the preferred style for churches, certainly in the north of England, but that this stylistic preference was in

8. 1: South Crossland, West Yorkshire, Holy Trinity (Peter Atkinson jnr, 1827-9). This is a particularly dreary example of the type of Gothic church being produced by many of Chantrell's contemporaries. (*Leeds University Library, Special Collections*).

8. 2: New Mills, Derbyshire, St George (R.D. Chantrell, 1827-31), a very successful example of Chantrell's cheap churches of the 1820s. It actually cost less, per sitting, than the Atkinson example shown in 8.1 and reveals something of Chantrell's exceptional skill with the Gothic repertoire.

contradiction to the prevailing fashion for Classicism in all other building types. It was a preference decidedly dictated by the congregations – as opposed to their architects – for whom it was widely seen as the natural setting for worship. And to satisfy the huge demand for new churches from a rapidly expanding urban population, architects had to master the unfamiliar principles of Gothic. For those like Chantrell who succeeded, it was no slight achievement. The architecture of the first half of the nineteenth century has often been caricatured as 'the battle of the styles' with an implication that the stylistic veneer of a building, whether Classical, Gothic or Exotic, required nothing more than the application of a few interchangeable details. This is a travesty. A successful Gothic composition not only required an understanding of that style's principles, but, perhaps more fundamentally, it involved a total *disregard* of the Classical rules in which almost every architect of this period had been schooled. Accepting such a profound theoretical shift was something many architects never achieved, and few understood it better than Chantrell.

He was then a pioneer in the design of sound, cheap Gothic churches. Their success was two-fold. They were functionally efficient, perfectly composed to provide maximum

8. 3: Guiseley, West Yorkshire, St Oswald. Chantrell's 1832 drawing shows his proposed new north aisle for the medieval church. It reveals his most accomplished Gothic designs were when, as here, he was given an opportunity to make his work blend with a medieval structure.

accommodation and the type of liturgical space that pre-Ecclesiological worship required. He also succeeded in giving these buildings a suitably convincing medieval atmosphere. But even the latter was fraught with difficulty. These were never intended to resemble medieval examples – the form of worship was very different from its pre-Reformation relative – and, perhaps more significantly, there was a line in the sand of medievalism which, if passed, would have brought forth the mindless charge of 'Popery', perhaps the ultimate criticism. We should see Chantrell's late-1820s churches, like those at Morley, Kirkstall and New Mills (**8.2**), as among the best of their type anywhere in the country when assessed in the context of the period's requirements. His diligent archaeological researches and thoughtful application of appropriate details produced some exemplary designs. But perhaps his true sympathy with Gothic is revealed in a restoration like that proposed for Guiseley (**8.3**) where, working with a genuine medieval structure, he could compose new work in the spirit of the old, unfettered by the concerns of rampant Protestants.

At the rededication of Leeds Parish Church in 1841, Chantrell must have believed that he had produced a church that forever would be seen as one of the great monuments of the age, perhaps its greatest church. However, its reception and legacy were hijacked by the Ecclesiologists, a group that had not even been dreamed of when he started the building, but by the time of its opening was influential and would soon occupy an unassailable position in directing attitudes to church design and forms of worship. For an architect considering posterity's assessment of his greatest project, the timing could not have been worse. His massive church, huge budget and innovative arrangements produced no legacy whatsoever. No wonder he later referred to *The Ecclesiologist* as 'a mischievous tissue of imbecility and fanaticism'.[4]

Yet Chantrell was not always in opposition to the new Ecclesiological agenda. Shortly before Leeds Parish Church, he built Christ Church, Skipton. Guided by the project's patron, Christopher Sidgwick and his friend the Revd Hammond Roberson, well known for his commitment to the observance of the Prayer Book rubrics, Chantrell produced a remarkable church that predicted many of the Cambridge Camden Society's innovations in church arrangements; Sidgwick's language in describing the project also anticipates its publications. It is a project that deserves a much more prominent place in the history of Victorian Anglicanism.[5] And through the 1840s, his churches continued largely to be in line with the latest Camdenian pronouncement. Georg Germann concluded that, as the early leaders of the Cambridge Camden Society were still in their early twenties, 'the ideas which they advanced were not put into practice until upwards of ten years later.'[6] This is questionable, but if it were true, it would make Chantrell's work all the more remarkable. His frequent specification of: long chancels with an altar raised on several steps; aisles and clerestories; asymmetrically placed towers; open roofs with 'all their honest nakedness'[7] demonstrated that he had enthusiastically embraced the new imperatives.

8. 4: Leeds Parish Church (R.D. Chantrell, 1837–41). Lithograph, by Richardson, 1841.

Chantrell is also significant for his antiquarian and academic work. His 'geometric principles' was taken very seriously in the middle of the century and it enabled him to move in a circle of some of the biggest architectural names of the period, for instance C.R. Cockerell, Edward Cresy and R.W. Billings, and it included several prominent continental theorists too.[8] Chantrell's other published works, on a variety of antiquarian topics, enabled him to speak with great authority and brought him much prestige at a time when few architects engaged with these areas of investigation. Despite twentieth-century scholars' dismissal of the idea that a ubiquitous mystical system of church design ever existed in the Middle Ages, Chantrell's own 'discovery' seems to have been the means by which he was able to produce a whole sequence of exceptionally accomplished church designs in the 1840s.

The exploitation of new materials was another area of practice which might have come to have been celebrated for the technological progress it represented, yet it failed the stringent Ecclesiological test: such innovations lacked 'reality', and were thus discredited.[9] However, the post-Waterloo period expended much energy on their development, and with good reason.[10] They were not simply cheaper than traditional alternatives, but had many practical advantages. Nevertheless the elegant columns of cast iron, embellished with wooden mouldings to resemble stone, which Chantrell exploited so effectively in a number of his early churches came to be seen as an embarrassment rather than a celebrated innovation. The rich interior of Leeds Parish Church (**8.4**) could never have been achieved without other novel methods of construction. For instance, the intricate gallery fronts, bristling with arches, pinnacles and crockets, would have been prohibitively expensive in carved wood, but in a moulded, *papier maché*-type composition, they could be endlessly and uniformly reproduced at an acceptable cost. Cast iron was also exploited for mass-produced decorative features elsewhere in the church. At the time this was not seen as deception, it was a celebration of the age's inventive genius, but, only a few years later, the Ecclesiologists and William Morris saw things differently, and convinced popular opinion in their favour.

Finally, we need to consider Chantrell in the context of professional practice. He was not quite the first architect to set up office in an expanding industrial town – as opposed to a county town frequented by the local nobility and gentry, like York – but he was certainly a pioneer. He and his colleagues had to establish the demand for their services and then satisfy it. Importantly, they had to convince local individuals and building committees that they could provide a level of service, on both a professional level as well as an aesthetic one, well beyond that of the builder/architects who were their main competition. Chantrell succeeded admirably. There was no hint that his integrity was ever seriously questioned, his buildings were greeted enthusiastically by the local newspaper, and as an antiquary and careful restorer, he enjoyed considerable status in the town. Alongside many substantial commissions, we have already noted his being consulted about leaking roofs and the erection of a schoolyard wall. While a later generation of

Leeds architects would shun these menial jobs, the most instructive interpretation of his involvement in such work is surely that there were no established rules about what a provincial architect should or shouldn't do; Chantrell was literally helping to forge a new, and very significant chapter in the history of the emerging profession of architecture.

A central theme of the Pugin/Ecclesiological hegemony was that only a *Christian* architect could design a first-rate church. It was not enough that such an architect regularly attended a church, but he should devote himself to God's work to the exclusion of all other. The image of the medieval architect's office replete with its own altar and religious statuary that formed the frontispiece to Pugin's *True Principles* in 1841 was a potent one. Its implications were radical. This was the age of the general practitioner, a concept confirmed by several pattern books that offered guidance in the design of every structure a town could conceivably require, from a church to a gas works.[11] Although instances of an architect entirely rejecting secular commissions are rare, the ideal is a further indication of the philosophical shift that was taking place after 1840. Although the protagonists of this re-orientation of practice would have been horrified to acknowledge it, Chantrell had been fundamentally committed to such a path for more than a decade.

In September 1841, at the time of the rededication of Leeds Parish Church, Chantrell must have believed his fame was assured; he had created a lasting monument to his own genius. There was another brief moment at the end of 1847, his first year in London, when he might, with only a little arrogance, have believed himself to be in the very top echelon of the select group of antiquarian-architects. Of those whom he would have seen as rivals for this crown, Rickman had died in 1841 and Cottingham earlier in 1847; Blore was still active and unquestionably had extensive knowledge, but has not unreasonably been dismissed for allowing 'a dull competence to pervades all his work',[12] and from the early '40s he was pilloried by *The Ecclesiologist* which regularly savaged his church work.[13] Scott had certainly achieved successes, but could still just about be dismissed as a youngster, and the new generation of Carpenter and Woodyer had yet to make its mark. Pugin was an obvious rival, but his qualifications were much diminished by his Catholicism. Chantrell, on the other hand, could review with satisfaction a year in the capital punctuated by high-profile lectures and antiquarian publications. Yet on both occasions, Chantrell's ambitions were not to be fulfilled. The remarkable authority of the Ecclesiologists very effectively marginalised his achievements and thus his reputation, condemning him to be a part of the 'lost generation' of late-Georgian architects whose successes, in many cases, still remain to be fully appreciated.

CATALOGUE

Adel, Leeds, St John the Baptist
Rebuilt W gable and bellcote, 1838-9

This is an important example of a Norman village church, but by the 1830s its original roofs had long since been replaced by ones of a much flatter pitch with 'a large rude wooden belfry like a farm pigeon house.' (Chantrell, 'Observations' p. 111). at the W end. This 'fell through decay in 1838, and a vestry meeting … [of] 1 September 1838 … resolved that the plans presented by Mr Chantrell … placing a double-niched bellcote to the crown of the west gable, should be adopted.' (G. Lewthwaite, 'Adel Church'). Chantrell's working drawings are dated 8 September 1838 (RDP2) and show his intention to build the new bellcote on the existing W gable and renew the westernmost roof truss designed to follow the pitch if the gable. Rather inelegantly, but no doubt for economy, the new section of roof was designed to merge into the existing shallow pitch. However, when work began, 'it was found that the groiling [this seems to be a local term to describe the rubble infill] between the wall faces had been reduced to powder … [and] it was necessary to take [the gable] down to the square of the roof to enable it to bear the additional weight which had been proposed for it.' (G. Lewthwaite, *op. cit.*). *LI,* 17 August 1839 announced that 'Adel Church … [has] just been improved by the erection of a turret at the west end of the church, exactly corresponding with the ancient style of architecture.'

DRAWINGS: WYASL, RDP2/68.

REFERENCES: W. H. Lewthwaite, 'Discovery of the Norman Roof at Adel' in *YAS Papers,* 1843; R.D. Chantrell, 'Observations on the Ancient Roof of the Church of Adel … ' in *YAS Papers,* n.d. but probably 1845, reprinted in *YAS Papers* 1887, reprinted in *Institute of British Architects Papers,* 1847; G. Lewthwaite, 'Adel Church: Its Fabric, Restorations and Discovery of Norman roof' in *YAS Papers,* 1887; *LI,* 17 Aug. 1839.

Adel, Leeds, St John the Baptist
New chancel roof, 1843

The original roof of the Norman church at Adel had been replaced at an unrecorded date by one of much flatter pitch. Chantrell's work on the building in 1838-9 (see above) had recreated the original pitch at the W end and perhaps as a result of this, probably in late 1842 or early 1843, 'the rector determined to raise the roof of the chancel to its former pitch.' (G. Lewthwaite, 1887). Establishing the form of the original roof was problematic as there was no example that could be referred to with authority. 'In this state of the case, Mr Chantrell … had presented an elaborate design [showing] a treatment which he thought would best harmonize with the style of the building … ' Prior to work commencing, Chantrell 'was invited with some amateur members [of the YAS] to a consultation on the spot in the course of which it was determined to examine the existing roof … [which] had been lowered and new fir trusses inserted.' (*ibid.*). This examination revealed to Chantrell fragments of a much older roof structure, largely decayed or dismantled but not removed in the later re-roofing. From this it proved possible to envisage the form of the original roof. Chantrell considered that these were the original timbers of the Norman roof and this led him to the conclusion that this roof had been an open one. On this basis he 'restored this roof with partly new oak using the old materials as far as practicable, and the effect is good, harmonizing with the general form of the building and its ornaments.' (*ibid*.).

REFERENCES: W.H. Lewthwaite, 'the Discovery of the Norman Roof at Adel' in *YAS Papers*, 1843; R.D. Chantrell, 'Observations on the Ancient roof of the Church at Adel' in *YAS Papers*, n.d. but probably 1847, reprinted in *Institute of British Architects Papers*, 1847, reprinted in *YAS Papers*, 1887; G. Lewthwaite, Adel Church: Its Fabric, Restorations and Discovery of Norman Roof' in *YAS Papers*, 1887.

Almondbury, West Yorkshire, All Hallows
Alterations including repewing, 1829
All Hallows is a large, mostly late-medieval church.

An application was made to the ICBS for a grant for alterations creating 260 extra seats, 100 of them free. At its meeting on 23 May 1829, the ICBS offered a grant of £50 (ICBS, MB4). Confirmation of completion and creation of extra seats was sent in a letter of 29 October 1829. It was signed by, among others, 'John Wade, Surveyor'. This was accompanied by two plans dated 1829 and signed 'John Wade, Clerk of Works, acting for Mr Chantrell, Architect' (ICBS, file 01089).

DRAWINGS: ICBS, file 01089.

REFERENCES: ICBS, file 01089; ICBS, MB 4, p. 252, MB 5, p. 55.

Armitage Bridge, Huddersfield, Armitage Bridge House.
New house for William Brooke, 1828
'The late William Brooke Esq of Northgate House [erected] … Armitage Bridge House. [It was built] for the use of his eldest son John Brooke Esq … from the designes of R.D. Chantrell Esq … Leeds.' (Hulbert, pp. 275-6). Crump and Ghorbal (p. 92), give the date as 1828. It must have been finished by the summer of that year as the procession which went to the first stone-laying ceremony at the nearby Emmanuel Church, Lockwood, started from Armitage Bridge House (*LI*, 11 Sept. 1828).

The Brookes were a prosperous family who owned Armitage Bridge Mills and were instrumental in driving forward the erection of several new churches in the area, mostly designed by Chantrell, starting with those at Lockwood and Netherthong where he was appointed in 1826. It was, no doubt, these commissions which led to the meeting of Brooke and Chantrell.

The house is a Classical, two-storey, five-bay composition. There are wings at each side, probably later additions. The entrance front has a projecting central bay in which the door has an Ionic column and square Tuscan pilaster at each side. In the centre of the garden front is a large niche surrounded by projecting pilasters crowned by an entablature. The two principal rooms had shallow vaulted ceilings not unlike that designed by Soane for the Breakfast Room of 12 Lincoln's Inn Fields. These ceilings were removed when the house was converted to flats in *c*.1980.

There is a substantial stable block decorated with Soanian incised motifs in the blocking coarse. The gate lodge forms part of an impressive concave composition of gate piers and railings and although probably later than the house, might also be by Chantrell.

REFERENCES: C.A. Hulbert, *Annals of the Parish of Almondbury*, Longmans, 1882; W.B. Crump and G. Ghorbal, *History of the Huddersfield Woollen Industry*, 1935, reprint Kirklees Leisure Services, 1988.

Armitage Bridge, near Huddersfield, Armitage Bridge Mills
Unidentified work, including measuring, for William Brooke, 1829-38

The huge mill complex was begun *c.*1816-17 by the Brooke family, long-established manufacturers and merchants. Much additional building was being undertaken in the 1829-38 period including the six-storey, thirteen-bay Mill 2, the five-storey loomshop, the weaving shed and houses for the waterwheels and steam engines (RCHM). Most of the buildings are utilitarian in appearance but their sheer scale would suggest they would not have been constructed without the direction of an architect or civil engineer.

The Partnership Stock Book (1825-1922) of the Brooke family's company lists various references or payments to Chantrell 'for measuring', including in 1829 'Building Account as per Mr Chantrell's Measurement' which amounts to £6,852 for an unspecified but clearly substantial project and does not include any sum for an architect/designer. In 1831 Chantrell was paid £9/9/0 'for measuring'. In 1836 the book lists 'Particulars of Cost of Building the School, Power Loom, Wool … (?) , Meeting Rooms, … [words unclear] and additions to the Wool Warehouse'. This amounts to £1060, including £14/16/0 for Chantrell 'for measuring'. In 1838, £3,000 is listed as the cost of the Power Loom Mill, including £168/9/0 for Chantrell 'for measuring'.

These entries raise tantalizing questions about the designers of the buildings. Nowhere is a sum specified for a designer/engineer. Could Brooke have designed the buildings himself using Chantrell's professional services to check the accounts? On the other hand, Chantrell's 1838 fee of £168 represents more than 5% of the total cost of the £3,000 Power Loom Mill, an impossibly large sum just for measuring and generous even if Chantrell was the designer too. The School – see a later entry in this catalogue – is confidently attributed to Chantrell, but there is no reference to payments to an architect and there is no mention of Chantrell's work at Armitage Bridge House, although this could be explained as the school and house were private commissions rather than the business's.

REFERENCES: C. Giles and I.H. Goodall, *Yorkshire Textile Mills*, HMSO, 1995. The Brookes' Partnership Stock Book was held by John Brooke and Sons Holdings Ltd at the mill when seen in 1995.

Armitage Bridge, near Huddersfield, St Paul
New church, *c.* 1844-8

Decorated Gothic in style with W tower, nave with aisles and clerestory, chancel and S porch.

An application for a grant from the ICBS is dated 26 November 1844. The estimated cost was £3,200. The plans were approved by J.H. Good, the Society's surveyor on 5 December and a grant of £300 was confirmed on 16 December (ICBS, file 03527). At about the same time, a grant application was made to the CBC but at its meeting of 14 January 1845 it resolved to tell the applicants 'again' the estimated cost was too great and the accommodation of 430 too small for a grant to be given (CBC, MB 59, p. 253). The remainder of the final cost – '£5,000 we are told', according to *The Builder* – was paid for by the local mill owners John Brooke and Sons.

Tenders were invited in August 1845 (*LI*, 16 Aug. 1846) and the ICBS meeting of 19 June 1848 noted the receipt of the completion certificate. There is a detailed description of the finished church in *The Builder* (1848). Drawings were exhibited at the Free Architectural Exhibition in London on 1850; 'the tower is absolutely wretched' was *The Ecclesiologist's* opinion.

Archives at Wakefield include the only Chantrell bill to include details of site inspections. This itemises 15, although a letter in the archive suggests 24 visits, including the first stone-laying and consecration ceremonies. Even when he had moved to London, Chantrell still visited roughly every three months. Nevertheless, there are several letters from Chantrell written after the opening of the church in which he attempted to settle disputes over payments to tradesmen, suggesting a less than perfect management of the project.

The church was badly damaged by fire in the 1980s and the original design was adapted in the rebuilding.

DRAWINGS: ICBS, file 03527.

REFERENCES: ICBS, MB 13, p. 119; ICBS, file 03527; CBC, MB 59, p. 253; CBC, Armitage Bridge file 15078; CBC, Halifax file 16862; WYASW, WDP85 box 5; *Builder*, 5, 1847, p. 302; 6, 1848, p. 249; *Ecclesiologist*, 11, 1850, p.134; *LI,* 16 Aug. 1845.

Armitage Bridge, near Huddersfield, Vicarage
New vicarage, *c.*1848

The building is in Chantrell's characteristic Tudor style with elaborate gables and lozenge motifs, although in plan it is L-shaped whereas other houses of this period tend to be square.

While the church was largely paid for by Messrs John Brooke and Sons, the vicarage was paid for by William Brooke acting in a private capacity. There is no explicit reference to Chantrell as architect although church and vicarage were clearly parts of a single project as *The Builder* confirms.

REFERENCES: CBC, Armitage Bridge file 15078; *Builder*, 6, 1848, p. 249.

Armley, Leeds, Armley Chapel/St Bartholomew
Proposed alterations, probably unexecuted, 1823 (demolished)

The earliest part of the structure was built in 1630 as a Chapel of Ease to the Parish Church of Leeds, but it was not consecrated until 1674 (Taylor). The style might best be described as 'country Perpendicular'. It consisted of a nave 52 feet x 25 feet and a chancel 25 feet x 20 feet (these are approximate, internal dimensions). In 1737 a N aisle was added. The W gallery – which might have existed before 1737 – was extended into the two westernmost bays of the new aisle (Midgley). There was a small vestry in the NE corner between the end of the N aisle and the chancel.

In 1820 the 'officiating minister' had written to the ICBS enquiring about grants and in 1823, Chantrell produced a drawing showing proposed alterations which involved demolishing the vestry, extending the 1737 N aisle eastwards to meet the line of the existing E wall. This new structure was of the same dimensions and had the same window details as the 1630 chancel. It was intended to contain pews for Benjamin Gott's family and servants. A new vestry was to be added to the N side of the extension and a new entrance, to serve as both a private entrance to Gott's pews, and to the vestry was included.

Probably none of this was carried out as a similar scheme appears in a faculty in 1825. However, in connection with a further extension in 1833, Gott wrote to the ICBS stating that the chapel 'was last substantially repaired in 1823 at an expense of £260'.

DRAWING: BI, Faculty 1825/1

REFERENCES: Taylor, pp. 98-9; M. Midgley (ed.), *Armley Church and Schools*, J. Hunter, 1907; ICBS, file 00256.

Armley, Leeds, Armley Chapel/St Bartholomew
Extension, 1825 (demolished)

In 1825, an application was made for a faculty for an addition in the NE corner of the building, broadly similar to the 1823 scheme (see above). However, there are a number of differences, For instance, the vestry is smaller in the later scheme and differently configured. The 1825 scheme includes a substantial vault for the Gott family under the extension which is absent from the earlier proposal.

Drawings for the 1833-4 extensions (see below) include one recording the chapel 'in its present state'. This shows the vestry to have been built in a form that differs from those shown in both the 1823 and 1825 drawings.

DRAWINGS: BI, Faculty 1825/1; WYASL, Richmond Faculties, RD/AF/2/2, no. 7; WYASL, RDP4/131.

REFERENCES: BI, Faculty 1825/1; WYASL, Richmond Faculties, RD/AF/2/2, no. 7; WYASL, RDP4/131.

Armley, Leeds, Armley Chapel/St Bartholomew
Extension, 1833-4 (demolished)

Cat. 1: Armley, Leeds, Armley Chapel, largely rebuilt by Chantrell in 1833-4. The square-headed nave windows differ from the pointed ones shown in Chantrell's drawings and it is nor clear if they were subsequently altered to this form or whether Chantrell amended his earlier design. Late-nineteenth century photograph. (*Mike Collins*).

Taylor (p. 100) states that 'the church was almost entirely rebuilt in 1834-5 [this should be 1833-4] with the exception of the chancel and vestry at the east end, and in the same style as the old chapel, consisting of two parallel naves of the same size … ' On 16 May 1833 Chantrell wrote to the ICBS that it was his intention to: 'build a new north wall and fix the new line of iron pillars, take down the west wall and build up the new wall … build in the gallery … take off the old south roof and place it on the new north side than take down the south wall … rebuild the south wall and place a new roof on this part … estimated cost £1,030'. Eight days later, Benjamin Gott wrote to the ICBS 'on behalf of himself and the township of Armley' applying for a grant. He explained that the building 'was now dilapidated owing to the N and S walls being badly built and graves excavated below their foundations.' The ICBS's meeting of 17 June 1833 awarded a grant of £250, subsequently raised to £300 since John Gott promised to give an extra £100. The reopening was announced on 8 November 1834 'after rebuilding and considerable enlargement.' (*LI*). The ICBS received the certificate of completion and agreed payment at its meeting on 16 March 1835. The N wall had been moved out 13', the whole roof raised by 14' and 395 additional sittings created of which 300 were free (Gott papers). With the earlier seats, the total accommodation amounted to a staggeringly large 963 seats (Midgley).

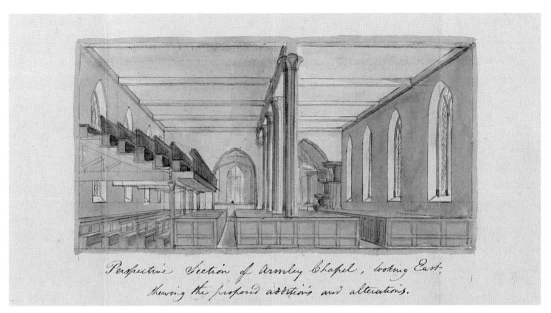

Cat. 2: Armley, Leeds, Armley Chapel. Chantrell's 1833 drawing, an unusual interior section, shows the extended nave on the right and his new north aisle and gallery on the left. (*Lambeth Palace Library*).

DRAWINGS: ICBS, file 00256.

REFERENCES: ICBS, file 00256; ICBS, MB 6, pp. 208, 220 and MB 7, p. 119; Taylor; M. Midgley (ed.) *Armley Church and Schools*, J. Hunter, 1907; UL SC, Gott Papers, 15/234; *LI,* 8 Nov. 1834.

Armley, Leeds, Armley Chapel/St Bartholomew
Extensions, 1844 (demolished)
This final involvement of Chantrell at Armley Chapel comprised a modest monument recess for John Gott. This necessitated taking out the N window of the N chancel aisle, building a three-sided recess approximately three feet deep extending N, reusing the old window in the new gable wall. It also required that the door to the vestry be moved about 6 feet further N. The scheme as set out above is shown in a drawing in the parish records (no. 131), assumed to be by Chantrell. It is accompanied by another, signed by Chantrell and dated June 1844. This shows a broadly similar plan but the sheet is dominated by a perspective drawing of tremendous virtuosity. Its low view point gives this relatively modest building a awesome quality. In it the monument recess gains an E window in the style of the two existing E windows and buttresses, the vestry acquires a new N window and double pitched roof to take on the form of a transept and, most strikingly of all, a massive tower – much in the style of the one he had recently built at Leeds Parish Church – rises from the W end to dominate the entire composition. This perspective drawing might represents nothing more than a piece of fanciful, even light-hearted speculation. There is no other indication that such a dramatic remodelling was ever contemplated.

A faculty was applied for in 1844 but the drawings for this are by R. W. Moore, Chantrell's former assistant who had recently established an independent practice. Perhaps Chantrell was too busy on grander schemes elsewhere. Moore's scheme merely repeats the simpler of the two Chantrell drawings.

Drawings from the 1870s for an entirely new church by Walker and Athron show the plan of the old chapel. They reveal the monument recess built as set out in the Chantrell/Moore designs (Parish records, 132).

DRAWINGS: WYASL, RDP4/131.

REFERENCES: BI, Faculty 1844/1; WYASL, RDP4/131 and 132.

Bakewell, Derbyshire, All Saints
Alterations, probably unexecuted, *c*.1830
All Saints is a substantial cruciform medieval church with a central tower and spire. Its dilapidated state prompted the parish to seek proposals from Francis Goodwin in 1824. He produced an elaborate scheme for rebuilding the W end which included removing the tower and building a new one at the W end (WDRO). These were not adopted, but the spire was removed in 1825 and the tower in 1830 (Combes). No doubt seeking a cheaper scheme than Goodwin's, Chantrell was approached and in *c*.1830 a design was produced for a new gallery, new or refaced columns in the nave and new windows in the three sides of the nave. The drawing is not dated but the paper is watermarked 1828. It is signed (by Chantrell) 'John Wade Clerk of Works acting for Robert Dennis Chantrell, Architect' (Wade had been Clerk of Works for Chantrell at Lockwood and Netherthong, 1828-30 and had undertaken a survey similar to Bakewell's at Almondbury in 1829).
Much of the church was rebuilt by William Flockton in 1841-52. His 'before' drawings are similar to Goodwin's 'before' drawings so it seems unlikely Chantrell's proposals were adopted. There is no record of payment to him in the parish records. However, they include a bill from Wade dated 8 May 1840 'for superintending the taking down of Bakewell Church Tower', but no date is given for the work (WDRO).

DRAWINGS: West Derbyshire Records Office, Deposit 2057A/PI/689.

REFERENCES: WDRO, Deposit 2057A/PW 227-385; I.A.H. Combes, *Anglican Churches of Derbyshire*, Landmark Publishing, 2004, pp. 24-5.

Barmby on the Moor, East Yorkshire, St Catherine
Rebuilt nave and chancel, 1850-2
On 1 February 1850, Robert Taylor – the vicar – wrote to the ICBS requesting funds. 'The church has been closed a year and a half from its dilapidated and dangerous state.' Although J.B. Atkinson of York had earlier produced the dilapidation report, it was Chantrell who was asked to supervise the repairs. He had produced a plan dated 20 November 1849 and signed the grant application that accompanied Taylor's letter. On it he notes the present church as 'late second pointed … 14th cent. … Present Accommodation: 130 in 10 square pews + Singers' Gallery'. He proposed increasing this to 287 at an estimated cost of £955. The ICBS agreed a grant of £120 at its meeting of 18 March 1850 and the board subsequently noted the completion of work and reopening on 15 April 1852.
Chantrell kept the old tower and spire, but a new undivided nave/chancel was built, along with a N vestry and S porch. The gallery was removed. He created an elaborate hammer-beam roof. Neave concludes Chantrell's work is 'conservative for its date, i.e. not yet influenced by the Ecclesiologists.' (p. 271).

DRAWING: ICBS, file 04227.

REFERENCES: ICBS, file 04227; ICBS, MB 13, p. 302, MB 14, p. 197; *Yorkshire Gazette,* 17 April 1852; N. Pevsner and D. Neave, *Yorkshire: York and the East Riding*, Penguin, 1995, p. 271.

Batley Carr, West Yorkshire, Holy Trinity
New church, 1839-41

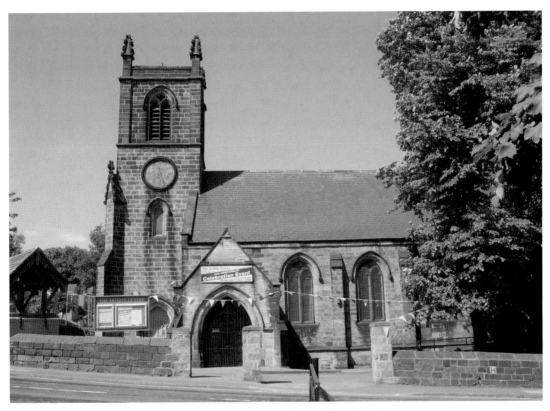

Cat. 3: Batley Carr, West Yorkshire, Holy Trinity (R.D. Chantrell, 1839-41).

The church consists of an aisleless nave with W gallery, W tower and a chancel that is exceptionally long for its date. Internally, the 'open' nave roof is unusually elaborate; the trusses are much embellished with Gothic tracery, and the connection of truss to purlin has decorative diagonal bracing. The S porch is a later addition. The distinctly Classical character of the upper stage of the tower is, no doubt, an overt reference to the mother church in Dewsbury.

The *LI*, 2 February 1839 announced that £600 had been raised for building a new church at Batley Carr in the Parish of Dewsbury. On 4 May 1839 the vicar of Dewsbury applied to the CBC for a grant towards an estimated cost of £1,750 for a church to hold 600 plus 200 children (CBC, Batley Carr file, 17831). Chantrell's association is first noted when the vicar wrote to the CBC on 23 Oct 1839 to say plans had been obtained from him. On 3 January 1840 he wrote again to say 'Mr Chantrell is preparing plans which will be forwarded to you in the next fortnight'. The CBC's printed form, signed Chantrell and Son on 7 February 1840 gives the cost as £1500, including £260 for the tower 'the church will contain 611 sittings and be in the style of the 15th century.' In the meantime, an application had also been sent to the ICBS – form signed 17 January 1840 – and on the 17 February, the ICBS offered a grant of £250, subsequently raised to £300. The drawings were discussed at the ICBS's surveyor's Committee of 7 February 1840: 'not objected to … [although] the walls could be thicker.' (ICBS Surveyor's Report Book 5, no. 87). The foundation stone was laid on 19 May 1840 and a short account of the ceremony appeared in *LI* four days later. The vicar wrote to the CBC on 25 May 1841 to confirm completion, except for painting. The CBC's certificate of completion – dated 22 Oct 1841 – gives the total cost as £2,027/15/5d 'including the land and repair fund'.

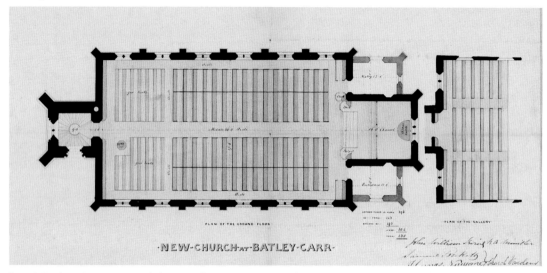

Cat. 4: Batley Carr, West Yorkshire, Holy Trinity (R.D. Chantrell, 1839-41). The west gallery is shown on the extreme right. (*Lambeth Palace Library*).

Consecration took place on 5 October 1841, an event anticipated in *LI* three days earlier. This report included: 'It has been erected from the design and under the direction of R.D. Chantrell of this town. It contains 636 sittings and has a tower … the building is Gothic of the date of Leeds Parish Church and is a neat ecclesiastical looking structure. It is said to be the best specimen of a village church [built] at a comparatively small cost … in the neighbourhood.' Taylor used this account as the basis of his own assessment; coming as it did 34 years later, when tastes had changed, it was remarkably complementary:' … a fine church. It is said to be the best specimen of a village church at a comparatively small cost erected in the neighbourhood … it is considered a much more ecclesiastical structure than most of its date.' (p. 161). Perhaps he was swayed by the progressive chancel.

DRAWINGS: ICBS, file 02590.

REFERENCES: Taylor, pp. 166-8; CBC, Batley Carr file, no. 17831; CBC, Surveyor's Report Book 5, no. 87; ICBS, file 02590; ICBS, MB 13, p. 346, MB 14, p. 255, MB 15, pp. 54, 142, 164; *LI* 2 Feb., 13 July, 8, 23 Oct. 1839, 16, 23 May 1840, 25 Sept., 2 Oct. 1841.

Birkenshaw, West Yorkshire, St Paul

Repairs, 1835

The church was built for the CBC to the designs of Atkinson and Sharp of York in 1829-30. On 7 January 1835 the incumbent wrote to the CBC to say that the building was affected by dry rot. He goes on to explain that the original floor had suffered from an earlier infestation, had been replaced at a slightly higher lever – presumably to allow better ventilation – and this second floor was now rotting. This higher floor might have been carried out by the surveyor Jeremiah Marriott of Dewsbury, but the papers are not explicit. On 26 February 1835 Chantrell submitted an estimate for 'replacing part of the floor, pews and skirting' for £195/7/0. On the same day he wrote to the CBC telling it of his successful eradication of dry rot at Rudding Park (see below) and advocating the same procedures at Birkenshaw. On 18 May 1835 he again wrote to CBC to say that the outbreak was more extensive than he anticipated and that a further £30 would be needed. His letter confirming the completion of the work is dated 30 September 1830.

REFERENCE: CBC, Cleckheaton file 15199.

Birkenshaw, West Yorkshire, St Paul
Repairs, 1840
The storm of 7 January 1839, which damaged several churches in the area including Holy Trinity, Leeds, 'blew half the slates from the roof' and brought down the spire which fell through the roof and demolished half of the west gallery.' Remarkably, the church remained in use while fundraising was organised with the congregation 'bringing umbrellas' (ICBS). On 10 February 1840, the incumbent finally applied to the ICBS which offered £50 towards Chantrell's estimated cost of £140 for repairs and a further £100 for a hot water heating system. Chantrell's undated report notes the 'upper stage of the spire was badly constructed'. The completion certificate was signed by Chantrell and others on 24 March 1841.

REFERENCES: ICBS, MB 10, p. 10, MB 10, p. 257; ICBS, file 02652.

Birstwith, near Harrogate, North Yorkshire, unidentified house
New house, 1840
Advertisements appeared in the *LI* and *LM* inviting tenders 'for a house at Birstwith to be sent to Chantrell and Son ... Plans to be seen at the house of Robert Surr at Birstwith'.
No house likely to be by Chantrell has been identified in the area.

REFERENCES: *LI,* 29 Aug. 1840; *LM,* 5 Sept. 1840.

Bramley, Leeds, Bramley Chapel
New belfry, 1821 (demolished)
The medieval chapel at Bramley was largely rebuilt in the 17th century and further extended in 1731-2 (Friedman, p. 43). 'The next alteration was made in 1821. In October John Waddingtom, chapelwarden, paid R D Chantrell £76 for taking down the old belfry upon Bramley Chapel, designing a new belfry and erecting it.' (Dobson, p. 31). It can be assumed that the £76 was the total cost of the project rather than Chantrell's fee. This belfry – in all probability Chantrell's first executed Gothic design – was an irregular octagonal in plan with four long and four shorter sides. Each of the long sides had a pointed arched opening and all eight sides had a gable. The structure was crowned by a low, 4-sided spire. By the following year the new belfry was causing problems: 'the turret, although a recent erection, is yet much out of line' (ICBS). See Bramley, 1822, below.

REFERENCES: A. Dobson, *A History of the Ancient Chapel of Bramley* ... , privately printed, 1964; ICBS, file 00413.

Bramley, Leeds, Bramley Chapel
Proposed enlargement, 1822, unexecuted
Having been asked to advise on the best ways of increasing accommodation in the Chapel, Chantrell produced a report dated 14 August 1822. In it he offered two alternatives, firstly 'an addition the whole length of the south front 10 feet 6 inches wide to accommodate 130 on the ground floor and 120 in the gallery, plus a Christening pew, total 265'. The scheme also included a small W tower, 16 feet by 8

feet and 55 feet high — crowned by the reused 1821 belfry — containing a chancel at ground level. This would have an estimated cost £1,280. Alternatively, a new church 65 feet by 42 feet, capable of holding 800 worshippers, could be built on new ground using the materials from the old chapel at an estimated cost of £1,870 (although elsewhere in the correspondence with the ICBS, Chantrell gives the cost of a new church at £3,000). Chantrell recommended a new church as the ground surrounding the existing one was 'very irregular'. An application, dated 16 August 1822, was made to the ICBS for assistance and the structural problems in the 1821 bell turret, noted above, used as evidence of the poor state of the existing structure! The Society offered a grant of £100 but sufficient funds from other sources were not forthcoming and no building work was carried out at this time.

DRAWINGS: Chantrell's suggested extension is illustrated in ICBS, file 00413.

REFERENCES: ICBS, file 00413, ICBS, MB 6, pp. 218, 224; *LI,* 13 May 1822.

Bramley, Leeds, Bramley Chapel

New church, 1824, unexecuted

Following the lack of progress with the two alternative proposals of 1822, in 1824 the chapelwardens again determined to address the accommodation problem. This time, it was the Church Building Commission that was targeted and on 9 November 1824 the Revd Humphreys, the incumbent, requested funds to build a new church capable of holding 800 worshippers, capable of being increased by a further 200. The proposal may well have been basically the same as the 'new church' alternative of 1822. Humphreys adds 'I should hope the Commissioners will determine to employ Mr Chantrell, of Leeds, as architect both because he is hereabouts regarded as conspicuous in his profession and likewise because we have given him a great deal of trouble with our projected new church for all of which I was not aware that he has ever been paid or has ever demanded a penny on which account I thought him entitled to this little notice.' The application was rejected.

REFERENCE: CBC, MB 15, pp. 113-15.

Bramley, Leeds, Bramley Chapel

New church, 1828, unexecuted

Yet another initiative for a new church — this time rather bigger than that envisaged in 1824 — was launched in 1828 with an application to the CBC. On 25 September 1828 Chantrell wrote to the Revd Humphries with advice on how best to word the application. He adds that the cost of a new church will be about the same as Kirkstall's — £3,600 for 1200 sittings (WYASL). Clearly Chantrell produced drawings for this project as an undated letter from him states 'the plan is in progress and will be ready this afternoon' (WYASL). A draft copy of the CBC Application notes 'the enclosed plan' (now no longer present) and shows the estimated cost as £3,750 for 1200 sittings (WYASL). The application was considered by the CBC at its meeting of 7 October 1828 and on 21 October the Secretary wrote to the Revd Humphries stating the Commission's inability to make a grant as funds were too low (WYASL).

REFERENCES: WYASL, RDP14/142; CBC, MB 32, p. 356.

Bramley, Leeds, Bramley Chapel

Alterations, 1833, (demolished)

Following the failure to raise sufficient funds from either the CBC or the ICBS for a new church, the chapelwardens resolved to pursue more modest ambitions and on 2 April 1833 established a building

Cat. 5: Bramley, Leeds, Bramley Chapel. Chantrell's 1833 drawing shows the small transept with gallery and organ that he added that year. (*Lambeth Palace Library*).

committee to raise funds to extend the chapel (WYASL). No doubt in anticipation of this development, on 30 March 1833 Chantrell produced a drawing showing an addition to the organ gallery situated over the altar, against the E wall, and three days later he produced two drawings for a more ambitious scheme to open up the S side of the chapel to form a transept with an organ gallery on its upper floor (ICBS).

The building committee's meeting of 18 April 1833 resolved to adopt the 'transept' scheme and proposed placing the main entrance to the chapel in the S wall of the transept (WYASL). The faculty was obtained on 1 May 1833 (ICBS) and *LI*, 4 May 1833 noted that 'a handsome subscription had been raised'. An application dated 17 June 1833 was sent to ICBS which included Chantrell's estimate of £450, comprising £280 to extend the building and £170 to repair it. The ICBS offered a grant of £100 providing the 150 extra seats, 80 of which were to be free, were included. The certificate of completion was dated 19 Oct. 1833 (ICBS) and *LI* of 2 November contained an account of the reopening which occurred on 27 October and noted that 150 extra seats had been obtained. The final cost was £582/10/0 of which Chantrell received £12/0/0 (ICBS).

The E and W walls of the extension reproduced – or perhaps reused – the simple rectangular windows found elsewhere in the chapel, but for the S wall of the transept, Chantrell produced a more sophisticated, though modest, Gothic composition of doorway with blank pointed arch above it. Crowning the gable was the troublesome 1821 bell turret which had been given an elongated spire.

The whole building was demolished in 1861 when Perkin and Backhouse's new church was consecrated, although the bell turret and spire survive in the present graveyard as a landscape feature.

DRAWINGS: ICBS, file 00413 notionally contains four drawings but three of them have, for many years, been housed at the Society of Antiquaries Library, London; WYASL, RDP14/144.

REFERENCES: ICBS, file 00413; ICBS, MB 7, pp. 23, 29; WYASL, RDP14/143, 144, 145; A. Dobson, *A History of the Ancient Chapel of Bramley,* privately printed, 1964; *LI,* 4 May, 14 Sept., 19 Oct., 26 Oct., 2 Nov. 1833, 14 April 1834.

Bramley, Leeds, Parsonage
New parsonage, 1823

Cat. 6: Bramley, Leeds, Bramley Parsonage (R.D. Chantrell, 1823).

Chantrell surveyed the old parsonage and his report refers to it as 'dilapidated ... hardly suitable for a minister' (BI). He produced a design for a new parsonage in 1823 comprising a two-storey, three-bay composition with a small service wing to one side. The central block was an orthodox, symmetrical arrangement, but the sash windows had Tudor arched tops and the front door had a Batty Langley-type Gothic surround. It cost £744 'including gate posts' (BI).
The building survives, though much altered.

DRAWINGS: BI, MGA 1823/3.

REFERENCES: BI, MGA 1823/3; *LI,* 8 May 1823.

Bruges, Belgium, Cathedral of St Saviour
Restoration following fire and new tower, 1839-47

A comprehensive account of this major project in Chantrell's career can be found in: A. Van den Abeele and C. Webster, "'A portentous Mass of Bastard Romanesque Frippery": an Early Ecclesiological Export', in *Architectural History,* 42, 1999, pp. 284-92. The following is a much-abridged version of it.

The medieval church of St Saviour – raised to cathedral status only in 1834 following various ecclesiastical suppressions and demolitions of the Napoleonic era – was badly damaged by fire on 19 July 1839. The worst of the damage occurred in the wooden roof and the wooden upper section of the Romanesque tower.

Many of Chantrell's relatives lived in Bruges and two of his brothers – William and George – had achieved

Cat. 7: Bruges, Belgium, St Saviour's Cathedral, Chantrell's 1847 drawing for his proposed completion of the west façade. (*Groeninge Museum, Bruges*).

considerable prominence in the business and social life of the city by this time. William had substantial experience in major construction and road-building projects, and he secured the commission to repair the damaged roof, despite no apparent architectural expertise. From the outset it seems William anticipated assistance from his brother in Leeds; certainly the latter was soon involved and it is known that he made several visits to supervise the project. Within a year, the roof was completed and amid general rejoicing at the speed and efficiency of the work, attention then turned to the tower. By this stage, R.D. Chantrell had certainly assumed architectural leadership. On examining it he found it to have 'remained nearly perfect to a height of 150 feet from the ground'. On it he added 'a termination of massive proportions' bringing the total height to 250 feet 'with the detailed decoration resembling the towers of Ely, Norwich, Rochester and Durham' (*LI*, 30 Oct. 1847). The choice of English Romanesque details was a curious one, but it was selected in preference to several locally produced Gothic schemes (Devliegher). Work on the tower occupied 1843-6. In October 1847, Chantrell had a design 'in the course of preparation' from which 'the west end [i.e. the W ends of the aisles] is about to be completed' (*LI*, 30 Oct. 1847), but nothing of this scheme was carried out.

DRAWINGS: State Archives of Bruges: Archives of the Province of West Flanders, 3rd Division, file 1242; Groeningemuseum, Bruges, Steinmets Cabinet, 0.2662.II. The three drawings are catalogued as nos 605, 606 and 607.

REFERENCES: A. Van den Abeele and C. Webster, *op. cit.*; A. Van den Abeele, 'Entrepreneurs brugeois au XIX siecle: George et William Chantrell' in *Bulletin Trimestriel du credit Communal de Belgique*, 146, Oct. 1983; L. Devliegher, 'De Restauratie van de Toren' in *In de Steigers*, 1, Sept. 1994, pp. 13-16; W. Papworth, *Dictionary of Architecture*, London, 1852-92, p. 157; Diocese of Bruges, Cathedral Archives, *Resolutions of Church-Wardens*, 5/10/1840-32/12/1850 [specifically 7 July 1840]; F. Koller, *Anneraire des Familles Patriciennes de Belgigne*, Bruxelles, 1941, vol. 2, p. 70; State Archives of Bruges, Archives of the Province of West Flanders, 3rd Division, file nos. 385, 1242, 1243; C. Van de Velde, *Stedelijke Musea Brugge, Steinmetzkabinet, Catalogue ven des tekeningen*, Bruges, 1984, p. 47; J.-L. Meulemeester, 'Een Onbekende Ontwerptekening voor de Westgevel van de Brugse Sint-Salvatorskathedraal' in *Biekorf*, 1984, 2, pp. 156-9; *Ecclesiologist*, 11, 1850, p. 174; *LI*, 30 Oct. 1847.

Chapel Allerton, Leeds, Chapel Allerton Chapel/St Matthew

Alterations, 1839-41

This chapel, of 1737, was in an unsophisticated Classical style with round-topped windows and a Gibbs surround to the entrance.

The first meeting of the committee for enlarging the chapel was on 15 March 1839 when it was resolved 'that Mr Chantrell's plan for procuring additional accommodation by erecting a gallery on the south side and raising the roof at an estimated expense of £500 appears desirable to be erected' (Parish Papers, 73). The faculty noted the alterations would produce nearly 150 extra sittings. Tenders exceeded the estimate and on 8 April 1839 the committee requested Chantrell 'to check the specification and ascertain in what items the difference chiefly consisted'. Eventually, on 24 April 1839 the Committee 'adopted … Chantrell's plans'. *LI* of 4 January 1840 announced 'the extensive improvements and enlargements … are now nearly complete … the chapel will open tomorrow week'. Printed accounts of 21 May 1841 record the total cost as £1,082/5/5 including £39/6/6 architect's commission.

DRAWING: BI, Faculty 1839/1; WYASL, RDP19/88/3.

REFERENCES: WYASL, RDP19/73 and 127; *LI*, 21 May 1841.

Cleckheaton, West Yorkshire, St John

Repairs, 1840

This Gothic church, financed in part by the CBC, was built to the designs of Atkinson and Sharp of York in 1830-1.

A storm on 9 January 1839 resulted in the top 9 feet of the spire being dislodged, much of it falling through the roof. On 7 November that year, the incumbent wrote to the CBC to inform it that the church was affected by dry rot. Chantrell produced a report dated 29 February 1840, but this is exclusively concerned with the spire. In it he states the original construction was faulty, especially the iron bar meant to hold the top-most section in place. On 3 March 1840, he informed the CBC that tenders for the necessary work amounted to £127/0/0 plus 10% architect's commission. He does not state whether these concerned the spire, dry rot or both. The Commissioners' meeting of 10 November 1840 noted the completion of work.

REFERENCES: CBC, Cleckheaton file 15199; CBC, MB 52, p. 297.

Cowling, near Skipton, North Yorkshire, Holy Trinity
New Church, 1839-45

The finished building consisted of a low nave, without clerestory, double-pitched N and S aisles, W tower, chancel and a vestry. There was a W gallery. The pinnacles of the tower were damaged in a storm in 1894 and the upper section of the tower was subsequently rebuilt to a slightly higher level incorporating a clock. Although the vicar of Kildwick, in whose parish Cowling was situated, first applied to the CBC in 1825 with a design perhaps by William Bradley of Halifax, it was not until 26 April 1836 that he wrote again to thank the commissioners for their offer. His letter continues 'will you furnish a plan or would you

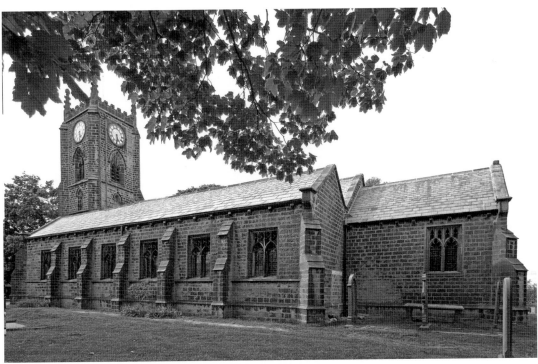

Cat. 8: Cowling, North Yorkshire, Holy Trinity (R.D. Chantrell, 1839-45). (*Roger Hatfield*).

wish me to apply to Mr Chantrell of Leeds, or to some other architect?' (Cowling is an isolated Pennine community about 10 miles from Skipton – the closest substantial town – where Chantrell was at this time designing Christ Church). The Ripon Diocesan Church Building Society offered a grant of £250 towards an estimated requirement of £1,400 (*LI*, 5 Oct. 1839), but early the next year the vicar was still unable to begin work. He applied to the ICBS and its meeting of 27 April resolved to grant £250 for a church with 500 sittings, 300 of which were to be free. Not until 1 February 1842 was he able to tell the CBC that Chantrell 'is now preparing the plans' and 25 days later told the commission the money had been raised and a new and better piece of land obtained. He wrote on 21 June 1842 that 'estimates … were under consideration', but only on 11 February 1843 did *LI* invite tenders in the name of Chantrell and Shaw. Clearly funds remained tight and the vicar wrote again to the ICBS requesting permission to omit the

W gallery to save £100; the ICBS meeting of 18 March 1844 refused. The foundation stone was laid on 25 May 1844 and the CBC's completion certificate was signed by J.B. Chantrell on 20 September 1845. This gives the style as '15th century' and states 533 seats were provided at a cost of £1,908/8/7 including architect's commission of £106/19/7. The ICBS's certificate of completion was received at the meeting of 17 November 1845 and records that all 500 sittings were free. One wonders how the two certificates could reveal a difference of 33 seats.

REFERENCES: CBC, Cowling file, 15542; ICBS, MB 10, p. 24, MB 12, p. 35, 47, 222, 227; *LI,* 5 Oct. 1839, 11 Feb., 9 Sept. 1843.

Denholme Gate, West Yorkshire, St Paul
New church, 1843–6

The church is Early English in style and consists of nave with clerestory, aisles and W gallery, a substantial chancel with five steps to the altar and stalls at either side, W tower with generous spire. The nave and chancel have impressive vaulted ceilings of wood and plaster. It is the writer's belief that Chantrell was the designer, although perhaps not the superintendent of this project.

The earliest document in this project is a request to the CBC for a grant application form dated 12 July 1842. This produced £500 and the Ripon Diocesan Church Building Society also made an unspecified grant, reported in the *LI* of 5 November 1842. An application was also made to the ICBS, discussed at its meeting of 3 July 1843 which produced a grant of £200 for a church to hold 624 including 543 free seats. The CBC's form of enquiry, signed 10 May 1843, notes an estimated cost of £2,181/6/3 for a church to hold 643 worshippers, suggesting the design was produced early in 1843. Tenders were advertised – to be returned to Chantrell and Shaw – in *LI* of 2 September 1843 and the CBC's certificate of completion was signed by J.B. Chantrell on 24 December 1846. The latter gives the cost as £3,700 for 704 seats, although the accounts in the CBC file suggest a cost of £4,169, including 'J.B. Chantrell, architect: £147/19/9, Messrs Chantrell and Shaw, architects: £3/3/0, Messrs Chantrell [probably H.W. Chantrell] and Burrell, clerks of works: £29/16/0'. The ICBS's certificate of completion was not dated until 19 February 1847. Signatories included 'J.B. Chantrell, late Chantrell and Shaw, architect'. *The Ecclesiologist* lists the architect as 'Mr John Chantrell jun.'; it was not at all impressed with the church. Thus far, R.D. Chantrell's involvement is questionable. However, there are two interesting letters in the ICBS file. The first, from H.B. Bennett of Halifax, perhaps the secretary of the local committee, who signed many letters for the project, is dated 27 March 1847. It refers to some confusion over who should have signed the certificate of completion as architect and states, 'Sir, the Certificate you returned to Mr Chantrell (who is not the architect of this church, but his son Mr J.B. Chantrell of Leeds) has not reached the Committee … ' Sadly, the wording is not helpful to us. Less ambiguous is a letter from R.D. Chantrell to the ICBS dated 19 March 1847. 'Sir, I beg to return to you the Plan and Papers for Denholm Gate Church for which I made the design only for Messrs Chantrell and Shaw of Leeds, but I observe that the plan is signed by Mr John Chantrell of Leeds … ' It would seem clear, then, that the design was RDC's but the execution was not. Whether he was annoyed that JBC had signed the plan rather than it being given to himself, is also ambiguous.

DRAWINGS: ICBS, file 03257 [signed by J.B. Chantrell].

REFERENCES: CBC, Denholme file, no. 15573; ICBS, file 03257; ICBS, MB 11, MB 12, p. 357; *LI,* 5 Nov. 1842, 2, 9 Sept. 1843; *Ecclesiologist,* 11, 1850, pp. 143–4.

Dewsbury, West Yorkshire, All Saints
Designed monument to Mrs Allbutt, 1843

The *LI,* 23 September 1843 noted 'A very chaste and elegant marble monument in the Early English style was placed in the Parish Church of Dewsbury to the memory of the late Mrs Abbutt (sic). The monument has been executed by Mr D. Wilson of Leeds from a design by R.D. Chantrell, Esq.' Mrs Allbutt was the wife of the Revd Thomas Allbutt, vicar of Dewsbury 1835-52, for whom Chantrell had undertaken several school and church commissions. The monument, a modest Gothic composition in dark and light marble, survives in the SW corner of the nave. It records Marianna Allbutt who died in 1843, aged 41.

REFERENCE: *LI,* 23 Sept. 1843.

Dewsbury, West Yorkshire, National School

New school, 1842-3

The *LI,* 10 September 1842 requested tenders for 'the Church of England School at Dewsbury … to be sent to Chantrell and Shaw'. The edition of 8 October 1842 announced the completed building would be '105 feet by 30 feet … [it will be a] very handsome Gothic structure'. It added that the cost was estimated at £1,100 and it was designed by 'Messrs D. Chantrell and Shaw'. The building's date stone records its erection in 1843. The building, situated off Daisy Hill, survives as the Howland Centre for the Disabled.

REFERENCES: *LI,* 10 Sept., 8 Oct. 1842.

Dewsbury, West Yorkshire, St John, Dewsbury Moor

Repairs, 1839-40

The church was built to the designs of Thomas Taylor in 1823-7.

Benjamin Healey, a surveyor, produced a report dated 2 June 1838 on the outbreak of dry rot in the floor (CBC). This seems not to have been acted on immediately. Then, on 7 January 1839, the storm brought down three of the tower's pinnacles, one of which fell through the nave roof and the other through the tower floor. The documentation then becomes confusing but it seems an application was made to the CBC for a grant for the dry rot repairs and an enquiry was sent to the ICBS for the tower repairs, although

Cat. 9: Dewsbury, West Yorkshire, Dewsbury Moor vicarage (R.D. Chantrell, 1840).

the two documents include almost identical sums. In April 1839, Chantrell obtained estimates amounting to £277/10/0 for the necessary repairs for the CBC application, which makes no mention of the tower; the vicar wrote to the CBC on 27 April 1840 anxious for work to begin on Chantrell's proposals 'for repairing and re-arranging the interior'. Chantrell signed the CBC certificate of completion on 21 August 1840. For the ICBS's enquiry, which mentions only the roof, Chantrell's estimate was £275. It seems a formal application to the ICBS was not made. It is possible that the CBC filing system confused this church with Dewsbury, Earlsheaton (see below).

REFERENCES: CBC, Dewsbury file, no. 18258; ICBS, file 02709.

Dewsbury, West Yorkshire, St John, Dewsbury Moor, Vicarage

New vicarage, 1840-1

The new vicarage was paid for by the Queen's Anne Bounty. The drawings are dated October 1840 and the contractor, Thomas Healey of Dewsbury, agreed to have the building finished 'on or before 1st July 1841' for the sum of £840. The building was in a free Tudor style, with a shaped gable in the centre of the principal, symmetrical, two-storey façade.

DRAWINGS: WYASL, 555/9.

REFERENCE: WYASL, 555/9.

Dewsbury, West Yorkshire, St Peter, Earlsheaton

Repairs, 1840

The church was built in 1825-7 to the designs of Thomas Taylor.
A CBC Minute Book includes a 'Statement' written by Chantrell and read at the Commissioners' meeting on 10 November 1840 'of sums of money due to the undermentioned persons for several works' which are assumed to have been repairs. These amount to about £275 plus £21/19/0 for Chantrell. (See Dewsbury Moor church, above).

REFERENCE: CBC, MB 52, p. 298.

East Ardsley, West Yorkshire, St Michael

Report on old church and designs for new one, unexecuted, 1843-7

The churchwardens' accounts note a payment on 26 May 1843 'To the expenses of Mr Chantrell for examining the church: £-/10/-' (WDP 16). His report contained: 'The whole of the chancel walls are in a dilapidated state and will not admit of any repair. The south wall of the nave is very unsafe. The north aisle has been rebuilt but without character … ' (ICBS). The following year, the *Intelligencer* announced – somewhat optimistically as it turned out – that the church was 'intended to be rebuilt. The plans of the new structure, which will be on a larger scale than the old one are designed by Mr Chantrell'. However, it was not until 1845 that applications for grants were submitted to the CBC and ICBS. The former was rejected at the Commissioners' meeting of 10 June 1845 (CBC) but the latter secured a grant of £200 (ICBS). The intended new church would have accommodated 450 (old church 207) at an estimated cost of £1,700. A full set of plans must have been produced as they were examined by the ICBS's surveyor on 12 May 1845 who 'saw no objection to them'. Perhaps an amended scheme was conceived as on 29 May 1847, the vicar told the ICBS that 'plans, 6 in number, are to be sent with the free seats marked on them'. Finally, he wrote again on 29 October 1850 to say that insufficient funds had precluded further developments.

REFERENCES: ICBS, MB 12, p. 197; ICBS, file 03455; CBC, MB 60, p. 115; Churchwardens' Accounts WYASW, WDP16/5/2; *LI,* 13 July 1844.

Fangfoss, East Yorkshire, St Martin
Rebuilt church, *c.*1849-50
The dilapidated Norman church was rebuilt 'strictly [in] the Anglo Norman style' comprising of nave and chancel with a small W tower with a stone pyramid roof.

Chantrell must have acquired the commission *via* his work for the ICBS and although his report does not survive (but see below), there is an attractive watercolour perspective by him of the old church in its picturesque, dilapidated state. The Revd Wood-Rees, writing in 1913, notes, 'The restoration was entrusted to Mr Chantrell a well-known London architect of that time who, in his initial Report, observes "Fangfoss is perhaps the most interesting building to the antiquarian that can be found in the County and it has so much beautiful carved material in a perfect state that I should be glad to undertake its restoration. Fangfoss has once been a gem of Norman architecture." ... A report by the Revd Robert Taylor who commissioned Chantrell says, "Chantrell discovered a *vesica piscis* (a fish's bladder) which he states is an ancient symbol of Christianity. We also found the master mason's private mark ... Chantrell, in his rapture, declared these last to be of great value."'

An application 'for rebuilding' was submitted to the ICBS dated 12 January 1849, to which is added, 'Plan to be sent by Mr Chantrell 5 March 1849'. It estimates the costs at £871 plus architect's commission, plus clerk of works, £87, total £958. The application was considered at the ICBS meeting of 19 March 1849 when a grant of £80 was offered providing 98 new seats were added to the previous total of 84. The certificate of completion was attached to a letter from the vicar dated 17 August 1850, 'The Church was much admired by the Clergy and Gentry present att the opening ... The total cost was £863 ... sufficient old carved stone was found to form the arches of the portal ... ' The certificate is signed by Chantrell and others.

A detailed account of the new church, probably written by Chantrell, appeared in the *Yorkshire Gazette* and was reprinted in the *Architect and Builders' Gazette.*

DRAWINGS: ICBS, file 04114.

REFERENCES: ICBS, MB 13, p. 193, MB 14, p. 4; ICBS, file 04114; BI, faculty papers; *Yorkshire Gazette,* 14 Oct. 1848, 10 Aug. 1850; W.D. Wood-Rees, 'Fangfoss Church' in *Yorkshire Archaeological Journal,* 22, 1913, pp. 253-5; *Architect and Builders' Gazette,* 24 Aug. 1850, pp. 399-400.

Farnley Tyas, West Yorkshire, St Lucius
New church, 1838-40
This small village church has a nave, chancel and W tower with spire. The majority of windows in this low walled church are three-light, square-headed ones with simple Perpendicular tracery.

This new church in the parish of Almondbury was the result of 'the liberality of the Earl of Dartmouth' who not only was to finance the building but also 'keep [it] in repair and endow [it].' (*LI,* 19 May 1838). Tenders were advertised on 3 March 1838 (*LI*), the foundation stone was laid by the vicar 'before an assembly of 5,000 people' on 11 May 1838 (*LI,* 19 May 1838), and was consecrated on 28 March 1840 (*LI,* 4 April 1840).

REFERENCES: *LI,* 3 March, 19 May 1838, 4 April 1840.

Frodingham, Lincolnshire, St Lawrence

Rebuilt church, 1840-2

Chantrell rebuilt the dilapidated medieval church which, in 1913, was enlarged by Sir Charles Nicholson who added a very substantial N extension. Much of Chantrell's work survives on the S side.

Correspondence starts in May 1840 when the incumbent, the Revd Sheffield, wrote to Charles Winn on Nostell Priory, West Yorkshire – who, as rector, was responsible for the maintenance of the chancel – reporting the decayed state of the church. He informed Winn that the town intended to repair the nave, adding casually, would you like our tradesmen to repair the chancel for you, or 'do you prefer to undertake the work yourself?' It was an ominous start to what should have been a straightforward project. Chantrell's initial estimate of 19 June 1840 gave the cost of the nave repairs as £697/15/- and those for the chancel as £227/10/-. Two days later Winn decided to undertake the chancel with his own team and asked for two separate reports from Chantrell. Winn wrote to Chantrell on 5 August confirming his appointment. On 8 November 1840 Chantrell wrote to Winn to say he had sent over a complete set of plans and specifications, and would be visiting again to discuss estimates with the workmen.

What followed was probably one of Chantrell's most frustrating commissions, from the beginning beset with problems caused by having two patrons, two sets of plans for different parts of the building and two sets of workmen meeting at the chancel arch. Initially time was lost in sending drawings – each apparently of little use without the corresponding set – on long journeys seeking the approval of all concerned for a faculty. On 1 February 1841, Chantrell wrote to Sheffield asking him to try to persuade Winn to use the same contractors, but to no avail. The problem was highlighted in a letter from Chantrell to Winn of 20 May 1841: the chancel arch, for which neither set of tradesmen had assumed responsibility, had fallen. Chantrell was anxious to get the two groups of workmen together so that a joint strategy could be evolved, 'it is desirous that the two parts should proceed together'. Worse was to come. The rebuilt chancel arch was both wider and higher than Chantrell had specified. However, rather than 'making the contractors rebuild the arch agreeable to the intended plan', Chantrell apparently allowed it to remain, necessitating changes to the form and pitch of the roofs, changes which reached only one set of contractors! Fudging the join of the two roofs led to further problems and appears to have caused much ill feeling between the parishioners and 'the gentleman from Leeds'. Only in December was Chantrell stating that he had 'written to the parties to find the exact dimensions of the arch and pillars ... which I will have put right'. Chantrell suggested oak be used in the chancel which appears to have been adopted. It seems to have been completed by April 1842 when Sheffield confirmed his overall approval. Winn and Chantrell also seem to have parted on good terms as Winn sought Chantrell's advice on professional matters ten years later.

Coming at a time when Chantrell was already heavily engaged elsewhere, especially at Leeds Parish Church, and in settling his father's estate in Bruges, perhaps the project received rather less attention that it should have. Furthermore, the correspondence makes it clear that the unnamed Clerk of Works was not present all the time, and Frodingham was not easy to reach from Leeds. But the project also reveals all too clearly the minefield produced by a system of church maintenance in which different sections of a church are the responsibility of different parties.

REFERENCE: WYASL, 1352/A/1/8/8.

Glossop, Derbyshire, All Saints

Rebuilding of nave and repairs, 1827-32

Following Chantrell's appointment to for the new church at New Mills, Derbyshire, in the Parish of Glossop, he was soon asked to advise on the state of its parish church. His report of 19 June 1827 notes: 'the tower, chancel and remains of the pillars and arches at the west end of the building are of Early English character ... with additions in the 16th and 17th centuries ... the building has been taken down and rebuilt most injudiciously and is in very bad taste; there are 6 cast iron columns on each side which support the new roof … wall piers are not lined up with columns … cost of rendering the building perfect, including taking down the window piers to the cills and making other such alterations as are indispensable, £1,348.' (ICBS). The 'injudicious rebuilding' Chantrell referred to had been undertaken by Edward Drury of Sheffield only a few years earlier. The parish applied to the ICBS on 29 June 1827 and the following day the vicar wrote to the bishop of Lichfield to say 'the plans were laid before the vestry and [were] highly approved.' (ICBS).

Chantrell's drawings of 12 June 1827 show his intention to rebuild the N and S walls to enable the piers to line up with the columns supporting the gallery and roof. During the operation, the gallery and roof were to remain undisturbed. Presumably from a lack of funds, it was not possible to order the commencement of work until 'the close of 1830'(ICBS) and the foundation stone was laid in May 1831 (Churchwardens' Accounts). The certificate of completion was signed on 6 November 1832 (ICBS). Chantrell was paid £101/3/0 in 1832 having been paid £15/15/0 a year earlier 'for plans and report … 1827.' (ICBS). Unusually, Chantrell produced a report at the end of the project dated 6 November 1832. In it he notes ' the gallery is as first designed, but the ground floor is a new design … the chancel is about to be taken down and rebuilt', although the chancel seems to have survived into the early 20th century before being renewed.

DRAWINGS: ICBS, file 00456.

REFERENCES: ICBS, MB 2, pp. 102, 117, MB 4, p. 38, MB 6, pp. 162, 179; ICBS, file 00456; Churchwardens' Accounts, Derbyshire County Records Office, D2448 A/PW 2.

Golcar, West Yorkshire, St John the Evangelist
Repairs, 1842-4

The church was built to the designs of Peter Atkinson of York in 1828-9. A short account of subsequent events provides a useful context for Chantrell's work. According to the incumbent, the 'church never dried out after being built – it was always damp. Rain comes through the steeple, steeple floor and the frame of the bell was rotten soon after the church was erected.' (CBC). These defects might explain why the spire was blown down, part of it coming through the roof and damaging the galleries, in December 1833 (*LI*, 28 Dec. 1933). It was repaired under the direction of Pickersgill and Oates of York (*LI*, 5 July 1834). In February 1835 the church was again 'considerably damaged' by a storm (*LI*, 14 Feb. 1835) and repaired by an unknown architect. Pritchett of York was consulted about repairs (CBC). Nevertheless, by 1842 it was 'very dilapidated, owing to the faulty construction of the roof' (ICBS). Chantrell examined the church on 14 December 1842 and deduced that the problems arose from the pitch of the roof being too low and there being insufficient overlap in the Westmorland slates. Water penetrated the roof and many of the timbers had rotted. It 'is in so dangerous a state that it may be destroyed by the first high wind.' He advised building a new roof and re-pointing much of the stonework (ICBS). The ICBS initially turned down the application – presumably as no more seats would be provided – but following the intervention of the bishop of Ripon, £50 was offered on 3 July 1843. A CBC meeting later that month also approved the repairs 'under the direction of Chantrell and Son'. The completion certificate was signed by Chantrell and Shaw, and others, and was dated 21 August 1844 (CBC). J.B. Chantrell signed the accounts for the CBC dated 16 November 1844. They show the total cost as £360/11/11, plus £31/12/0 architects' commission.

REFERENCES: CBC, MB 11, pp. 263, 311, 341, MB 57, p. 158, MB 59, p. 155; CBC, Golcar File, 26725; ICBS, file 03196.

Guiseley, West Yorkshire, St Oswald
Alterations, 1830–33

The first church was built in the 12th century and had undergone various phases of rebuilding and enlargement in the medieval period.

Following a number of earlier meetings about the accommodation in the church, on 22 October 1830 the parishioners resolved that 'Mr Chantrell be instructed to give an estimate for repairing the church … on the following plan: the church floor to be levelled, the pulpit moved to the centre of the transept, pews to occupy the whole of the middle aisle as far as the west window, [more details of re-arrangement of pews] … Mr Chantrell give a valuation of all the materials of the present pews … ' (WYASB). On 19 January 1831 the wardens were authorised to proceed with the plan 'with the exception of the suggested woodwork in the tower.' (WYASB). A faculty was applied for 26 November 1831 (BI) and on 26 March 1832, the wardens resolved to let the work, with Chantrell employed to supervise the project (WYASB). Although tradesmen were appointed, probably before work commenced a grander scheme was envisaged and on 4 July 1832 an application was made to the ICBS for a grant to: 'widen the church, erect a gallery on the north side, rebuild the north wall and other repairs' as well as 'repewing on a more commodious plan [and] occupying the centre aisle with pews.' (ICBS). Chantrell described the church as 'very dilapidated … the north wall is badly inclined' and estimated the costs at £998 (ICBS). His drawings reveal a scheme which would have replaced the irregular and inelegant N wall with a new one, somewhat to the N of the old one, with four new Decorated ones to harmonise with the details of the tower. Chantrell's drawings reveal a design that was both elegant and convincingly medieval, his most sophisticated restoration to date. The N arcade of three arches was to be demolished and replaced by a new higher one of four arches– to accommodate the proposed N gallery – to correspond to the four bays of the existing S wall and the four bays of the new N wall (ICBS). However, there was much concern in the parish about the higher costs of this more extensive scheme and on 30 July 1832, the wardens resolved that, unless the vicar could confirm that the parish's rate-payers would not be responsible for the extra costs, the second scheme was to be abandoned and the 'plan of repewing originally agreed upon be forthwith proceeded with.' (WYASB). Since the vicar could offer no such reassurance, the original repewing scheme was then undertaken, modified slightly by the removal of some of the ceiling and the taking down the W gallery thereby 'throwing open' the W window and 'much improving the church both in light and beauty.' (ICBS). The total cost was £550 including £137 for the organ and £60 'expenses of Mr Chantrell and obtaining the Faculty.' (ICBS). As if to confirm Chantrell's assessment, 'In the 1850s, the north wall gave way and had to be rebuilt.' (Dobson and Rawnsley, p. 4).

DRAWINGS: BI, Faculty, 1833/1; ICBS, file 01472.

REFERENCES: A. Dobson and R.G. Rawnsley, *The Church of St Oswald*, privately printed, 1971; ICBS, file 01472, ICBS, MB 6, pp. 144, 160; Churchwardens' Accounts, WYASB, BDP29/102.

Halifax, King Cross Church
Survey and report, 1826

At its meeting of 21 October 1828, the CBC discussed the viability of acquiring the lately erected church at King Cross and making it available for Anglican worship. It noted that Chantrell had examined the tower and spire and pronounced them sound. His report is dated 30 November 1826 (CBC). Was this the 'Christ Church near King Cross' built independently by the Revd Jonathan Ackroyd in 1826 and eventually sold to the Wesleyans in 1842 for £900 (White) and/or the 'new church at King Cross' whose opening was noted in *LI* of 4 January 1827?

REFERENCES: CBC, MB 32, pp. 422-3; W. White, *Directory and Gazetteer of Leeds, Bradford … William White*, 1853, p. 685; *LI,* 4 Jan. 1827.

Halifax, St John
Repairs, 1818-20

St John is the substantial late-medieval parish church of Halifax.

Writing about Gothic architecture in 1847, Chantrell stated: 'In the year 1818 in restoring the parapet and pinnacles of the parish church of Halifax, I copied the half decayed fragments which remained, and this my first attempt, is more satisfactory than any Gothic work I designed, till within the last five years.' (*Builder*). In 1818 Chantrell was working as an assistant to William Bradley of Halifax. The churchwardens' accounts record numerous payment to Bradley for work in connection with the tower from 1818 to 27 January 1820 when he was paid £5/1/7 'in full' for the steeple' and does not appear again in the accounts. Since Chantrell was not a principal of the firm, it is to be expected that he would not be named in the accounts. However, on 25 March 1820 – two months after Bradley was paid 'in full', the Accounts record that Chantrell was paid £3/10/0 'for plans etc'. Whether or not this was for work on the tower is not clear.

REFERENCES: Churchwardens Accounts, 1760-1832, WYASW, WDP53/7/1/6.

Halifax, St Paul, King Cross
New church, 1844 (or perhaps 1840)-7

Early in 1840, the Ripon Diocesan Society for Church Building gave £300 for a new church at King Cross estimated to cost £2000 (*LI,* 28 March 1840), but it was more than four years before the vicar of Halifax applied to the CBC and ICBS for further funds. The CBC application form, dated 17 July 1844, notes an estimated cost of £2,030 for 586 seats as does the ICBS's dated a day earlier. The CBC discussed the application at its meeting of 21 July 1844 noting that plans were included. The CBC architect's form records the style as 'Gothic of the 13th century', length 139 feet, tower 63 feet plus 54 feet for the spire, 596 seats and a cost of £2,031. It is signed 'Chantrell and Shaw'. Amended plans were sent to the CBC on 7 August which included a modified roof construction, presumably following criticism of the initial one. Tenders were advertised in the *LI* of 31 August 1844.

In February 1845, during construction, the partnership between J.B. Chantrell and Shaw was dissolved, apparently because of 'Shaw's blunders'. A few days later, Chantrell wrote to the CBC; among other things, the letter claims authorship for Chantrell senior: 'In consequence of the several alterations made by Shaw and his setting all plans and specifications at nought, my son John has separated from him and I am examining all their works (as many as those which I entrusted to them) and rectifying the blunders committed by Shaw; I find that the drawings and specifications (copies) given by Shaw to the contractors for King Cross Church, Halifax, (while I was in London and my son was on the Continent to be at variance with my original designs that I shall be obliged by your allowing me to have those sealed by HM Commissioners for a few days to enable me to see what the difference is and to correct those copies and I will return them to you; I have arranged to have a Clerk of Works [the reliable John Wade] to sort out Halifax Church with the masons and to superintend them, as I find that Shaw had told the [local] committee that no clerk of works was necessary.'

As the church neared completion, Chantrell twice wrote to the local committee about a decorative scheme for the E end. 'The reveals of the windows should be coloured light blue … I would like to see it carried out with scrolls and scriptural texts as at Rise and Leven and other churches, and which would give a beautiful finish to the chancel' A few days letter a second letter included, 'the letters should all be capitals and coloured red. They are the Novissima Monachalis of the 12th century [taken to mean 'the latest monastic fashion of the 12th c.'] and are found at [various ancient churches]'. It is not clear if the decoration was completed (WYASW).

The church was consecrated on 26 April 1847 (*LI*, 24 April 1847) although the edition of the following week gives the date as 28 April. This edition continues: 'The style of the fabric is Early English and Mr Chantrell is the architect. It contains 600 free seats ... the exterior is handsome with a neat east window by Williamson [Willement] of London.' A lengthy description, probably by Chantrell, appeared in *LI* of 8 May 1847. The CBC certificate of completion gives the accommodation as 635 and the cost £3,650. However, the account for the remission of duties in the CBC gives the cost as £4,681/4/7 plus architect's commission.

DRAWINGS: ICBS, file 03474; WYASW, WDP72/60 (for decoration).

REFERENCES: WYASW, WDP72/60; ICBS, MB 12, p. 131, MB 13, p. 24; ICBS, file 03474; CBC, MB 58, p. 484; CBC, Halifax, St Paul, file 16867; *LI*, 28 March 1840, 31 Aug. 1844, 24 April 1847, 1, 8 May 1847; *Builder*, 5, 1847, p. 300; *Civil Engineer and Architect's Journal*, April 1846, p. 100.

Harrogate, Bath House for the Poor

New baths, 1821, unexecuted

The Harrogate Baths Charity was started on 7 October 1818 with Montague Burgoyn as its chairman (*LI*, 26 Oct. 1818). On 3 September 1821 the *Intelligencer* reported that: 'at a meeting of the subscribers ... on 31 Aug, the Earl of Harewood in the chair, it was resolved that it would be expedient to erect Baths for the separated use of the poor resorting to Harrogate ... Mr Chantrell having produced a plan and estimate of the building which seems to be generally approved is desired to submit it to the next meeting ... ' There were various reported attempts to raise money for this charity over the next few years, but eventually the project was abandoned and the money raised diverted to the Harrogate Hospital Charity (*LI*, 7 April 1825) which opened on 6 April 1826 (*LI*, 30 March 1826), but was designed by Samuel Chapman.

REFERENCES: *LI*, 3 Sept. 1821.

Headingley, Leeds, St Michael

New church, 1836-8

The completed building had a narrow aisleless nave with W gallery, chancel, W tower with spire and, unusually, N and S transepts. Also usual was a semi-circular stair to the gallery housed in a canted bay extending from the N wall. The chancel appears to have been built on the old foundations, as was the easternmost part of the nave. The long chancel should not be seen as prophetic of ecclesiology; it housed large box pews facing W to the three-decker pulpit. The building was demolished in 1884.

Probably in the middle of 1836, Chantrell surveyed the old Headingley Chapel and produced designs for a bigger replacement. On 28 November 1836 the building committee resolved 'that Mr Chantrell be appointed architect and that the plan submitted by him ... be adopted'. It wanted the new church to have 600 places, with sufficient height to add galleries later if required (WYASL). The *LI* of 3 December 1836 was able to report that: 'the proposition to erect a new church in the township [of Headingley] has been so warmly supported that the estimated cost of £2,000 has been nearly raised by voluntary subscription and the work will be forthwith commenced.' Dated 14 December 1836, Chantrell produced an additional plan and a report on the old church to accompany the faculty which was dispatched five days later. He found the old chapel 'much decayed' and suggested building a new structure using some of the old materials rather than trying to repair the old one (BI, Faculty 1836/3). The following April 'workmen began to unroof the Episcopal Chapel at Headingley preparatory to the erection of a more spacious edifice on the site' (*LI*, 8 April 1837), and the foundation stone was laid on 19 April (*LI*, 22 April 1837). It was opened on 31 January 1838 and a full account of the dedication service appeared in *LI* three days later. The initial estimated cost was £2,020 according to the faculty, the work was let for £2,307/6/0 and the final cost was

£2,510/9/6 including extras (WYASL). Chantrell's fee was £118/5/0 but he waived half of this making him one of the principal subscribers (*ibid.*).

DRAWINGS: BI, Faculty 1836/3; WYASL, RDP39/86.

Cat. 10: Hemsworth, West Yorkshire, St Helen, one of Chantrell's 1842 drawings for the restoration of the chancel. (*WYASW*).

REFERENCES: ICBS, file 02091; WYASL, RDP39/67, 84 and 86; BI, Faculty 1836/3; *LI*, 3 Dec. 1836, 8, 22 April 1837, 13, 27 Jan., 3, 10 Feb. 1838.

Headingley, Leeds, unidentified house
New house, 1842

The *LI* of 25 June 1842 advertised for tenders 'for a house in Headingley' to be sent to Chantrell and Shaw. The house has not been identified.

REFERENCE: *LI*, 25 June 1842.

Heckmondwyke, West Yorkshire, St James
Repairs, 1840

The church was built to the designs of Atkinson and Sharp in 1830-1. On 11 June 1840 Chantrell produced a report: 'I find the church affected by Dry Rot like Cleckheaton and Birkenshaw due to insufficient ventilation … the estimated cost of repairs is £167/12/9'. The report goes on to suggest alterations to the internal layout for a further £10. It is signed in the names of R.D. Chantrell and J.B. Chantrell in JBC's hand. The certificate of completion was signed by RDC on 22 August 1840 (CBC).

REFERENCE: CBC, Cleckheaton file, no. 15199.

Hemsworth, West Yorkshire, St Helen
Repairs to chancel, 1842, possible unexecuted

A seating plan of 1811 by Thomas Billington of Wakefield has, sketched over it, proposed alterations of 1842, signed 'C&S', taken to mean Chantrell and Shaw. The parish records also include a series of sketches for the rearrangement of the chancel and roof reconstruction. The latter is annotated in what is almost certainly Chantrell's hand, although it is not signed. The churchwardens' accounts make no mention of payments to architects or builders at this time. Glynne, visiting in 1860, referred to it as 'a poor church', and perhaps the work was not carried out. That Chantrell was the author of these proposals is strengthened by the fact that, subsequently, Chantrell made several references to Hemsworth's open roof as a model worthy of emulation, e.g. at Middleton (ICBS).

DRAWINGS: WYASW, WDP36/125.

REFERENCES: WYASW, WDP36/124 and 125; Glynne, p. 217; ICBS, file 03514.

Holbeck, Leeds, St Matthew
New church, 1827-32

The finished church consisted of aisleless nave with galleries on three sides, shallow chancel with vestries at each side, W tower. The overall design is close to those of Chantrell's contemporary churches at Kirkstall, Morley and New Mills, although almost all of the details are different. A spire was part of the original design, but was omitted to reduce the cost. The present spire, designed by William Hill, was added in 1860 (Linstrum, p. 374).

Chantrell was asked to 'make an estimate of the sums necessary to build a plain new chapel for 1200 persons and the cost of repairing the old [chapel]'. His report of 31 May 1827 stated the old chapel was 'unsound and neglected'; the necessary repairs would cost £150 but would last only 'for a few years' (CBC, Holbeck file 17593). He estimated a new church would cost £4,950 and on 12 June 1827, the Commissioners approved a grant of £3,000 (CBC, MB 25, p. 244). Six days later Chantrell produced a more detailed estimate: 'for a chapel to contain 1200 seats, one half of them free, in plain Gothic, Early English of the Thirteenth century, with lancet windows and plain flat buttresses, a small tower and spire at the west end … £4,950 if in wallstone, £5,200 if in ashlar' (CBC, Holbeck file). Perhaps disappointed at the level of grant, Chantrell was induced to write to the CBC to say 'a church having the required character cannot be built for less than £4,000. The letter was discussed by the Commissioners on 23 August 1827 (CBC, MB 26, p. 131) and at their meeting of 25 September 1827, increased the grant to £4,000 (CBC, MB 26, p. 359). On 20 September 1828 Chantrell informed the Commissioners: 'I have this day forwarded the drawings and specifications and detailed estimates for the new church proposed to be built at Holbeck … in the design I have adhered to the style of Henry III which is the most economical that can be adopted and it possesses a degree of elegant simplicity rarely found in the Decorated examples of the 14th century as far as respects contour.' (CBC, MB 32, p. 300-1). The Commissioners approved 'the general style and character and plan' at their meeting of 30 September 1828 (*ibid.*). However, it seems there was a call from some quarter for greater economy as the incumbent, the Revd Bushby, informed the Commissioners in a letter of 7 February 1829 that 'Mr Chantrell says a plain substantial building can be erected for about £3,500.' (CBC, MB 33, p. 299).

Tenders were advertised in the *LI* of 21 May 1829 and the foundation stone was laid on 3 August 1829 (*LI*, 6 Aug. 1829). Even by the *Intelligencer's* standards, its praise for the Chantrell was unusually laudatory: 'an approved and elegant design furnished by a well known and justly esteemed, highly talented architect … ' (*ibid.*).

During construction problems arose: on 24 December 1830 Chantrell wrote to the Commissioners saying water found on the site had unsettled the foundations and he proposed to omit the spire and use the money saved to strengthen the W end of the church. He included with his letter a plan of the old coal pits on the site which he believed were causing the problems (CBC, Holbeck file). The consecration took place on 3 January 1832. The building had cost £3,734/18/4 of which Chantrell received £167/3/0 (*ibid.*).

DRAWING: CBC, Holbeck file no. 17593

REFERENCES: CBC, Holbeck file, no. 17593; CBC, MB 25, p. 244, MB 26, pp. 131, 359, MB 30, p. 155, MB 32, pp. 300-1, MB 33, p. 299; *LI*, 21 May, 11 June, 30 July, 6 Aug. 1829.

Holbeck, Leeds, St Matthew
Consultation regarding pew rents, 1855
On 7 May 1855 J.H. Good, the CBC surveyor, wrote to the Commissioners concerning alterations to pew rents that would result from the placing of an organ in the W gallery. He stated: 'Mr Chantrell, the architect of this church, has certified in the plan provided for the scale of pew rents that only 5 free sittings are lost'.

REFERENCE: CBC, Holbeck file, no 17593

Holbeck, Leeds, National School
New school, 1839-40, demolished
As early as 1834 there was discussion about building a school attached to St Matthew's Holbeck (*LI*, 25 Jan. 1834), but it was not until the middle of 1839 that a subscription was opened (*LI*, 18 May 1839). The *LI* of 4 July 1840 announced that the new school would open on 10 July adding, ' … the style of architecture is such as to reflect great credit on the taste of Mr Chantrell under whose superintendence the building has been erected. The foundation stone was laid on 26 March and the entire edifice will cost about £1000. The school is very large, capable of containing 600 children and presents a very handsome front of cut stone, forming one of the most handsome superstructures in the township … ' *LI*, 18 July 1840 contained an account of the opening.

REFERENCES: *LI,* 25 May 1834, 18 May 1839, 4, 18 July 1840.

Holmbridge, near Huddersfield, West Yorkshire, School

New school, *c.*1837, unexecuted

Following the Holmbridge church debacle (see below), Chantrell submitted his account for time spent on the aborted project. In addition to work on the church design, his bill included, '1837, for drawings etc also for Holmbridge School, £7/0/0, as per account rendered'. Although there is a school at Holmbridge of *c.*1840, presumably this, like the church, was designed by William Wallen.

REFERENCE: ICBS, file 01422.

Holmbridge, near Huddersfield, West Yorkshire, St David

New church, 1837–8, unexecuted

Holmbridge was an isolated village in the parish of Almondbury. The design was a simple, lancet-style church to hold 776, with W tower and optional spire, aisleless nave with galleries on three sides, shallow chancel with vestry at each side. It had much in common with his churches at Morley and Holbeck of a decade earlier, but was on a smaller scale.

It had been intended to build a church at Holmbridge in the early 1830s to a design by Henry Ward, then working in Huddersfield. However, the project was postponed as a suitable site could not be found. When, in 1837, a site was found, Ward had moved to Staffordshire; his scheme had always been thought of as expensive and Chantrell was asked to submit an alternative one (ICBS). His drawings and specifications are dated 1 June 1837. The estimated cost was £1,540 plus £150 for the spire (WYASW). The ICBS had already approved a grant for the Ward scheme and a second application was made in respect of Chantrell's design. On 26 July 1837, the ICBS surveyor informed the Board he saw no objection to Chantrell's structure, but elsewhere objections must have existed as on 6 December 1837, Chantrell wrote to the ICBS with new plans which he 'hoped would be found acceptable'. The vicar was minded to write on 2 January 1838 requesting that the ICBS make their objections explicit to Chantrell so he could satisfy them. On 7 February, Chantrell wrote to ICBS saying he had obtained the consent of the vicar for the preparation of 'a plan that will be more equitable to the ICBS's Regulations … ', but further delays ensued. The documentation does not identify the issues, but certainly the N and S galleries of this small church were only 20 feet apart, rather than the 24 feet specified by the ICBS's rules. Eventually, the vicar obtained from the ICBS the plans of Ward's church, claiming, rather deviously 'they may suit for another design of a church on a large scale in the neighbourhood' and only days later, gave them to the Huddersfield architect William Wallen, although the vicar had earlier suggested Chantrell execute Ward's plan, a proposal which Chantrell dismissed as 'quite unprofessional'. Wallen then wrote to the ICBS on 17 March 1838 to say the local committee had 'relinquished all other plans' previously submitted and had resolved to erect Ward's original design 'to which the [ICBS's] official seal is attached' (ICBS). The Ward/Wallen church opened in July 1840 (*LI,* 1 Aug. 1840).

On 21 January 1839, Chantrell submitted his bill to ICBS. This comprises a detailed breakdown of the time spent and is thus a rare and informative example of Chantrell's office practice (ICBS).

Although the vicar was clearly frustrated by the course of events, it seems Chantrell's reputation was unaffected; early in 1840 he was asked to design a new church at nearby Honley, and subsequently received other commissions in the parish of Almondbury.

DRAWINGS: WYASW, WDP24/87; ICBS, file 01422.

REFERENCES: ICBS, file 01422; ICBS, MB 6, pp. 140, 155, 262, MB 8, p. 260, MB 9, p. 330; *LI,* 28 Jan. 1837, 26 May, 2, 9 June 1838, 5 Oct. 1839, 1 Aug. 1840.

Honley, near Huddersfield, St Mary

Report on the Old Chapel, 1830

While nearing the end of the commissions for new churches at Lockwood and Netherthong, Chantrell was asked to examine the old chapel in nearby Honley, also in the parish of Almondbury. He 'advised the entire reconstruction', although repairs were undertaken. Only in 1840 was a new church agreed upon.

REFERENCE: M. Jagger, *The History of Honley,* privately printed, 1914, p. 184.

Honley, near Huddersfield, St Mary

New church, 1840-4

The finished church is Early English in style and consists of W tower, nave with aisles and galleries on three sides, a shallow three-sided chancel. Despite some later 19th-century re-ordering of the E end, this attractive interior is much as Chantrell left it.

Although some repairs were carried out in 1825 (Town Book), by 1830 the church's condition was again causing concern and Chantrell was asked to inspect it (Jagger, p. 184). He advised the entire reconstruction' although in 1831 the decision merely to repair again was taken (Town Book). In 1840 Chantrell was again asked for advice and his report, dated 12 March offers various costed alternatives, but recommends a new church at an estimated cost of £2,600 (Parish papers, 23). John Brooke who had already given Chantrell much employment in Armitage Bridge and who contributed to other Chantrell churches in the parish gave generously (Parish papers, 24) and a new structure was agreed upon. This was announced in *LI,* 28 November 1840 but already Chantrell was busy as the vicar of Almondbury wrote to ICBS eight days earlier to say he had 'just' received plans from his architect (ICBS). Only on 6 November 1841 were tenders advertised (*LI*); perhaps Chantrell had caused delays as the vicar wrote to the ICBS on 1 December 1841 to say he had been 'for months ready to bring an application' but 'have been unable to obtain from Mr Chantrell the needful plans'. However, the building accounts – an unusually detailed document – which record all the costs of postage and carriage of plans, show Chantrell sent plans to Honley in the previous September, October and November Eventually, plans were sent to the ICBS on 15 December 1841. Work would take 12 months and cost £3,000. On 10 January 1842, contractors began to dismantle the old chapel (Jagger, p.184). On 25 January 1842 the ICBS's surveyor informed the board he saw no objections to the proposed construction but he identified a problem 'conveying condensation to the outside'. Furthermore, the pews were only 2 feet 6 inches wide, not 2 feet 9 inches and the gallery fronts were only 21 feet 9 inches apart, not the requisite 24 feet (ICBS). The issues must soon have been resolved as the *LI* of 29 January 1842 reported the award of the ICBS grant, and the edition of 28 October 1843 reported the consecration two days earlier. The completion certificate was signed on 3 February 1844 (ICBS).

Jagger gives the total cost at 'over £4,000'. Chantrell was paid £230. His son, Henry William, acted as clerk of works. Thomas Shaw, J.B. Chantrell's partner, was paid 1/- per week for 33 weeks for unspecified work (Building Accounts).

DRAWINGS: ICBS, file 01484.

REFERENCES: ICBS, file 01484; ICBS, MB 11, p. 28, MB 12, pp. 46, 62, 65; Parish papers, nos 17, 23, 24 (seen at the church in 1977 and not, apparently, among the papers subsequently deposited at Wakefield); *LI,* 28 Nov. 1840, 6 Nov. 1841, 29 Jan. 1842, 21, 28 Oct. 1843; M. Jagger, *The History of Honley,* privately printed, 1914.

Horwich, Lancashire, Holy Trinity

New church, 1828, considered as potential architect

At the meeting of the CBC on 23 January 1827, the Commissioners noted a request from the parish of

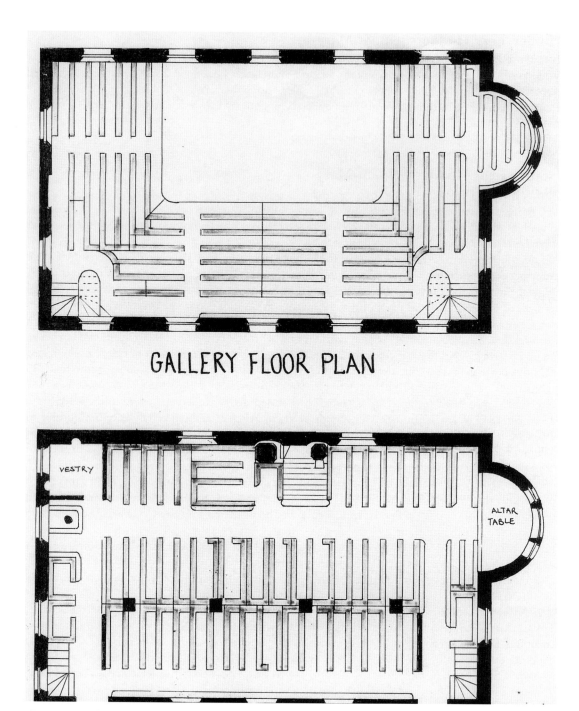

GALLERY FLOOR PLAN

VESTRY

ALTAR TABLE

Cat. 11: Hunslet, Leeds, Hunslet Chapel, a re-drawing of Chantrell's seating plan of 1826, the completion of a project started earlier by Benjamin Jackson.

Dean in Lancashire for a design for its proposed new church at Horwich. This was an unusual request; the Commission usually relied on applicants to acquire their own designs. At the Commissioners' meeting in June 1828 it received a report from its surveyor J.H. Good: 'Having pursuant to the instructions of the board, examined the drawings in the office to ascertain whether there be any design of Mr Chantrell applicable for the new church proposed to be erected at Horwich in the parish of Dean, to accommodate 1,500 persons, I beg to report that there appears to be no design of Mr Chantrell in the office for a church calculated to accommodate more than 1000 persons … ' It is of interest that Good was asked specifically to look at Chantrell schemes; it suggests he was held in high regard by the Commissioners. There is no evidence that, subsequently, Chantrell was invited to design a larger church and eventually Holy Trinity was erected to a new design by Francis Bedford.

REFERENCES: CBC, MB 23, p. 237, MB 31, pp. 146-7.

Hunslet, Leeds, St Mary
Completion of alterations, 1826

Hunslet Chapel was built in *c.*1636 and in 1744 was doubled in size, 'a very plain unpretending edifice of brick' (Taylor).

The minor architect/surveyor Benjamin Jackson had been appointed, probably in 1823, to survey the chapel roof; subsequently, he was appointed to carry out a more extensive scheme of raising the outer walls 16 feet, re-roofing and inserting galleries on three sides. However, unspecified problems arose and Chantrell was 'called in to extricate the chapel from its difficulties and manage the accounts' (ICBS). Chantrell's report of 4 March 1826 notes 'Jackson's Report [about the roof] is perfectly correct … the new roof is entirely finished and the gallery framing nearly so, both of which are executed in a substantial and workmanlike manner … vestry requires only its last coat of plaster … there remains only the ceiling under the gallery and the framing of the seats and the tower which can be left till the interior is perfected … ' It is hard to understand the 'difficulties' referred to earlier, unless they were primarily financial. Then on 27 March 1826, an application was submitted to the ICBS requesting funds towards the £1,521 cost of the enlargement and £800 of repairs. The total of £2,321 was a huge sum for such a relatively modest project. Furthermore, the ICBS did not normally give grants retrospectively and Chantrell had already confirmed that much of the work was completed. Indeed, *LI,* 11 May 1826 announced the enlargement was 'completed'. Nevertheless, the ICBS gave a grant of £300. This was based on the claim that an additional 555 free seats would, by the end of the project, have been created. However, correspondence between the incumbent and ICBS in connection with further proposed repairs in 1843 says 'numbers in the 1826 Grant Application were never accurate … the wardens had exaggerated them.'

DRAWINGS: ICBS, file 00742.

REFERENCES: ICBS, MB 3, p. 101, 169; ICBS, file 00742; *LI,* 11 May 1826; Taylor, p. 395.

Hunslet, Leeds, St Mary
New tower, *c.*1830-2

Chantrell's 'before' drawing shows a plain rectangular Georgian 'box'. The W wall represented something of a blank canvas for the new tower, but Chantrell composed a particularly interesting design, and one of his most Soanian, replete with elements of the Dulwich Picture Gallery on which Chantrell had worked as a pupil. The entire chapel was demolished in 1862-4.

The addition of a tower had been contemplated in Jackson's *c.*1823-6 alterations, but probably through a shortage of funds, it was postponed. The Leeds architect John Clark submitted three alternative designs dated 26 August 1830 for towers costing between £350 and £750 (WYASL); perhaps other architects did likewise, but Chantrell was selected for the job. In Nov. 1830 the faculty application was submitted and tenders were requested in the *LI* of 10 March 1831. Completion is not recorded, although Taylor states the tower was built in 1832-3.

Cat. 12: Hunslet, Leeds, Chantrell's new tower added to the plain, eighteenth-century chapel in 1830-2. Watercolour by W.R. Rhodes. (*Leeds Library and Information Services*).

DRAWINGS: WYASL, RDP44/75.

REFERENCES: WYASL, RDP44/75 and 76; *LI*, 10 March 1831; Taylor, p. 396.

Hunslet, Leeds, St Mary
Alterations, 1843

By 1843, the internal layout of St Mary's must have seemed old-fashioned and inappropriate for those sympathetic to new Camdenian ideas. In particular, the gallery of W-facing benches built over the shallow chancel and the entire seating arrangement focused on the pulpit on the N wall would have been condemned. Chantrell was asked for suggestions and produced a report dated 15 June 1843 in which he proposed 'to remove the east gallery and open up the chancel … remove the organ into the tower … alter the windows … add Baptistry with 2 lofty arches' (ICBS). He adds the chapel should have been 'pulled down instead of repaired 17 or 18 years ago but now it must remain with proposed alterations …' He estimated the cost at £400 (ICBS). An application to ICBS followed. A letter from the incumbent to ICBS of 3 October 1843, says they 'intend to repair the free sittings which are, according to Mr Chantrell … very old and decayed'. He mentions architect's plans – 'at present' and 'as intended' – but these are no longer in the file. The application was rejected and it is not clear if any of the proposed repairs/alterations were undertaken.

REFERENCE: ICBS, file 03293.

Hunslet, Leeds, St Mary
Proposed new church, 1843-4

The Revd John Clark, the incumbent at Hunslet, wrote to the ICBS on 1 December 1843 saying 'The architect says a good church could be erected similar to Denholme for £2000. Another letter from him of 15 August 1844 repeats his desire for a new church, either on this site or a new one. 'I have consulted with Mr Chantrell. He says that a church could be built like Denholme Church but rather larger for £2000 exclusive of the old materials which would be worth about £400 – such a church to contain 500 free sittings on the ground floor and about 350 sittings in a west gallery which could be let.' He goes on to ask if a grant could be given, but no application appears to have been made. The old church remained until a new one was erected in 1863-4.

REFERENCES: ICBS, files 03292, 03484.

Hunslet, Leeds, School
New school, c.1840-3 (demolished)

The *LI* of 30 November 1839 noted that subscriptions were being collected for a new school at Hunslet and on 27 June 1840 both *LI* and *LM* invited tenders to be sent to Chantrell and Son. However, more than two years later contributions were still needed to meet the estimated cost of £1,400 (*LI*, 5 Nov. 1842). Not until 28 January 1843 was *LI* able to announce 'building will begin in the spring' and the edition of 9 September that year announced the completion: It is 'entirely of stone and was erected from the designs and under the superintendence of R.D. Chantrell. It is 120 feet long, 30 feet wide and 30 feet high. The style is Elizabethan and the cost is £1,500.'

REFERENCES: *LI,* 30 Nov. 1839, 27 June 1840, 5 Nov. 1842, 28 Jan., 9 Sept. 1843; *LM,* 27 June 1840. The school is illustrated on a transfer-printed tile in the Thoresby Society collection.

Hyde, Cheshire, St George
Design for new church, 1828, unexecuted

The vicar of the parish in which Hyde was situated wrote to CBC on 20 July 1826 asking for a plan for the proposed new church. Subsequently, CBC asked Chantrell to go to Hyde 'to look at the site and make proposals' (CBC [letter from Chantrell, 11 Jan. 1834, requesting payment]). The *LI* of 4 September 1828 reported the request with great pomp: 'His Majecty's Commissioners … have ordered a design and estimate to be prepared for a new church at Hyde … a sketch has been prepared by Mr Chantrell of this place in the Gothic or Early English style … ' On 20 September 1828 Chantrell submitted his designs and attached the following letter. 'I beg leave to tender my most grateful acknowledgements to His Majesty's Commissioners for their honour they have conferred upon me by requesting an estimate for a new church at Hyde where I attended immediately after the receipt of your letter and obtained every information necessary to enable me to make calculations. I have in progress a design in the Early English style (Henry III) partly on the model as far as respects the west front of Ripon Minster and the E part a composition from buildings of the same date which abound in this county. Although two towers are shown (which may appear extravagant at first sight) on inspection of the plan it will be seen that they are mere elongations of the entrance and the staircase walls, and the gallery, which by this method of arrangement is brought to the front of the towers giving nearly 70 additional sittings and pews. In the ordinary manner the placing of the tower in the centre of the west front, 10 feet or more on the total length would be requisite and the expense of extra foundations, and these which are 74 feet appear as lofty as a central tower 100 feet and can be erected for less than one half of the expense of an ordinary tower.' (CBC, MB 32, pp. 301-2). This was discussed by the Commissioners at their meeting on 30 September 1828; also discussed was a scheme for Hyde from Messrs Atkinson of York. Chantrell sent his finished plans on 11 October 1828. However, at their meeting of 11 November 1828, the CBC selected the Atkinsons' more orthodox scheme to be built.

Although a number of architects produced 'two tower' designs around this time, usually they were variants on King's College, Cambridge, with the 'towers' really just modest octagonal turrets. Designs with two substantial towers were rare and never again did Chantrell pursue this idea.

REFERENCES: CBC, Hyde file; CBC MB 21, p. 270, MB 32, pp. 301-2, MB 33, p. 145; *LI,* 4 Sept. 1828.

Keighley, St Andrew
New church on old foundations, 1845-9
See Chapter 7 for a fuller account of this commission.

At the end of 1844 or early 1845 the Bradford architect Walker Rawsthorn, who had been appointed to rebuild the church, was dismissed. *LI* announced on 11 January 1845 that 'Messrs Chantrell and Shaw have received instructions to prepare plans etc for the rebuilding of Keighley Parish Church'. In March 1845, 'Mr Chantrell [was] busily engaged in preparing plans ... [intended to] add 715 extra seats. This will cost £3,000 using the old tower, foundations and materials. On 5 March 1845 the vicar asked if the £400 grant was still available adding 'The Bishop has, I believe, made you acquainted with the circumstances which compelled us to employ a new architect – the justly celebrated Mr Chantrell. Good approved Chantrell's designs on 12 May 1845 and the faculty was applied for with two drawings signed 'Chantrell and Son, June 1845' accompanied by an explanation: 'the removal of the nave and choir, or as much of the said parts as may be necessary and ... rebuilding on the site of the present church ... a new church and chancel ... 141 feet long and 62 feet wide' (BI). Tenders were advertised in the *LM,* 20 September 1845 and the demolition of the old church commenced in December that year (churchwardens' accounts). *LI,* 28 February 1846 carried an account of the foundation stone-laying which took place four days earlier. *LI* of 4 December 1847 was able to announce 'the beautiful building is now fast approaching completion', although the edition of 29 July 1848 still described it as 'nearly complete' adding 'the church is a fine specimen of Perpendicular Gothic of the 15th century, the whole being carried out with the greatest accuracy and will long be remain a striking proof of the great fame of this celebrated architect ...' the church was consecrated on 11 August 1848, an event recorded in *LI* eight days later. The completion certificate is dated 3 February 1849 and was signed by Chantrell from his office in Lincoln's Inn Fields.

The finished church is Perpendicular with tower (largely rebuilt), nave with aisles, clerestory and galleries on three sides, long chancel with Camdenian arrangements. It is one of Chantrell's most successful late designs.

DRAWINGS: BI, Faculty 1845/1; ICBS, file 00818.

REFERENCES: BI, Faculty 1840/2 [Rawsthorn's scheme]; BI, Faculty 1845/1; ICBS, file 00818, ICBS, MB 4, p. 66, MB 9, p. 220a, MB 12, p. 190, MB 13, pp. 156, 178; Churchwarden's Accounts, WYASB, BDP57/2/1/2; *LM,* 20 Sept. 1845; *LI,* 11 Jan., 1 March 1845, 28 Feb. 1846, 4 Dec. 1847, 29 July, 19 Aug. 1848; *Civil Engineer and Architects' Journal,* April 1846, p. 100; *Builder,* 5, 1847, p. 300; *Ecclesiologist,* 11, 1850, pp. 64-6.

Kirkstall, Leeds, Chapel
Unexecuted design for Sir James Graham, *c.*1820
The only known reference to this project comes in a letter from Chantrell to Soane, 6 January 1821: '... I was lately introduced by Mr Gott ... to Sir James Graham for whom I have designed a small church

Cat. 13: Kirkstall, Leeds, Parsonage House (R.D. Chantrell, 1834–5). The watercolour by W.R. Robinson reveals Chantrell struggling to adapt Gothic forms to a modest structure, a problem he would later overcome by exploiting the Tudor style for small-scale houses and schools. Compare with Cat. 15. (*Leeds Library and Information Services*).

proposed to be erected on his property near Kirkstall Abbey … '

REFERENCE: SM, Private Correspondence, xv, A, 32.

Kirkstall, Leeds, Parsonage
New parsonage, 1834–5 (demolished)

On 8 November 1834, 'Mr Chantrell, architect, waited upon the Committee with plans for the Parsonage House when the plan marked A was unanimously adopted' (WYASL). Contracts with the tradesmen were signed in Chantrell's office on 25 November 1834 (*ibid.,* p. 66) and the first stone was laid on 7 March 1835. The parson took up residence on 13 November 1835 (*ibid.,* p. 1). It cost £1,128/15/2 (parish papers no. 44) of which Chantrell received £35/0/0 plus £10/10/0 for a 'further 5 and 3/4 days attendance'. Fenteman described it as 'a beautiful Parsonage in the style of the church', although the Early English idioms produced a curious design.

REFERENCES: WYASL, RDP50/23, pp. 63, 97, RDP50/44; T. Fenteman, *Historical Guide to Leeds,* Thomas and Sons, 1858, p. 138.

Kirkstall, Leeds, St Stephen
New church, 1827-9

Lord Cardigan gave a piece of land for a new church in 1826 (*LI*, 29 Feb. 1826) and on 2 June 1827, the 'inhabitants of Kirkstall' enquired of Chantrell what would be the estimated cost of a new church for the village to which he replied ' … I beg to acquaint you that a plain structure in the Early English style 70 feet long, 45 feet wide to contain 1000 with galleries … without tower £2,900. A tower 60 feet high is … extra £700 and a spire £160 … total £3,760.' (CBC). On 12 June 1827 an application was submitted to CBC and on 20 July a parishioner Mr Wilks informed the Commissioners 'plans were being prepared' (CBC, MB 26, p. 132), although it was not until 8 December 1827 that Chantrell sent his drawings which were approved by the board on 18 December 1827 (CBC, MB 27, p. 446), and by the surveyor on 11 February 1828 (CBC, Surveyor's Report Book 2, no. 209). By March the cost had been reduced to £3,180 to include a tower and spire (ICBS). Tenders were invited in *LI* of 3 April 1828 and the first stone was laid on 7 July 1828 (*LI*, 10 July 1828). The *LI* of 1 January 1829 gives an interesting account of construction: 'The roof of the new church at Kirkstall is upon the ground and would have been raised before this day had it not been for repeated difficulties in procuring stone, for want of which, a number of men have been discharged frequently. The sides of the church are levelled up to the square but stone cannot be got so as to enable the contractors to proceed regularly with the east and west ends. This appears rather mysterious as it is in the immediate vicinity of the stone quarries.' The church was consecrated on 25 September 1829, an event reported fully in the *LI* of 1 October. The total cost was £3,206/4/5, of which Chantrell was paid £146/19/6 (CBC, MB 36, p. 207).

The finished church consisted of tower with spire, aisleless nave with galleries on three sides, shallow chancel with vestries at each side. The overall design is similar to Holbeck, New Mills and Morley although the details are different. The E end of the church was altered radically in 1863 and 1894.

DRAWINGS: CBC, Kirkstall file, no. 18274.

REFERENCES: CBC, Kirkstall file, no. 18274; CBC, MB 25, p. 269, MB 26, p. 132, MB 27, p. 446, MB 33, p. 35, MB 36, p. 207; CBC, Surveyor's Report Book 2, no. 209; WYASL, RDP50/23, 39 and 44; *LI*, 29 Feb. 1826, 3 April, 3, 10 July 1828, 1 Jan., 11 June, 24 Sept., 1 Oct. 1829; Taylor, pp. 444-52, includes a description of the church before the 1863 alterations.

Kirkstall, Leeds, St Stephen
Repairs to spire, 1833

Taylor (p. 444) gives a dramatic account of the 'catastrophe' of 29 April when the spire was struck by lightning. Chantrell examined the church the following day and reported, '… the upper part of the spire about 15 feet inn length is totally destroyed and the lower part is cracked on the north side of the octagon down to the level of the tower … pinnacles and cornice … thrown through gallery roof … necessary to take down spire and north-east angle of tower, west end above staircase on north side and broken ceiling joists … cost £385.' (ICBS). On 15 May an application was made to ICBS which elicited a grant of £150. The *LI* of 1 June 1833 announced work would 'proceed immediately' and the edition of 1 September 1833 noted the church was now open.

DRAWINGS: ICBS, file 01562.

REFERENCES: ICBS, file 01562, ICBS, MB 6, pp. 195, 240; WYASL, RDP50/23; *LI*, 1 June, 1 Sept. 1833; Taylor, p. 444.

Leeds, Bond Street, shops with living accommodation

Row of four new shops for William Hey, 1820, unexecuted

WYASL has a set of four drawings showing two alternative schemes for this project signed 'R.D. Chantrell, 20 April 1820'. Both show a three-storey block of four shops, the upper floors are plain but the ground floors reveal elegant shop-fronts replete with a range of fashionable motifs largely drawn from Soane's repertoire; the principal difference is that one set show an alleyway to the right-hand side of the design. Confusingly, the intended site was subsequently renamed as numbers 4, 5, 6 and 7 Commercial Street, but Chantrell's scheme was not built. A very similar scheme was executed in 1823 to the designs of Atkinson and Sharp of York (Beresford) of which a substantial part of numbers 4 and 7 survives.

DRAWINGS: WYASL, DB 75/9.

REFERENCES: WYASL, DB 75/10, DB 75/19; M. Beresford, 'The Birth of Commercial Street' in *The Dial; The Leeds Library Magazine,* 3, 1993, p. 8.

Leeds, Central Market

Unsuccessful competition entry, 1824

As early as 2 September 1822 the *LI* noted the proposal to erect a new covered market in the town centre, but it was not until April 1824 that architects were invited to submit plans (*LI,* 22 April 1824). Chantrell's scheme was, apparently, selected although he was not formally appointed as architect. Subsequently, there was disagreement between Chantrell and the committee which resulted in Francis Goodwin from London being appointed; his design was executed in 1824-7. According to the account in *LI* of 7 July 1825, the stumbling block to Chantrell's employment was that 'Mr Chantrell would not furnish working drawings … that injurious delay was the result, and that the Committee were compelled to apply to another quarter:- to which it is replied, that he in the outset had furnished all the Drawings, Plans, Estimates, etc. customary in such cases – that he only waited till he should be actually appointed architect, to furnish the Working Drawings – That the latter would have been very expensive, and that in no instance are they supplied before the architect is chosen.' On the face of it, the issue seems to have been nothing more than a misunderstanding capable of easy resolution; that it was not resolved would suggest a more complex set of issues between Chantrell and the committee. This was a huge commission to lose; Goodwin's scheme cost £30,000 (Grady, p. 170). (See also Leeds, Commercial Buildings, below, for further examples of tension between Chantrell and prominent Leeds citizens).

REFERENCES: *LI,* 2 Sept. 1822, 22 April, 17 June 1824, 7 July 1825; K. Grady, ' … The Provision of Markets … in Leeds, 1822-9', in *Thoresby Society Miscellany,* 16 pt 3, 1976, pp. 165-95.

Leeds, Christ Church

New church, 1821-6

See Chapter 7 for a full account of this commission.

The *LI* of 6 March 1820 announced that in answer to an application from the vicar of Leeds, the Commissioners for building new churches 'had declared their readiness to build a church in Leeds … to contain … 2000 people.' However, within three months CBC had made fresh proposals which involved the erection of three churches, each capable of holding 1,200. Suitable sites had already been identified (*LI,* 10 June 1820). Fund raising to buy the sites followed and on 20 November 1820, the *LI* invited architects to submit plans. The following May it was reported that Chantrell had been chosen for the Meadow Lane church [Christ Church], Mr [Edward] Gyfford [of London] for that at Woodhouse and Mr [C.A.]Busby for Quarry Hill (*LI,* 14 May 1821). Subsequently, both Gyfford and Busby were replaced. Relatively minor concerns of the CBC's surveyor and Board of Works necessitated much amending of plans and not until

September 1822 was Chantrell's scheme approved (CBC, MB 6, p. 143). On 4 November 1822 *LI* invited tenders adding that all candidates were required to 'provide the names of two respectable persons as sureties …' Additionally, Chantrell was required to comment on the character of those tendering; his long letter on the subject dated 9 November 1822 occupies nine pages of the Minute Book! (CBC, MB 6, pp. 233-41). On 29 January 1823 the first stone was laid, an event accompanied with a great procession of civic dignitaries, clergy and tradesmen, and much euphoria in the newspapers (*LI*, 30 Jan. 1823). By 29 September 1825 the *LI* noted Woodhouse and Meadow Lane churches had 'for some time been completed in the interior'. But the archbishop refused to licence them until they were 'properly enclosed'. Eventually, consecration took place on 12 January. 1826, reported in *LI* 7 days later. The final cost was £10,555 of which Chantrell was paid £553/16/7 (CBC, Surveyor's Book 2, no. 100).

This was Chantrell's first new church and was much admired. 'As [it] was the first of the parliamentary churches founded in Leeds, so it is the first in architectural beauty, and undoubtedly does great credit to the architect, R D Chantrell' was a not untypical assessment (Heaton). It consisted of 'a nave and aisles, with a massive tower rising to a height of 127 feet, and is of the Decorated style of the 14th century. The main entrance in Meadow lane consists of a pointed arch flanked by small panelled buttresses … above are some very curious work in quatrefoil panelling, over which a pointed window of three lights, with cinquefoil heads, a transom and tracery in the sweep of the arch, besides many other adornments. The interior has a very commanding aspect. The aisles, which are divided from the body of the church by six depressed pointed arches … ' (*Historical Guide*, pp. 58-9). The church was demolished in 1972.

REFERENCES: CBC, Leeds Christ Church file, no. 20548; CBC MB 4, pp. 91, 254; CBC MB 5, pp. 222, 290, 332, 339, MB 6, pp. 143, 233-41, MB 7, pp. 76, 272, MB 17, p. 224; CBC Surveyor's Book 1 [no page numbers], Surveyor's Book 2, p. 100; *LI*, 14 May, 2 July 1821, 4 Nov., 30 Dec. 1822, 2, 9, 30 Jan 1823, 27 May 1824, 16 June, 4, 18 Aug., 29 Sept., 6, 13, 20 Oct. 1825 9 Nov. 1826; *LM* 2 July 1825; WYASL, RDP56/45 and 54; T. Fentemen, *An Historical Guide to Leeds,* Thomas and Sons, 1858, pp. 58-9; *Walk Through Leeds*, J. Heaton, Leeds, 1835, pp. 104-7. For material on the Busby/Goodwin relationship see: M. Port, 'Francis Goodwin, 1784-1853', in *Architectural History*, 1, 1958, pp. 60-72; *Monthly Magazine*, 54, 1822, pp. 211-12; Busby's pamphlet defending his actions, a copy of which is in the V&A Library, Box I 35J.

Leeds, Christ Church
Alterations, 1828
At its meeting of 8 January 1828, the Board of the CBC approved the spending of £94 of 'extra work' at Christ Church, Leeds to be carried out under Chantrell's supervision.

REFERENCE: CBC, MB 28, p. 14.

Leeds, Christ Church
New perimeter wall, 1829
The *LI,* 19 March 1829 reported that at the recent 'Vestry Meeting … Mr Chantrell had been employed to make plans and specifications for enclosing Christ Church … ' It added, interestingly, that there was likely to be 'some delay' as he 'was absent from home'. It gives no further details of his location. The Leeds Parish Church churchwardens' accounts note a payment to Chantrell of £5/0/0 on 7 February 1830 which could relate to this commission.

REFERENCES: WYASL, RDP68/41/3; *LI,* 19 March 1829; LPC, 41/3.

Leeds, Christ Church
New N and S galleries, 1836

The *LI,* 4 June 1836 requested tenders for 'new galleries for Christ Church … Plans to be seen at Mr Chantrell's office.' The edition of 26 November 1836 noted the 'improvements' were 'nearly completed'. On 24 December 1836, the paper gave more details: ' … during the past year the original design of Mr Chantrell has been completed by the erection of north and south galleries and the church has been likewise lighted by gas … Christ Church is now decidedly one of the most beautiful and commodious places of worship in the Parish of Leeds … ' The cost of the work was £853 (WYASL).

REFERENCES: *LI,* 4 June, 26 Nov., 24 Dec. 1836; WYASL, RDP56/45.

Leeds, Christ Church

Repairs, 1839

The *LI* of 12 January 1839 contained a full account of the violent storm which hit the town five days earlier. It noted damage to several churches, including Holy Trinity and St George's, and noted that at Christ Church, 'three of the pinnacles of the tower wee dislodged, one falling through the roof and almost totally demolishing the organ.' A bazaar in the Music Hall intended to raise money for repairs had already been arranged and, remarkably, the edition of 9 March was able to record that 'The damage is repaired …' However, a letter from the vicar of Leeds, accompanied by a letter from Chantrell, requesting assistance, was discussed at the CBC meeting of 12 February 1839. It was rejected.

REFERENCES: *LI,* 12, 26 Jan., 9 March, 25 May 1839; CBC, MB 50, p. 2.

Leeds, Christ Church, School

New school, 1839-42

The intended new school is first mentioned in *LI,* 12 January 1839 when the bazaar was proposed to raise funds to repair various churches following storm damage [see above] 'and provide a school for each of them'. The edition of 1 June 1839 noted further funds were required for a school at Christ Church which 'will be plain and substantial … [and] cost about £1000'. These details suggest Chantrell was involved by this date. Fund raising progressed slowly; *LI,* 5 December 1840, noted money was still required. However,

Cat. 14: Leeds, Christ Church, Meadow Lane, National School (R.D. Chantrell, 1839-42).

Chantrell was paid £30 'on account' on 3 November 1841 (Parish papers) and by early 1842, the building was 'rapidly approaching completion' and promised to be 'an elegant structure' (*LI,* 15 Jan. 1842). The edition of 2 April 1842 recorded the opening and gave a particularly rhapsodic assessment – at least in part, probably written by Chantrell himself – of this distinctly unremarkable design: 'the commodious building ... is situated immediately behind the church. It is capable of holding 7-800 children [and] cost about £1900 ... It is worthy of the attention of admirers of the ancient style of architecture ... 150 feet long ... high pitched roof after the Tudor style ... and while it is simple almost to severity, the chasteness of the design, the noble proportions and the characteristic disposition of what forms at once the structure and the ornament of the building are such as to provide a most imposing and pleasing effect. There is nothing wasted in decoration and enrichments, yet nothing wanting to satisfy the eye. In its very simplicity it bespeaks the genius of the designer as forcefully as more elaborate work and it will constitute another monument to the talent of the architect, Mr Chantrell.' The final cost was £2,100/14/9 of which Chantrell received £72/7/10 (WYASL).

REFERENCES: WYASL, RDP56/45; *LI,* 12 Jan. 1839, 5 Dec. 1840, 15 Jan., 2 April 1842.

Leeds, Claremont,
Design for a gate lodge, probably unexecuted, 1838
WYASL, contains a drawing by Chantrell for a Tudor-style gate lodge and gates intended to be built 'on the estate of the late John Atkinson Esq's trustees'. It is dated 19 April [possibly September] 1838. There is no evidence it was built.

Cat. 15: Leeds, Claremont, unexecuted gate lodge (R.D. Chantrell, 1838). This is an early example of Chantrell's adaptation of Tudor, a style he used regularly in the late 1830s and 1840s. (*WYASL*).

DRAWINGS: WYASL, DB5/23.

REFERENCE: WYASL, DB5/23.

Leeds, Commercial Buildings

Unsuccessful competition entry, 1825

The move to erect the Commercial Buildings – or Exchange Rooms as it was sometimes called – was a further aspect of the initiatives to improve the marketing and commercial facilities of the town in the 1820s (see Grady). As a major public building in Leeds, the project received extensive coverage in *LI*. The scheme 'was actually set on foot between May and Nov. 1824 (Grady, p. 167), and on 7 January 1825 a meeting was held 'to prepare instructions for architects' (*LM*, 8 Jan. 1825). Subsequently, these were sent to the six men invited for the limited competition. *LI*, 3 March 1825 noted drawings were to be submitted by the end of March and anticipated that the completed building would 'probably form as splendid a specimen of modern architecture as any in the North of England.' The building committee met on 10 May 1825 to inspect the plans (*LI*, 12 May 1825) and the following month, the shareholders met to consider the proposals of Barry, Chantrell, Clark, Goodwin, Salvin and Taylor, intending to produce a shortlist (*LI*, 23 June 1825). However, there was much debate and a decision was postponed; *LI* of 30 June and 7 July contained lengthy articles about each of the six schemes. Of Chantrell's it said: 'Our chief objection to is, that too florid an order of Architecture has been adopted and the ornaments are too numerous. In internal arrangements, the position of the Coffee-Room relatively to the News Room, appears to us a striking defect. At the same time, the general merits of the design are so great that we only regret our inability to do justice to them at present'. The *Mercury* went so far as to say Chantrell's scheme was 'enthusiastically received by many shareholders.' (*LM*, 2 July 1825). Only on 14 July 1825 was the preference of the shareholders published in *LI*: Clark's design was deemed best followed – in order – by those of Taylor, Goodwin, Chantrell, Salvin and Barry. *LI* of 7 July noted 'some prejudice prevails against' Chantrell and that 'in consequence, if his Designs and Plans … were unexceptionable, they would still be rejected … ' adding the 'prejudice' resulted from his 'professional conduct relative to the Philosophical Hall and Central Market' and proceeded to defend Chantrell's actions. See also entries for Leeds, Philosophical Hall and Central Market, and Chapter 4).

REFERENCES: *LM*, 8 Jan., 2 July 1825; *LI*, 3 March, 12 May, 23, 30 June, 7, 14 July 1825; K. Grady, 'The Provision of Markets in Leeds, 1822-29', *Thoresby Society Miscellany*, 54, pt 3, 1976, pp. 165-95.

Leeds, Conservative Pavilion

Temporary pavilion, 1838

The *LI* of 24 March 1838 reported that, for the 'Third Annual Conservative Dinner … [the] Leeds Tradesmen's Conservative Association have great pleasure in being able to announce that they are making arrangements for accommodating 1500 persons in a handsome pavilion to be erected for the purpose …' For the next five weeks the paper carried lengthy and enthusiastic accounts of the project's progress and for the four weeks from 31 March 1838 carried an engraving of the intended building, possibly the first ever illustration in the paper. The gushing reports in the Conservative-supporting *Intelligencer* need to be set against those in the Liberal *Mercury* which referred to the pavilion an 'the rat trap' and at least two editions encouraged rumours that the building would not be completed on time, and if it was, was likely to be unsafe (*LI*, 24 March 1838). The *LI* of 31 March 1838 contained the following description that should, no doubt, be viewed as biased: ' … a Grecian exterior [with] a Hexastyle Portico *in antis*, which is surmounted by a pediment bearing the Royal Arms … within the portico is a spacious hall, leading, to the left, to the gentlemen's room adjoining the Saloon and the Ladies' Cloak Room communicating with the gallery.

On the right of the Entrance Hall is the Receiver's Room for Ticket, Waiters' Apartments, Bar, Scullery, Pantries etc. The Saloon is 120 feet long by 80 feet broad … the Gallery will comfortably accommodate 500 ladies … the interior walls of the Saloon will be lined with white calico and the pillars and pilasters painted deep crimson … the effect will be similar to the accounts of Pompeii and Herculaneum, and the exterior will be coloured to represent Greek Polychromatic Painting. The whole edifice will be of timber and plank, framed together in the most secure and substantial manner … for the entire design of this truly chaste and Classical building, the inhabitants of Leeds and the gentry of the county are indebted to Robt Dennis Chantrell Esq. Arch. of this town who has, in the most handsome manner, gratuitously offered to the Committee his valuable services.' The festival took place on 16-20 April and by 12 May the dismantling of the pavilion was in progress (*LI*, 12 May 1838). The estimated cost was £395 (*LI*, 24 March 1838). Despite its modest cost and limited life-span, Chantrell must have been pleased with it; subsequently he presented a drawing of it to the IBA, the only one of his commissions to be marked in this way.

DRAWINGS: RIBA Drawings Collection.

REFERENCES: *LI*, 24, 31 March, 7, 14, 18 April [an extraordinary edition], 21, 28 April, 12 May 1838.

Leeds, Court House
Additions, 1827–34

At the justices' meeting of 7 February 1827 it was resolved that 'it is highly desirable the enlargement of the Leeds Court house should take place [for an additional Court and rooms for public business] … [and] that the plans which were some time ago prepared by Mr Taylor, the architect (now deceased) be handed to Mr Chantrell with a view of obtaining his professional assistance in effecting the contemplated improvement … that the Mayor and Mr Sadler be a committee to confer with Mr Chantrell on the subject … ' (Magistrates' minutes). At their meeting of 2 March 1827 the justices examined Chantrell's plan and resolved 'that without formally adopting it', an application would be made 'at the next Pontefract Riding Sessions for a grant of £1,000 towards the cost'. However, because of the general shortage of funds for public works at this time, it was agreed the 'scheme shall be abandoned' when the justices met on 5 March. The project was revived at the meeting on 3 April 1829 where it was resolved that the 'plans … now produced' be submitted to Mr Hartley, the Riding Surveyor and that Hartley, Chantrell and the justices were to meet 'to settle on the plan'. This would suggest new – perhaps more modest – proposals were then envisaged. The design was approved by the justices at their meeting of 23 April 1829 but they noted on 25 June that the Riding refused to make a grant. The *LI*, 16 April 1829 gave more details: 'The Court House is to be extended with the addition of another story on the wings … estimated cost £3000.'

Five years later, the alterations remained to be started and on 20 March 1834 the justices resolved that additions to the Court House be made 'with as little delay as possible' and at their meeting of 21 April, Chantrell's plans were formally approved and estimates from tradesmen accepted. The *LI* of 22 March 1834 described the scheme: 'The additions are to be made after the ensuing sessions. The Rotation Office is to be enlarged and fitted up for a second Court at the Sessions, and – beside other alterations in the present building – over the wings are to be erected a Grand-Jury Room, and a Waiting Room for witnesses'. Work began on 25 April 1834 (*LI*, 3 May 1834) and must have been completed by 4 November 1834 when the justices ordered Chantrell to measure the work and 'bring in' the accounts. The building was demolished in 1901.

REFERENCES: WR Magistrates' Minutes 1827-42, WYASL, P36/c/3/1; *LI*, 16 April 1829, 22 March, 3 May 1834; *Architectural Magazine,* 1, 1834, p. 211.

Leeds, Court House
Alterations 1840-1
At the meeting of the Repairs and Alterations of Corporate Buildings Sub-committee on 21 November 1840 it was 'Resolved that Mr Chantrell be appointed to examine the Court House and make a Report as to the best means of warming and ventilating the Council Room, Large Court and Rotation Office, and the estimated expenses thereof.' This came after four years of discussions in the sub-committee on this subject and the ensuing submission of estimates from various tradesmen for different schemes. Chantrell attended the meeting of 22 December 1840 and reported that 'the apparatus of Mr H.C. Price of Bristol for both warming and ventilating is best calculated for these buildings'. He estimated the cost at £260. He added that 'there was in the course of erection at Brunswick Chapel certain works intended to warm and ventilate the building on an improved and efficient principle' and he suggested that the sub-committee should 'examine and test the apparatus of that plan'. The meeting of 4 January 1841 resolved 'Mr Chantrell be directed immediately to prepare a plan' but when this was examined three days later the discussion was inconclusive. However, the meeting of 22 March accepted tenders from two contactors and resolved the work should commence immediately after the next court sessions.

REFERENCE: Repairs and Alterations to Corporate Buildings Sub-committee Minutes, WYASL, LLC16/1/1.

Leeds, Drying House in or near Meadow Lane
Designed or surveyed the building, c.1819
In connection with Chantrell's appointment to design Christ Church, Leeds, the CBC asked many questions about the proposed site and its geological make-up. He wrote a long letter which discusses the sub-soil in the area and adds: 'Having occasion to inspect the building of a drying house within 200 yards of the site of the church, the water was found to be 18 feet from the surface, the back wall of this building was erected in an old watercourse about 3 feet 6 inches deep. The bed had almost 14 feet of common alluvial deposit and below that a course of loose sand about 2 feet 6 inches deep. The footing stones were laid upon the gravel which appeared at this depth (about 7 feet from the surface) which proved sufficient to bear about 30 feet of wall. No defect being visible though executed more than two years and a half [i.e., late in 1819] … ' He does not go so far as to state he designed the drying house, although clearly he was well acquainted with its construction. The letter also discusses the properties of the ground on which the Public Baths in Leeds were built; this he certainly did design although he doesn't state it in the letter.

REFERENCE: CBC, MB 5, p. 332.

Leeds, Free or Grammar School
New perimeter wall, 1824
At the meeting of the Leeds Pious Uses Committee – which oversaw the school's operation and maintenance – on 1 September 1824 it was 'ordered that Mr Chantrell's plan for the school wall be adopted and that the wall be set back to range with the master's house, provided the [highways] commissioners will pay the charge of the wall – the railings will be furnished by the committee.' The meeting of four weeks later noted that: 'the vestry meeting had agreed to the surveyor paying out of the Highways Rate the sum of £34/18/0 for the Free School wall and ordered that the work be proceeded with without delay.'

REFERENCE: Pious Uses Committee Minutes, WYASL, DB197/2

Leeds, Free or Grammar School
Repairs, 1825
The churchwardens' accounts of Leeds Parish Church record that on 22 September 1825 'Mr Chantrell

[was paid] £12/12/0. It is not clear for what. It seems too large a sum for the new perimeter wall and in 1825, these accounts list several payments to tradesmen for repairs to the Free School and Masters' House; it seems more likely that Chantrell had supervised these.

REFERENCE: WYASL, RDP68/71/4.

Leeds, Free or Grammar School
Consulted about proposed extension, 1844
In the early 1840s, the Pious Uses Committee considered substantially enlarging the school 'on its present site'. There is a plan by Dobson and Shaw of *c*.1844 proposing a doubling of the accommodation. The committee meeting of 10 April 1844 'Resolved that the School Sub-committee be requested to communicate with Mr Chantrell on the best means of doing this with reference to the plans laid before the meeting and to report to the next meeting.' However, subsequent meetings did not pursue the matter, either with or without Chantrell's advice.

REFERENCE: WYASL, DB 197/2, pp. 420-1.

Leeds, General Cemetery
Unexecuted design, 1833
Seventeen architects submitted designs for the competition for a new privately owned cemetery to be built near Woodhouse Moor. Proposals were to include a chapel, superintendent's house and mausoleum etc. and drawings were required to show the proposed layout of the whole site (Fletcher). Chantrell's submission included 'a ground plan, a bird's perspective of the site, general elevation (which is a mere sketch)' and a written description. In it he explained: 'In compiling my design I have considered economy, at the same time giving all the effect possible and I hope, taken every advantage of applying what I have found deficient in many which I have visited, and suggested such arrangements as were usual in the days of the Romans.' (LU SC MS 421). All the plans were examined on 13 November 1833 by a sub-committee which produced a shortlist of six schemes – which didn't include Chantrell's – and from these, the general committee awarded first prize to Clark at its meeting on 18 November 1833. The sub-committee made brief comments on each submission, noting any perceived weaknesses. Several of those rejected at an early stage were deemed 'too costly' or were noted as failing to include costs of 'drainage, planting and laying-out' from their estimate. Another contained a 'basic mistake in the ground plan'. It seems somewhat strange that Chantrell's plans were quickly discarded even though its cost was not excessive, it contained 'full plans' and no specific criticism was identified and noted.

REFERENCES: UL SC MS 421/140/1, SC MS 421/33; *LI*, 23 Nov. 1833; R.F. Fletcher, 'The History of the Leeds General Cemetery Company, 1833-1965', unpublished M.Phil thesis, University of Leeds, 1975.

Leeds, Holy Trinity
Repairs and new upper stage of tower, 1839-40
Holy Trinity, built 1723-7, was designed by William Etty. Although in place by 1726, the spire was, according to Whitaker 'no part of the original plan [and] unquestionably one instance of many of private interference, by which the better judgement of real architects is often overruled ... ' (Friedman). The spire was damaged in 'the hurricane' of 7 January 1839 along with the towers of several Leeds churches (*LI*, 12 Jan. 1839). Further damage was caused in the gale of 30 January. However, within two days the spire had 'been secured and strengthened in the inside under the superintendence of Mr Chantrell, the architect. He is of the opinion that the congregation and the inhabitants of the neighbourhood have no further cause for alarm and the temporary repairs will secure the spire until the weather is favourable for taking it down.'

(*LI*, 2 Feb. 1839). Having removed it, two predictable options existed: replace the spire with something similar; simply leave the tower with no spire, as Etty first intended. However, the outcome was an unlikely one: the erection of a three-stage, stone 'spire', a composite of the various steeples designed by James Gibbs and published in his *A Book of Architecture,* 1728. This outcome is deemed 'unlikely' for two reasons: firstly, at a time when money for church and church-school building was limited, spending almost £800 on the spire – the cost of a medium-sized school – might be interpreted as an extravagant solution; secondly, in 1839, the Baroque of Gibbs and his contemporaries was far from fashionable. Chantrell's steeple certainly respects Etty's design for the rest of the church, but while Etty's work is essentially a toned down version of metropolitan Baroque, Chantrell's steeple is as unquestionably exuberant. Sadly, the church records give no hint as to whether the project was driven by Chantrell or the parishioners, but it seems unlikely that laymen would have had such sophisticated taste. Work progressed through 1839 with the *LI* of 14 December 1839 reporting that, although the scaffolding was yet to be removed, the new work was 'so creditable to the architect'. It has remained an important – and almost universally admired – addition to the Leeds skyline ever since. The total cost was £797/11/6 of which Chantrell received £39/5/6.

REFERENCES: WYASL, RDP35/35; *LI,* 12 Jan., 2 Feb., 14 Dec. 1839; T. Friedman, *Church Architecture in Leeds 1700-1799,* Thoresby Society, Leeds, 2nd ser., vol. 7, 1996, pp. 58-102.

Leeds, Holy Trinity

Repairs, 1841-2

The churchwardens' accounts record various payments during 1841 and 1842 to tradesmen for such things as stone repairs and pointing, roof repairs, repairs to the ceiling, painting etc. The total spent was £867/12/6, a huge sum when it is remembered that at this time, the church at Poole, near Leeds, was rebuilt at an estimated cost of only £308. For supervising the work at Holy Trinity, Chantrell received £38/17/6.

REFERENCE: WYASL, RDP35/35._

Leeds, Leeds Library

Alterations, 1821

No doubt following discussions begun earlier, on 11 June 1821 the Library's committee 'Resolved to erect a gallery and set up a sub-committee to do this. The library will be closed from 3 July to 4 September for work to proceed.' The *LI* of 27 August 1821 announced: 'Our library is to be re-opened shortly, newly fitted up; and with the addition of a handsome gallery at the eastern end'. Tradesmen's bills totalled £63/1/7. On 10 September 1821, Chantrell presented his bill for 7 gns – 3½ days at 2gns per day. The project included an innovative iron spiral staircase.

REFERENCES: Leeds Library, Committee Minute Book; Leeds Library, Account Book; *LI,* 27 Aug. 1821.

Leeds, Leeds Library

Alterations, 1828

The *LI* of 17 July 1828 carried an advertisement calling a 'Special General Meeting of the Leeds Library to determine upon the proposition made for altering the windows in the shops below the library.' The library's account book records a total outlay of £152/16/7 – less £16/15/0 from the sale of the old windows – including £6/12/0 paid to Chantrell.

REFERENCES: Leeds Library, Account Book; Leeds Library, unclassified papers.

Cat. 16: Leeds, Leeds Library, east staircase and gallery which Chantrell added to Thomas Johnson's 1807–8 library in 1821. (*Blacksheep Photography*).

Leeds, Leeds Library
Alterations, 1835

The *LI* of 30 May 1835 reported that 'the Library Committee was authorised to lay out a sum not exceeding £300 in the erection of a new gallery on the north and west ends of the room, to correspond to that at the east end.' The edition of 31 Oct 1835 announced the reopening. Library papers note payment of £180 'for gallery' and £6/6/0 to Chantrell for 'architectural services'.

REFERENCES: *LI,* 30 May, 31 Oct. 1835; Leeds Library, Account Book; Leeds Library, unclassified papers.

Leeds, Music Hall
Alterations, 1821

LI, 16 December 1824 stated, 'The Committee of the Northern Society [for the Encouragement of Arts] have in conjunction with the Trustees of the Music Hall, directed Mr Chantrell, architect, to improve the Saloon be the addition of a lantern similar to those in the Gallery and Cabinet erected by him three years ago.'

REFERENCE: *LI,* 16 Dec. 1824.

Cat. 17: Leeds, the Gallery of the Music Hall, Albion Street, where Chantrell rebuilt to roof to add 'lantern lights' in 1821. This watercolour, by Joseph Rhodes, shows the Gallery in 1839, set out for the Northern Society for the Encouragement of Arts' exhibition that year. (*Leeds Museums and Galleries*).

Leeds, Music Hall
Alterations, 1824–5

The passage from the *LI*, 16 December 1824, quoted above, concludes '[The addition of a lantern in the Saloon] will enable us to boast of as complete a suite of exhibition rooms as any in England.' On 28 April, the *LI* was able to announce 'The old gloomy entrance or anti-chamber leading to the gallery of the Northern Society exhibition rooms has been completely remodelled and presents as light and elegant an appearance as either of the others.'

REFERENCES: *LI*, 16 Dec. 1824, 28 April 1825; *LM*, 28 May 1825; T. Fawcett, *The Rise of English Provincial Art*, Oxford UP, 1974, p. 114.

Leeds, Music Hall
Alterations, 1840

LI, 9 May 1840 reported 'the [Music Hall] has been undergoing extensive alterations during the last six weeks under the direction and according to the designs of Mr Chantrell, architect. The Saloon has been greatly enlarged and would now accommodate to dinner one quarter more persons than could have dined there two months ago. There are other improvements which we shall notice hereafter.' However, the promise of the last sentence appears not to have been fulfilled.

REFERENCES: *LI*, 9 May 1840.

Leeds, Philosophical and Literary Society Hall
New hall, 1819–21

A writer in the *LM* 'at the close of 1818' suggested the formation of the society (Laws) and on 11 December 1818 a meeting was held at the Court House of 'Gentlemen favourable to the formation [of such a society] and it was decided that an institution be established' (*LI*, 4 Jan. 1819). In January, a subscription was opened for the erection of a suitable hall (*LI*, 18 Jan. 1819) and on 8 March the paper was able to announce that £3,000 had been raised. On 7 May a meeting was held to examine the plans submitted by architects (*LI*, 3 May 1819). On 14 May Chantrell was appointed architect (Clark, p. 20) and at the same time, asked to 'prepare drawings for the different parts of the building and to advertise for estimates' (Building Comm. MB). Tenders were requested in editions of the *LI* on 17 May, 7 June and 21 June 1819. The foundation stone was laid on 9 July (*LI*, 12 July 1819) and work progressed sufficiently for the building committee to be discussing designs for mantle pieces in February and March 1820 (Clark). On 30 July 1820 a meeting was held to inform members of progress; of the £5,000 necessary to complete the building, £3,800 had been raised and a further £700 was promised at the meeting (*LI*, 7 Aug. 1820). The first meeting was held in the new hall on 6 April 1821 (*LI*, 2 April 1821) and the total cost of the building was £6,150/10/3 (Building Comm. MB). Chantrell received 100 gns, although for many years after, he claimed additional fees for 'extra work' with limited success (Council Minutes).

The building was of two storeys, the lower one was rusticated and on the upper one, Doric pilasters supported a debased entablature. The side elevation was of three bays with the centre one projecting slightly. The front elevation, facing Park Row, was of five bays with the middle three projecting. The accommodation consisted of: 'a vestibule or entrance hall 22 feet by 16, leading to a commodious lecture hall, 44 by 31½ feet, having seats for 300 persons; the council-room 12¾ by 14½ feet; library 24 by 13 feet; and ante-room 15½ by 14½ feet. The principal apartments are in the upper storey, and consist of curator's room 24 by 13 feet; geological room 49 by 15 feet; do., 24½ by 20 feet; and zoological room, 42 by 31 feet.' (Fenteman, p. 86). Soon after its completion Baines described it as 'a handsome stone edifice [which] claims a prominent rank amongst our public buildings', a sentiment repeated in directories for many years.

It was altered and extended in 1861-2 by Chorley and Dobson; following damage in enemy action, the site was cleared in the 1960s.

DRAWINGS: Leeds City Museum.

REFERENCES: LPLS papers, LU, MS 1975/1, especially Council MB (no. 3), Building Accounts (no. 4), Building Comm. MB (no. 6), also nos 236 viii, 236 x; *LI*, 4, 18 Jan., 8 March, 3, 17 May, 7, 21 June, 12 July 1819, 7 Aug. 1820, 2 April 1821, 1 July 1825; *Laws and Regulations of the Philosophical and Literary Society*, Leeds, 1841; E.K. Clark, *A History of One Hundred Years of the Leeds Philosophical and Literary Society*, Leeds, 1920; T. Fenteman, *Historical Guide to Leeds*, Thomas and Sons, 1858; E. Baines, *History, Directory and Gazetteer of the County of York*, E. Baines, 1822, vol. 1.

Leeds, Philosophical and Literary Society Hall
Alterations, 1826, unexecuted

In the *Report for the Year 1825-6*, the Council noted: 'The inconvenience of the present Museum and Lecture Room, but especially the former, being found very pressing, it was concluded that ... some steps might be immediately taken, with a view to making such alterations in the original building, as would render it more adequate to the requirements of the Institution.' On 1 June 1826, the building committee 'resolved that Mr Chantrell be appointed architect ... for the alterations', adding 'on condition that he enters into a bond to complete the work for the estimated cost' (Building Comm. MB). At the building committee's meeting of 5 July 1826 it was noted that 'Mr Chantrell having declined to enter into a bond ... Watson and Pritchett [architects of York] be applied to' and the meeting on 14 July 1826 'adopted Mr Pritchett's plan for the proposed alterations'.

REFERENCE: LPLS papers, LU, MS 1975/1, Building Committee MB, no. 6.

Leeds, Philosophical and Literary Society Hall
Alterations, 1839-40

At the society's council meeting of 15 March 1839, it was 'resolved that the Curator be requested to obtain a plan and specification of the proposed alterations'. The *LI* of 16 March 1839 noted a subscription for improving the museum had been opened and the edition of 4 May 1839 reported that 'alterations and repairs' would soon commence. At the council meeting of 17 May 1839 'Mr Teale [the society's curator] having laid before the Council the plan by Mr Chantrell for the proposed alterations ... it was resolved [he] should proceed immediately with the alterations to the Museum, Vestibule and Lecture Room, according to the plan and estimates.' The Council's *Report for the Year 1838-9* gives more details of the intended changes: 'It is now proposed to make such alterations in the Hall as will afford not only considerably more room but also of a kind better suited for the arrangements and exhibits of specimens. This will be accomplished by converting the large room into the Geological Museum. To adapt it for this purpose it will be necessary to build up the windows and to admit light from the roof by lanthorns by which a very considerable space of wall room will be gained. The estimated cost of these alterations and repairing the roof and skylights on the Zoological and Mineral Rooms, which are in the most defective condition (having been badly constructed at first) is more than £700.' The council's *Report for the Year 1830-40* recorded that 'the long room, formerly for antiquities and works of art, has been rendered more lofty. A new roof with three lanthorn lights has been substituted for the old one and the side windows closed up ... In the Zoological Room, the large [defective] lanthorn light ... has been replaced by an entirely new one ... The Society is indebted to the great liberality of Mr Chantrell for providing plans and superintending the alterations'.

REFERENCES: LPLS papers, LU SC MS1975/1, Council Minute Book 3, Reports 1838-9 and 1839-40; *LI*, 16 March, 4 May 1839.

Leeds, Philosophical and Literary Society Hall
Design of pedestal for statue of M.T. Sadler, 1843
The *LI* of 22 April 1843 announced that 'The statue of M.T. Sadler by [Patrick] Park [of Edinburgh] is now in the Philosophical Hall'; the edition of 27 May 1843 noting that it had been placed on a 'classical and appropriate' pedestal 'designed by Mr Chantrell'. Gunnis refers to a bust of Sadler carved in 1837 and placed in Leeds Parish Church from where, presumably, it was relocated.

REFERENCES: *LI,* 22 April, 27 May 1843; R. Gunnis, *Dictionary of British Sculptors 1660-1851,* Abbey Library, 1964, p. 291.

Leeds, Public Baths
New bath building, 1819–21
A meeting 'to make arrangements for the erection of cold and warm baths' was held in the Court House in Leeds on 30 November 1818. Present were many of the town's leading men who 'resolved that the establishment of cold and warm baths will be very conducive to the health and comfort of the inhabitants of the town and that immediate steps be taken to effect so desirable an object' (Bath Committee MB). The committee met on 14 January 1819 and decided on the precise facilities required (these are listed in detail in the MB). They agreed the building was 'to be of brick with a handsome stone front and covered with blue slate'. The cost was not to exceed £2,500. They resolved to place advertisements inviting architects to submit plans (*ibid.*). Certainly one appeared in *LI* of 18 January 1819, but there must have been wider publicity as 14 architects from London and the provinces responded, 12 of them with designs (Baths Committee MB). Chantrell wrote from Halifax asking for particulars on 20 January; he must have been eager to begin his design as he wrote again on 24 January (Baths Company papers). In fact he submitted no less than three alternative schemes and accompanied them with a letter: 'As it is unusual that candidates for public works in architecture should annex their names to their performances, I shall distinguish my design by the word "Ionia". R.D. Chantrell, Saddle Yard, Briggate, or Blackwall, Halifax, till 15 March.' (*ibid.*). The letter is of interest for three reasons: it gives a precise date for Chantrell's removal to Leeds; his departure from Halifax clearly pre-dates his victories in either the Baths or Phil. and Lit. Hall competitions; there is a certain naïve high-mindedness in the wording of Chantrell's letter which suggests his thinking was still closer to the world of Soane than the more prosaic practises of the West Riding. The building committee met on 18 February 1819 and noted the submissions received, but deferred a decision until 4 March 1819 when it agreed to award Chantrell first prize, James Elmes of London, second prize, and Lindley, Woodhead and Hirst, third prize. Success was a remarkable achievement for the young Chantrell who had also triumphed over the leading Yorkshire practice of Watson and Pritchett, Rickman from Liverpool and a handful of London architects including Decimus Burton. Tenders were advertised in *LI* of 5 April 1819 and the foundation stone was laid on 12 May (*LI,* 17 May 1819). On 31 July 1820, the building 'although not finished, was opened for the reception of the public' (*LI,* 7 Aug. 1820), and it seems still not to have been completed a year later; inevitably, costs had risen although the committee appeared satisfied with its choice of architect. Justifying Chantrell's position in the face of delays and rising costs, on 27 August 1821 the building committee reported that 'Mr Chantrell's plan was adopted and he was appointed architect and it is but justice to this gentleman that your Committee should declare, that his attention to his duty has fully warranted their warmest approbation … It was the wish of your Committee not to have exceeded £5,000 … but it will not be affected for less than £7,000.' In fact the total cost was £7,053 (Baths Committee MB). The completed building contained 'two separate and complete suites of apartments … for ladies and gentlemen' (Baines) and Heaton described it as ' … a highly elegant and classical, though diminutive building … the entrance is marked by two couples of Ionic columns supporting an entablature, and a richly chiselled panel, where among the foliage is seen the Esculapian serpent; at the ends of the building are coupled pilasters. The interior is fitted up with considerable taste … 'The building, situated in

Wellington Street, near the present City Square, was demolished in 1857 (White).

REFERENCES: Leeds Public Baths Committee Minutes, 1818-27, WYASL, DB276; *LI,* 30 Nov., 7 Dec. 1818, 18 Jan., 5 April, 17 May 1819, 7 Aug. 1820, 16 March 1833, 16 July 1836; E. Baines, *History, Directory … County of York,* Baines, 1822; J. Heaton, *Walks Through Leeds,* J. Heaton, 1835; W. White, *Leeds Trades Directory, 1857-8,* William White, 1857, p. 28.

Leeds, Public Baths

Minor works, 1824-5

In response to 'an application from Mr Beverley who is about to erect a building adjacent to the Baths and wishes to build on the wall of the Baths', on 19 March 1824 the committee resolved to 'decline the request and the new building is to be kept distinct under the superintendence of Mr C[h]antrell.' (Baths Committee MB).

At its committee meeting on 4 May 1825, 'It having been represented … that a beneficial enlargement of the Baths Building may be effected by building over the front so as to make accommodation for the Mechanics Institute or other purpose, it was resolved [that a sub-committee be formed] and that the committee of management be directed to obtain plans and specifications of the improvement capable of being made to the present building.' Given its recourse to Chantrell in 1824, it seems most unlikely the committee would not have consulted him on this initiative too. However, nothing more appears on the topic in the minutes.

REFERENCES: Leeds Public Baths Committee Minutes, 1818-27, WYASL, DB276.

Leeds, South Market

New market complex, 1823-4

See Chapter 7 for a full account of this building.

A public meeting at the Court House on 16 June 1823 resolved that it was 'highly desirable that a public market should be erected in the south division of the town'. A plan by Charles Fowler, dated April 1823, [now in the TS Collection, Box A] indicating how the market might be laid out was exhibited, a suitable plot of land was identified and £7,050 in £50 shares 'was raised in the room' towards a predicted cost of £15,000 (*LI,* 19 June 1823). Demonstrating a speed remarkable in such projects, only a week later the *LI* invited architects to submit plans with premiums of 20, 10 and 5 gns offered for the best designs. Chantrell was announced the winner in the *LI* of 28 August 1823 and the edition of 4 September invited tenders. On 25 September it announced the work was let and that work would commence 'this week'. The first stone was laid at the end of October (*LI,* 30 Oct. 1823), and the cross for the sale of butter was opened on 10 July 1824 (*LI,* 8 July 1824), although the edition of 16 December 1824 referred to the complex as 'nearly completed'. White records the final cost as £22,000.

The market was on an irregular site and consisted of 18 three-storey shops with houses above facing outwards to Meadow Lane and Hunslet Lane, 9 slaughter houses, 118 stalls in roofed enclosures, and at its centre, the remarkable circular cross of concentric Doric columns, topped by an upper floor of twelve attached columns crowned by a hemi-spherical dome surmounted by a tall statue – in essence, 'a circular temple' (Heaton). Within this cupola was a committee room.

The market never achieved popularity with the public, although from 1827, the quarterly leather fairs achieved some success. Parsons recorded in 1834 'This speculation has been a decided failure … ' The central section was demolished in the early 20th century, although some of the surrounding shops survived until the 1960s.

DRAWINGS: TS Box A; TS 39B 38.

REFERENCES: *LI,* 19, 28 June, 28 Aug., 4, 5 Sept., 30 Oct., 13 Nov. 1823, 4 March, 27 May, 1, 8 July, 15 Sept., 16 Dec. 1824; J. Heaton, *Walks Through Leeds,* J. Heaton, 1835, p.102; W. White, *Directory and Gazetteer of Leeds …* , W White, 1853, p.24; E. Parsons, *The Civil, Ecclesiastical … History of Leeds …* , Frederick Hobson, 1834; K Grady, 'The Provision of Markets in Leeds' in *Thoresby Society Miscellany,* 54, pt 3, 1976, no. 122, pp. 165-95.

Leeds, St George

Unexecuted design for new church, 1836

The *LI* of 16 April 1836 stated that 'Plans are invited for a new church at Mount Pleasant, Leeds.' The edition of 18 June 1836 reported that: 'Mr Clark's plan has been chosen for the new church at Mount pleasant … Mr Chantrell came second in the competition with an excellent plan in many respects, also in the Gothic style. The principal point of preference was, that Mr Clark's plan needs no interior pillars'.

REFERENCES: *LI,* 16 April, 18 June 1836.

Leeds, St John

Repairs and alterations, 1837-8

As a result of the parish church's closure prior to rebuilding, 'the parochial services were transferred to [St John's], in which additional galleries were erected for the occasion, and all available space filled with seats and benches' (Moore). St John's is a rare surviving example of a Gothic church built in the 1630s. The LPC Building Committee MB records 'Expenses of St John's Church: … Chantrell, architect's commission £15/7/6 [total £375/10/10, the biggest item of which is] Russell, joiner £179/9/6'.

REFERENCES: WYASL, RDP68/41/7; R.W. Moore, *A History of the Parish Church of Leeds,* Richard Jackson, 1877, p. 7.

Leeds, St Mark, Woodhouse

Alterations, 1827

St Mark is a Gothic church, built 1823-5, by Atkinson and Sharp of York. It was one of the three churches built in Leeds from the first Parliamentary grant. On 30 March 1827, the incumbent wrote a long letter to CBC about his recently opened church. He reports that Chantrell had 'advised' on laying out the pews and moving the pulpit to enable the congregation to hear, and have a better view of, the services.

REFERENCES: CBC, Leeds, Meadow Lane, Quarry Hill and Woodhouse file, no. 20548.

Leeds, St Mark, Woodhouse

Minor work, 1827-8

Chantrell estimated the cost of installing a floor in the tower to create a ringing chamber, and a bell, would be £65. The expenditure was approved by J.H. Good, the CBC surveyor, on 14 January 1828 (CBC, MB 27), and passed for payment on 20 May 1828 (CBC, MB 30). The CBC meeting of 8 January 1828 also approved the expenditure of £8/10/- for a font 'to be erected under the supervision of Mr Chantrell' (CBC, MB 28).

REFERENCES: CBC, MB 27, p. 210, MB 30, p. 220, MB 28, p. 14.

Leeds, St Mark, Woodhouse

New W gallery, 1832-3

St Mark's Vestry Minute Book record that 'On 16 June 1833 the gallery at the west end of the church was opened … the gallery was erected according to plans prepared by Mr Chantrell, architect.' The expenditure, approved at the vestry meeting of 8 September 1833, amounted to £210 of which Chantrell received £13/9/5. Chantrell's bill (WYASL) gives considerable detail of the time he spent on the project.

DRAWINGS: WYASL, RDP108/53, 1-3.

REFERENCE: WYASL, RDP108/53/1–3; Vestry Minute Book WYASL, RDP108/45; *LI,* 15 June 1833.

Leeds, St Mark, Woodhouse

New S gallery, 1836-7

The *LI* of 24 Sept 1836 reported: 'At a meeting of the subscribers to the fund for building a new south gallery … it was unanimously determined to commence the work immediately according to the plans and designs by Mr Chantrell which have received the sanction of the Archbishop of York.' However, it seems likely there were delays as the *LI* of 29 April 1837 noted 'the new gallery … is now rapidly advancing, the church being closed on account of the work … it will open on May 12th. The vestry minutes of 26 May 1837 record 'The Gallery on the south side was opened … the Gallery was erected according to the plans prepared by Mr Chantrell (who gave his professional services). The cost … is £374.'

REFERENCES: Vestry Minute Book, WYASL, RDP108/45; *LI,* 24 Sept. 1836, 29 April, 6, 27 May 1837.

Leeds, St Mark, Woodhouse

New organ screen, 1838

The *LI* of 20 October 1838 noted 'St Mark's organ [was built] by F. Booth of Wakefield … Its exterior appearance is all that could be desired – harmonising with the beautiful architecture of the structure in which it is placed. The honour of the elegant design belongs to Mr Chantrell; the ornamental parts are by Messrs Bullman and Son.' A document records the 'design and drawings for the case [were] presented by R.D. Chantrell, Esq.' (WYASL).

REFERENCES: WYASL, RDP108/55, RDP108/56/1-2; *LI,* 20 Oct. 1838.

Leeds, St Mark, Feather Hill School

Enlargement, 1832

The school was built in 1784. Its Managers' Minute Book records: 'May 9th 1832 … that Mr Chantrell be requested to prepare a specification of the works to be done in enlarging the school before contracts are made.' Their meeting of 29 May 1832 confirmed the tenders. The *LI* of 2 August 1832 noted 'Feather Hill Sunday School enlarged … 'There were subsequent extensions in 1846 and 1873.

REFERENCES: School Manager's MB, WYASL, RDP108/94; *LI,* 2 Aug. 1832; *Yorkshire Evening Post,* 25 July 1934.

Leeds, St Mary, Quarry Hill

Overseeing the purchase of a new burial ground, 1829

The *LI* of 19 March 1829 noted Chantrell had been appointed to ' … purchase burial land for St Mary's

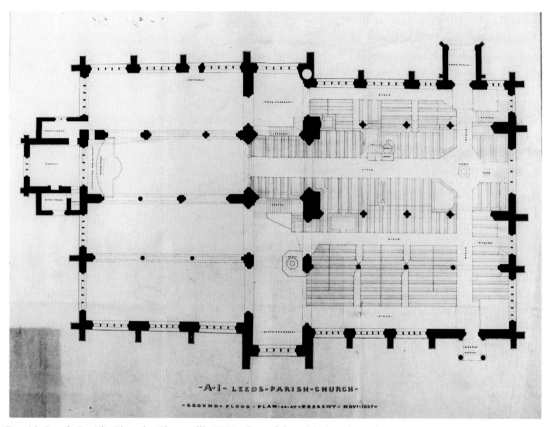

Cat. 18: Leeds Parish Church, Chantrell's 1837 plan of the old church. (*BI*).

… ' Leeds Parish Church Churchwardens' Accounts note Chantrell was paid £5/0/0 on 7 February 1830 which might relate to this commission.

REFERENCES: *LI,* 19 March 1839; WYASL, RDP68/41/3.

Leeds, St Mary, Quarry Hill, School

New school, *c.*1829

The parish papers include a drawing by Chantrell for a new school. On the reverse, in a hand not Chantrell's, it states 'The original designs for Quarry Hill School, 1829'. The CBC meeting of 12 January 1830 agreed that land for the school could be transferred to the school's trustees, but it is not clear if the school was finished by this date. The drawing shows a single storey rectangular building with six paired lancet windows on the long E side and a tripartite lancet window with door below in the N gable. The school was enlarged – including an upper storey – by C. W. Burleigh in 1848 (*LI*).

DRAWING: WYASL, RDP66/16.

REFERENCES: CBC, MB 36, p. 439; *LI,* 13 May 1848.

Catalogue

Leeds, St Peter
Rebuilt church, 1837–41

For a full account of this building, see Chapter 7 and C. Webster, *The Rebuilding of Leeds Parish Church 1837-41, and its place in the Gothic Revival,* The Ecclesiological Society, 1994.

The medieval parish church of Leeds, with a cruciform plan and central tower, and, unusually, an 'extra' N aisle, was both physically neglected and internally ill-suited to the more progressive liturgical thinking at the beginning of Victoria's reign. Most detrimentally, the narrow arches of the crossing tower effectively cut the church in two; in the nave a 'preaching box' auditorium had been created in the 18th century with galleries on all four sides focused on the pulpit, while the E end – a vast space equal to the area of the nave – was more or less abandoned, used only for the rarely celebrated communion.

The driving force behind the rebuilding was the new vicar, Dr W.F. Hook. He was inducted to the living on 15 April 1837 and within two weeks announced ambitious plans. Hook was a man of great energy 'the greatest parish priest of the nineteenth century', according to Rusby – the writer of the monumental 1896 *History of Leeds Parish Church* – and believed 'a handsome church [was] a kind of standing sermon' (*LI,* 11 Nov. 1837). Details of the initial scheme were announced in *LI* of 29 April 1837 – essentially re-pewing and raising part of the roof to accommodate more gallery space – at a cost of £2,000-2,500. By early October discussion included rebuilding the tower and re-siting the organ as well, and the cost had risen to £4,500. So far, there is no mention of professional assistance for the vicar's ideas. However, on 19

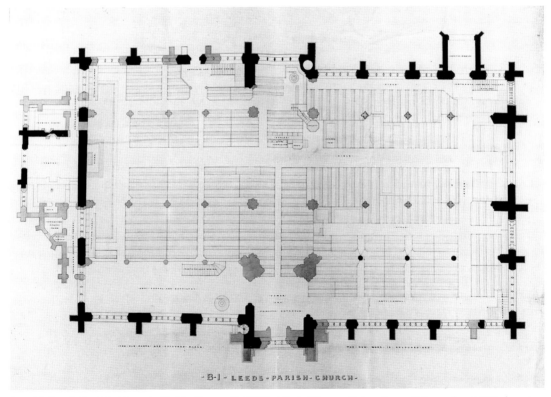

Cat. 19: Leeds Parish Church (R.D. Chantrell, 1837-41). A Chantrell drawing of November 1837 showing his initial intention to keep most of the exterior walls, shown in black, with a new tower on the north side, new columns in the nave and chancel, and new tracery in some windows, shown in grey. At this early stage of the project, the east end was to be filled with congregational seating, there were no choir stalls or steps up to the altar, and there was to be only limited space around the alter. (*BI*).

279

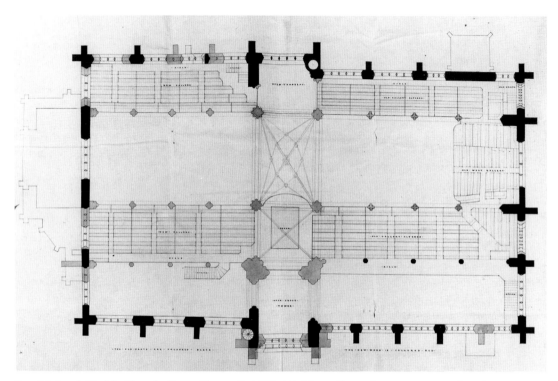

Cat. 20: Leeds Parish Church (R.D. Chantrell, 1837-41). The gallery plan to correspond with Cat. 18. At this stage of the project, it was intended to have new north and south chancel galleries running up to the east wall with the organ in the middle of the north gallery. The north and south nave galleries are marked 'old gallery altered' while the old west gallery is labelled 'unaltered'. (*B1*).

October 1837 he had a meeting with some of the leading townsmen and it was suggested Hook procure plans from Chantrell, a task the latter accepted enthusiastically as only two days later, the *Intelligencer* could report a plan 'to raise the whole roof [and a new internal] arrangement' at a cost of £6,000. Hook called a public meeting for 8 November which gave him enthusiastic support and formally adopted Chantrell's scheme. Later in November, Chantrell produced plans for the faculty which show the removal of the tower from the crossing to the N transept, a much wider crossing, the inclusion of the old chancel into a single huge 'body' pewed throughout, and with substantial galleries on three sides continuing to the E wall and enclosing the altar. All the internal columns were to be new and most re-sited; they would support new clerestories and they, in turn, a series of new, higher, roofs; but very significantly, all the outer walls were to be kept, changed only by the introduction of a small number of new windows, and new tracery in most of the old windows. Despite Hook's reputation for advanced liturgical practices, thus far the proposals could hardly be seen as moving much beyond the principles of the Commissioners.

The *LI* of 17 February 1838 invited tenders 'for renovating the eastern part of the church'. However, the following week, the paper published a letter from 'an old inhabitant' suggesting that this was an ideal opportunity for building an entirely new church. The same edition quoted 'a member of the Building Committee' as saying this was quite out of the question. The church closed in March and work began. Only as plaster and wooden casings were stripped out did the full extent of decayed stonework and poor foundations become evident. Despite the emphatic rejection of 'the old inhabitants' proposal, just two weeks after his letter another appeared signed 'Dionysius' – almost certainly Chantrell using the Latin form

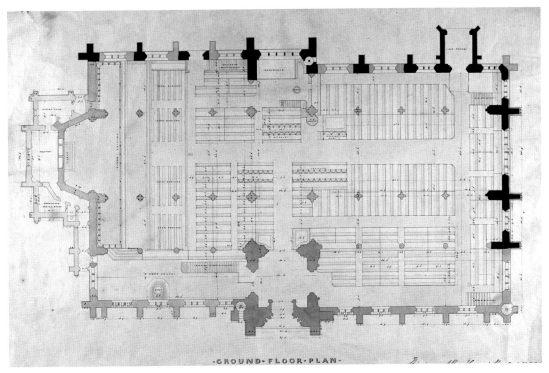

Cat. 21: Leeds Parish Church (R.D. Chantrell, 1837-41). This plan, perhaps of early 1839, shows that by this stage, the whole of the north and east sides were to be rebuilt, the canted bay behind the altar formed part of the design, and there is much more open space in front of the altar than shown in Cat. 18. However, it seems that, at this stage, it was still planned to retain much of the old church. For instance, some of the gallery staircases are annotated 'old staircase' while others were to be new ones. The organ was still intended for the middle of the north gallery. (*Lambeth Palace Library*).

of his Christian name – stating that 'the south wall alone is to be retained, the remainder being razed to the foundations'. The same edition invited further tenders, this time for renovating the whole building. Hook later explained, 'Bit by bit, we found the church crumbling about us, and were placed in the predicament of building a new church, not repairing an old one.' The crucial – but unanswerable – question is this: had Hook and Chantrell known at the beginning of the project that almost nothing of the old church would survive, and that an awesome £30,000 would be spent, would a very different church have been designed? The answer is almost certainly 'yes'; notwithstanding the extent of the new work, the footprint of the finished church followed almost exactly that of the old one. Yet despite rising costs and lengthening project times, there was universal enthusiasm for the scheme – at least in the pro-Tory *Intelligencer*. The recipients of the praise were threefold: the vicar for his vision, Chantrell for the way he overcame a litany of problems, and the subscribers to the rebuilding: 'it is truly an honour to Leeds, and those who have contributed to the work ought to consider it as one of the privileges of their lives', waxed the *Intelligencer* of 4 September 1841.

The finished church is cruciform in plan with an outer or additional N aisle in both the nave and chancel. The tower is in the middle of the N front. There is no structurally separate chancel although there is a canted bay at the E end and much of the eastern arm of the church is raised on steps both before and inside the altar rails. The final internal arrangement was influenced by Hook's friend John Jebb and involved the omission of many of the pews and areas of gallery at the eastern end which appear in the 1837 faculty's

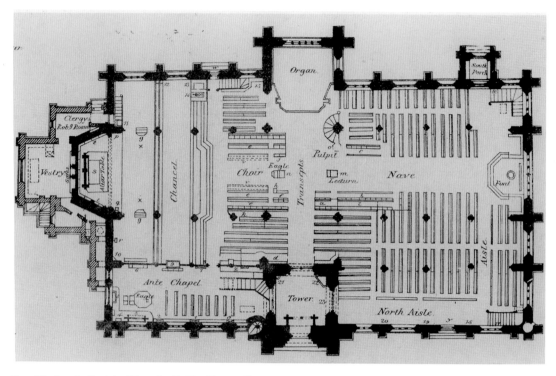

Cat. 22: Leeds Parish Church (R.D. Chantrell, 1837-41). Plan of the finished church by which time virtually all the old masonry had been replaced. Note the choir stalls, south transept, organ, open space in front of the altar, none of which were present in Cat. 20. (R.W. Moore, *Leeds Parish Church and its Ancient Pillar*, 1877, opp. p. 9).

plans. Indeed, only in August 1840 was the decision taken to include choir stalls, steps up to the altar flat and then to the altar, altar rails etc. The style, according to Chantrell, is 'the transition from Decorated to Perpendicular … which has its peculiarities, though unnoticed by modern writers'.

The rededication of 2 September 1841 was an event of national importance, attended by an archbishop, three bishops and 300 clergy. It was the country's biggest new church since St Paul's Cathedral, but its significance rests also with its date: the early 1840s was a period of real importance for Anglicanism: the establishment of the Oxford Movement had helped to give new momentum to reformers; Pugin's Gothic proselytising was generating much support on both sides of the religious divide; Leeds Parish Church and its energetic vicar, Hook, were anticipated to offer a lead in the Church of England's drive to win back the industrial towns from Non-conformity; and finally, the Cambridge Camden Society's agenda of liturgical and architectural innovations was beginning to be noticed. Yet despite the general euphoria that greeted the opening, its architectural influence was negligible. It came just too soon to capitalise on the Camdenian revolution; had building started five years later, it might have been a flagship for the new movement; as it was, it was old-fashioned almost as soon as it was opened. Commenting in 1847, a writer in *The Ecclesiologist* felt, not unfairly, that it could be seen 'only as an historical monument. It had certainly been important as the first great instance … of catholic feeling in a church … and yet it had not been able to compass those points of church arrangement which are the result of study and patient research … [it is not] a protestant preaching hall; nor …a church as we should like to build.' Both literally and conceptually, the central space is a crossroads: the eastern arm anticipates much that we associate with Victorian church arrangements; the western one is still fundamentally a preaching box.

Despite failing the Camdenian test, in a number of important respect, the design anticipates much that became commonplace later. The space around the altar and the number of steps on which it is raised has already been mentioned. Additionally, Chantrell makes explicit the greater importance of the building's eastern arm via a series of often subtle differences in decoration, for instance in the decoration around the clerestory windows, or on what appear to be the huge beams supporting the roof – in reality, the lower parts of the roof trusses. Even the bases of the two eastern crossing piers are more richly carved than their western counterparts.

The total cost was £29,770/6/8½ of which Chantrell received £1570 (Building Accounts).

DRAWINGS: BI, Faculties 1837/5, 1841/2; ICBS, file 02293; also ICBS drawings at the Society of Antiquaries; WYASL, RDP68/52/3, WYASL, DB/M 380.

REFERENCES: ICBS, file 02293; ICBS, MB 9, pp. 55, MB 11, p. 6; Accounts of Building Committee WYASL, RDP68/41/5; Building Committee MB WYASL, RDP68/41/7; Building Committee Rough Minutes WYASL, RDP68/41/13 and 41/14; Misc. papers concerning rebuilding, WYASL, RDP68; *LI,* 31 July 1809, 25 June 1819, 11 May 1812, 20 Feb. 1823, 14 Jan. 1830, 29 April, 26 Aug., 7, 21, 28 Oct., 11, 18 Nov. 1837, 17, 24 Feb., 3, 10 March, 21 April 1838, 20 April, 26 Oct., 30 Nov. 1839, 4 April, 3 Oct. 1840, 1, 8 May, 19 June, 10, 24, 31 July, 28 Aug., 4, 11, 18 Sept., 23 Oct. 1841, 8 Jan., 25 June 1842, 20 July 1844; *Ecclesiologist,* 8, 1847, pp. 129–34; *Gentleman's Magazine,* 27, 1847, p. 190; R.W. Moore, *A History of the Parish Church of Leeds,* Richard Jackson, 1873; J. Rusby, *History of the Parish Church of St Peter at Leeds,* Richard Jackson, 1896; N.Yates, *Leeds and the Oxford Movement,* The Thoresby Society, Leeds, 1975; H.W. Dalton, *Anglican Resurgence under W.F. Hook in Early Victorian Leeds,* The Thoresby Society Leeds, 2nd ser., vol. 12, 2002.

Leeds, St Peter

Monument to Ralph Thoresby, 1841

The *LI* of 23 October 1841 reported 'Mr Gott's monument to [Ralph] Thoresby [was] designed by Mr Chantrell so as to exhibit a model of what a Gothic monument ought to be … 'Whether 'Mr Gott' refers to the sculptor Joseph Gott as carver of the monument, or a member of the prominent Gott family as patron of the project is not clear. The oft-repeated story that the monument was constructed from the piscina from the old parish church seems most unlikely; the size of the monument and the crispness of the carving would appear to contradict these accounts.

REFERENCE: *LI,* 23 Oct. 1841.

Leeds, St Peter, Oratory

New oratory, 1838

At its meeting of 5 March 1838, the Leeds Parish Church Building Committee 'Resolved to build an oratory of brick in the new church yard and request Mr Chantrell to make out and furnish a plan and estimate of the same'. It was proposed that the oratory could be used for worship while the Parish Church was being rebuilt, despite the oratory's limited size and the decision to transfer services to St John's. The Building Committee's meeting of 19 March 1838 suggested 'old oil paintings from the [Parish] church … could be used to decorate the chapel to be erected in the burial ground'. The Building Committee's account book notes payments for the oratory between April and October 1838 and show the total cost to have been £192/11/0 of which Chantrell received £9/0/0.

The internal dimensions were about 18 feet x 30 feet. It was demolished when the railway line was constructed through the burial ground in *c.*1870.

REFERENCES: LPC Building Committee Minutes, WYASL, RDP68/41/7; LPC Building Committee Account Book, WYASL, RDP68/41/5.

Leeds, St Philip

New church, 1845-7

The Gott family, owners of the vast mill complex at Bean Ings, gave liberally to the erection of schools and churches in the area around the mill, the St George's district. The *LI* of 28 February 1843 invited architects to submit plans for a new chapel of ease for the district, although there was no announcement of the outcome. On 23 August 1843, the Revd Sinclear, the incumbent of St George's, wrote to the CBC about church provision for his flock: 'It is proposed to use a portion of the National School [at Bean Ings] as a temporary place of worship for the second new parish … and the expense of the requisite fittings and some alterations for the purpose of giving an ecclesiastical character to the building have been undertaken … also an adjoining plot of land to the school has been purchased for the intended church'. Not until 11 January 1845 did the *Intelligencer* announce proposals for a new church at Bean Ings and two months later Sinclear completed the CBC's application form. It is 'signed' R.D. Chantrell, although not in his hand. A further copy of the application form was submitted on 3 September 1845 – this time signed by Chantrell. In it, the size, cost and accommodation differs significantly from that in the March form suggesting a major redesign of the project. Meanwhile, an application had been made to the ICBS which offered a grant of £200 in May 1845. The foundation stone was laid on 10 November 1845 (*LI*, 1, 15 Nov. 1845). Correspondence with both the CBC and Ripon Diocesan Church Building Society of March and April 1847 suggests there were further alterations to the internal layout, probably seating. The *LI* of 20 June 1847 noted 'The noble structure is now so far advanced towards completion that it will soon be [finished] … The builder has completed setting the spire'. The 9 October 1847 edition carried a lengthy description following the consecration. The CBC completion certificate was signed on 31 December 1847; it records 587 seats at a cost of £3,371. However, the CBC file notes the cost as '£5,231 … including site and architect's fees'. The difference is perplexing, especially since the site was apparently given by John Gott. The church occupied a small, irregular site, with existing buildings on some of its boundaries; Chantrell was faced with real problems both in fitting a church onto it and in arranging the windows to light the building adequately. It consisted of nave with aisles, clerestory and small W gallery, principally for the organ. There was a long chancel and a substantial tower – forming the principal entrance – and spire projecting from the S aisle. It was demolished in the 1930s.

DRAWINGS: CBC, Leeds, St Philip, file 20547; ICBS, file 03601.

REFERENCES: CBC, MB 57, p. 454; CBC, Leeds, St Philip's, files 3791 and 20, 547; ICBS, file 03601; ICBS, MB 12, p. 184, MB 13, pp. 69, 73; *LI*, 28 Jan. 1843, 11 Jan., 2 Aug., 1, 15 Nov. 1845, 17 April, 20 June, 9 Oct. 1847; *Builder*, 5, 1847, pp. 454, 508; 6, 1847, p. 485; *Civil Engineer and Architect's Journal*, April 1846, p. 100; *Ecclesiologist*, 8, 1847, pp. 109-10.

Leeds, St Philip's School

Extension, 1843

The school was built in 1839-40 (*LI*, 18 May 1839 and 18 Jan. 1840). No architect was recorded, although Chantrell may well have designed it as he produced many schools in Leeds around this time and received much employment from the Gott family. However, in 1843 it was extended. On 23 August 1843, the incumbent at St George's, in which district the school was situated, wrote to the CBC about church provision: 'It is proposed to use a portion of the National School as a temporary place of worship for the second new parish [which eventually became St Philip's] … and the requisite fittings and some alterations for the purpose of giving an ecclesiastical character to the building have been undertaken'. The link to Chantrell is that his plan of St Philip's church (CBC) includes part of the nearby school. Most of the school is included only in outline, but one section is shown in the same colour and degree of detail as the church, suggesting it was related to the building of the church. On it Chantrell has written: 'Entrance Corridor To

School'. This corridor faced the church and contained three shallow pointed arched windows and a small groined porch at its far end, all in keeping with the style of the church.

DRAWINGS: CBC, Leeds St Philip, file no. 20547.

REFERENCES: CBC, Leeds St Philip, file no. 3791.

Leeds, unidentified house

New house, 1825

The *LM* of 16 April 1825 carried the following advertisement: 'Joiners and carpenters required for a large dwelling house about 1 mile from Leeds. Apply to Mr Chantrell … Cottages will be provided on the spot for such workmen as may require them at the customary rent.' The building has not been identified, but the provision of cottages suggests the building was, indeed, a 'large' one.

REFERENCE: *LM,* 16 April 1825.

Leeds, unidentified houses in Woodhouse Lane

New houses, 1842

The *LI* of 23 July 1842 invited 'Tenders for two houses in Woodhouse Lane' to be submitted to Chantrell and Shaw. The houses have not been identified.

REFERENCE: *LI,* 23 July 1842.

Leeds, Vicarage, 6 Park Place

Repairs, 1826

The accounts of the Commissioners of the Leeds Improvement Act include a payment to 'Mr Chantrell for plans and designs' of £102/18/0. The payment was approved on 29 March 1827 for unspecified work undertaken in the previous year. The only project in 1826 that would have involved architectural expertise was 'the fitting up and repairing the new vicarage premises recently bought', a substantial late-Georgian brick terrace house in Park Place, where £637 was spent. Nevertheless, this alone would not account for the whole of Chantrell's fee.

REFERENCE: WYASL, LC/Tr 324.

Leeds, Yorkshire Agricultural Society Pavilion

Temporary pavilion, 1839

The *LI* of 20 and 27 July 1837 announced that: 'Arrangements are made for an Agricultural Dinner, upon an extensive scale, on 28th of August, the day of the Society's Show'. The edition of 31 August reported the proceedings and, most unusually included an illustration of the dinner in progress. It added the 'spacious pavilion was … erect[ed] in the Barrack Yard, under the immediate superintendence of R.D. Chantrell Esq., MIBA, architect … The pavilion was 113 feet long and 108 feet wide. The exterior was quite plain, in the interior there were covers laid for 1800 persons. The roof is supported by 2 rows of pillars … '

REFERENCES: *LI,* 20, 27 July, 31 Aug. 1839.

Leven, East Yorkshire, Holy Trinity.

New church, 1840-5

On 26 September 1840, the vicar, the Revd Wray, enquired about a ICBS grant and at around the same time asked Chantrell to survey the old church. His report of 10 November 1840, noted its poor condition. 'The north wall has given way and is supported by two massive brick buttresses, the west wall has been cut to admit of a large Venetian window ... the east wall of the tower is unsafe ... I most strongly recommend that bell-ringing be discontinued'. Since 'it could not possibly be repaired', he recommended it should be rebuilt, and preferably on a new site nearer the village it served. 'The body of the church can be taken down and the materials used in the new building ... the estimate for a building (using the old materials) in the Anglo-Norman or Lancet style (plain) 54 feet by 36 feet with a tower 13 feet square and 36 feet high, and a chancel 27 feet by 20 feet outside, to contain 274 sittings, is £996/0/0' (BI). A petition to rebuild, dated 21 January 1841, was sent to the archbishop (BI), and there are several Chantrell drawing dated later in 1841 (ERYRO). On 13 April 1842, the vicar wrote again to ICBS to enquire about a grant adding, 'I am particularly anxious to ascertain whether any and what modifications the Society has adopted in regard to tie-beams and other parts of the roof. My present plans are constructed with tie-beams – but from the [?] recent lectures of the Oxford and Cambridge Architectural Societies, I am led to hope that those tie-beams are not now insisted on.' Leven is Chantrell's first appearance of a type of roof structure that he used extensively in the 1840s, based, as he says, on examples seen at 'Howden, Hemsworth, Cottingham, Fenton, the Augustines, London, and many others ... ' Although Wray refers to 'my present plans' he probably means those that Chantrell has given him, although he seems to have demonstrated an interest in the latest ideas from Oxford and Cambridge.

On 12 November 1842, the ICBS received the completed application which stated 'building work will be completed in twelve months ... estimated cost £1,500.' A grant was approved, but on 15 November 1842 J.H. Good reported he was unhappy with the proposed roof construction. Chantrell's reply of 8 December

Cat. 23: Leven, East Riding of Yorkshire, Holy Trinity (R.D. Chantrell, 1840-5).

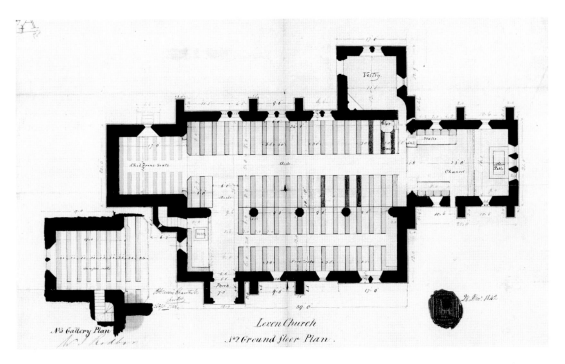

Cat. 24: Leven, East Riding of Yorkshire, Holy Trinity (R.D. Chantrell, 1840-5). (*Lambeth Palace Library*).

1842 stated he was enclosing both the old and the new plans and pointed out that the roof was 'to be constructed on the system of old churches in this part of the country' (ICBS). The foundation stone was laid on 11 July 1843 by Richard Bethell of Rise Park, lord of the manor of Leven (*Gentleman's Magazine*) and an account of the consecration appeared in *LI* of 7 June 1845. The finished church is Early English in style. Its plan is strangely irregular for a new church, although Chantrell referred to it as 'little more than the restoration of the old church' (*GM*) despite being moved about a mile, perhaps the parish was keen to replicate the old church as far as possible. It consists of a nave with S aisle but no clerestory, a substantial but low tower containing a gallery projecting slightly into the nave, a long chancel lined with stalls, a S porch and a large vestry projecting from the NE corner of the aisle.

DRAWINGS: ICBS, file 02784; East Riding of Yorkshire Records Office, PE 128/53.

REFERENCES: ICBS, file 02784; ICBS, MB 11, pp. 176, 229, 248, MB 12, p. 259; BI, Faculty 1843/2; ERYRO, PE 128/53; *LI,* 15 July 1843, 7 June 1845; *Gentleman's Magazine,* 20, 1843, p. 301; *Civil Engineer and Architect's Journal,* April 1846, p. 100; *Builder,* 5, 1847, pp. 301-2;

Lockwood, Huddersfield, Emmanuel
New church, 1826-30

Thomas Taylor of Leeds had submitted proposals to CBC for a new church at Netherthong (CBC, MB 17, p. 185) in 1825 and might also have had discussions with the Commissioners about Lockwood too prior to his death in 1826 (*LI,* 30 March 1826). However, at the CBC meeting of 26 September 1826 a letter from the vicar Of Almondbury, in whose parish Lockwood was situated, informed that 'Mr Chantrell will soon furnish you with plans for Lockwood and Netherthong.' (CBC, MB 22, p. 17). The CBC Building Committee approved the plans on 15 May 1827, noting the estimated cost as £3,630 (CBC, MB 24,

Cat. 25: Lockwood, Huddersfield, Emmanuel (R.D. Chantrell, 1826-30). (*Albert Booth*).

p.420). The CBC printed form records the dimensions as 99 feet by 48 feet, accommodation for 920, cost £3,600 including £62 for the bell turret. The CBC surveyor approved the scheme on 17 December 1827, by which time the cost was reduced to £3,300/15/4 (CBC surveyor's Report Book 2, no. 207). Interestingly, the Surveyor's Committee meeting of 14 January 1828 considered the Lockwood design as one of ten potentially suitable for a site in Rochdale, although nothing seems to have come from this. Tenders were advertised in *LI* of 11 September 1828 and it was consecrated in the spring of 1830. *LI* of 7 January 1830 said it was expected to be ready … in Easter Week', but the paper does not seem to have reported the consecration. The CBC meeting on 25 May 1830 approved the builders' accounts and Chantrell's fee of £136/6/5.

The finished building is Decorated in style with a nave without aisles, but galleries on three sides and a shallow chancel. A vestry was directly beyond the chancel. The corners of the nave and slightly projecting E and W gables are accentuated with eight octagonal turrets, there is square bell turret with low spire in the W front. The interior has two lines of columns to support the galleries and roof. These are simple cast-iron pipes with wooden mouldings bolted to them to produce a suitably 'ecclesiastical' appearance. Most of the galleries remain, shortened slightly at the E end. *The Ecclesiologist* would have been damning, but the intimate interior is not without a certain Gothick charm. The chancel was added by Chantrell in 1848-9 (see below).

REFERENCES: CBC, Crossland, Linthwaite, Lockwood and Netherthong file, no. 15548, pt 2; CBC, MB 22, p. 17,

MB 24, p. 420, MB 33, p. 299, MB 36, p. 188, MB 37, p. 292; CBC, Surveyor's Report Book 2, nos 207, 210; WYASW, WDP18/42; *LI,* 12 June, 11 Sept. 1828, 7 Jan. 1830. There are plans showing pew rents, produced by Chantrell's clerk of works, WYASW, WDP97/42.

Lockwood, Huddersfield, Emmanuel
New chancel, 1848-9

The contracts with workmen are dated 28 September 1848, suggesting the design was produced earlier that year. Most of the payments were made in March, April or May 1849 which suggests completion of the project early in the year. Throughout the documentation, the architect is referred to as 'Mr Chantrell of London'; there is no mention of Chantrell and Son of Leeds. The cost was £574/16/8, although the accounts note 'architect to be paid' suggesting Chantrell had not at this point submitted his bill. John Wade was clerk of works – as he had been when the church was originally built, and on many other Chantrell projects – and he was paid £25/7/0, '5% for superintending', suggesting he had day-to-day control. The new two-bay chancel uses the same system of tracery as the 1820s nave, but the roof is more steeply pitched and has a hammerbeam form, and there are buttresses and other 'correct' details. It was a very early example of a Camdenian re-ordering and included steps to the altar and misericords.

REFERENCE: WYASW, WDP97/72.

Lothersdale, near Skipton,
Unexecuted design for new church, 1829-30

In February 1829, J.B. Sidgwick and his brother Christopher, two members of a prominent local manufacturing family, wrote to ICBS to suggest the building of a small chapel to hold 300. The letter notes plans have been obtained, but mentions no architect. On 4 April 1829, a letter from the Revd Hammond Roberson, the energetic champion of church extension in West Yorkshire, wrote to support the Sidgwick's initiative, confirming 'the soundness of their principles and their undeviating habits'. Clearly in answer to some question from the ICBS, Sidgwick wrote on 12 June 1830 to say 'I have written to Mr Chantrell for the particulars which have been omitted.' The ICBS meeting of 21 June 1830 approved a grant of £350 towards an estimated cost of £1,350 (ICBS, MB 5, p. 186). Sidgwick replied on 17 July 1830 with thanks for the offer but pointed out it was not enough! The parish had raised £350 itself, and even if the tower was omitted to save £250 – although 'this alteration would at once destroy the character of a building belonging to the Establishment' – there was still an impossible shortfall. Noting this at its meeting on 18 Oct. 1830, the ICBS decided to cancel its offer (ICBS, MB 5, p. 219). Subsequently, a church was built in Lothersdale, but on a new site (see below).

REFERENCES: ICBS, file 01074; ICBS, MB 5, pp. 186, 219.

Lothersdale, Christ Church
New church, 1837-8

Following the abortive attempt to build a church in the area in 1829-30 (see above), a fresh initiative was launched in 1837 and the vicar of Carlton, in whose parish Lothersdale lay, wrote to the ICBS seeking funds for a 'district church' on a different site. The application form, dated 22 April 1837, estimated the cost at a modest £650. In answer to the question 'What plans enclosed?' is stated: 'The plans, it is hoped, will not be insisted upon especially in this district as the expense of an architect attending and of their production would be most inconvenient'. This statement and the difference between the £650 quoted here and the £1,350 estimated in 1830 suggests there was no attempt to use the designs from the earlier application. However, plans must have been produced quickly as Chantrell's scheme was approved by the

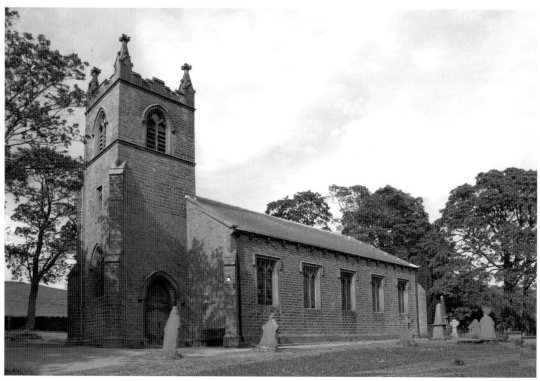

Cat. 26: Lothersdale, near Skipton, North Yorkshire, Christ Church (R.D. Chantrell, 1837-8). (*Roger Hatfield*).

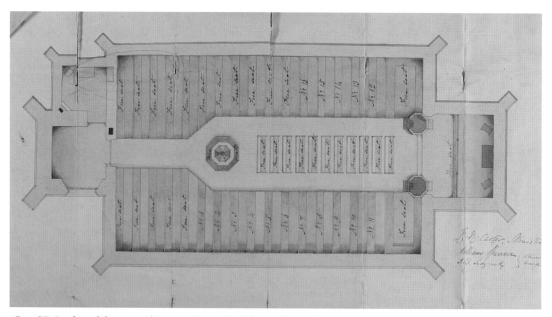

Cat. 27: Lothersdale, near Skipton, North Yorkshire, Christ Church (R.D. Chantrell, 1837-8). The plan is an unusual one, perhaps indicative of a local tradition. (*Lambeth Palace Library*).

ICBS surveyor on 25 July 1837, further plans being sent by Chantrell on 11 August 1837. A grant of £250 had been approved on 15 May 1837. The foundation stone was laid on 6 April 1838 (*LI,* 21 April 1838) and the church was consecrated on 22 October 1838 (*LI,* 3 Nov. 1838). The finished church consists of a nave, a small chancel which is almost square in plan, a W tower which serves as the porch, and small vestry attached to the N wall of the tower. The unusual seating arrangement – which might reflect an idiosyncratic local tradition in this remote area – survives. It consists of a central aisle which is relatively narrow at the W end, with slightly raised pews on either side, and which then splays out around the font to produce a much wider aisle which runs to the chancel arch. In this wider section of aisle it was intended to place free benches. The chancel was altered in 1883 (Wilson). The church was designed to hold 319 seats, 220 of which were free. There was, apparently, room for a further 80 free seats on additional benches.

REFERENCES: ICBS, file 02173; ICBS, MB 8, p.170, MB 9, pp. 128, 178, 211; *LI,* 21 April, 3 Nov. 1838; K. Wilson, *A History of Lothersdale,* privately printed, n.d., p. 138. There is a seating plan in the ICBS file, but it is not by Chantrell.

Lund, East Yorkshire, All Saints
Rebuilt chancel, 1845-6

According to Steel's booklet, 'On the underside of the altar table … is written "Through the unremitting exertions of the Revd J. Blanchard, vicar, this chancel was rebuilt by subscription, 1845-6. R.D. Chantrell, architect, … [list of tradesman]".' The chancel is of three bays with a fine Decorated E window. The chancel roof is supported by what Chantrell referred to as his 'perfect trusses' in a *Civil Engineer and Architect's Journal* 1846 article, although he doesn't mention his work at Lund in it.

REFERENCE: A. Steel, *History of All Saints Church, Lund,* privately printed, n.d., unpaginated.

Cat. 28: Lund, East Riding of Yorkshire, All Saints. The chancel is a rebuilding of 1845-6 by Chantrell.

Cat. 29: Middleton, Leeds, St Mary's Vicarage (R.D. Chantrell, 1845-8). Now demolished. The illustration is taken from an old photograph.

Malton, North Yorkshire, St Michael

New chancel, 1858

The medieval church still has much evidence of its Norman origins on the inside, although various insensitive additions and repairs to the outside might suggest otherwise. It was described as being 'in a miserable state' in 1838. Whellan tells us that 'In 1858 ... Mr Chantrell, the architect of the Incorporated Society' rebuilt the chancel 'somewhat smaller than the old one'. He put in the chancel walls five round-topped widows, some with stained glass, which give the chancel 'a dim religious light'. The unattractive re-facing of the nave (also 1858) and the addition of the transepts, were not part of Chantrell's commission.

REFERENCES: *Architectural Magazine,* 5, 1838, p. 163; T. Whellan, *History and Topography of York and the North Riding,* John Green, 1859, vol. 2, p. 218.

Middleton, near Leeds, St Mary

New church, 1845-6

See Chapter 7 for a fuller account of this commission.

The *LI* of 5 October 1839 noted the Ripon Diocesan Society for Church Building had given a grant of £350 for a new church at Middleton, estimated to cost £900. Whether this project was closely related to the 1845 scheme is not clear. There is no further news until 28 February 1845 when Chantrell, writing to the CBC about the new church at Halifax he adds, 'I ... have the plans for Middleton Church nearly ready.' (CBC, Halifax, St Paul file, no. 16867). Tenders were requested in *LI* of 28 June 1845 and the edition of 12 July 1845 sought further subscriptions for the church and parsonage estimated to cost £3,000.

The first stone of the church was laid on 28 July 1845 (*LI*, 26 July 1845) and it was consecrated on 22 September 1846. *LI*, 26 September 1846 reported the ceremony adding 'The church has been executed in strict accordance with the plans approved by the various societies who have contributed to its erection. It consists of a nave and side aisles, with a good chancel and a tower [which] is surmounted by a well proportioned broach spire ... it can accommodate 500-600 ... in every respect it does great credit to the architects, Messrs Chantrell and Son of Leeds.' Like Chantrell's contemporary St Philip's, Leeds, the tower is attached to the S aisle and forms the porch. While such an arrangement was, to a considerable extent, dictated by the cramped site at St Philip's, here it seems the decision was aesthetic as the site is expansive. Chantrell noted that the open roof was copied 'from those at Howden, Fenton, Hemsworth, Cottingham and numerous other churches of the 13th and 14th centuries' (ICBS). By the early 20th century nearby coal mining had created structural problems with the tower; the spire was removed in 1939 and a parapet created to terminate the tower.

DRAWINGS: WYASL, RDP78/21; ICBS, file 03514.

REFERENCES: WYASL, RDP78/21; ICBS, MB 12, pp. 196, 332; ICBS, file 03514; *LI*, 5 Oct. 1839, 28 June, 12, 26 July, 22 Nov. 1845, 19, 26 Sept. 1846.

Middleton, near Leeds, St Mary's Vicarage
New vicarage, 1845-9

The vicarage was always an integral part of the new church project, but it had to be delayed to allow for further fund raising. However, 'Messrs Chantrell and Son of Leeds' invited tenders in *LI* of 26 August 1848, repeated on 2 and 16 September (these were the first tenders advertised since R.D. Chantrell left Leeds at the end of 1846). The Leeds builder George Nettleton won the contract for 'mason's, bricklayer's and digger's work for a parsonage ... according to the plan and specification of Mr Chantrell , architect of Leeds' at a price of £430 on 23 September 1848. The building was a symmetrical Tudor style composition of brick with stone dressings. It was demolished in the mid-20th century.

DRAWING: It is included in the perspective of the church, WYASL, RDP78/21.

REFERENCES: Nettleton Papers, WYASL, 376, acc 1339, no. 3; WYASL, RDP 78/21-2; *LI*, 26 Aug., 2, 16 Sept 1848.

Morley, near Leeds, St Peter
New church, 1828-30

See Chapter 7 for a fuller account of this commission.

Probably it was at the beginning of 1828 that Chantrell first became involved with this scheme in which the earl of Dartmouth not only gave the land but also played a prominent role in driving the project. Chantrell wrote to the local committee for the Morley and Churwell District on 19 February 1828 saying that a church 85 feet by 55 feet with 1,000 sittings would cost 'about £4,000', but a building 70 feet by 45 feet, still capable of seating 1,000 could be built for £3,000. He pointed out that the savings would result from lighter walls, less substantial timbers and a tower that need not be so high in the smaller church (CBC). In a letter to CBC four days later he gave more details: 'The cost of a church as His Majesty's Commissioners propose would cost £4,000, but a chapel the size of that intended for Kirkstall could be erected for the sum specified if very plain.' Presumably the 'sum specified' was £3,000, the figure mentioned in the earlier letter. Chantrell completed the printed application form on 20 May 1828; by this time the plan must have been advanced as here he quotes £3,065 for a church with 1,000 seats (CBC). Tenders were invited in *LI*, of 29 June 1828, the foundation stone was laid later in that year and the consecration took place on

Cat. 30: New Mills, Derbyshire, St George (R.D. Chantrell, 1827-31).

28 August 1830. Its report added the church 'is what is generally termed Gothic in the style of the 13th century but of the plainest class. The windows are lancet headed and simple. The three chancel windows are united in a moulding.' (*LI*, 2 Sept. 1830). The church had a rectangular body without aisles and with galleries on three sides, a shallow chancel and a tower with spire. In 1885, Walter Hanstock of Batley extended the chancel, rearranged the seating at the E end and removed the side galleries.

REFERENCES: Hanstock's plans, which show Chantrell's church, are in WYASL, RD/AF/2/8 no. 13; CBC, MB 30, p. 231, MB 36, p. 80; CBC, Morley file, no. 15678; *LI*, 29 June 1828, 5, 24 Aug., 2 Sept. 1830.

Netherthong, near Huddersfield, All Saints
New church, 1826-30

Thomas Taylor of Leeds had been appointed to build a new church at Netherthong and after his death in 1826 it was a commission which Chantrell inherited. The CBC meeting of 26 September 1826 noted a letter from the vicar of Almondbury, in whose parish Netherthong is situated, stating 'Mr Chantrell will soon furnish you with plans for Lockwood and Netherthong.' These were approved by the CBC surveyor on 11 November 1826 who noted the estimated cost at £3,362/15/6. However, it was not until 15 May 1827 that the plans were approved by the Building Committee, by which time the cost had been reduced to £3,000 (CBC, MB 24, p. 420). *LI* of 20 November 1828 noted that the foundation stone will be laid 'in the course of the next or following week', although the *Centenary Souvenir* states 'the first foundation stone was laid on 14 January 1829 … the second on 13 March 1829 … it was consecrated on 2 September 1830.' The finished church is in the Decorated style, 88 feet by 45 feet and cost £2,988 of which Chantrell received £130/3/3. It had a body, containing galleries on three sides, which projected slightly at the E and W ends, the former being a shallow chancel. The corners are marked by octagonal towers. There is a bell-turret at the W end which was damaged in a storm in April 1847 and replaced by a new one designed by Chantrell (see below). The church subsequently underwent several unsympathetic re-orderings and the resulting interior is not attractive.

REFERENCES: CBC, MB 22, p. 17, MB 24, p. 420, MB 38, p. 39; CBC, Crossland, Linthwaite, Lockwood and Netherthong file, no. 15548; CBC, Surveyor's Report Book 2, no. 137; *LI*, 20 Nov. 1828, 7 Jan. 1830, *Centenary Souvenir 1830-1930*, WYASW, WDP18/ 23 and 41.

Netherthong, near Huddersfield, All Saints
New bell turret, probably 1847

The meeting of the CBC on 11 May 1847 discussed a request from the vicar of Netherthong for financial assistance with repairs to the church following lightning damage on 23 April 1847. The application was rejected. (CBC, MB 63, p. 155). However, on 20 December 1847, the ICBS confirmed a grant of £70. The parish records include an undated perspective drawing of the W end signed by Chantrell. The present appearance of the bellcote corresponds almost exactly with this drawing. The ICBS papers mention one Thomas Dunthwaites as surveyor for the project, a surprising choice given that John Wade was currently employed at nearby Lockwood.

DRAWING: WYASW, WDP18/41.

REFERENCES: CBC, MB 63, p. 155; ICBS, MB 13, pp. 69, 72; ICBS, file 03911; WYASW, WDP18/41.

New Mills, Derbyshire, St George
New church, 1827-31
An application was made to the CBC for assistance towards the erection of a new church at New Mills in the parish of Glossop, dated 8 May 1826. It stated the new church would hold 1,000 worshippers and cost an estimated £3,667. The plans – by someone other than Chantrell, but it is not clear who – were approved at the CBC meeting of 13 June 1826 (MB 21), but then rejected at the meeting of 15 May 1827 when 'Mr Chantrell was requested to go to Glossop to view the site and prepare new designs.' (MB 24). The meeting of 4 September 1827 noted the letter from Chantrell saying: 'I hope this style, which is a collection from some specimens of the thirteenth century, will meet with [your] approbation as it is substantial and economical. The elevation is an improvement upon that one which I submitted to the Bishop of Lichfield and Coventry … ' (MB 26). Chantrell estimated the cost at £3,297 in a document dated 7 January 1828 and the drawings were considered to be 'now satisfactory' at the surveyor's meeting of 18 February 1828. It was not until 29 May 1828 that the *LI* invited tenders. The first stone was laid on 21 September 1829 (*LI*, 1 Oct. 1829), and it was consecrated on 25 July 1831. Port gives the cost as £3,398 of which Chantrell received £150 (MB 39).
The finished church is in the Early English style, similar to Morley, Kirkstall and Holbeck. It consists a large body and retains all three galleries. There was a shallow chancel and a W tower with spire. It is a rare example of a Commissioners' church that is little changed and its interior is very satisfactory.

REFERENCES: CBC, New Mills file, no. 18103; CBC, MB 21, p. 129, MB 24, p. 421, MB 26, p. 234, MB 27, p. 445, MB 30, p. 197, MB 39, p. 458; CBC, Surveyor's Report Book 2, no. 214; *LI*, 29 May 1828, 1 Oct. 1829.

Peasenhall, Suffolk, St Michael

Rebuilt church, except for the tower, 1860–1

This is Chantrell's last known commission. He was encouraged out of semi-retirement for his long-time patron John Brooke for whom Chantrell had done so much work at Armitage Bridge, Yorkshire, in the 1820s and 1830s, and who at retired to nearby Sibton Park in Suffolk. The rebuilding of the medieval church cost 'upwards of £2,000' and was paid for by Brooke. The nave followed the dimensions of the original one, but the chancel was lengthened about 10 feet and the tower was raised in height. *The Builder* gave a detailed description of the church, its windows and other fittings. Uniquely in Chantrell's output, the building is of knapped flints with white stone dressings.

REFERENCES: *Ipswich Journal,* 13 July 1861, p. 5; *Builder,* 19, 1861, p. 621; *Illustrated London News,* 39, 7 Sept. 1861.

Pontefract, All Saints

Restoration, 1831–3

The original building was largely Decorated and Perpendicular in style and cruciform in plan with a central tower crowned by an octagonal upper stage. When finished it must, according to Glynne, 'have been a noble structure'. The church was damaged during the Civil War in one of the sieges of the nearby castle and remained in a ruined condition except that some repairs were carried out to the tower in the seventeenth century. At the same time, the nave was roofed for use at funeral services. Probably early in 1831, Chantrell was asked to advise on the practicality of restoring part of the building to form a chapel of ease and on 16 April 1831, the vicar of Pontefract wrote to the ICBS to request assistance. He adds that Mr Chantrell has drawn the plans and estimated the cost at £1,200. The scheme proposed the restoration of the crossing and transepts, the construction of a short polygonal chancel in the old one and a porch projecting slightly into the original nave. There were to be galleries on three sides. Dated 1831 is a lithograph of the proposed interior, from a drawing by Chantrell – perhaps produced as part of the fund-raising initiative – which shows the interior largely as built and reveals the elaborate plaster vaulted interior and rich decoration was part of the original project. Tenders for 'the restoration of the transepts' were invited in the *LI* of 26 May 1831, and work must have commenced shortly after. However, only after work had started was it possible to examine the old structure in more detail and discover the extent of the decay, a point Chantrell made to the ICBS in a letter of 10 January 1832 which explains the new estimate of £2,100. A further letter from him seven days later adds 'the south transept had to be taken down and rebuilt as it was in worse condition than had been originally thought … [and] the west entrance had to be extended so as not to interfere with a [burial] vault.' A progress report appeared in *LI* of 22 March 1832: 'The new work is executed in the original Gothic style under the direction of that able superintendent, Mr Green [the clerk of works who was also paid 'for carving']; the tower will appear entirely new when completed, and the ornaments are beautiful, and in the Gothic style.' The vicar wrote to the ICBS in July 1832 seeking extra funds: 'the extra expense could not be blamed on Mr Chantrell who spent 2 days examining the church for his original estimate … no other architect would have been able to foresee the difficulties encountered.' On 20 January 1833 a letter to the ICBS signed by the vicar, wardens and Chantrell confirmed the building was finished and recorded that the total cost was £4,162. Given the shortage of funds and the escalation of costs, it seems surprising that no attempt was made to economise with the lavish interior decoration. George Pace made various additions in the 1960s.

DRAWINGS: ICBS, file 01347.

Cat. 31: Pontefract, West Yorkshire, All Saints. Chantrell restored the central tower and transepts, 1831–3, to create a small church within the ruin of this medieval structure.

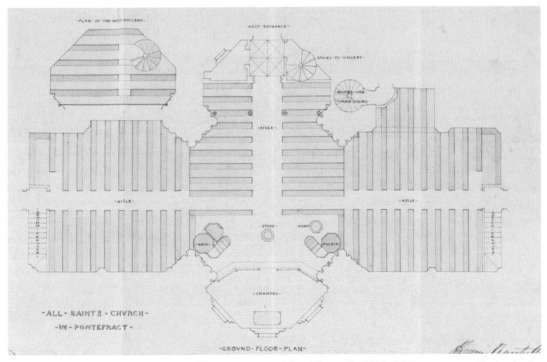

Cat. 32: Pontefract, West Yorkshire, All Saints, restored by Chantrell, 1831–3. There were galleries in the north, south and west wings of this approximately cruciform plan. (*Lambeth Palace Library*).

Cat. 32: Pontefract, West Yorkshire, All Saints, restored by Chantrell, 1831–3. There were galleries in the north, south and west wings of this approximately cruciform plan. View looking south. (*Lambeth Palace Library*).

REFERENCES: ICBS, file 01347, ICBS, MB 6, pp. 18, 89, 174, 182, 190; *LI*, 29 May 1831, 22 March 1832, 13 May 1837, 22 Sept. 1838; Glynne, pp. 327–9.

Poole, near Otley, West Yorkshire, St Wilfred
New church, 1838–40
An application to the ICBS for assistance with rebuilding to create additional seats was made on 4 June

Cat. 34: Poole, West Yorkshire, St Wilfred (R.D. Chantrell, 1838-40). (*Leeds University Library, Special Collections*).

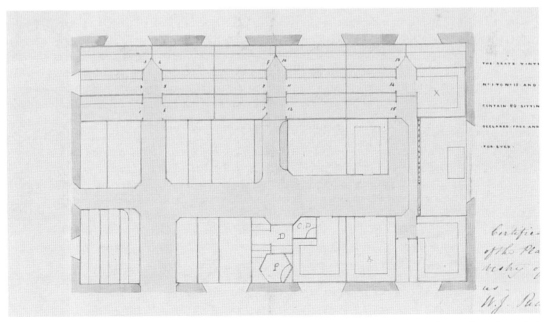

Cat. 35: Poole, West Yorkshire, St Wilfred (R.D. Chantrell, 1838-40). The seating was focused on the pulpit on the south wall, an arrangement fairly common in the eighteenth century, but old-fashioned by the mid-nineteenth. It might reflect the plan of the earlier chapel which Chantrell replaced. (*Lambeth Palace Library*).

1838. It stated the chapel was built 'about 1684' and last repaired in 1800. It stated Chantrell had examined the old church and pronounced it to be in a good condition, except that there was slight dilapidation in the roof. To produce a building with the desired capacity, Chantrell proposed demolition and the reuse of materials to double the accommodation to 200, including 80 free seats, at an estimated cost of £308. A grant of £50 was awarded. The ICBS surveyor approved the design on 22 June 1839 and the new church was opened on 14 June 1840 (*LI,* 20 June 1840). The completion certificate was signed on 20 October 1840. The finished church was small and economically designed. It consisted of a rectangular body and W tower – which served as a porch – with spire. The windows were lancets, mainly in pairs and with three in the E window. The plan is of some interest as a late example of a type popular in Yorkshire in the 18th century in which the altar is at the E end but the focus of the seating is the S wall where the three-decker pulpit is placed. The interior was re-ordered and the present chancel added by Healey and Healey in 1891 (WYASL).

DRAWING: ICBS, file 02028.

REFERENCES: ICBS, file 02028, ICBS, MB 9, p. 71, MB 10, p. 125; WYASL, RDP86/27. *LI,* 20 June 1840.

Rawdon, near Leeds, St Peter
Alterations, 1821-6
The old chapel was consecrated on 4 May 1684 (Lawton, p. 86-7). An application was made to the ICBS dated 1 June 1821 for 'extending the building 4 yards in width and 2 yards in height, the four walls to be carried up new with Gothic windows … [there were to be new galleries and pews] … estimated cost £942/0/0'. Presumably, plans were requested and on 13 June, R. Fawcett Esq. wrote to say 'I have this day sent by the mail plans and estimates for the enlargement'. The author of the plans is not recorded but the detail given so far suggests an architect was involved. The ICBS meeting of 17 September 1821 granted £500. However, finding additional funds was problematic and the Revd Schomberg, the vicar, wrote on 23 December 1822 asking for more time before the grant offer was withdrawn. Then on 15 April 1824 the Revd Ibbotson, the new incumbent at Rawdon, wrote to the ICBS: 'Revd Schomberg's plan was to widen the church but he has now gone away. Now this plan was not approved by the parishioners [presumably because of the financial burden that would fall on them] neither do I think it prudent or necessary. The walls, except the east end which is very much exposed to the weather, are very good and in my opinion, and that of the churchwardens and Mr Chantrell architect of Leeds, [it] should be imprudent to remove either the north or the south wall. The place wants enlarging and repairing, for it is in a most deplorable condition, but the present plan [he does not say what this is, but it might well have been primarily re-pewing, perhaps with a new gallery] I feel personally is the more advisable and may be done with half the expense. The east end wants rebuilding and in doing so, the walls might be extended a few yards.' A letter to the ICBS from the chapelwarden Mr M. White dated 14 July 1826 states 'Mr Oswald Emmett [the patron] has lately repaired the chapel completely and thoroughly at his own private expense … ' and thus the ICBS ceased its involvement. The Revd Fawcett gave more details in a letter to the archbishop of 5 April 1827: 'we have now got the chapel comfortable in the interior and for its exterior, the walls are in a complete good state of repair; as (?)sound as when new.' (ICBS). Thus the extent and time span of Chantrell's employment at Rawdon is unclear.

REFERENCES: ICBS, file 00301, ICBS, MB 1, p. 260, MB 2, p. 79, MB 3, p. 138.

Rise, East Yorkshire, All Saints
New church, 1844-6
Chantrell had previously been appointed to build the new church at nearby Leven (see above), a project

partly funded by Leven's lord of the manor, Richard Bethal Esq. Thus, when Bethal's attention turned to rebuilding the church at Rise, where he lived – a project he was to fund entirely – Chantrell was the obvious candidate as architect. The *LI* of 27 April 1844 invited tenders 'for taking down and rebuilding Rise Church, Holderness' to be sent to Chantrell and Shaw. The church was consecrated on 12 November 1845 by Bethell's brother, the bishop of Bangor (*Ecclesiologist*). It cost 'about £4,000' and had places for 220 worshippers (*Civ. Eng. Journal*). *The Builder* noted the opening and carried a neutral description, as did *The Ecclesiologist*. Subsequently, the *Civil Engineer and Architect's Journal* published a long letter from Chantrell which began 'Will you allow me to notice the inaccuracy of the account of All Saints Church, Rise, extracted from *The Ecclesiologist* and given in your last number? He then proceeds to give his account of the building ending with 'From the account in *The Ecclesiologist*, one should be lead to suppose that this was a small extravagant building … ', although it is difficult to see how he comes to this conclusion. He then proceeds to discuss his 'discovery' of 'true Masonic principles' concluding that they are readily adaptable and beneficial in the design process. Chantrell describes the church thus: 'it consists of a chancel (correctly proportioned), nave, with south porch, massive tower, and broach spire, [in the] first pointed style.'

It is an attractive design, superficially similar to his other churches of the mid-1840s, but the unusually generous budget was put to good effect on the decorative details, both inside and out.

REFERENCES: *LI,* 27 April 1844; *Builder,* 3, 1845, p. 585; *Ecclesiologist,* 5, 1846, pp. 78-9; *Civil Engineer and Architect's Journal,* April 1846, p. 100.

Roberttown, West Yorkshire, All Saints

New church, 1843-5

The vicar of Liversage wrote to the ICBS seeking a grant on 13 September 1843 and on 4 November *LI* noted a contribution from the Ripon DCBS. An application was also made to the CBC with drawings from Chantrell and Shaw, covering letter signed JBC, on 25 November. The CBC form records 500 seats at a cost of £1,421/0/0. LI of 23 December 1843 invited tenders to be sent to Chantrell and Shaw and the edition of 13 April carried an account of the foundation stone-laying. During construction, the partnership between JBC and Shaw was dissolved and, in an attempt to share out the current projects equitably, Roberttown was given to Shaw. The CBC certificate of completion was signed by Shaw on 24 November 1845. The CBC's remission of duties form notes the cost as £2,076/16/11.

Of all the churches from the period of the Chantrell and Shaw partnership, this is the only one where there is no reference to RDC in the documentation. It is also the cheapest of churches of this period; if RDC really was going to trust the new partnership with an ecclesiastical design of its own, perhaps this was it. On the other hand, the general features and proportions of the church are entirely compatible with RDC's work of the 1840s.

DRAWINGS: (by Chantrell and Shaw) CBC, file 16067.

REFERENCES: CBC, Roberttown, file 16067; ICBS, file 03286; *LI,* 4 Nov., 3, 23 Dec. 1843, 22 Nov. 1845; WYASW, WDP193 box 4.

Rudding Park, near Harrogate, North Yorks

Alterations for Sir Joseph Radcliffe, after 1824-*c*.1835

Rudding Park is a medium sized Neo-classical country house, an 'impeccable design' (Hussey) of the finest ashlar for the Hon. William Gordon. Construction began in 1807 replacing an earlier house on the site. The architect was not recorded but Hussey links it to the Wyatts or their circle. It was advertised for sale in *LI* of 15 March 1818 where it was described as 'newly erected'. It was eventually bought by Sir Joseph Radcliffe, Bt in a sale on 18 June 1822 (*LI,* 20 May 1822). Hussey asserts that at Radcliffe's acquisition, 'much of the interior was unfinished', although a sale of furniture and effects from the house was held on 28 June 1819 (*LI*, 28 June 1819) suggesting at least a part of it was habitable. Hussey continues: 'In 1824-5 Sir Joseph needed to complete an unfinished house. His architect was R.D. Chantrell … the work was said to have been done "with the utmost discretion in the manner of the original design", so that its extent cannot now be certainly distinguished, but was probably restricted to fittings and decorations.' Colvin (2nd ed.) refers to '[Chantrell] drawings formerly at Rudding', but these have not been traced. However there are Chantrell documents from the 1830s. On 22 August 1834 he wrote to Radcliffe concerning the positions of some chimney flues adding 'I will visit again next week' (WYASL). Additionally, on 26 February 1835 Chantrell wrote to the CBC about the eradication of dry rot at St Paul, Birkenshaw: 'I recommend the removal of joists as at Rudding Park, a case which I have now in progress of a new building [in which] it appears evident that the infection was communicated by some of the oak timbers of the old mansion, which was taken down because of dry rot, having been used with the new wood, probably from their sound appearance.' (CBC). His Birkenshaw report includes: 'during the last year I have had a case of considerable magnitude in this county where I have had to take out all the floors of a large mansion …' An 'Abstract of Tradesmen's Bills' signed by Chantrell but not dated, amounts to £11,047; it does not include architect's commission and adds there are further accounts to be settled. This was a huge sum to spend merely to 'complete' an existing structure and the inclusion of more than £2,500 for masonry suggests substantial additions to the structure. The stable block has a distinctly Soanian quality and could well be Chantrell's work.

REFERENCES: WYASL, Radcliffe of Rudding II/399, 400; *LI*, 15 March, 18 Aug. 1818, 28 June 1819, 20 May 1822; CBC, Cleckheaton file, no. 15199; C. Hussey, *English Country Houses: Late Georgian,* Antique Collectors' Club, 1986, pp. 74-82.

Shadwell, near Leeds, St Paul

New church, 1839-42

The *LI* of 5 Oct. 1839 noted a grant of £100 from the Ripon DCBS towards an estimated cost of £480 for a new church for Shadwell. Tenders were invited in *LI* and *LM* of 19 September 1840. The consecration of 21 July 1842 was reported in the *Intelligencer* of 23 July 1842 adding ' … there is no vestry. It is a neat little edifice, built in the early Norman style, very much after the ancient church at Adel. It has been erected in a very substantial manner under the architectural superintendence and from the designs of R.D. Chantrell, MRIBA [*sic*] at a cost of between £600 and £700 and it holds rather more than 200 … ' The final cost of £871/1/5 was reported in *LI* of 13 Aug. 1842. It has a four-bay nave with W gallery, a chancel in the form of a canted bay and a bellcote at the apex of the W gable.

REFERENCES: *LI,* 5 Oct. 1839, 19 Sept. 1840, 11 June, 16, 23 July, 13 Aug. 1842.

Sheffield, St Jude, Moorfields

Revision of original design by Flockton and Mitchell, *c.*1852-3

A new church was designed by the Sheffield firm of William Flockton and Joseph Mitchell, and the project began in 1848. From the outset, the ICBS Architects' Committee was concerned that a suitably sturdy church could not be built for the estimated sum and, unusually, seem to have carried out several inspections – although it is not clear by whom – with reports in early 1849, and in July and August 1849. The committee's fears were fulfilled when the tower of the nearly completed building collapsed in the autumn of 1852. An anonymous report was written on 15 November and Chantrell was there to inspect the ruin nine days later. His diagnosis was that the piers were too slight, there was insufficient abutment and the foundations were inadequate. In addition to this report, the ICBS file contains a long and detailed letter from Chantrell in which he assesses the culpability of the architects and each of the principal tradesman,

Cat. 36: Shadwell, near Leeds, St Paul (R.D. Chantrell, 1939-42). Unsigned watercolour. (*Leeds University Library, Special Collections*).

as well as sketching defective constructional details. However, Chantrell went beyond identifying the faults and made a number of recommendations which Flockton – by then, it seems, working without Mitchell – adopted. The result was a church with significant differences from that conceived in 1848.

Flockton wrote to Chantrell on 4 April 1853, 'I think you will find [the plan] mainly in accordance with your suggestions … I have retained the inverted arches shown on your sketch', and he wrote again on 17 January 1854 thanking Chantrell for 'your kind offer of assistance … I send the entire [set of] plans [for your inspection]'. Chantrell's final report for the ICBS, undated but probably of 1855 states, 'This church has been rebuilt according to the Sketches I [produced] for the Rev. Lyon requesting him to place them in the hands of some local architect; Mr Flockton of Sheffield has carried out the design and the work is very good and substantial … this church is placed on new foundations [not on the old ones which were left in the ground] … all is now sound.'

Although the completed church shares aspects of the collapsed design, for instance, the window details, the new one differed in important ways: the crossing tower and transepts were abandoned. This, plus the fact that Chantrell reports that the whole church was shifted within the site confirms a substantially new design in which he can claim a not insignificant role.

REFERENCES: ICBS, files 04172, 04623.

Skipton, North Yorkshire, Christ Church
New church, 1835-9

The driving force behind the erection of this important church, well ahead of its time so far as its high church arrangements were concerned, was Christopher Sidgwick. He had a clear vision for the project – 'It has been my endeavour to produce plans for a true Christian edifice' – and must have selected his architect with care. It is apparent that Sidgwick not only knew about church arrangements, but also had knowledge of the local building trades and their prices. While Chantrell was always listed as 'architect', it is likely that there was much collaboration between them throughout the project.

On 21 January 1835 Chantrell produced an estimate for the new church of '£2,590/13/6 plus £110 for groining'. The latter item – by no means usual was, perhaps, a specific request of Sidgwick. Probably the next 18 months were taken up with fundraising and on 1 August 1836, Sidgwick contacted the ICBS. He pointed out that there were 5,490 people in the town, but there were seats for only 1,100 in the parish church of which a mere 100 were free. As a consequence, there were then four dissenting chapels and plans for a Roman Catholic church in the town. He and his friends wished to build a second church and already had the sanction of the archbishop. 'The plans have been prepared by R.D. Chantrell' and he proceeds to give the dimensions and form of the intended church. 'There will be 630 sittings, 360 of which will be free … estimated expense is £4,000 plus £1,000 for endowment.' (ICBS). The printed ICBS form was completed on 21 February 1837 and signed by the archdeacon. It gave the estimated cost as £3,000-4,000 including extras, noting that prices had risen locally in the two years since Chantrell's earlier estimate of £2,590. This secured a grant of £350. There is an interesting letter from Sidgwick to the ICBS of 13 March 1837: 'I now send you the architect's estimates on which I think it is necessary to make the following remarks … ' He then proceeds to comment on each trade, e.g. 'His estimate for the mason's work above the ground line, according to the plans, I consider too much by £100 and therefore I take it at £1,262/13/6.' The others receive the same treatment and at the end he writes 'Architect (I shall myself look to the proper building of the church so that we shall only have to pay for plans and the occasional visit) say £100' the ICBS surveyor approved the design on 9 May 1837 and the foundation stone-laying took place on 21 June 1837. Chantrell was present and read out the inscription on the brass plate before putting it in place (*LI,* 24 June 1837). The building was consecrated by the bishop of Ripon on 25 September 1839. The service attracted an unusually prominent congregation, considering Skipton's somewhat isolated location, including Dr W.F. Hook, vicar of Leeds, and the Revd Hammond Roberson. The *LI* of 28 September 1839 gave a full report: ' … it was erected by our distinguished townsman Mr Chantrell … [gives dimensions and accommodation] the interior arrangements were made under the direction of Christopher Sidgwick whose object it has been to make it precisely conformable to what was designed by the Reformers of the Church of England, and to render it easy for the officiating minister to observe the Rubrics to the strictness of the letter. His readings on the subject have been extensive. The chancel is large and raised above the floor of the church by four steps. On top of the steps are placed the desks, which instead of been close boxes are open work … The reading-desk is so arranged that the minister can look to the people when addressing them in the absolution, etc. and look from them when praying. In the chancel beside the altar is a side table and two chairs … The pews are all single pews looking eastwards, and convenient kneeling boards are provided in all the free seats. The style of the church is 1300; the whole ceiling groined; and great care has been taken to preserve uniformity throughout the building … As we suspect the arrangement of this church will be a model for others, we have entered into a detailed description of it.' An almost identical account appeared in the *Gentleman's Magazine.* Rather belatedly, the *LM* of 18 January 1840 reported the opening under the heading 'Popery in an Anglican Church' noting with outrage that the chancel occupied one third of the total length and was raised on four steps, and that there was a lectern. *The Ecclesiologist* did not mention the church until 1846; the approval of the writer was not surprising as Sidgwick had predicted so many of the ecclesiologists' 'innovations'. 'This church has many good points, and displays so much of true church feeling in its arrangements as almost to disarm criticism. But there is unfortunately several architectural defects which mark a want of knowledge rather than a want of feeling in those who planned it … [long, non-judgemental description] the altar is of stone with two candlesticks … [there is] a credence … lectern and Litany-desk facing east … The tower has rather heavy pinnacles … the chancel [is raised] on several steps, below is a crypt in which the funeral service is performed.'

DRAWING: ICBS, file 02047.

REFERENCES: ICBS, file 02047; ICBS, MB 8, p. 144, MB 9, pp. 294-5; *LI*, 24 June 1837, 28 Sept. 1839; *LM*, 18 Jan. 1840; *Gentleman's Magazine*, 147, 1839, p. 532; *Ecclesiologist*, 6, 1846, pp. 154-5.

Skipton, North Yorkshire, Ermysted's Grammar School

New schoolroom, 1839-42

This modest commission must have come *via* Christopher Sidgwick, the driving force behind the erection of Christ Church, Skipton (see above); one of his brothers was the master at the school and the other one was a trustee. The school's trustees' meeting of 8 July 1839 resolved 'that Mr Chantrell's Plan for erecting a new school immediately adjoining the old one be adopted' and its meeting of 21 August 1839 noted the estimated cost at £420. However, the meeting of 20 June 1840 heard that the tenders amounted to only £250/14/0, not including clerk of works or architect's fee. Finally, the meeting of 29 July 1841 was told the accounts of the new building amounted to £317/4/4, exclusive of 'fitting up and furnishing'. It seems reasonable to conclude the building opened for the new academic year in 1841. The schoolroom was added to the existing range of buildings and is typical of Chantrell' scholastic Tudor style. The school moved in the nineteenth century and the schoolroom survives, ignominiously, as an electricity sub-station.

REFERENCES: Ermysted's Grammar School Trustee's Minute Book, in the possession of the school's governors in 2006; C. Webster, 'The new schoolroom at Ermysted's Grammar School, Skipton', in *Craven History*, 2, 2008, pp. 28-32.

Tuxford, Nottinghamshire, St Nicholas

Re-seating, 1844

The vicar of the interesting medieval church at Tuxford – who did not reside in his parish as he gave his address as Botham, York – wrote to the ICBS on 14 January 1843 enquiring about a grant. 'The church is a fine large building in excellent repair and preservation. The comparatively small number of persons [that can be] accommodated appears chiefly attributable to the pewing of it. [I] propose to substitute open sittings and stalls for the … if funds can be raised. The expense of the works according to a plan and estimate of Mr Chantrell, the architect of Leeds, [is] £250.' The vicar requested an application form, but does not appear to have submitted it.

REFERENCE: ICBS, file 03173.

Wortley, Leeds, Unidentified House

New house, 1844

The *LI* of 6 July 1844 requested 'Tenders for a house at Wortley' to be sent to Chantrell and Shaw. The house has not been identified, but, on stylistic grounds, it is likely to be Greenhill House, Greenhill Lane, built for Matthew Hall, a surgeon. The original design appears to have been a symmetrical, two-storey Tudor-style composition, with tall, centrally-placed chimney stacks. In 1853, following Hall's death, his widow sold the house to Robert Ingham whose family lived there for many years and substantially altered the house, adding a SW wing and various embellishments to the original structure. It was refurbished and converted to flats in *c.* 2006.

REFERENCES: *LI*, 6 July 1844. West Riding Registry of Deeds, LR 704 696, NK 640 281, OZ 684 691, PN 36 42, RZ 164 181.

INSPECTIONS FOR THE ICBS

In his capacity as a member of the Incorporated Church Building Society's Committee of Architects from 1849-63 (see Chapter 5), Chantrell was responsible for overseeing projects in the York and Ripon dioceses. The committee as a whole examined the submitted drawings at its regular London meetings, sometimes finding many faults with submissions and provoking correspondence with the church's architect that could run for several years. Where an architect seems to have been inexperienced in church work, the committee, or individual architects on it, might significantly revise a scheme before returning the drawings to the local architect for implementation. In these cases, communication between the ICBS and the applicant or applicant's architect seems to have been written by the committee's secretary. However, sometimes the committee's architect responsible for the diocese wrote personally. Additionally, individual architects were responsible for visiting projects in their area and writing a report prior to the payment of grants. So far as Chantrell was concerned, the examples listed below are only a small proportion of the ICBS projects in 'his' dioceses in this period, and it is not clear whether Chantrell also inspected these others but his reports have not survived. Certainly a small number of cases have been noted where another member of the committee carried out an inspection, e.g. Barwick in Elmet, near Leeds (1854-7), where it seems G.G. Scott undertook the inspection, and Hollis Croft, Sheffield (1854-60), where Ewan Christian produced the final report. Perhaps in some cases, grants were paid without any inspection.

Ackworth, West Yorkshire, St Cuthbert
Inspection and report, 1855
The church was rebuilt by J.W. Hugall of Oxford and Reading in 1850-7. In a letter to the secretary of the ICBS dated 7 August 1855, Chantrell mentions that it has been suggested to him that he inspect the churches at Spofforth and Ackworth. He certainly visited Spofforth and it is thus likely he also went to Ackworth, although his report appears not to have survived.

REFERENCES: ICBS, files 04359, 04779.

Brampton Bierlow, South Yorkshire, Christ Church
Inspection and report, 1855
The church was built by Pritchett and Pritchett of York in 1853-5. An undated letter in file 04727 includes 'The Committee would beg to suggest that in carrying out [Brampton Bierlow] church special study should be given to the general architectural character which as it now stands appears to evince some degree of haste and want of mature study of the parts as to refinement and beauty.' The letter proceeds to specify concerns. A second letter, also containing criticisms, was sent. A letter from Chantrell to the secretary of the ICBS, dated 14 August 1855 includes, 'I have examined Skipton … and tomorrow I take in Sheffield and Brampton Bierlow'. Perhaps it was following this visit that Chantrell wrote an undated note in the ICBS file which states: 'This church was only begun in the spring and the works are scarcely above ground'.

REFERENCES: ICBS, files 04292, 04727

Eastwood, near Keighley, West Yorkshire, St Mary the Virgin
Inspection and report, 1850s
The church was built to the designs of Perkin and Backhouse of Leeds in 1850-5. There is a partial note, commenting on the proposed construction, cut off at the bottom and without signature or date, but

probably by Chantrell and written in 1851-2. It elicited a reply from Perkin and Backhouses dated 12 February 1853. Another note from Chantrell, similarly now devoid of its signature or date but probably early 1855 states, 'This church is not more than five feet above the ground'. Chantrell visited the church on 13 August 1855 and this report includes, 'This church has been previously examined and reported on; all appears substantial and free from settlings … '

REFERENCE: ICBS, file 04292.

Heptonstall, West Yorkshire, St Thomas Becket
Inspection and report, 1854
The church was rebuilt to the designs of Mallinson and Healey of Bradford in 1853-6. Chantrell inspected the church on 25 May 1854. His report includes 'This is one of the finest specimens of a late [Perpendicular] Church that has been designed … the seats are ample, properly placed and the fir is all stained … the building is substantial and nearly complete.' Healey, apparently responsible for all the firm's churches, had been a pupil of Chantrell's and the former teacher was always complimentary about Healey's work.

REFERENCE: ICBS, file 04000.

Knaresborough, North Yorkshire, Holy Trinity
Inspection and report, 1853-5
The church was designed by Joseph Fawcett of Thirsk and Knaresborough in 1852-7. An undated comment from the Committee of Architects elicited a reply from Fawcett of 9 April 1853. A note from Chantrell of 28 May 1854, apparently written after a site visit, records, 'This church is not yet commenced', but one of 9 November 1855 states, 'This church is unfinished but as far as completed, the works are substantial and well (?) ---- it is lofty and well proportioned.' He seems to have made a visit earlier in that year as a letter from Chantrell to the ICBS secretary of 7 August 1855 includes 'the Yorkshire churches I have inspected are: … Knaresborough … '

REFERENCES: ICBS, files 04617, 04779.

Leeds, St Barnabas, Brewery Field
Inspection and report, 1855
The church was built to the designs of J.T. Fairbank of Bradford in 1851-6. A note from the Committee of Architects, initialled by Chantrell and T.H. Wyatt, probably written in late 1852, included, 'This church is so unpleasing in its treatment, so sham in its proposed groining and so much below the average of its Ecclesiastical knowledge and taste of the present day that it cannot be supposed for a moment that the committee will make a grant to such plans.' It proceeds to a detailed criticism, answered in a letter from the incumbent of 14 February 1853. A further critical report was produced by the committee, probably in early March 1853. A new design was produced but the committee claimed it was 'not … by any means of average merit' and proceeded to catalogue its defects. Chantrell seems to have visited on 24 May 1854 but found the works had not commenced. A letter from Chantrell to the ICBS's secretary of 7 August 1855 includes 'the Yorkshire churches I have inspected are: … Leeds, Brewery Field … ' A further inspection on 14 November 1855 recorded that 'This church is nearly completed. The stonework is substantial and well executed and the carved work superior … '

REFERENCE: ICBS, file 04779.

Leeds, St John the Baptist, New Wortley

Inspection and report, 1854

The church was built to the designs of Jeremiah Dobson of Leeds in 1847-54. Chantrell inspected the church on 24 May 1854. His report starts with a description and notes about the materials used then includes, 'It is of a fair Character with geometric tracery and in harmony throughout; it appears substantial and free from defeacts ... the whole of the works are executed in a substantial and satisfactory manner.'

REFERENCE: ICBS, file 03976.

Sheffield, St Luke, Hollis Croft

Inspection and report, 1855

The church was built to the designs of Joseph Mitchell of Sheffield in 1850-60. The ICBS file includes a long critical report on the submitted plans written by the Committee of Architects, probably in the early 1850s. There followed much correspondence between the committee and Mitchell. Chantrell inspected the church in the summer of 1855, although his report has not survived; a letter from Chantrell to the secretary of the ICBS included, 'The churches in Yorkshire which I have inspected are: ... Sheffield, Hollis Croft ... ' Chantrell made another visit on 12 November 1855 and reported, 'The church is in an unfinished state and on enquiring is stated to have been discontinued for some time past'. The report proceeds to be critical of the construction. Subsequently these are several letters from Chantrell, written from his home address in Canonbury, to Mitchell, one of which included sketches and a description of the best way to construct piers. Mitchell's replies survive. In the late 1850s, Ewan Christian seems to have taken over from Chantrell as supervising architect – the correspondence from Mitchell suggests his relationship with Chantrell had broken down – and Christian produced the final report of 5 December 1860. He notes the defective pier 'alluded to by Mr Chantrell ... has been taken down and rebuilt ... and all the recommendations of the Committee of Architects have been duly carried out.'

REFERENCES: ICBS, files 04323, 04779.

Sheffield, St Matthew

Inspection and report, 1855

The church was built to the designs of Flockton and Flockton of Sheffield in 1853-5. Chantrell inspected the church on 12 November 1855. His report confirms the work as satisfactory and adds that although the window arrangement is unusual because of the close proximity of other buildings, it is not unlike 'the old churches of All Saints, North Street and St Mary, Castlegate, in York.'

REFERENCE: ICBS, file 04744.

Skipton, North Yorkshire, Holy Trinity

Inspection and report, 1855

The medieval church was repaired by J.A. Cory of Durham in 1854-6. Chantrell inspected the church on 11 August 1855. His report includes, 'the repairs to this church are conducted in the best manner possible: the roof has been judiciously cleaned and restored, and new oak timbers [used], all defective stonework substituted ... '

REFERENCE: ICBS, file 04843.

Spofforth, near Harrogate, North Yorkshire, All Saints

Inspection and report, 1855

The medieval church was rebuilt to the designs of J. W. Hugall of Oxford and Reading in 1854-5. Chantrell inspected the church on 8 September 1855. His report includes, 'This church has been rebuilt in the style corresponding with the nave ... One unsightly box pew remains in the chancel, claimed by the owner of Rudding Park who will not permit its removal, though a special object of deformity now that the rest of the interior has been properly remodelled.'

REFERENCE: ICBS, file 04779.

Thorner, near Leeds, St Peter

Inspection and report, 1855

The medieval church was extensively restored by Mallinson and Healey of Bradford in 1854-6. Chantrell inspected the church on 8 November 1855. His report included, 'This church has been nearly rebuilt. The work is ... substantial and of good character, in harmony with the nave and tower of the 15th c. ... the whole well executed with the best materials and is in every respect satisfactory.'

REFERENCE: ICBS, file 04834.

Whitby, North Yorkshire, St Michael

Inspection and report, 1855

The church was built to the designs of J.B. and W. Atkinson of York in 1847-8 with a small grant from the CBC (Port, p. 343). However, it was not consecrated until 1855 because 'the project was not properly funded' meaning, perhaps, that either the church was unfinished or that there were no funds to sustain a minister. The ICBS files contain correspondence and other references to applications from Whitby for assistance in building 'a chapel', but rarely is it clear whether this refers to St Michael's or St John, built 1848-9, also to designs by the Atkinsons. However, it seems reasonable to conclude that in answer to a request for further funds from both the CBC and ICBS for St Michael's in the mid 1850s, Chantrell was asked to assess the church in his capacity as the ICBS's inspecting architect for the diocese of York, to assist the grant makers. It seems it was the ICBS that commissioned the report, but it was subsequently passed to the CBC. It is dated 27 August 1855 and concludes that the building had been well constructed and its internal arrangements were appropriate.

REFERENCES: ICBS, MB 13, p. 13, MB 14, p. 4, MB 15, pp. 173, 188; ICBS, file 03860.

Withernwick, East Yorkshire, St Alban

Inspection and report, 1855 and earlier

The church was rebuilt in 1853-5 by Mallinson and Healey of Bradford in 1853-5. Chantrell might have inspected the church in the summer of 1855, but it is not clear. A letter from Chantrell to the ICBS's secretary, dated 7 August 1855 includes states 'The churches in Yorkshire which I have inspected [in the past few days] are:' ... Withernwick ... ' However, in another letter dated 14 August 1855 he discusses the problems of travel and includes ' ... Withernwick will take about 20 miles by carriage from the Bridlington railway and as it is in the hands of Mr Healey there will be no doubt that the Report will be favourable as the old church which I examined a few years ago had little to recommend it, being rough cast and almost void of character.'

REFERENCES: ICBS, files 04292, 04763 and 04779.

Cat. 37: Halifax, West Yorkshire, Sion Chapel, 1819. Most of the chapel shown to the left of the photograph has been demolished, but the stone principal front survives, replete with all its Soanian motifs, now incongruously forming part of the bus station

ATTRIBUTED BUILDINGS

Armitage Bridge, near Huddersfield, School
New school for William Brooke, *c.* 1835 (demolished).

This was a single-storey, eight-bay schoolroom in a debased Tudor style. It was 'built in 1835 due to the instrumentality and generosity of Messrs J. Brooke and Sons' (Ahier). However, CBC file for Armitage Bridge states that while the church was paid for by J. Brooke and Sons, William in his private capacity paid for the school and vicarage. Given the dates of the two sources, the CBC file is likely to be the more reliable.

The attribution is made on the basis of strong stylistic links to Chantrell's documented schools of the *c.*1830-40 period, including those at St Mary, Quarry Hill, Leeds, and Skipton. Furthermore, Chantrell undertook much building for the Brooke family at Armitage Bridge and in 1836 was paid 'for measuring' work which included the school. Since the school was a 'private' commission from William Brooke, the absence of any mention of an architect's fee for Chantrell in the Partnership Stock Book should not be seen as significant.

REFERENCES: P. Ahier, *History and Topography of South Crosland, Armitage Bridge and Netherton*, Longman, 1938; CBC, file 15078; the Brooke family's Partnership Stock Book, 1825-1922 (see references for Armitage Bridge Mills); CBC, Armitage Bridge file 15078.

Armley, Leeds, Almshouses and School
New buildings for Benjamin Gott, 1832 (demolished)

The scheme was U-shaped in plan with the school in the centre with the almshouses 'for 12 poor women' forming the two flanks. The style was debased Tudor. The complex 'was founded by … Benjamin Gott Esq. in 1832.' (Taylor).

The attribution is based on the regularity with which Gott employed Chantrell at this time and the stylistic similarity between the Armley buildings and Chantrell's documented school buildings of this period.

REFERENCE: Taylor, p. 99.

Halifax, Sion Chapel
New chapel, c.1818-20

The story of this once very impressive building begins in 1816 when a faction of worshippers at Square Chapel decided to purchase a small chapel in Wade Street from the Methodists (Wadsworth, p. 20). The dynamic Revd Edward Parsons began his ministry there on 21 December 1817. This active preacher and educator 'first intended to enlarge the old building to the necessary extent, but upon examination it was found necessary to erect an entirely new chapel … the foundation stone was laid on 10 May 1819 … it was opened on 7 June 1820 … it cost £4,514 (Dale, pp. 28-31). No reference to an architect seems to have survived.

Dale's dates suggest the following chronology: in 1818 the old chapel was examined and pronounced unsatisfactory; a new chapel was designed and an estimate established; fundraising began. Early in 1819 the old chapel was demolished and groundwork was commenced for the foundation stone-laying in May. Since initially extension was proposed, it is unlikely that the congregation would look outside the locality for an architect making John Oates and William Bradley the only contenders. On pronouncing the old building un-enlargeable, the architect of the report was an obvious contender for the new chapel.

The remarkable aspect of this building was the extent of Soanian motifs, both on the façade and in the elaborate plaster ceiling. Nothing like these appears in Oates or Bradley's other work, or indeed in the work of any other architect operating at this time in the area. It is therefore suggested that Bradley was asked to assess the old chapel and subsequently obtained the job on the new one but allowed his assistant Chantrell to do most of the design work. Alternatively, the decision to build a new chapel more or less coincides with the commencement of Chantrell's practice; perhaps independently he secured the new chapel commission.

REFERENCES: B. Dale, *Jubilee Memorial of Sion Chapel and Sunday Schools,* privately printed, 1867; G.P. Wadsworth, *The History of Square Road Congregational Church, Halifax,* privately printed, 1889.

Headingley, Leeds, Kirkstall Grange (now Beckett's Park), lodge.
New estate cottage for William Beckett, 1838

The building is attributed to Chantrell on two counts: firstly its similarity to the documented gate lodge design for Claremont, Leeds of the same year; secondly Chantrell was well acquainted with Beckett. In 1838, Chantrell had just completed the rebuilding of Headingley Chapel, Beckett's local church. Becket, later thanked for 'the great zeal he had shown in … promoting [the rebuilding]' initially chaired the rebuilding committee and was subsequently its treasurer. Unusually, Chantrell donated half is fee to the rebuilding fund for the church which surely ingratiated him with Beckett. By 1838, Chantrell was busy with the prestigious rebuilding of Leeds Parish Church where Beckett owned three pews and which was his favoured place of worship.

Headingley, Leeds, School in Hollin Lane
New school and mistress's house, *c*.1840

The school is attributed to Chantrell because of its similarity with his documented schools of *c*.1840. For instance, the idiosyncratic finials seen at Claremont's Lodge and Skipton school reappear here. Furthermore, the school is just beyond the boundary of William Beckett's mansion. Beckett's monument in Leeds Parish Church records him as 'the founder of several schools' and it is improbable that he was not involved with his local one, certainly he gave £100 to the building fund. In 1840 Chantrell had recently completed the new chapel in Headingley, a project in which Beckett was heavily involved, and perhaps Beckett's lodge (see above). A date of 1839 is given in an old parish magazine, but building accounts suggest 1840-1. These accounts do not list an architect; perhaps Chantrell gratuitously designed this little building – he had earlier donated half his fee for rebuilding nearby Headingley Chapel – as a favour to Beckett.

REFERENCES: WYASL, RDP39/112; *St Chad's Magazine*, Dec. 1892; D. Hill, *Far Headingley*, Far Headingley Village Society, 2000, p. 50.

Keighley, Eastwood House
New house for William Sugden, 1819

Cat. 38: Headingley, Leeds, Kirkstall Grange (now Beckett's Park), lodge, 1838.

Cat. 39: Keighley, West Yorkshire, Eastwood House, *c.*1819.

The date of 1819 for the house has been published widely, but whether this refers to the whole house, to the centre only or the addition of wings is not clear. Certainly the house *appears* as if the centre and wings are by two independent designers, although an inspection of the roofs and internal walls might lead one to conclude the whole building was erected as a single project. Angus Taylor – or more likely his editor, Janet Martin, since discussions with Taylor revealed he had only limited belief in the attribution – claims the house for the Websters. However, it is well outside their sphere of operation in 1819 and has little to link it stylistically with their documented work. It is far more likely that a Keighley client proposing to build a modest house would look to nearby Halifax, the closest location of an architect. There the choice was between the young John Oates or the more experienced William Bradley, the latter having in his office as his assistant, Chantrell. The use of the dominant semi-circular motif in the wings has an obvious affinity to the Halifax Sion Chapel of precisely the same date (see above) and these, plus the form of the pilasters and the Soanian motifs on the parapet all suggest buildings of the period of Chantrell's pupilage with Soane.

Leeds, Broomhill, Harrogate Road
New house for John Skelton, *c.*1838
The building is attributed to Chantrell on two counts: its similarity to various documented Chantrell houses, for instance the vicarage at Middleton, and a family connection between the Chantrells and Skeltons. The Skeltons bought the Broomhill farm from Sir Stanford Graham in 1838 and the new house 'erected by John Skelton' (1804-64) was probably begun almost immediately (property deeds), perhaps in time for his marriage to Ruthetta Smithson Barstow. It seems the Barstows and Chantrell's were related (see Chapter 2), indeed Ruthetta's younger sister – Mary Ann – married Chantrell's second son, John Boham, in 1844. John and Ruthetta had only one child, a daughter Margaret Annetta Smithson Skelton, who bequeathed

Cat. 40: Leeds, Broomhill, Harrogate Road, *c.*1838.

Broomhill to 'my cousin' William Smythson Chantrell, Chantrell's grandson, who inherited it in 1920. The building survives largely unaltered and is currently the presbytery of the nearby Sacred Heart of Mary Roman Catholic church.

REFERENCE: Unclassified papers in the Leeds diocesan archives.

Leeds, Race Ground

New grandstand, *c.*1822

An illustration of the grandstand, from a drawing by Chantrell, decorates Charles Fowler's *Plan of Leeds Race Ground* of 1823. It appears to be an elegant structure and could well have been a Chantrell design. *LI,* 31 July 1823 noted that 'we are happy to announce that a race ground will shortly be opened … the glass house mansion will form the grandstand.' However, an article in *LI,* 24 June 1824 includes, 'the "grand stand", which has been described as a permanent, safe and elegant erection, and which is calculated to contain about 1000 persons, is simply a boarded (unpainted) stage erected in front of the old house.' It is thus unclear whether the illustration in Fowler's map was a Chantrell scheme that was not executed, or perhaps Chantrell asked to provide a bit of 'artistic licence' in drawing a plain, functional structure that already existed? The issue is further complicated by a short article in the *LM* in 1825 which claimed, 'a complete range of stands substantially constructed of brick and wood have risen up.'

REFERENCES: *LI,* 31 July, 20 Nov. 1823, 5 Feb., 24 June 1824; *LM,* 11 June 1825.

Cat. 41: Leeds, The Bank National School, c.1840.

Leeds, St Peter's School, The Bank

New school, c.1840

The *LI* of 11 April 1840 announced the opening of 'the new National School of St Peters [at] The Bank, Leeds', but gave no more details. This is unusual as new schools normally attracted the paper's interest and this one was exceptionally large. As its name suggests, it is close to Leeds Parish Church. As Chantrell was in the middle of the rebuilding of the church when the school was erected, and secured a number of National School commissions within the parish at this time, he would have been the obvious choice as architect. The attribution is strengthened by its similarity to documented Chantrell schools, especially *via* the octagonal turrets which reappeared at Hunslet a few years later.

Morley, near Leeds, St Peter's National School

New school, 1832

LI, 9 August 1832 reported the opening of the 'Morley and Churwell District National School. The style of architecture corresponds with that of the church.' The building includes a date-stone which confirms the date as 1832. However, *LI* of 1 June 1833 noted 'the new National District School House at Morley cum Churwell opened on Whit Monday.' This is perplexing as there is no other evidence to suggest that two independent schools were built at this time. The school in the corner of the church yard at St Peter's is attributed to Chantrell firstly on the grounds that, as architect of the church opened only two years earlier, he would be the most likely candidate for the job. Secondly, stylistically the building has much in common with Chantrell's documented school at St Mary, Quarry Hill, Leeds of 1829-30, for instance the tripartite window in the principal gable end, the form of the corner buttresses and the details of the 'kneeler' stones at the bottom of the gables.

REFERENCES: *LI,* 9 Aug. 1832, 1 June 1833.

Cat. 42: Thorner, near Leeds, Fieldhead, *c.*1839–40.

Thorner, near Leeds, Fieldhead
New house for Henry Skelton, *c.***1839–40**

The house is attributed to Chantrell on the basis of its similarity to documented Chantrell designs, particularly the lodge for Clarement, Leeds, and the Skelton connection noted at *Broomhill* (see above). The house was built on part of the estate of Henry's father, also called Henry (b. *c.*1777), and was completed in time for the marriage of Henry junior (b. *c.*1806) to Anna Maria Kitson on 25 August 1840.

REFERENCES: T.W. Brown, *The Making of a Yorkshire Village: Thorner*, Thorner Historical Society, 1991, p. 114; J. Gilligham, *Highways and Byways from Leeds*, Kingsway Press, 1994, p. 37.

Abbreviations

BI	Borthwick Institute, University of York.
CBC	Church Building Commission.
Colvin	H.M. Colvin, *A Biographical Dictionary of British Architects 1600-1840*, Yale, 2008.
Glynne	S. Glynne [L. Butler ed.] *The Yorkshire Church Notes of Sir Stephen Glynne (1825-1874),* Yorkshire Archaeological Society and Boydell Press, 2007.
ICBS	Incorporated Church Building Society papers, at Lambeth Palace Library.
LI	*Leeds Intelligencer.*
LM	*Leeds Mercury.*
Lawton	G. Lawton, *Collections relative to Churches and Chapels within the Diocese of York,* Rivington, 1842.
LPC	Leeds Parish Church.
Linstrum	D. Linstrum, *West Yorkshire Architects and Architecture*, Lund Humphries, 1978.
SM	Sir John Soane's Museum, London.
Taylor	R.V. Taylor, *The Churches of Leeds*, Simpkin, Marshall and Co., 1875.
UL SC	University of Leeds Library, Special Collections.
WYASB	West Yorkshire Archives Service, Bradford.
WYASL	West Yorkshire Archives Service, Leeds.
WYASW	West Yorkshire Archives Service, Wakefield.

Notes

Introduction

1. CBC, Golcar file.

Chapter 1: Architecture in Post-Waterloo England

1. J. Summerson, *Architecture in Britain, 1530-1830,* Penguin, 1970, p. 497.
2. D. Watkin, *The Buildings of Britain: Regency,* Barrie and Jenkins, 1982, p. 7.
3. Published by Zwemmer.
4. Yale, 1995, p. 312.
5. Watkin [note 2].
6. T. Brittain-Catlin, *The English Parsonage in the Early Nineteenth Century,* Spire Books, 2008, identifies the 1830s as a period ripe for re-examination – 'one of the most obscure chapters in English architectural history' he claims on p. 9.
7. Among recent books, F. Salmon, *Building on Ruins,* Ashgate, 2000, is almost alone in seeking to re-establish the importance of Classicism in the second quarter of the nineteenth century.
8. William Wilkins held the post for two years between them, but did not deliver any lectures.
9. See R.A. Kindler, 'Periodic criticism 1815-40: originality in architecture' in *Architectural History,* 17, 1974, pp. 22-37. Kinder points out that examples quoted were 'largely drawn from one variety or other of the Classical tradition … one is barely aware of the rising groundswell, the love of antiquarianism' (p. 31). While new Gothic work might, occasionally, be mentioned, it was not subjected to any sort of critical scrutiny in the way that Classical buildings were. Only the *Gentleman's Magazine* maintained a consistent interest in Gothic.
10. There is an interesting article on this topic in *Colburn's Monthly Magazine,* 1821, p. 50, quoted in Kinder [note 9], p. 27. George Wightwick put it succinctly: in seeking to explain the 'misplaced popularity' of the Classical style among architects, he claimed it was because it relied on 'mathematical certainties' whereas the great monuments of English Gothic were the products of 'so many examples of independent genius … [By following] Vitruvius, [architects] are enabled to realise perfection without troubling their inventive powers' (*Architectural Magazine,* 3, 1836, pp. 453-4).
11. Details of the books quoted in the following sentences can be found in John Archer, *The Literature of British Domestic Architecture, 1715-1842,* MIT Press, 1985, and E. Harris and N. Savage, *British Architectural Books and Writers, 1556-1785,* Cambridge UP, 1990.
12. Published by J. Taylor, plates 133-5.
13. A.G. Cook, *The New Builder's Magazine and Complete Architectural Library,* Thomas Kelly, 1820, pp. 307-8.
14. Cook [note 13]. For Carter, see J.M. Crook, *John Carter and the Mind of the Gothic Revival,* Maney and the Society of Antiquaries, 1995.
15. Vol. 2, pp. 517.
16. *Ibid.,* pp. 448-9.

17. Although the numbering is not entirely consistent.
18. Alluding to Giacomo Barozzi da Vignola (1507-73), the leading Roman architect after the death of Michelangelo, and confirming the book's Classical bias.
19. pp. 27-9.
20. Aside from educational buildings, Thomas Rickman's Gothic Newsroom and Library in Carlisle (1830-1) and the design for a 'Town Hall and Market House' in the 'Anglo Norman style' included in P.F. Robinson, *Village Architecture,* James Carpenter, 1830, Design X, are rare exceptions.
21. The same is true of A. Pugin and J. Britton's *Illustrations of the Public Buildings of London,* John Weale, 2 vols, 1825-8.
22. However, Dobson did produce the occasional Gothic design and Foulson's remarkable 'experimental group' of Greek, Roman, Gothic, Oriental and Egyptian buildings in Kerr Street, Plymouth should not be overlooked. For the latter, see, J.M. Crook, *The Dilemma of Style,* John Murray, 1987, p. 34.
23. C. Brooks, *The Gothic Revival,* Phaildon, 1999.
24. *Ibid.,* pp. 5-6.
25. *Ibid.,* pp. 64-5. The important link between British patriotism and Gothic architecture during and after the Napoleonic wars is emphasised in Crook [note 14], e.g., p. 36.
26. *Ibid.,* p. 118.
27. *Ibid.,* pp. 127-52.
28. See R. Sweet, *Antiquaries: the Discovery of the Past in Eighteenth Century Britain,* Hambleton and London, 2004.
29. R. Hill, *God's Architect: Pugin and the Building of Romantic Britain*, Penguin, 2007, p. 51. E.J. Willson, in the Introduction to vol. 1 of A. Pugin, *Examples of Gothic Architecture*, published for the author, 1831, p. xi, wrote: 'the study of ancient architecture is not now confined to the mere antiquary, but has become almost a part of polite education.'
30. P. Bicknell (ed.), *The Illustrated Wordsworth's Guide to the Lakes,* Webb and Bower, 1984, p. 34.
31. See C. Hussey, *English Country Houses: Late Georgian,* Antique Collectors' Club, 1986, pp. 161-3.
32. The importance of fashion is discussed in J.M. Robinson, *The Regency Country House from the Archives of Country Life,* Aurum Press, 2005, p. 21. 'Novelty and richness were what mattered, and the pace was set by the Prince Regent'.
33. For instance, many of the principal Gothic and Tudor houses have 'modern' (i.e. Classical) interiors designed for comfort rather than style, e.g. Belvoir, Ashridge and Tregothnan.
34. Robinson [note 32], p. 9.
35. *Architectural Magazine,* 5, 1838, p. 50. The writer continues, 'but since that period many men of elegant genius and unswerving industry, in answer to calls from an already prevailing taste [have come forth].'
36. This comes from J. Britton, *The History and Antiquities of the Cathedral Church of York,* Longman *et al.,* 1819, p. v, but similar sentiment is found elsewhere in his publications.
37. D. Watkin, *The Rise of Architectural History,* The Architectural Press, 1983, p. 60.
38. J. Britton and T.E. Jones, *A Descriptive Account of the Literary Works of John Britton,* for the Subscribers, 1849, p. 69. However, the fifth volume of the *Architectural Antiquities*, of 1825, did include a 'Chronological History and Graphic Illustration of Christian Architecture in England'.
39. N. Pevsner, *Some Architectural Writers of the Nineteenth Century,* Oxford, 1972, p. 25.
40. Britton and Jones [note 38], p. 75.
41. J. Britton, *The History and Antiquities of the Cathedral Church of Wells,* Longman *et al.,* 1824, p. vii., Later in the book he goes further, adding 'the church [is] worthy of the most careful attention by the professional architect.' p. 91.
42. Britton and Jones [note 38], p. 90.
43. A. Pugin, *Specimens of Gothic Architecture,* London, 1825, vol. 1, p. vi. Benjamin Ferrey, one of Pugin's pupils recorded 'Mr Nash … feeling the want of practical works upon Gothic architecture (for although beautiful pictorial illustrations of our cathedrals were in course of publication by Britton,

no book yet existed in which the details were so drawn as to enable the practical architect to make working drawings of them), suggested to Pugin [senior] that by applying himself to this particular purpose he would do the profession a great service and secure a profitable occupation.' B. Ferrey, *Recollections of A.N. Welby Pugin*, Edward Stanford, 1861, p. 5.

44. Hill [note 29], p. 51.
45. Pugin [note 43], p. v.
46. *Ibid.*, p. xx. He continues: ' In designing and adapting Gothic Architecture to modern edifices, it is of primary importance to calculate on the size, proportions, object and situation of an intended building; and to select a class or style applicable to those points. The next requisite is to preserve harmony, or consistency of style, throughout all the members and details of the work. Disregarding this, or ignorant of its principles, many builders, miscalled architects, have committed egregious blunders, and having jumbled together, in one design, not only the styles of different ages, but mixtures of castellated, domestic, and ecclesiastical architecture. Indeed, it is to the tastelessness of persons, who occasionally compose, or rather build, such edifices without well-planned and well-digested designs, that "modern Gothic" has been treated with sneers and contempt.'
47. Published by M. Taylor, pp. 10-11.
48. The book includes designs for simple non-conformist chapels and a variety of Anglican churches. The best are Classical, although these are hardly sophisticated; the Gothic ones are little more than paired-down versions of Battey Langley's interpretation of the style.
49. For instance: J.B. Papworth's *Rural Residences* of 1818; J.C. Loudon's *Encyclopaedia of Cottage, Farm and Villa Architecture* of 1833.
50. Watkin [note 37], p. 56.
51. J. Britton, *Architectural Antiquities of Great Britain*, Longman *et al.*, vol. 5, 1826, pp. 31-102.
52. H-W. Kruft, *A History of Architectural Theory*, Zwemmer, 1994, pp. 323-7.
53. Pevsner [note 39], pp. 16-100.
54. Watkin [note 37], pp. 56-69.
55. The idea of a set of consistent rules was implied by Palladio and developed by his followers. However, the more intelligent architects came to realise that the concept of Classical 'rules' was an elusive one and Soane is explicit about this in his second RA lecture. J. Soane, *The Royal Academy Lectures,* Cambridge, 2000, p. 62.
56. C.R. Cockerell, 'William of Wykham' in *Proceedings of the Annual Meeting of the Archaeological Institute* ... , John Henry Parker *et al.*, 1846, p. 32.
57. *Archaeologia,* 16, 1812, p. 298. The paper was delivered in 1809, although not published until three years later.
58. J.M. Neale, *Church Enlargement and Church Arrangement,* Cambridge Camden Society, 1843, p. 8.
59. J. Elmes *Lecture on Architecture,* Priestley and Weale, 1823, p. 374. Despite the book's general concentration on Classical architecture, he conceded: Gothic is 'one of the most important although heretical inventions ... in the annals of architecture ... [although] Wren called Gothic a gross concameration of heavy, melancholy and monkish piles [it can be] grand [and] impressive.' (pp. 372-5).
60. J. Kendall, *Elucidation of the Principles of the Principles of English Architecture,* J. Murray *et al*, 1818, p. 21.
61. *Ibid.,* pp. 27-30.
62. J. Soane (D. Watkin ed.), *The Royal Academy Lectures,* Cambridge, 2000, p. 120.
63. Wightwick [note 10].
64. *Architectural Magazine,* 2, 1835, p. 429.
65. M.H. Port (ed.), *The Houses of Parliament,* Yale, 1976, p. 31.
66. For instance: R. and A.J. Brandon, *An Analysis of Gothic Architecture*, Pelham Richardson, 1847; G.A. Poole, *A History of Ecclesiastical Architecture in England,* Joseph Masters, 1848. Perhaps the most useful was: R. and A.J. Brandon, *Parish Churches ... English Eccesiastical Structures Drawn to a Uniform Scale* ... , David Bogue, 1851. The Brandons' *Analysis* begins: 'Of the numerous works recently called into

existence by the prevalent spirit of enquiry and research into the Ecclesiastical Architecture of the Middle Ages, none has supplied such as analysis of details as is absolutely essential, no less for the complete abstract elucidation of the principles of this great art, than for a correct practical application.' (p. v).

67. The first edition stated its object was 'to defuse among the general reader a taste for architecture' as well as addressing itself to the architect, surveyor, builder and upholsterer (p. 1).

68. However, in his *Treatise* of 1806 he pronounced 'the general effect of a [Gothic] cathedral … far surpasses that of any Grecian building in producing that exhilarating sublimity which is so analogous to the purpose for which they are erected.' pp. 101-2.

69. *Architectural Magazine,* 2, 1835, pp. 333-6.

70. *Ibid.,* 2, pp. 5-11.

71. *Ibid.,* 3, 1836, pp. 147-50.

72. *Ibid.,* 2, 1835, p. 339.

73. *Ibid.,* 3, 1836, p. 147.

74. *Ibid..* 1, 1834, pp. 318-9.

75. *Ibid.,* 1, 1834, pp. 273-4.

76. *Ibid.,* 2, 1835, p. 384.

77. *Ibid.,* 5, 1838, p. 49.

78. *Ibid.,* 5, 1838, p. 114.

79. Much space was devoted to the consideration of the best methods of warming and ventilating buildings, to making them more resistant to fires and to the most expedient means of exploiting new materials, like corrugated iron sheeting for roofing or iron chains for bridges. There was also articles on, for instance, innovative cooking stoves, furniture made of slate, and the eradication of dry rot.

80. There were numerous articles demanding the proper regulation of competitions and the formation of a professional body to oversee architects, e.g. 1, 1834, p. 12, or 2, 1835, pp. 12-14.

81. Summerson [note 1], p. 343.

82. See S. Sawyer, 'Delusions of National Grandeur: Reflections on the Intersection of Architecture and History at the Palace of Westminster, 1789-1834' in *Transactions of the Royal Historical Society,* 13, 2003, pp. 237-50.

83. See D. Stroud, *Sir John Soane, Architect,* Faber, 1983, p. 108.

84. The best account of the competition is: M.H. Port (ed.) [note 65], especially chs. ll and lll. Also useful are: H. de Hann and I. Haagsma, *Architects in Competition,* Thames and Hudson, 1988, pp. 30-40; C. Riding and J. Riding, *The Houses of Parliament,* Merrell, 2000, pp. 99-111.

85. *Architectural Magazine,* 2, 1835, p. 314.

86. The committee included no architects and several of its members were keen amateur Goths.

87. K. Clark, *The Gothic Revival,* John Murray, 1975, p. 114. Clark proceeds to quote from F. Goodwin's *Rural Architecture,* 1835, no. 5: 'For civil purposes, public or private, the town hall, exchange or senate house; the Greek, Roman or Italian styles are universally admitted as applicable.'

88. Quoted in G. Germann, *Gothic Architecture,* Lund Humphries, 1972, p. 67.

89. *Architectural Magazine,* 2, 1835, p. 381.

90. *Ibid* p. 383.

91. *Ibid.,* 2, 1835, p. 273.

92. *Ibid.,* 2, 1835, pp. 506-7.

93. *Ibid.,* 2, 1835, pp. 509-10.

94. *Ibid.,* 2, 1835, p. 507.

95. *Ibid.,* 3, 1836, p. 100.

96. Clark [note 87], p. 115.

97. *Architectural Magazine,* 3, 1836, p. 187.

98. Certainly Lewis Vulliamy did not enter on these grounds. (*Architectural Magazine,* 3, 1836, p. 309).

99. *Architectural Magazine*, 3, 1836, p. 294-303.

100. Quoted in Haan and Haagsma [note 84], p. 35.

101. *Architectural Magazine*, 5, 1838, pp. 51-6 and 110-1.

102. *Ibid.*, 2, 1835, p. 273.

103. *Ibid.*, 2, 1835, pp. 509-11.

104. His 'A Letter to A.W. Hakewill' was reviewed in *Architectural Magazine,* 2, 1835, pp. 507-9.

105. *Architectural Magazine*, 3, 1836, p. 296.

106. For the formation of the Institute see B. Kaye, *The Development of the Architectural Profession in Britain,* George Allen and Unwin, 1960, pp. 79-80; M.H. Port, 'RIBA Founders', *ODNB On Line,* 2009.

107. Port [note 65], p. 1.

108. Medieval styles were 'adapted to the Gothic origin and time-worn buttresses of our constitution' dating from a 'time when classic architecture was unknown in this country', quoted in Port [note 69], p. 30.

109. Cook [note 13], pp. 307-8. The text, including the comparison between St Paul's and Westminster Abbey, is largely plagiarising John Carter's *Builder's Magazine* from the 1770s. See also Crook [note 14].

110. The subject is covered with exemplary thoroughness in M.H. Port, *Six Hundred New Churches: The Church Building Commission 1818-1856,* Spire Books, 2006.

111. Within the broad heading of 'Baroque', some churches tended towards a stricter Classicism and others Early Christian. However, all were explicitly not Gothic.

112. Port [note 110], p. 41.

113. *Ibid.*, p. 50.

114. *Ibid.*, pp. 85-8.

115. *Ibid.*, p. 87.

116. M. Mansbridge, *John Nash: A Complete Catalogue,* Routledge, 1991, p. 214.

117. See also R. Liscombe 'Economy, character and durability: specimen designs for the Church Commissioners, 1818', in *Architectural History,* 13, 1970, pp. 43-57. 'The stylistic diversity of the designs by Soane and Nash, and possibly the monotony of those by Smirke, may have encouraged the Commissioners to assume a position of stylistic neutrality. The specifications distributed to architects competing for individual commissions began with the question: 'Whether the Church or Chapel is to be of Grecian and of what order or Gothic and of what century?' (p. 50).

118. CBC, first *Annual Report*, 1821.

119. Soane Museum, Private Correspondence, xv, A, 32.

120. *Builder*, 5, 1847, p. 300.

121. The writer is grateful to Dr Friedman for sharing this unpublished information with him.

122. A writer in the *Gentleman's Magazine*, July 1790, p. 600, reviewing Thomas Harwick (junior's) new Classical church at Wanstead, noted: 'it may be considered as a pattern church to any parish in the kingdom, where the subject is too small for a Gothic building, or where, for other reasons, it cannot properly be admitted.' This seems to imply that, in normal circumstances, the Gothic style would be the natural choice. See T. Friedman, 'Thomas Hardwick Jr's early churches', in *Georgian Group Journal,* 8, 1998, pp. 43-55.

123. John Carter, 'York', *Gentleman's Magazine*, 76, 1806, I, p. 322, quoted in Crook [note 14], p. 33.

124. J. Carter, *The Builder's Magazine,* For the authors, 1774-8, caption to plate CLXXXV.

125. J.C. Loudon, *A Treatise on Farming, Improving and Managing Country Residences,* Longman *et al.*, 1806, p. 101-2.

126. J. Britton, *Salisbury Cathedral,* Longman *et al.*, 1814, p. 2.

127. J.P. Neale, *Views of the most interesting Collegiate and Parochial Churches of Great Britain,* 1824, quoted in J. Macaulay, *The Gothic Revival 1745-1845,* Blackie, 1975, p. 262.

128. G.A. Poole, *the Appropriate Character of Church Architecture,* T.W. Green, 1842, p. 86.

129. The story is told in Port [note 110], pp. 74-8.

130. D. Watkin, *C.R. Cockerell,* Zwemmer, 1974, p. 250. Watkin incorrectly records Cockerell's successor in 1823 as Hodgson Fowler. However, Fowler – not born until 1840 – was responsible for alterations *c.*1880 (East Riding of Yorkshire Archives, DDX234/2) and Colvin includes Birdsall among Oates' commissions. I am most grateful to David Neave for clarifying this matter for me.

131. St Mary's was the Commissioners' church chosen by Pugin in *Contrasts* to exhibit all that was wanting in modern Gothic. See also B.F.L. Clarke, *Parish Churches of London,* Batsford, 1966, p. 140, which includes the Summerson quotation.

132. Colvin, p. 114.

133. T. Faulkner and A. Gregg, *John Dobson Architect of the North East,* Tyne Bridge Publishing, 2001, pp. 75 and 78.

134. Port [note 110], p. 97-8.

135. F. Beckwith, *Thomas Taylor, Regency Architect,* Thoresby Society, 1949, p. 92.

136. SM [note 119].

137. Pevsner [note 39], p. 85.

138. *Architectural Magazine,* 3, 1836, p. 396. The article is by T. Sopwith who, interestingly, ten years earlier published *A Historical and Descriptive Account of All Saints Church in Newcastle upon Tyne,* an innovative circular Classical church of the 1780s. See T. Friedman, *The Georgian Parish Church: 'Monuments to Posterity',* Spire Books, 2004, pp. 133-47.

139. *Architectural Magazine,* 5, 1838, p. 223.

140. W. Bardwell, *Temples Ancient and Modern,* for the author, 1837, pp. viii-ix. An underlying theme of the book is the superiority of Classicism for churches.

141. W.P. Griffith, *The Natural System of Architecture,* for the author, London, 1845.

142. W.V. Pickett, *New System of Architecture Founded on the forms of Nature and Developing the Properties of Metals … ,* Longman and Co., 1845. Remarkably, vol. II of the Ecclesiological Society's *Instrumenta Ecclesiastica* of 1856 included a design for an iron church.

143. C. Wren, *Parentalia,* 1750, p. 320, quoted in G. Beard, *The Work of Christopher Wren,* Bartholomew, 1982, p. 22.

144. Port [note 110], pp. 62-3.

145. Furthermore, the Commissioners were not keen on cross plans because of the difficulties of congregations who were sitting in the transepts having a clear view of the altar.

146. Pocock [notes 47 and 48].

147. *The British Critic,* 28, 1840, p. 471, quoted in Colvin, p. 769.

148. Even in the 1830s the situation was little better, e.g. P.F. Robinson *Village Architecture,* James Carpenter, 1830 (which included only one church, in the 'Anglo Norman style'); G.E. Hamilton, *Designs for Rural Churches,* John Weale, 1836 (with 12 very crude Gothic designs). G. Godwin, *The Churches of London,* 2 vols, C. Tilt, 1838-9, represents an admirable illustrated survey of the capital's post-Reformation churches, but contains no plans.

149. See J. Myles, *L.N. Cottingham, Architect of the Gothic Revival,* Lund Humphries, 1996.

150. See J. Allibone, *Anthony Salvin, Pioneer of Gothic Revival Architecture,* Lutterworth Press, 1987.

151. See A. Taylor, *The Websters of Kendal,* Cumberland and Westmorland Antiquarian and Archaeological Society, 2004.

152. Such an attitude was still the standard one in the middle of the 20th century. See the otherwise balanced H.S. Goodhart-Rendel, English Architecture since the Regency, Constable, 1953, p. 50 where he concluded, 'these early 'Commissioners' Churches' are mere preaching-houses of little architectural worth.' However, he does offer some lukewarm praise for them on pp. 51-3.

153. See C. Webster, *'Temples … worthy of His presence': the early publications of the Cambridge Camden Society,* Spire Books, 2003, pp. 9-31.

154. Quoted in M. Port, 'Francis Goodwin (1784-1835)' in *Architectural History,* 1, 1958, p. 71.

155. 'The business of the architect is to make the designs and estimates, to direct the works and to measure

and value the different parts; he is to be the intermediate agent between the employer, whose honour and interest he is to study, and the mechanic, whose rights he is to defend, his situation implies great trust; he is responsible for the mistakes, negligences, and ignorances of those he employs; and above all, he is to take care that the workmen's bills do not exceed his own estimates. If these are the duties of the architect, with what propriety can his situation and that of the builder, or contractor be united? J. Soane, *Plans, Elevations and Sections of Buildings,* Messrs Taylor, 1788, p. 7.

156. Much of Pecksniff's character is revealed in chapter II. His pomposity is admirably conveyed in the illustrations by 'Phiz' which appear in many editions of the book. See also A. Saint, *The Image of the Architect,* Yale, 1983, pp. 51–5.

157. J.M. Crook, 'The pre-Victorian architect: professionalism and patronage' in *Architectural History,* 12, 1969, p. 66.

158. *Ibid.*

159. Port [note 65].

160. R Hill, 'Architecture in the 1840s' in R Hill (ed.) *The 1840s,* The Victorian Society, 2008, pp. 7–17. The book contains other illuminating essays about aspects of the decade, including M. Hall, '"Our own": Thomas Hope, A.J. Beresford Hope and the creation of the High Victorian style', pp. 60–75.

161. An anonymous review article 'Principles of Gothic Architecture' in *Quarterly Review,* 69, no. 137, 1841, pp. 111–49, suggests the days when Gothic could be seen as 'clumsy, nonsensical, impertinent and incongruous … unworthy of the name architecture' were over and the 'return to the habits of other days is full of meaning and interest.' The writer points to 'the numerous churches which are rising … the two societies recently established at Oxford and Cambridge …[and] the restorations … in our cathedrals and collegiate buildings' reveal that 'something better is indicated by these facts than a mere caprice of fancy.' (p. 113.)

162. Hill [note 160], p. 8. 'Perhaps it was not until the 1960s that another decade had its tone so much determined by the rising generation.' p. 7.

Chapter 2: Childhood, Architectural Education and the Beginnings of a Career

1. City of Bruges, Public Records, Register of Deaths, 1811.
2. F. Koller, *Annaire des Familles Patriciennes de Belgique,* Brussels, 2, 1941, pp. 67–70.
3. City of Bruges, Public Records, Register of Deaths, 1830.
4. Koller [note 2].
5. *Ibid.*
6. *Ibid.*
7. *Ibid.*
8. In the twenty years between 1797 and 1817, either Robert or Robert Dennis are recorded as being at the '10th house, Crown Row', '24th house, Crown Row', 7 Crown Row, 9 Crown Row, 20 Crown Row, 6 Crown Row. (This information comes from a variety of sources including *Newington Parish Rate Books* and birth certificates). Conceivably the family owned the entire street. At the time of R.D. Chantrell's death in 1872, his estate included 'Property in Crown Row, Walworth'.
9. He was baptised at Newington parish church on 24 Jan. 1793. Unusually, the day of birth is not recorded, neither is the family's address. LMA, P92/MRY/14.
10. Koller [note 2].
11. LMA, P92 MRY/14, p. 138. He was baptised on 3 Sept. 1795. Like Robert Dennis, no address is given.
12. It is possible they were staying with Mary's relatives which would also explain the absence of an address in the births register.
13. Newington parish rate books for 1797 and 1798, John Harvard Library, Newington.

14. *Holden's Triennial Directory*, William Holden, 1799, p. 122.
15. This can be explained as the information in directories was often collated many months prior to publication.
16. Koller [note 2].
17. *Ibid.*
18. *Ibid.*
19. *Ibid.*
20. According to Chantrell, the indigenous residents abandoned the traditional practise of burning wood for domestic heat in favour of 'coal [which] is of comparatively recent introduction by the English residents' (R.D. Chantrell, 'On the domestic buildings of Western Flanders in the sixteenth century illustrating the ornamental brickwork of the period', unpublished paper, read to the IBA 2 June 1856, RIBA Archives, CHR/1; another version is in MS SP.12, no. 17).
21. A. Van den Abeele, 'Entrepreneurs Brugeois au XIX siècle: George et William Chantrell' in *Bulletin Trimestriel du Crédit Communal de Belgique*, 146, 1983, p. 240.
22. *Ibid.*, p. 244
23. Chantrell [note 20].
24. The sale catalogue of 1840 says he began the collection 'about 40 years ago'.
25. A copy of the sale catalogue is in the Van de Muser Library, Bruges. It lists only paintings, but it seems unlikely there were not also drawings and prints; perhaps they were sold separately.
26. *Ibid*, p. 1. The introduction to the catalogue begins: 'The collection of pictures of Mr Robert Chantrell is too well known in the country and abroad for it to be necessary to enter into detail here of the merits of the majority of the canvases which compose this collection ... ' (p. 3) The Catalogue notes the collection included Dutch, Flemish, Italian and French Schools and included examples of Bruegal, Cuyp, Van Dyke, Greuze, Pousin and 12 Van Ousts, the latter secured high prices. There were also 45 oil sketches by Rubens (p. 3).
27. RIBA Archives, LC/2/3/3.
28. Chantrell [note 20].
29. There is an intriguing Chantrell connection that takes us back to the seventeenth century: a legal document concerning property in the manors of Bingley, Cottingley etc [north-west of Bradford, 16 miles from Leeds] refers to 'and also the moiety of the Chantrell of the parish church of Bingley ... ' WYASB, STST/2/161.
30. This, and subsequent genealogical material comes from a variety of web sites specializing in this sort of material.
31. Leeds City Library, Sykes Collection, vol. 1, pt 2, pp. 78-80.
32. John Bigland, *The Beauties of England and Wales, Yorkshire,* vol. 16, Longman *et al.*, 1812, p. 611.
33. Robert Chantrell wrote to Soane on 16 May 1820: 'I have lately been so fortunate to acquire by purchase 40 sketches by Rubens on paper. I have also acquired some other good paintings by good masters which I shall take the liberty of showing you in the course of a few months when I hope to visit your city. I beg leave to tender my best services here ... ' The letter goes on to say that a Bruges artist Mr – the writing is unclear but it is probably De Meulemeester (1771-1836) – will soon have for sale sets of engravings after drawings from the Vatican which Chantrell would 'submit' to Soane for 'inspection' (SM, Private Correspondence, XV.B.32.1)
34. George Basevi, one of Chantrell's fellow pupils, also had a father who was interested in the arts, had business interests on the Stock Exchange and 'knew Soane very well'. (A.T. Bolton, *Architectural Education a Century Ago,* n.d., p. 3). Charles Tyrrell, another contemporary pupil, was the 'son of Timothy Tyrrell, a solicitor who was an old friend of ... Soane.' (Colvin, p. 846). The *Westminster Review*, XLI, 1844, p. 73, in an article critical of the state of architectural education, states: 'the choice of instructor in the art [of architecture] is entirely guided by family connections or acquaintances.'
35. The majority of architects combined the designing of buildings with the supply of labour and/

or materials making the concept of the architect as an intermediary between the client and the building tradesmen quite impossible. See J.M. Crook, 'The pre-Victorian architect: professionalism and patronage' in *Architectural History,* 12, 1969, pp. 62-78.

36. All of Soane's pupils, assistants and clerks are listed, with brief biographical details, in A. Bolton, *The Works of Sir John Soane ... ',* Sir John Soane Museum, n.d., pp. xxxix-xlvii.

37. J. Soane, *The Royal Academy Lectures,* (D. Watkin ed.), Cambridge U.P., 2000, p. 19.

38. SM, Private Correspondence, XV.C.16

39. 'board, lodgings and wearing apparel' seems to have been a standard part of Soane's indenture agreements. However, this should not be taken literally; it is quite certain that the pupils did not live with Soane and his family at Lincoln's Inn Fields.

40. SM, Private Correspondence, XV.16

41. Malton and Bailey also came at 14, Basevi and Tyrrell were 16 and Adams was 21. Bolton [note 34], p. 3.

42. In the 1800-20 period, 150 gns was the norm; some paid 125 or 175 gns, but no one had paid as little as Chantrell since 1792. There is no apparent rationale behind Soane's fees structure.

43. A.T. Bolton, *Works* [note 36], p. xxxix.

44. C. Webster, 'The Architectural Profession in Leeds, 1800-50' in *Architectural History,* 38, 1995, pp. 178-9.

45. *Bentley's Miscellany,* 32, 1852, p. 25. While the architect Seth Pecksniff in Charles Dicken's *Martin Chuzzlewit* (1st ed., 1844) might be seen as a caricature, he was surely a readily identifiable character for Dicken's readers. Also in 1844 the *Westminster Review* (41, p. 73-4) made the following cynical observations about architectural education: 'A young man designing to enter the profession is apprenticed for seven years to an architect, not on account of his eminence, for none of our great architects have a school of followers, nor do any of them take more pupils than are required to perform the drudgery of the office ... this period of service is spent in copying papers or designs of the most commonplace buildings, and in working out the details of carpentry and bricklaying. It is not pretended that the pupil is sent there to be instructed in the history of his art, nor to be taught the art of designing buildings according to any fixed theory; and if during his apprenticeship he picks up any artistic notions on the subject, he must have more enthusiasm or better opportunities than fall to the lot of most men. Pupils are taken to assist the master in carrying out his own designs, and to acquire what knowledge might stick to them in so doing; whatever they learn beyond that is their own ... '

46. Soane [note 37], p. 28.

47. Between 1806 and 1820 over 1,000 of these watercolours were produced, many 3 or 4 feet long.

48. The Exhibition *Catalogues* record Chantrell exhibited a 'Design for a Cenotaph' in 1812 (no. 857) and in 1813 he exhibited a 'Design for a Church' (no. 843) and a 'Design for a Public Library' (no. 887).

49. M. Richardson, 'The Progress Tracers' in *The World of Interiors,* May 2008, pp. 246-51, discusses this aspect of training; F. Nevola, *Soane's Favourite Subject: The Story of Dulwich Picture Gallery,* Dulwich Picture Gallery, 2000, illustrates many student drawings connected with the Dulwich project, including several by Chantrell.

50. Bolton [note 34], p. 3. Bolton adds that George Basevi 'had a day's work with the head of the office measuring mason's work', although there is no record of similar experience for Chantrell.

51. Richardson [note 49], p. 250.

52. *Ibid.*, p. 251.

53. SM, day books.

54. Watkin, discussing the creation of the RA lecture diagrams, suggests that, at a time when the war with France restricted architectural commissions, they 'helped train the young men in the office in the absence of real jobs'. (Soane [note 37], p. 6). However, even in this relatively fallow period of Soane's career, there was no shortage of commissions on which the pupils could have been engaged had he thought it expedient. This writer would argue that by this stage of Soane's career only rarely were

the pupils given any meaningful role in their master's commissions regardless of the quantity of work passing through the office.

55. Printed in full in Soane [note 37].
56. See D. Watkin, *Sir John Soane, Enlightenment Thought and the Royal Academy Lectures,* Cambridge U.P., 1996.
57. Soane produced a total of twelve lectures in two series of six. While only the first set was delivered during Chantrell's time with Soane, the second set, first delivered in 1815, was in preparation during Chantrell's pupilage.
58. Soane [note 37], pp. 28-9.
59. Watkin [note 56], p. 1.
60. Soane [note 37], p. 62.
61. *Ibid.,* p. 249.
62. *Ibid.,* pp. 28-9.
63. *Ibid.,* p. 55.
64. C. Webster, 'The Influence of Sir John Soane' in *Late Georgian Classicism,* The Georgian Group, 1988, pp. 28-30. The writer is pleased to note his conclusions about Soane's conservative thinking are confirmed, although with much profound amplification, in Watkin's 'Introduction' to Soane [note 37].
65. A. T. Bolton (ed.), *Lectures on Architecture by Sir John Soane,* Sir John Soane's Museum, 1929, p. 7.
66. The day books record several days spent drawing churches, but these were probably Classical ones. In 1807, Chanttrell spent a week 'about Ramsay Abbey', a house which Soane Gothicised in 1804 and on 6 Feb. 1813, inexplicably, the entire office spent the day on drawings of Stockport church, rebuilt in the Gothic style by Lewis Wyatt from 1813 to 1817.
67. Soane [note 37], p. 122.
68. *Ibid.,* p. 120.
69. *Ibid.*
70. *Ibid.* pp. 122-3.
71. *Ibid.,* p. 123.
72. These two fascinating quotations appear in Watkin [note 56], p. 391.
73. Soane [note 37], p. 131.
74. *Ibid.,* p. 166.
75. *Ibid.,* pp. 215-6.
76. *Ibid.,* pp. 271-2.
77. *Ibid.,* p. 261.
78. *Ibid.,* p. 274. Of his own foreign travel Soane latter wrote 'it was the most fortunate event of my life … [for] it was the means by which I formed those connections to which I owe all the advantages I have since enjoyed.' Quoted in D. Stroud, *The Architecture of Sir John Soane,* Faber, 1961, p. 22.
79. RIBA Fellowship Nomination Papers, 1834-42, in the RIBA Library.
80. Bermondsey Parish Records, St Mary Magdalene, register of marriages, 1813-22. LMA, 71/MMG.
81. *The Exhibition of the Royal Academy, 1814,* p. 32, exhibit no. 706. Graves incorrectly records this item as a 'Design for a Villa' by Chantrell.
82. He was also called Robert Dennis, was born 30 Dec. 1815 and was baptised on 27 Feb. 1815 at St Mary, Newington. Newington parish registers, p. 173. LMA, P92/MRY/22.
83. This was subsequently erected to the designs of William Brooks. In 1823 Chantrell exhibited a 'View of an edifice designed for the London Institute of Literature and Philosophy' at the Northern Society for the Encouragement of Arts, almost certainly one of the unsuccessful competition entries.
84. J. Summerson, *Georgian London,* Penguin, 1969, pp. 154-62. He notes that state expenditure on building was withdrawn while an acute shortage of Baltic timber and high taxation on building materials discouraged private building projects.
85. *Ibid.,* p. 155. Summerson lists Gandy, Tatham, Bond and Sanders in this category.

86. Newington already had a well-established surveyor, Francis Hulbatt (*c*.1754-1834), who is known to have produced some executed designs and probably satisfied the limited demand for architectural services in the parish.
87. Newington parish registers, register of births, p. 270. LMA, P92/MRY/22.
88. *Builder,* 5, 1847, p. 300.
89. WYASL, DB 276, Leeds Public Baths, committee minute book, 1818-27.
90. SM, Private Correspondence, XV.A.32. The letter is dated 4 Jan. 1821. The wording of this letter is ambiguous: 'since I had the pleasure of waiting upon you' might suggest Chantrell's move to Halifax occurred soon after the expiry of his indentures, in Jan. 1814, yet we know he was still in London at least until 1816.
91. WYASW, WDP53/7/1/6, Halifax Parish Church Accounts 1760-1832.
92. Quoted in D. Linstrum, *West Yorkshire Architects and Architecture,* Lund Humphries, 1978, p. 35.

Chapter 3: Post-Waterloo Leeds

1. Interestingly, in the early 1840s, when the parishioners of Kirkstall decided a new school was needed, two members of the building committee believed they could proceed without the expense of an architect and produced a design of their own, essentially a pastiche of several earlier Chantrell schools. The committees minutes record a litany of problems: tradesmen failing to turn up and complete work; tradesmen failing to follow the specifications; parts of the unfinished building having to be demolished and rebuilt; tradesmen having to be replaced. WYASL, RDP50/43.
2. The best accounts are E.M. Sigsworth, 'The Industrial Revolution' in M.W. Beresford and G.R.J. Jones (eds) *Leeds and its Region,* The British Association, Leeds, 1967, pp. 146-55; S. Burt and K. Grady, *The Illustrated History of Leeds,* Breeden Books, 1994, pp. 87-132.
3. C.J. Morgan, 'Demographic Change, 1771-1911' in D. Fraser (ed.), *A History of Modern Leeds,* Manchester U.P., 1980, p. 48.
4. M.W. Beresford, 'The Face of Modern Leeds, 1780-1914' in Fraser [note 3], p. 73.
5. Quoted in M.W. Beresford, *East End, West End,* Thoresby Society, vols 60 and 61, 1988, p. 374.
6. Dividing building types into those that did or did not provide employment for architects is problematic, but there are some basic principles. So far as Leeds was concerned, all the churches and most of the nonconformist chapels can be linked to an architect. A single shop was unlikely to involve an architect, a row of shops might and a market certainly did.
7. For a detailed discussion of the provision of religious and public buildings in the town see M.W. Beresford [note 4] and K. Grady 'The Georgian Public Buildings of Leeds and the West Riding,* Thoresby Society, 62, 1989.
8. Watson and Pritchett of York produced plans for Hanover Square in 1823, the scheme for the 'New Town of Leeds', again by Watson and Pritchett, caused much excitement in 1828 and 1829 although little was built and as late as 1840 John Clark produced a design for Woodhouse Square.
9. Far more is known about architects' authorship of this type of house in Newcastle in this period, and there it is quite clear that their design formed a significant proportion of the leading architects' practices, for instance those of John Dobson or John Green.
10. See C. Webster, 'The Architectural Profession in Leeds 1800-50: a case study in professional practice' in *Architectural History,* 38, 1995, pp. 176-91.
11. *LI,* 9 Sept. 1811.
12. M.W. Beresford [note 4], p. 147.
13. A Raff Merchant was an importer of foreign timber.
14. J. Guest, *Historic Notices of Rotherham: Ecclesiastical, Collegiate and Civil,* Worksop, 1879, p. 542. I am most grateful to Dr Kevin Grady for this information.
15. ICBS, file 00818.

16. ICBS, file 00742.
17. ICBS, file 00456.
18. *The Newleafe Discourses* first appeared in *The Builder* between 11 July and 5 Sept. 1846. This passage is quoted in A. Saint, *The Image of the Architect,* Yale, 1983, p. 62.
19. W. White, *History, Gazetteer and Directory of the West Riding of Yorkshire,* William White, 1837, p. 496.
20. There are exceptions, mainly churches or chapels, and often such commissions can be explained as extensions of aristocratic or gentry patronage.

Chapter 4: Chantrell in Leeds

1. It seems likely that Chantrell was related to the Barstow family who, in the 1840s, were living in the parish of Guiseley; three of Chantrell's children are recorded in the 1841 census as living with the Barstows and there is a link between the Barstows and the Skeltons as John Barstow, head of the family in 1841, was a trustee of Margaret Blackburn's estate. John Boham Chantrell married one of John Barstow's daughters, Mary Anne. This information comes from census returns, the *National Register of Births, Marriages and Deaths Registers* and the deeds of the former Skelton residence, Broomhill, Harrogate Road, Leeds, now in the possession of the RC Diocese of Leeds.
2. The letter that accompanied Chantrell's baths drawings noted his address as, 'Saddle Yard, Briggate, or Blackwell, Halifax till 15th March'. (Leeds Public Baths, miscellaneous letters, WYASL, DB 276). By way of confirmation, Chantrell wrote to Soane on 6 Jan. 1821 ' ... during a residence in Leeds of 20 months ... ' (SM, Private Correspondence, XV. A. 32).
3. There were fifteen entries including six London firms, most notably J. Elmes and Decimus Burton, Rickman of Liverpool, as well as leading Yorkshire firms Watson and Pritchett, and Lindley, Woodhead and Hirst. (Leeds Public Baths, Committee Minute Book, WYASL, DB 276).
4. Although *LI* of 3 May 1819 announced the decision would be made at the meeting on 7 May, the Building Committee Minutes suggest Chantrell was not chosen until 14 May (UL SC, Phil. and Lit. Papers, no. 6).
5. The letter [note 2] can be dated to late January or early February.
6. Chantrell was probably aware of Taylor's increasing specialisation in ecclesiastical commissions, an area of practise Chantrell perhaps viewed with little interest at this time, and as if to confirm the opportunity that Leeds offered, Taylor did not submit an entry for the baths competition. Whether he entered the Philosophical Hall competition is not known as the unsuccessful entries were not recorded.
7. E. Baines, *History, Directory and Gazetteer of the County of York,* E. Baines, 1822, p. 22.
8. J. Heaton, *Walks Through Leeds,* J. Heaton, *c.*1835, p. 7.
9. Leeds Public Baths, *Committee Minute Book,* WYASL, DB 276.
10. *LI,* 2 April 1821.
11. Two sets of drawings for slightly different schemes are in WYASL, DB 75/9 Hey Estate. They were not built.
12. The town houses, which were re-fronted in the mid-nineteenth century and became the Leeds Club, were built for Hey's son and grandson. (Ex inf. Leeds City Library, Local Studies Dept; WYASL, DB75/19).
13. Pattern books that Chantrell might have used for additional inspiration can be found in D. Dean, *English shop Fronts 1792-1840,* Tiranti, 1970.
14. These included various alterations to Armley Chapel, a new school and alms-houses in Armley and the new church at Bean Ing, on the western fringe of Leeds.
15. SM, Private Correspondence, XV. A. 32, Chantrell to Soane.
16. Chantrell 'was paid £76 for taking down the old belfry upon Bramley Chapel, designing a new one and erecting it.' (A. Dobson, *St Peter's Church, Bramley,* privately printed, 1964, p. 31). However, it seems

more likely that £76 was the cost of the entire job, rather than just Chantrell's commission.

17. An advertisement inviting architects to submit plans did not appear in *LI* until 20 Nov. 1820. It asked for designs capable of holding 1200 people, with a capacity to be increased to 2,000. These were to be submitted by 10 Jan. 1821, although this was later extended to 1 March 1821. (*LI*, 11, 18 and 25 Dec. 1820).

18. SM, Private Correspondence [note 15].

19. *Builder*, 5, 1847, p. 300. He was probably right; 98 of the 99 churches erected in the West Riding aided by the Commissioners between 1821 and 1856 were Gothic.

20. SM, Private Correspondence, XV.B.32.1.

21. SM, Private Correspondence [note 15].

22. The dedication page carries the date of 'June 1821' putting publication in the second half of the year.

23. For instance, Chantrell's illustration of the Philosophic and Lieterary Society's hall appears on Fowler's 1821 map of Leeds, his drawing of the toll houses at Barnsdale appears on Fowler's 'Plan of Several Turnpike Roads between Leeds and Doncaster', published in 1822 and a view of the grandstand appeared on Fowler's 'Plan of the Leeds Race Ground' of 1823.

24. *LI*, 9 Sept. 1822.

25. See T. Fawcett, *The Rise of English Provincial Art*, Oxford U.P., 1974.

26. *LI*, 27 May 1822. Taylor's contribution included a 'correct and spirited representation ' of the interior of York Minster.

27. ' … foremost among the local men who were practising [architecture] in Leeds and the surrounding county and exhibiting designs for churches and other buildings of importance was R.D. Chantrell'. (W.H. Thorp, *John N Rhodes*, Richard Jackson, 1901, p. 14).

28. *LI*, 15 Jan. 1841. Completion was still more than a year away.

29. *LI*, 2 April 1842: 'It is simple almost to severity, the chasteness of the design, the noble proportions and the characteristic disposition of what forms at once the structure and the ornament of the building are such as to produce a most imposing and pleasing effect. There is nothing wasted in decoration and enrichment, yet nothing wanting to satisfy the eye. In its very simplicity it bespeaks the genius of the designer as forcefully as a more elaborate work and will constitute another monument of the talent of the architect, Mr Chantrell.'

30. *LI*, 26 Nov. 1821.

31. House numbering in this period was by no means consistent. The 1826 directory gives Chantrell's home address as 1 Park Row and his office as '11 and 12 Benson's Buildings, 2 Park Row'. Whether these are the properties first occupied in 1821 is not clear.

32. *LI*, 9 Jan. 1823.

33. *LI*, 16 Jan. 1823. The 'plates' were engraved brass plates noting the date and details of the building's designer and patron, to be fixed on or buried with the foundation, or 'first' stone.

34. *LI*, 2 Dec. 1824.

35. *LI*, 17 June 1824.

36. *LM*, 16 April 1825.

37 *LI*, 27 May 1824.

38. K. Grady, 'the Provision of Markets in Leeds, 1822-9', *Thoresby Society Miscellany*, 16, pt 3, 1976, p. 170.

39. *LI*, 7 July 1825. Much more of this article appears below in connection with the Commercial Buildings competition.

40. *LI*, 2 Dec. 1824.

41. Grady [note 38] p. 170, gives the finished cost at £34,000.

42. *LI*, 30 June, 7 July 1825.

43. *LI*, 7 July 1825.

44. *LM*, 2 July 1825.

45. *LI*, 7 July 1825.

46. *LI,* 14 July 1825

47. The precise dated of Clark's removal to Leeds is not known but he continued to appear in the *Edinburgh and Leith Post Office Directory* through the 1820s, but is absent for the edition of 1830-1. His obituary in the *Building Chronicle,* May 1857, pp. 197-8, notes '[the Commercial Buildings] was Mr Clark's introduction to Leeds [and] soon brought him a large amount of architectural business.'

48. *LI,* 8 Sept. 1825.

49. *Ibid.*

50. A full obituary appeared in *LI,* 30 March 1826.

51. For Taylor, see F. Beckwith, *Thomas Taylor, Regency Architect,* The Thoresby Society, 1949.

52. The Preface is dated 'Morley, 1st of December, 1827'.

53. Published by Longman *et al.,* p. 46.

54. *LI,* 5 March 1825.

55. Hammerton had been Taylor's assistant at a number of projects.

56. CBC MB 22, p. 17. Lockwood and Netherthong were two districts within the extensive parish of Almondbury. Certainly Taylor had submitted proposals to the CBC for Netherthong (CBC MB 17, p. 185), but it is not certain that he had done the same for Lockwood.

57. The words 'new designs' are significant as the parish had already approached John Day of Stockport to design the new church. He signed the CBC's Application Form on 8 May 1826. (CBC New Mills file 18103). It is not clear why he was dismissed.

58. *LI,* 28 Sept. 1839.

59. H. Roberson, *Prospectus for the Intended Church at Liversedge,* 1811, quoted in Beckwith [note 51], p. 94. Roberson continued this theme: writing 27 years later, he referred to 'Church Accommodation [as that which offers] the celebration of the Services, Sacraments, Rites and Ceremonies of the Church according to the Rubric', and which differed from the principles of non-conformity. (H. Roberson, *A Third Address to the Clergy and Influential Laity ... ,* J. Brook, 1838, p. 3).

60. A letter from the architects Perkin and Backhouse concerning the Leeds Industrial Schools competition refers to Clark as 'once the best architect in Leeds' (*LI,* 3 March 1848).

61. *LI,* 14 March 1835.

62. *LI,* 13 Feb. 1836.

63. UL SC, MS.421/140/1: Leeds General Cemetery papers.

64. Sadly, the house was neglected for many years and when converted to flats in the 1980s, the decayed ceilings were destroyed.

65. For instance, the mason's work at St Paul, Halifax cost £2,098 (CBC file 16,862).

66. *LI,* 28 Jan. 1843.

67. *Leeds Grammar School Registers, 1820-1900,* vol. 14, library of the Thoresby Society, Leeds.

68. He is recorded as a 'Proprietor' in 1827 with share no. 90. He might have joined several years earlier, but records before 1827 are incomplete. He continued to be a proprietor until at least 1846 and in 1854, his son John requested that the father's share be passed to himself (*Leeds Library, Register of Members, 1854-87,* held at the library).

69. The LPLS archives have only an incomplete set of *Annual Reports.* He was a member for the 1825-6 season, but *Reports* for 1827-30 are missing. He was not a member by the time of the 1831-2 *Report.*

70. *LI,* 9 Nov. 1839.

71. *LI,* 7 July 1831.

72. *LI,* 3 Jan. 1835.

73. *LI,* 7 March 1835.

74. It would seem his interest in its affairs diminished as the year passed. Much of the business concerned the proposed new Water Works, a project on which no significant progress was made, a fact which engendered much criticism in the *Intelligencer.*

75. *Lodge of Unanimity, Wakefield, List of Joining Members,* John Goodchild Archive, Wakefield.

76. A. Scarth and C.A. Bain, *History of the Lodge of Fidelity*, Beck and Inchbold, 1894, p. 220. Enquiries to the Librarian of the Library and Museum of the Grand Lodge of England reveal that Chantrell was a member of the lodge of Fidelity 'until 1844, left in 1845, rejoined 1846 than membership ceases 1849.'

77. *LI,* 20 May 1837.

78. *LI,* 27 May 1837.

79. *LI,* 23 Dec. 1837.

80. RIBA, Fellowship Nomination Papers, 1834-42.

81. RIBA Archives, EW 2399.

82. It was read on 18 December 1837, RIBA Archives, MS SP 6/9.

83. An even more eccentric gesture was the 1840 presentation to the Institute of a piece of decayed oak from Bruges. Chantrell seemed to believe its powdery state and pungent smell were worthy of note (RIBA Archives, LC/2/3/3).

84. ICBS, file 01422. This file records that Chantrell called at the ICBS offices in London 'when returning from the Continent' on 8 Aug. in connection with the Holmebridge church project; it also tells us he was at the same office on 17 July, so his trip cannot have been a long one.

85. J. Rusby, *A History of Leeds Parish Church,* Richard Jackson, 1877, p. 6.

86. W.R.W. Stephens (ed.), *The Letters of Walter Farquhar Hook,* Richard Bentley and Son, 1879, p. 409.

87. *LI,* 11 Nov. 1837.

88. To taker just one example, the Vicar of Birkenshaw referred to Chantrell as 'the eminent architect of Leeds' (ICBS, file 02652).

89. See H.W. Dalton, *Anglican Resurgence under W.F. Hook in Early Victorian Leeds: Church Life in a Nonconformist Town, 1836-1851,* Thoresby Society, 2nd ser., vol. 12, 2003; N. Yates, *Leeds and the Oxford Movement,* Thoresby Society, 1975.

90. On 25 June 1842, in a letter to the editor of the *Intelligencer* defending the vicar of Leeds from accusations of 'Popish interests', Chantrell claimed it was his own decision to reuse the old piscina and sedilia at Leeds Parish Church, acting 'as an antiquary'.

91. *LI,* 13 April 1839. The lecture was given on 19 April.

92. *LI,* 14 March 1840.

93. Leeds Philosophical and Literary Society, *Annual Report,* 1841-2.

94. *LI,* 15 April 1843.

95. J. Gibbs, *A Book of Architecture,* [no publisher recorded for the first edition], 1728, contains several designs for church towers, including alternative ones for St Martin-in-the-Fields, plates 29-30.

96. R.W. Moore, *A History of the Parish Church of Leeds ... ,* Richard Jackson, 1877, p. 54.

97. The first reference to the new firm appeared in a request for tenders in *LI,* 25 June 1842.

98. The subject is discussed in detail in Chapter 7.

99. This is the wording of the beginning of the YAS's first rule.

100. See H. Murray, *The Yorkshire Architectural and York Archaeological Society 1842-1992,* YAYAS, 1992.

101. See K. Taylor, 'A Pious Undertaking: the Retrieval of a Medieval Bridge Chantry', *Ecclesiology Today,* 16, 1998, pp. 8-11.

102. The dates of his membership appear in G.K. Brandwood, 'A Camdenian Roll-Call' in C. Webster and J. Elliott (eds) *'A Church as it should be': the Cambridge Camden Society and its influence,* Shaun Tyas, 2000, p. 380. A list of members was published only periodically; Chantrell was a member at the time of the 1856 list, but was not when that for 1864 appeared. *The Ecclesiologist* published several reviews of Chantrell's churches which were, at best, neutral in their assessment. These are noted in the Catalogue.

103. *LI,* 15 April 1843.

104. A review of the lecture appeared in *Gentleman's Magazine,* 28, 1847, pt 2, p. 67.

105. *Builder,* 5, 1847, pp. 300-2.

106. *LI,* 2 Jan. 1847.

107. *Memoirs Illustrative of the History and Antiquities of ... York communicated at the Annual Meeting of the*

Archaeological Institute of Great Britain and Ireland … York, July 1846, Archaeological Institute, London, 1848, p. vii.

108. *Ibid.,* p. xii.

Chapter 5: Chantrell in London

1. *LI,* 2 Jan. 1847.
2. Even 15 years later, he still believed 'the *far niente* never will agree with me.' ICBS Committee of Architects' Minute Book, letter from Chantrell, 9 Sept. 1863.
3. In May 1845, Chantrell wrote to the ICBS from 20 Lincoln's Inn Fields – although perhaps this should have said '21' (ICBS, file 03527), on 5 May 1845 he wrote from Tavistock, Covent Garden (ICBS, file 03455), and on 3 Sept. 1845, wrote from 21, Lincoln's Inn Fields (ICBS, file 20547).
4. In addition to material in [note 3], on 8 Dec. 1842, Chantrell wrote to the ICBS and apologised for his late reply as he 'had been away in London'. (ICBS, file 02784.); on 3 July 1844 and 2 May 1845 Messrs Horsfall and Harrison, solicitors, who handled the financial and legal affairs of the Leeds Parish Church rebuilding, wrote to Chantrell in London concerning payments for the project; 11 Aug 1845 Chantrell wrote to the ICBS ' … on my return from London last month … ' (ICBS, file 00818).
5. Records of his addresses held in the membership records of the RIBA more or less agree with *Kelly,* although the RIBA has him at Bruton Street in 1851.
6. The final reference appears in *Slade and Roebuck's Directory* of 1851, p. 182, probably compiled in 1850.
7. *LI,* 26 Aug. 1848.
8. Interestingly, the Lockwood and Netherthong jobs were documented as by 'Mr Chantrell of London', not Chantrell and Son of Leeds.
9. For more details of Wade and the relationship between Chantrell and John see Chapter 6.
10. Chantrell's will suggests he had a not inconsiderable collection of drawing fragments and artefacts. It lists, after his household effects, 'books,, pictures, paintings, engravings, antiquities … '. (Principal Probate Registry).
11. See C. Webster, '"True masonic principles": a mid nineteenth century alternative to "true principles"' in *Ecclesiology Today,* 18, 1999, pp. 1-5. It is discussed more fully in Chapter 7.
12. *Gentleman's Magazine,* 1847, 28, pt 2, pp. 68-9.
13. *Builder,* 5, 1847, pp. 300-2.
14. *Gentleman's Magazine* [note 12], p. 67.
15. *Gentleman's Magazine,* 1847, 27, pt 1, p. 190.
16. R. W. Moore, *Leeds Parish Church and its Ancient Cross,* Richard Jackson, 1877, p. 54.
17. According to a letter from H. W. Chantrell which appeard in the *LI,* 1 Aug. 1866.
18. A. McGuire and A. Clark, *The Leeds Crosses,* Leeds City Museums, 1987, p. 48. To complete his arrival on the Institute's scene, Chantrell presented its library with a copy of Blondel's *De la distribution des maisons de plaisance, et de la decoration des edifices en general,* of 1737-8 during the 1847-8 season.
19. Although he wrote to the Institute's secretary about bells and bell-hanging in January 1856 (RIBA Archives, MS.SP/12/12) and on 2 June 1856 read a paper – his last known lecture – 'On the domestic buildings of West Flanders in the sixteenth century illustrating the ornamental brickwork of the period'. (RIBA Archives, CHR/1).
20. For instance: *Ecclesiologist,* 6, 1846, pp. 154 (Skipton); 8, 1847, pp. 109-10 (Leeds, St Philip); 11, 1850, pp. 64-6 (Keighley) and pp. 143-4 (Denholme Gate).
21. Committee Minute Book, ICBS, MB 13. (Lambeth Palace Library)
22. Committee of Architects Minute Book, 1848-1900, ICBS, MB 39.
23. *Ibid.,* meeting of 31 March 1849.
24. See the Catalogue for details.
25. Minutes [note 22].

26. The only reference to a fee is in the case of Fangfoss where the cost is recorded as '£871 plus £87 architect's commission and clerk of works, total £958.' (ICBS, file 04114.)

27. Quoted in W.D. Wood-Rees, 'Fangfoss Church' in *Yorkshire Archaeological Journal,* 22, 1913, pp. 253-5.

28. *Ibid.*

29. Perhaps Chantrell was introduced to Taylor earlier in the 1840s, possibly while he was working at Leven for the Revd Wray another clerical antiquary. The suggestion takes weight from Chantrell's paper 'On the Geometric System Applied to Medieval Architecture', delivered on 14 June 1847 – at least a year before the Fangfoss commission started – in which he talks knowledgeably about nearby East Yorkshire churches of Routh, Sancton and Walkington, as well as Barmby.

30. It was dated 29 May 1851 and was sent from Chantrell's London house in Canonbury. The whereabouts of the original letter is now unknown. The quotation comes from a copy made by Miss Doris King of Pocklington in *c.*1989 and given to David Neave. I am extremely grateful to Dr Neave for alerting him to this letter and generously taking to time to copy it for me.

31. T. Whellan, *History and Topography of York and the North Riding,* 1859, vol. 2, p. 218.

32. *Builder,* 19, 1861, p. 621.

33. *Ibid.*

34. *Ibid.,* p. 772.

35. *Ibid.,* p. 792.

36. *Ibid.,* p. 812.

37. Details of the memorial appear in B. Ferrey, *Recollections of A.N. Welby Pugin,* Edward Stanford, 1861, pp. 467-73. The date of the memorial's establishment is obscure; Pugin scholars suggest it was likely to have been in the late 1850s.

38. It is not clear precisely what was wrong with Chantrell's leg. However, an 1845 letter from one subscriber to the Lund restoration fund to another includes 'Mr Chantrell is slow in his movements!' (East Riding of Yorkshire Archives, DDGR 44/22).

39. ICBS [note 22]. The letter is dated 31 May 1863.

40. This and the preceding two letters come from the Minutes [note 22].

41. Reported in the *Gentleman's Magazine,* March 1863, p. 397.

42. Mary Elizabeth Dear was born on 12 Nov. 1832 and Christened at St Pancras old church, London, on 6 June 1833. As a painter she enjoyed some precocious success, exhibiting for the first time at the Royal Academy at 15, in 1848. She exhibited there a further 6 times and on 5 occasions at the Suffolk Street Gallery, for the last time in 1868. (A. Graves, *A Dictionary of Artists,* Kingsmead Press, 1984, p. 75). She sent her exhibits from various addresses in North London. (A. Graves, *The Royal Academy of Arts: A Complete List of Contributors ... ,* Kingsmead Press, 1970, vol. l, p. 283).

43. Principal Probate Registry.

44. *Ibid.,* Index of Wills 1872.

45. *Ibid.,* Index of Wills for 1874. Related to this is a line in R.W. Moore's *A History of the Parish Church of Leeds,* published in 1877, p. 55, which notes '... [Chantrell's house in Rottingdean] has been sold by order under the High Court of Chancery ... '

46. Principal Probate Registry.

47. National Register of Births, Marriages and Deaths Indexes, vol. 2B, p. 185. The writer is informed by Peter Chantrell, a distant descendant, that she subsequently emigrated to New Zealand.

48. A full account of the cross in Chantrell's garden, and of its subsequent return to Leeds in 1877 or 1878 appears in McGuire and Clark [note 18], pp. 6-9.

49. Note 42.

Chapter 6: Chantrell's Office and Professional Practice

1. Letter from Chantrell to Winn, 5 Feb. 1851, WYASL, 1352/A/1/8/8.

2. ICBS, file 01422.
3. WYASL, 1352/A/1/8/8.
4. See Chapter 1, Architecture: a Profession or a Trade?
5. E.g. *LI*, 28 June 1827.
6. The statement needs some qualification. At the time of joining, Chantrell was indeed the only FIBA in Leeds. However, William Hurst had joined in Feb. 1836 while based in Doncaster, although he had an office in Leeds from 1842.
7. *LI*, 17 May 1819.
8. The Saddle Yard was literally buried when the present railway embankment was built.
9. Bank Street ran from Boar Lane north to Commercial Street, almost opposite the Leeds Library. Only traces of the line of the street remain.
10. He wrote to Soane from this address on 6 Jan. 1821. SM, Private Correspondence, XV, A, 32.
11. This address appears in Parson's *Directory* of 1826, p. 27. Baines' *Yorkshire Directory* of 1822, p. 45, still lists Chantrell at Bank Street.
12. Parson and White, *Directory of the Borough of Leeds,* Parson and White, 1830, p. 127.
13. *LI*, 28 Jan. 1843 carried an advertisement stating that R.W. Moore, 'late pupil of R.D. Chantrell' was establishing a practice at 11 and 12 Benson's Building, or 2 Park Row.
14. Biographical information about Healey comes from: J. Lever (ed.), *Catalogue of the Drawings Collection of the RIBA, (G-K),* Gregg, 1973, p. 101. The collection includes many drawings by Healey from before his partnership with Mallinson, and suggests extensive sketching tours of Gloucestershire, Lincolnshire, Cheshire, Warwickshire, Herefordshire, Northamptonshire, as well as time spent in Yorkshire in the 1830s (pp. 101-4).
15. See the penultimate section of the Catalogue which lists inspections that Chantrell undertook for the ICBS, and which included several Healey churches.
16. *LI*, 28 Jan. 1843.
17. R.W. Moore, *A History of The Parish Church of Leeds* … Richard Jackson, 1877, p. v. Moore was given responsibility for counter-signing the contracts with the tradesmen for rebuilding LPC.
18. *Ibid.,* p. 54.
19. *Ibid.,* p. 54-5.
20. *LI*, 1 Feb. 1827. Despite keeping an office in Leeds until at least 1839, there is no record of his having done anything at all in the town.
21. WYASW, WDP18/42.
22. ICBS, file 01089.
23. Derbyshire Record Office, deposit 2057A.
24. ICBS, file 03527.
25. WYASW, WDP97/72.
26. WYASW, WDP231. Another interesting example is the reconstruction of All Saints, Pontefract (1831-3) where Benjamin Green was paid as both clerk of works (£153) and 'for carving' (£143) (ICBS, file 01347).
27. For instance the report for Golcar (ICBS, file 03196).
28. Gawthorp might also have written out the specifications for Guiseley church in 1830; certainly the are by neither Chantrell nor Wade (ICBS, file 01472).
29. Many of Chantrell's presentation drawings incorporate a form of inscription in which the letters are block capitals of thick lines, essentially rectilinear rather than curved, with each word separated by a dash. 'U's are written as 'V's. The Leeds South Market drawings illustrate this. All the better drawings with this form of lettering appear to be by Chantrell. However, the same style of lettering appears on more mundane drawings which were probably by a clerk.
30. Even a report for the prosaic job at Birkenshaw in 1840 was written by Chantrell (ICBS, file 02652), but for the equally mundane job of curing Golcar's leaking roof in 1843, the report in not in Chantrell's

hand (ICBS, file 03196). The ICBS Honley file (no. 01484) has plans that are neither produced nor signed by Chantrell, and the same is true of the plans in the Leven file (no. 02784).

31. As we have seen above, Chantrell used Shaw for assistance outside of the LPC job.
32. *LI*, 25 June 1842. Their office was at 6 Park Row.
33. *LI*, 23 July 1842
34. *LI*, 10 Sept. 1842.
35. *Civil Engineer and Architects' Journal*, April 1846, p. 100.
36. *Builder*, 5, 1847, p. 302.
37. CBC, Halifax file, no. 16867.
38. At Golcar, the initial report with a prescription for curing the problems is in Chantrell's hand, although the certificate of completion is signed by Chantrell and Shaw.
39. The formation of the partnership was announced in *LI*, 22 Feb. 1845. Their office was at 19 Park Row.
40. *Royal National Commercial Directory ... and Yorkshire*, Isaac Slater, 1848, p. 1191. *Slade and Roebuck's Directory ... of Leeds*, Slade and Roebuck, 1851, p. 182, gives the address as 12 ½ Park Row.
41. WYASB, 129/21/1-5.
42. ICBS, file 03257.
43. The information comes mainly from the RIBA's records of members and London directories. The inconsistencies are covered more thoroughly in the Chapter 5.
44. Dobson made extensive use of the talents of J.W. Carmichael. See T. Faulkner and A. Greg, *John Dobson Newcastle Architect 1787-1865*, Tyne and Wear Museums Service, 1987, pp. 9-10.
45. See the *Catalogues* of the Northern Society for the Encouragement of Arts, 1822, 1823, 1825, 1828 and 1830, plus the *Catalogue* of the public exhibitions in Leeds in 1839.
46. WYASL, RDP108/45.
47. ICBS, file 01422.
48. CBC, MB39, p. 155.
49. *Ibid.*.
50. See Chapter 5.
51. He produced an attractive perspective watercolour of the old, dilapidated church (ICBS, file 04114) suggesting a leisurely stay.
52. For instance, plans for King Cross, Halifax, church were sent to the ICBS by 'the railway' in 1844.
53. Note 1.
54. ICBS, file 01422.
55. This is a very crude calculation based on the fact that Holmbridge church consumed 22 days of office time before the job was put out to tender. Calculated from the other direction, if Chantrell received £250 for a £5,000 church – 5% – and expected to earn between £2 and £2/10/0 per day, this would equate to around 120 days of work, including the site visits.
56. He was in Rise sufficiently long for the solicitors handling the finances for the rebuilding of Leeds Parish Church to have felt it worth writing to him there rather than waiting for his return to Leeds. (WYASL, RDP68/41/13).
57. See C. Webster, 'The Architectural Profession in Leeds, 1800-50: a case study in provincial practice' in *Architectural History*, 38, 1995, pp. 176-91.
58. CBC, Golcar file.

Chapter 7: Chantrell the Architect

1. For instance, see Chantrell's letter to Soane, 6 Jan. 1821, quoted below.
2. His Conservative Pavilion in Leeds of 1838, although Classical, was only a temporary structure.
3. Its cost was £22,000. W. White, *Directory and Gazetteer of Leeds ...* , William White, 1853, p. 24.
4. *LI*, 19 June 1823.

5. Fowler, a minor Leeds architect, described by Linstrum as 'a civil engineer, valuer and agent, engineer and surveyor to several turnpike roads' (Linstrum, p. 376).

6. TS Collection, Box A.

7. These figures are based on those shown on the plan. Grady lists 49 shops and 88 stalls. (K. Grady, *The Georgian Public Buildings of Leeds and the West Riding,* The Thoresby Society, Leeds, vol. 62, no. 133, 1987, p. 165). These figures are repeated in J. Schmiechen and K. Carls, *The British Market Hall,* Yale, 1999, p. 274.

8. J. Heaton, *Walks Through Leeds,* J. Heaton, 1835, p. 102.

9. *LI,* 16 Dec. 1824.

10. I am most grateful to Oliver Bradbury for this suggestion.

11. Soane's interest in it might have been prompted by its inclusion in Sadby's RA lectures. It was illustrated in J.B. Fischer von Erlach's *Entwurff einer historischen Architecture* (first ed. 1721) of which Soane owned an English translation, and it is known that several of Soane's pupils were sent to make detailed drawings of it in 1817. See D. Watkin, *Sir John Soane, Enlightenment Thought and the Royal Academy Lectures,* Cambridge, 1996; C. Chippindale, *Stonehenge Complete,* Thames and Hudson, 1994, p. 138.

12. See Schmiechen and Carls [note 7], pp. 21-34.

13. SM, Private Correspondence, XV.A.32.

14. The Crown Architects rejected Busby's proposed iron roof-trusses and Gyfford failed to supply the Local Committee in Leeds with working drawings or his address (CBC, MB6, p. 42).

15. The story is told in M. Port, 'Francis Goodwin (1784-1835)', *Architectural History,* 1, 1958, pp. 61-72.

16. *Ibid.,* p. 66.

17. The possibility is considered, but dismissed in M. Port *600 New Churches,* Spire Books, 2006, p. 311, fn. 70.

18. In 1821 Goodwin was erecting churches in Ashton-under-Lyne, West Bromwich, Birmingham and Portsea that Chantrell might have seen on an extended tour.

19. Soane suggested that iron columns might be clad if 'the use of iron alone has not sufficient character and appearance of stability'. SM, Correspondence, X.B,8, quoted in M. Port [note 17], p. 63.

20. Volume 1, 1807, noted in Port, *600 New Churches* [note 17], p. 134.

21. Heaton [note 8], p. 104.

22. This was conveniently given a detailed description and several illustrations on Britton's *Architectural Antiquities of Great Britain,* 3, 1812, pp. 27-46.

23. The details of these octagonal towers probably came from plate VIII of the first edition (1817) of Rickman's *An Attempt.*

24. CBC, MB 32, pp. 300-1.

25. CBC, MB 26, p. 234.

26. CBC, MB 32, pp. 300-1.

27. Ripon's north-west tower – interestingly shown without its twin and the central gable that separates them, and thus looking much more like Morley's – is illustrated in Britton's *Architectural Antiquities,* 5, 1826, 'Chronological series of towers and spires' (no plate numbers).

28. *Ibid.*

29. CBC, MB 32, pp. 300-1. A similar arrangement of three lancet windows with continuous hood-mould and sill can be found in Britton's *Architectural Antiquities,* vol. 5 headed, 'Specimens of Windows and East Ends of Churches' (no plate numbers).

30. *The Church Intelligencer,* 11 Sept. 1841.

31. Poole is in interesting character and a pioneer Tractarian. In 1839 he *bought* St James, Leeds – a former proprietary chapel – and transformed its interior to conform to his more advanced principles. He was instrumental in establishing the Yorkshire Architectural Society and was its first Secretary. He was a ritualist and an advocate of altar candles. He left Leeds after only 4 years to take up the living of

Welford in Northamptonshire. See H.W. Dalton, *Anglican Resurgence under W.F. Hook in Early Victorian Leeds,* The Thoresby Society, Leeds, 12, 2001, p. 68. Dalton incorrectly states Poole was still at St James in 1848 (p. 117). Following his death in September 1883, a short obituary appeared in *Associated Architectural Society Reports and Papers,* 17, 1884, pp. xxviii, liv. Poole's books include: *The Appropriate Character of Church Architecture,* T.W. Green, Leeds, 1842; *Churches: Their Structure , Arrangements and Decoration,* James Burns, 1845; *A History of Ecclesiastical Architecture in England,* Joseph Masters, 1848; *A History and Description of York Cathedral,* Gunter, 1850; with J.W. Hugall, *Churches of Yorkshire,* T.W. Green, 1844. His remarkable contribution of 30 articles in various editions of *Associated Architectural Societies Reports and Papers* earned him the praise of the journal's indexer.

32. G.A. Poole, *The Appropriate Character of Church Architrcture,* T.W. Green, 1842, p. iv.

33. *Ibid.,* p. 12.

34. See G.K. Brandwood, 'The Establishment of the Society' in C. Webster and J. Elliott (eds), *A Church as it should be': the Cambridge Camden Society and its Influence,* Shaun Tyas, 2000, pp. 45-61.

35. *The Ecclesiologist,* 8, 1847, p. 132.

36. Anon., *The Leeds Guide,* Edwards Baines, 1803, p. 143.

37. T.D. Whitaker, *Loidis and Elmete,* Robinson, Son and Holdsworth, 1816, p. 176.

38. G.A. Poole, *Churches of Yorkshire,* T.W. Green, 1842-4, p. 34, although the pagination is not consistent. The book includes a plan of the church drawn by Chantrell.

39. R.D. Chantrell, 'Observations on the Ancient Roof of the Church of Adel … ', *YAS Papers,* n.d. but probably 1845, reprinted in *YAS Papers,* 1887, p. 111; also reprinted in *Institute of British Architects Papers,* 1847.

40. G. Lewthwaite, 'Adel Church: Its Fabric, Restorations and Discovery of Norman roof', *Associated Architectural Societies Reports and Papers,* 19, 1887, pp. 102-20. Chantrell's working drawings, dated 8 Sept. 1838 are in WYASL, RDP2/68.

41. Lewthwaite [note 40], p. 105.

42. *Ibid.*

43. *Ibid.,* p. 107.

44. Chantrell [note 39], p. 110.

45. *LI,* 17 Aug. 1839.

46. It was reprinted by YAS in 1887, but the date of the original printing is not clear.

47. RIBA Library, MS.SP/3/25.

48. J. Gwilt, *Encyclopaedia of Architecture,* Longmans, 1867, p. 972, and subsequent editions.

49. See C. Webster, '"True Masonic Principles": a mid-nineteenth century alternative to "True Principles"', *Ecclesiology Today,* 18, 1999, pp. 1-5.

50. Soane hints at this in his fifth RA lecture (J. Soane, *The Royal Academy Lectures,* (D. Watkin ed.), Cambridge, 2000, p. 119).

51. The significance of the these theories is underlined by their being discussed in considerable detail – no less than 61 pages of tightly-packed text – in Joseph Gwilt's influential *Encyclopaedia of Architecture,* in the editions from 1867.

52. The importance attached to it no doubt stemmed from Cesariano's commentary to his translation of Vitruvius in 1521. This was hardly a primary medieval source yet in the absence of anything of significance that was older, it represented a useful starting point for the study of medieval proportional systems. It was also mentioned by Dürer. For more recent works on the subject, see P.H. Scholfield, *The Theory of Proportion in Architecture,* Cambridge UP, 1958, pp. 82-9; B.G. Morgan, *Canonical Design in English Medieval Architecture,* Liverpool UP, 1961, p. 17.

53. Chantrell explains his version of it in tortuous detail in *The Builder,* 5, 1847, pp. 300-2; a slightly compacted version appears in Gwilt [note 48], 1867, p. 973, but neither is recommended for the faint-hearted!

54. Note 52.

55. Indeed, Carter had come to this view as early as 1814. See J.M. Crook, *John Carter and the Mind of the Gothic Revival*, The Society of Antiquaries and Lund Humphries, 1995, p. 44.

56. *The Builder* [note 53], p. 302. The previous year he wrote an article which added Keighley to this list. (*Civil Engineer and Architect's Journal*, April 1846, p. 100).

57. R. and J.A. Brandon, *The Open Timber Roofs of the Middle Ages*, David Bogue, 1849.

58. Lawton, p. 257.

59. *LI*, 1 March 1845.

60. ICBS, file 00818.

61. BI, faculty 1845/1.

62. BI, faculty 1840/2.

63. Tenders for its erection were advertised in *LI*, 12 June 1841.

64. *LI*, 1 March 1845.

65. *LI*, 4 Dec. 1847.

66. *The Ecclesiologist*, 11, 1850, pp. 64-6.

Chapter 8: Conclusion

1. T. Cocke, *The Georgian Group Newsletter*, Sept. 1995, p. 5.

2. By A. Pugin and J. Britton, 2 vols, W.H. Leeds, 1825-8.

3. By J.H. Shepherd and J. Elmes, published in several parts, Jones and Co., 1827-31.

4. Quoted in B.F.L. Clarke, *Church Builders of the Nineteenth Century*, David and Charles, 1969, p. 100.

5. G.A. Poole, whom we encountered in Chapter 7, included the church alongside Newman's chapel at Littlemore, Rickman's Hampton Lucy and Oulton, and Chantrell's Leeds Parish Church as 'encouraging signs [which] give … hope' for the future of church architecture. *The Appropriate Character of Church Architecture*, T.W. Green, 1842, p. 12.

6. G. Germann, *Gothic Revival*, Lund Humphries, 1972, p. 107.

7. *The Ecclesiologist*, 3, 1844, p. 102.

8. For a full discussion see J. Gwilt, *The Encyclopaedia of Architecture*, Longman, 1867, pp. 963-1024.

9. 'In GOD'S House every thing should be *real*', thundered *The Ecclesiologist*, 1, 1843, p. 11.

10. More examples are discussed in J.M. Robinson, *The Regency Country House*, Aurum Press, 2005, p. 21.

11. For instance, P.F. Robinson, *Village Architecture: being a Series of Designs for the Inn, Schoolhouse, Almshouses, Markethouse, Shambles, Workhouse, Parsonage and Church*, James Carpenter and Son, 1830; S.H. Brooks, *Select Designs for Public Buildings consisting of … Churches, Chapels, Schools, Almshouses, Gas-Works, Markets and other Buildings erected for Public Purposes*, Thomas Kelly, 1842.

12. H. Colvin, *A Biographical Dictionary of British Architects 1600-1840*, Yale, 3rd ed., 1995, p. 130.

13. For instance, see *The Ecclesiologist*, 7, 1847, p. 117.

Index

★ denotes architects.

Bold denotes pages with illustrations.

Individual works by Chantrell are indexed alphabetically by place under 'Chantrell's building and projects'.

Chantrell's family